Approaches to Teaching the Writings of Bartolomé de Las Casas

Approaches to Teaching World Literature

Joseph Gibaldi, series editor

For a complete listing of titles,
see the last pages of this book.

Approaches to Teaching the Writings of Bartolomé de Las Casas

Edited by

Santa Arias

and

Eyda M. Merediz

The Modern Language Association of America
New York   2008

For information about obtaining permission to reprint material from
MLA book publications, send your request by mail (see address below),
e-mail (permissions@mla.org), or fax (646 458-0030).

Library of Congress Cataloging-in-Publication Data

Approaches to teaching the writings of Bartolomé de las Casas /
edited by Santa Arias and Eyda M. Merediz.
p. cm. — (Approaches to teaching world literature ; 102)
Includes bibliographical references and index.
ISBN: 978-0-87352-944-0 (hardcover : alk. paper)
ISBN: 978-0-87352-945-7 (pbk. : alk. paper)
1. Casas, Bartolomé de las, 1474–1566—Criticism and interpretation.
2. Casas, Bartolomé de las, 1474–1566—Criticism, Textual.
3. America—Discovery and exploration—Spanish—Study and teaching.
4. Indians, Treatment of—Study and teaching. 5. American literature—
Colonial period, ca. 1600–1775—Study and teaching. 6. America—
History—To 1810—Study and teaching. I. Arias, Santa. II. Merediz,
Eyda M., 1964– III. Series.
E125.C4A55 2008
970.01'6—dc22   2008024220

Approaches to Teaching World Literature 102
ISSN 1059-1133

Cover illustration of the paperback edition:
Bartolomé de Las Casas, by Marta Gutiérrez. 2007.
Mixed media on paper: oil on computer-altered image

Published by The Modern Language Association of America
26 Broadway, New York, New York 10004-1789
www.mla.org

CONTENTS

Teaching Las Casas from a Comparative Perspective

PREFACE TO THE SERIES

In *The Art of Teaching* Gilbert Highet wrote, "Bad teaching wastes a great deal of effort, and spoils many lives which might have been full of energy and happiness." All too many teachers have failed in their work, Highet argued, simply "because they have not thought about it." We hope that the Approaches to Teaching World Literature series, sponsored by the Modern Language Association's Publications Committee, will not only improve the craft—as well as the art—of teaching but also encourage serious and continuing discussion of the aims and methods of teaching literature.

The principal objective of the series is to collect within each volume different points of view on teaching a specific literary work, a literary tradition, or a writer widely taught at the undergraduate level. The preparation of each volume begins with a wide-ranging survey of instructors, thus enabling us to include in the volume the philosophies and approaches, thoughts and methods of scores of experienced teachers. The result is a sourcebook of material, information, and ideas on teaching the subject of the volume to undergraduates.

The series is intended to serve nonspecialists as well as specialists, inexperienced as well as experienced teachers, graduate students who wish to learn effective ways of teaching as well as senior professors who wish to compare their own approaches with the approaches of colleagues in other schools. Of course, no volume in the series can ever substitute for erudition, intelligence, creativity, and sensitivity in teaching. We hope merely that each book will point readers in useful directions; at most each will offer only a first step in the long journey to successful teaching.

Joseph Gibaldi
Series Editor

ACKNOWLEDGMENTS

In the aftermath of the five-hundredth anniversary of Columbus's first voyage to the Americas, the most exciting discovery surrounding Bartolomé de Las Casas is a portrait that seems to reveal once and for all the famous Dominican friar's real face. In a portrait apparently painted from life, Las Casas, wearing his bishop's robes, holding papers in his hands, and bearing the burden of his years, casts his penetrating gaze directly at the viewer. The little history we know of this sixteenth-century oil painting is recent: it was part of a collection of artworks belonging to a German consul who had been posted to Montreal before World War II. The painting was seized by the Canadian government and eventually sold at a public auction. José Majzner, the Serbian painter and sculptor, came to know the picture in the process of restoring it; he subsequently purchased it in partnership with Nemanja Cvorkov and Gary Slimon of the Canadian Academy of Wilderness Artists and its museum. Shared ownership of the picture fell to Cvorkov and Slimon when Majzner died in the mid-1980s. In 1991, the discovery was presented at a symposium in San Francisco; a year later, Isacio Pérez Fernández published his findings about the portrait, thereby alerting the academic world to its existence ("Hallazgo"). To date, however, no art expert has studied the painting itself, and even Pérez Fernández, who advanced arguments in favor of the painting's authenticity, has never actually seen the original.

Determined to locate the portrait of Las Casas, we decided to launch our own investigation. We learned that Cvorkov took the painting with him when he relocated from Ottawa to Montreal, where he stored it in a secure location. Fighting in the Balkans made it necessary for him to travel to Kosovo to deliver a wheelchair to his sister, who lost both legs in the war: while there, Cvorkov was exposed to poisonous concentrations of spent uranium bombs, and he died very suddenly from the effects shortly after his return to Montreal. Unfortunately, Cvorkov neglected to share the secret location where he stored the painting, and Gary Slimon reports that it may have yet again disappeared. Pérez Fernández claims to have received information that the back of the painting carries the inscription "Fray Btme. de las Casas obispo de Chapa"; Slimon, on the other hand, tells us that the inscription was recorded not on the painting but on its fragile wood frame. He adds that on the occasion of his last viewing of the painting, the frame was missing in its entirety. The painting, as of this writing, has yet to resurface, leading one to suspect that it—along with the chance to verify its authenticity—has been lost to us. Once again, Las Casas seems to have eluded us. With this book, we aspire to approximate his intellectual portrait and legacy to provide new perspectives to the many instructors who teach Las Casas not only in Hispanic and Latin American studies classrooms but across the disciplines.

Oil portrait of Bartolomé de Las Casas (1484–1566), probably painted by N. Albítez between 1548 and 1558. Location unknown. Image courtesy of Gary Slimon

As we embarked on this project, we encountered challenges and obstacles but also rewards and satisfaction, for which we would like to express our gratitude. Thanks must go first to all survey participants for helping us frame this volume and identify relevant themes and difficulties in the teaching of Las Casas's writings. The contributors to the volume were enthusiastic and fully engaged with the project: we appreciate their efforts, rigor, and promptness. Recognition is also owed to several anonymous MLA reviewers, who significantly improved the content and organization of the volume. Joseph Gibaldi and the MLA deserve our gratitude for finding our proposal worthy and for fully supporting us along the way. Margit Longbrake has copyedited the final manuscript superbly, while initially we received great help from María Verónica Muñoz, whose sharp eye and organizational skills facilitated the timely delivery of the first draft.

We would like to thank Adán Griego for bringing us together and for helping resolve questions on missing materials, and we are grateful to the Colombian artist Marta L. Gutiérrez for conceiving another image of Las Casas for the cover. Finally, our thanks to Barney Warf, Tonny Lybek, and Chela Monzón for their caring and understanding during this long and arduous process.

INTRODUCTION

The writings of the Dominican intellectual Bartolomé de Las Casas are essential to understand the cultural and political history of the colonial period in the Americas. He is often considered the most significant Spanish religious and secular figure of the early years of the European colonization for his emphatic political interventions and his persuasive texts in defense of native populations. Las Casas's image, ideas, and personal history have transcended time and space. As a key transatlantic and hemispheric historian and advocate of Amerindian rights, this sixteenth-century friar still provokes much reflection and dialogue in the political and cultural arena, particularly in the study of imperialism and forms of colonialism and in the denunciation of human rights violations.

In recent discussions in postcolonial studies, Las Casas has been underscored as a decisive figure who articulates both sides of the imperial project, capable of being either an agent of hegemonic power or an antihegemonic force. For Michael Hardt and Antonio Negri in *Empire*, he serves as the example of political and cultural ambiguity when he describes Amerindian populations: "Las Casas can only think of equality in terms of sameness" (116), and he ultimately supports dominant Eurocentric ideology that aims to impose Christianity and European culture on the Amerindian populations. In contrast, Robert Young's chapter "Las Casas to Bentham," in his *Postcolonialism: An Historical Introduction*, emphasizes how anticolonialism begins within colonialism itself. For Young, Las Casas was the precursor of European anticolonialism when he questioned the moral and legal foundations of the conquest (75). Young's reading of Las Casas is insufficiently political, while Hardt and Negri applied to the sixteenth century an ideological apparatus that does not allow for nuances. Nevertheless, these two interdisciplinary studies document once more how Las Casas has been inscribed critically as a foundational figure in the long history of resistance to imperialism and colonialism.

In academic scholarship, the significance of Bartolomé de Las Casas's ideas has been a recurrent topic in the humanities and social sciences. There have been many conferences in Europe and Latin America commemorating the quadricentennial of his death in 1566, and later, quincentennial conferences were held based on his supposed birth date in 1474. The publication of Helen Rand Parish and Harold E. Weidman's research correcting Las Casas's birth date (placing it in 1484 ["Correct Birthdate"]) provided another occasion to call together Lascasistas from around the globe to reflect on and debate the friar's significance to contemporary thought and history. Many more academic or religious meetings have taken place since 1984: Las Casas is relevant for many constituencies and is part of the intellectual history in a number of national traditions.

In Latin America, political and social movements have been inspired by Las Casas, as in the case of the rise of the Zapatista rebellion in southern Mexico in the early 1990s. The bishop of San Cristóbal de Las Casas, Samuel Ruiz García (named to the same post that Las Casas held in the sixteenth century), served as mediator between the Zapatistas and the Mexican government during the initial indigenous uprisings. As Benjamin Keen has suggested, "the Mexican government decision to ask a Lascasian bishop—the only public figure who enjoyed the trust of the Mayan peasantry—to intervene in the Chiapas conflict suggests the continuing vitality and relevance of Las Casas's doctrines in the Modern World" (2). Ruiz is now retired but still speaks in public forums on the economic violence that the Mexican neoliberal government exercises. In a press conference published by José Antonio Román Enviado in 2005, Ruiz stated that because of high unemployment and extreme poverty, members of the indigenous communities are forced to leave the highlands and migrate illegally to the United States. Just as Las Casas did in colonial times, Ruiz uses every opportunity to offer a strong political critique of what he calls the new evil, the forced migration that is decimating Latin American indigenous communities.

Samuel Ruiz is one among many voices raising social consciousness in Latin America that already in the 1960s recognized Las Casas as the father of liberation theology because of his resounding call to emancipate indigenous communities from injustices and exploitation. Gustavo Gutiérrez and Enrique Dussel, key scholars in religion and philosophy respectively, have drawn on the Lascasian message to formulate a theory and praxis that are profoundly rooted in the Latin American colonial experience (Gutiérrez, *Teología* and *En busca*; Dussel, "Nucléo" and *Historia*). From the margins to the centers of power, Indian subjects continue to confront human rights violations, abuses of power in their communities, and even death in the long journey moving away from home, local discrimination, and social injustice. Poverty, inequality, and forced migration have not ended in Latin America, making it impossible to dismiss Las Casas's original message and legal demands.

Analogies with present-day situations, such as the complexities of neocolonialism in Latin America or even the injustice of today's wars, are a natural gateway to introduce Las Casas in the classroom. Nevertheless, teaching the literature of the colonial period is, above all, an interdisciplinary task. This volume pledges faith in that premise by collecting in its first section, "Teaching Las Casas across the Disciplines," complementary essays from scholars in literature, history, anthropology, and religion. Las Casas is also worth considering in discussions of early modern political theory, geography, and philosophy. Essays in subsequent sections of this collection guide the teaching of Las Casas from the multiple perspectives and intersections necessary to grasp the significance of his work. Lascasian texts are among the best examples of the interdisciplinary Hispanic intellectual tradition of the Renaissance, which blends humanism and scholasticism and helps us understand the "modernity" that defines the early modern period.

Las Casas commands much attention because of his multidimensional personality, his strong agency, and the intellectual depth he brings to some of the most polemical debates about human nature and actions. During his lifetime, he used his favored position at the court of Emperor Charles V to cast serious doubt on the ethics of colonization and its human, physical, and cultural destruction of the New World. The abuses that he graphically portrayed in his treatise *Brevísima relación de la destrucción de las Indias (Brief Account of the Destruction of the Indies)* called for justice and contributed to the spread of what has become known as the "Black Legend" of Spanish transatlantic history (anti-Hispanist and anti-Catholic sentiments advocated by sixteenth-century Protestants and emerging rival nation-empires). Therefore, we devote a whole section, "Teaching Las Casas's *Brevísima relación de la destrucción de las Indias*," to the Lascasian text most widely used in the literature classroom and in a variety of disciplines and national traditions. An enticing account in many ways, the *Brevísima relación* offers one of the most dramatic views of colonial violence and trauma. It is an essential and heartbreaking description that captures the many voices that joined Las Casas in testifying to the forms of aggression that took place during the first centuries of European domination. The *Brevísima relación*, in its many editions, is also a crucial text for tracking the importance of translation and political manipulation, since it has been widely translated, illustrated, edited, reprinted, and commented on since its first publication in 1552. During the eighteenth and nineteenth centuries, new editions in Latin America, Europe, and the United States fueled anti-Spanish sentiments, which served as the basis of nationalist movements for independence in the Spanish colonies and even as ammunition for the Spanish-American War of 1898. The essays in this section address the historical background surrounding the production of the text, look at the critical questions that it generates, and explore suggestive relating topics. They also help instructors make accessible the rhetorical techniques and persuasive language found in the *Brevísima relación*.

Because much teaching of Las Casas centers on the *Brevísima relación*—a text that, in many ways, is decidedly not representative of Las Casas's work as a historian, ethnographer, and canon lawyer—the following section, "Teaching Other Lascasian Texts," incorporates other forms taken by Las Casas's critique of the aggressive European practices in the New World: numerous letters, treatises, *memoriales* (petitions to the crown), and several voluminous and complex historical accounts that focus on the illegality and immorality of the Spanish conquest and colonization process. To address crucial issues in the teaching of the life and writings of Las Casas, we adopt a comparative approach and consider the *Apologética historia sumaria (Apologetic History)*, *De unico vocationis modo omnium gentium ad veram religionem (The Only Way of Calling All People to a Living Faith)*, and other treatises, such as the *Apología* and *Reglas para confesores (Rules for Confessors)*. His monumental *Historia de las Indias (History of the Indies)* is not featured independently here, but instead it serves as a basic source for many essays throughout as they touch on events and historical accounts narrated many times over and from different angles. The *Historia's* prologue, nevertheless, is discussed in detail in an introduction of Las Casas for historians. In addition, several essays work directly or tangentially with a selection of his *Remedios* and *Memoriales*. Such a comprehensive corpus is particularly illuminating, since it reveals both continuities and changes in Las Casas's ideology, but despite the importance of the petitions, these texts are often neglected or poorly integrated in the classroom. This volume attempts to correct that oversight.

Las Casas's writings generate rich discussions on broader issues pertaining not only to Renaissance humanism and political culture but also to national movements in Latin America, democratic processes, human rights, and the dynamics of globalization. Thus the section "Teaching Las Casas in the Broader Ibero-American Context" puts his contributions in dialogue with his contemporaries as well as with those who have used and abused his ideas in later centuries. Las Casas's writings are noteworthy: he presented in detail an exegesis of the Columbian enterprise, provided a comprehensive ethnography of the native cultures of the Americas, and elaborated a fervent critique of the evangelization process and of Spanish colonial rule, as well as constructed an apology for and a defense of his own actions as protector of the Indians.

The essays show first how Las Casas needs to be taught alongside historical figures such as Christopher Columbus, Gonzalo Fernández de Oviedo, Fray Toribio de Benavente (Motolinía), and many other secular and ecclesiastical historians of the sixteenth and seventeenth centuries. To understand the confrontational nature of the cultural contact, we need to look at how this Dominican historian manipulated his sources and established ardent oral and written dialogues with intellectuals of his day. His production was embedded in a network of contingent discursive practices that are often overlooked in common teaching designs. Furthermore, studies of the circulation and reception of Las Casas's texts at different times and in multiple regions are useful in the classroom. His work was of great influence during the independence periods: first, during the early nineteenth century, when most of Latin American territories achieved their sovereignty from Spain (1810–24), and later, toward the end of the century (1895–98), when Cuba and Puerto Rico were still struggling to achieve their independence from Spain. According to Simón Bolívar in his "Carta de Jamaica," Las Casas was the most "sublime" historian of his period (56), while decades later José Martí recommends to the youth of Latin America reading Las Casas because of his compassion and combative spirit ("El padre").

The essays here further develop Las Casas's interventions and subsequent appropriations in other positive and negative genealogies. His intellectual influence presents instructors with a predicament when his ideological transformations and the multifaceted, apparently contradictory nature of his thought are ignored. Besides being singled out as the promoter of the Black Legend, the other politically controversial aspect of Las Casas's life is his promotion of the African slave trade to replace the dying masses of Indian labor. Complementing a brief introduction to the subject at the beginning of the volume, this section amply contextualizes the institution of slavery, elucidating Las Casas's role in the arrival of African slaves in the Americas and discussing his place as a foundational figure in Caribbean discursive practices about race. Other essays tackle his ideas' contribution to the birth of liberation theology and to the emergence of literary movements such as *indigenismo* or the more recent testimonial-documentary genre and use the productive conversation between literature and film to address the controversial representation of Las Casas on both sides of the Atlantic.

The last section, "Teaching Las Casas from a Comparative Perspective," examines Las Casas in English, French, American, and Luso-Brazilian studies curricula. These essays look at the history of translations and printings, how to teach his writings using archival material and rare books, and the absence or partially acknowledged influence of Las Casas in the literary cultures of a range of national traditions.

Las Casas's life and works concern academic inquiry today as much as they influenced individuals and institutions during Spanish colonial rule and in national and transnational settings. His firsthand accounts of the history of the conquest and his legal treatises serve as an integral part of a variety of intellectual genealogies. As this volume makes clear, Las Casas was a product of his times; he was a Christian humanist who questioned, resisted, and attempted to reform Spanish policy in the Indies within a European legal, moral, and Christian framework. Beyond his active political life, Las Casas's writings ultimately presented a polemical defense of self-governance and property rights for Amerindians and advocated for restoration and restitution. Moreover, he narrated and described some of the most important events in the development of capitalism and articulated the most pervasive discourses on human rights and anti-imperialism across the centuries.

By addressing the increasingly interdisciplinary inclusion of texts from the Hispanic tradition in the global curriculum, this volume clarifies historical and critical issues and explores Las Casas's place and legacy in the intellectual culture of the Americas and Europe. Teachers in the field of colonial studies face the challenge of making historical figures, texts, and inquiries intelligible for contemporary students. It is not an easy task to navigate the permeable border between fiction and history, nor is it always possible to establish the rich connections between past and present in the classroom. For teachers of Bartolomé de Las Casas's writings, however, the endeavor is not only feasible but necessary.

SA and EMM

Part One

MATERIALS

Texts and Editions

In our review of the many editions of Bartolomé de Las Casas's writings and secondary sources, we found that an interdisciplinary approach to his texts is far from new. Some of the most widely read studies that successfully reconstruct, interpret, and recover Las Casas's texts fold in the rich cultural, political, and religious milieu of the European Renaissance, the Spanish Golden Age, and the colonial period of the Americas.

An indispensable tool that every library should have available to students and researchers is Bartolomé de Las Casas's *Obras completas*, published by Alianza under the direction of Paulino Castañeda Delgado. The fourteen annotated volumes, which appeared between 1988 and 1998, include critical introductory essays by prominent scholars such as Álvaro Huerga, Isacio Pérez Fernández, Vidal Abril Castelló, Ángel Losada, and Consuelo Varela, among many others. Our survey shows that most scholars still use the *Obras escogidas de fray Bartolomé de las Casas* edited by Juan Pérez de Tudela Bueso (in the Biblioteca de Autores Españoles series, 1957–58). Key texts included in this early edition are the *Historia de las Indias*, *Apologética historia sumaria*, and *Opúsculos, cartas y memoriales*.

Bartolomé de Las Casas's *Historia de las Indias* was and still is considered his most ambitious text. He unrelentingly maintained this account of the early years of contact and colonization for over thirty years (1527–61). In the seventeenth century, the Royal Historian Antonio de Herrera drew on Las Casas's detailed descriptions of the explored territories and on the Dominican's account of events in order to compose his own *Historia general,* and later the text was withheld from public view for over three centuries (Wagner xxi). The original manuscript (with revisions by Las Casas Himself) remains in the special collections at the National Library in Madrid (ms. 2812-2814); however, other copies are preserved at the Real Academia de la Historia, the British Museum, the New York Public Library, the John Carter Brown Library, and the Newberry Library. Its prologue, written in 1552, is an essential reading to understand Las Casas's intention, method, and ideas on the theory and praxis of Renaissance historiography.

Besides Alianza's outstanding edition of the *Historia de las Indias*, prepared by Isacio Pérez Fernández (*Obras completas*, vols. 3–5 [1994]), the standard modern edition has been Agustín Millares Carlo's, published by the Fondo de Cultura Económica (1951) with the introduction "Las Casas, historiador" by Lewis Hanke. This first twentieth-century edition of the *Historia* was revised in 1965 and then reprinted four times; today the 1995 reprint is still available. Another edition in Spanish worth recommending, although more difficult to obtain, is André Saint-Lu's, published by Ayacucho (1986). In English, Andrée Collard's translation of key parts of the *Historia* is commonly available at libraries (*History of the Indies*). In addition, George Sanderlin's *Bartolomé de las Casas: A Selection of His Writings* (1971) includes selections of the *Historia*, as well as the *Apologética historia sumaria* and some of Las Casas's *memoriales* and treatises.

Manuel Serrano y Sanz was responsible for the first complete edition of the *Apologética historia sumaria* in 1909. In the second chapter of the *Apologética*, Las Casas clarifies its textual origins as part of the *Historia de las Indias*. However, as Pérez Fernández states, seeds of the *Apologética* can be found in an earlier Lascasian treatise, "Del bien y favor de los indios," whose arguments were later restated in the *De unico vocationis modo* and in the *Historia de las Indias* ("Identificación"). Selections of the *Apologética* have been included in important ecclesiastical histories such as Jerónimo Román y Zamora's *República de Indias idolátricas y gobierno en México y Perú* (1569), Jerónimo de Mendieta's *Historia eclesiástica indiana* (1596), and Juan de Torquemada's *Monarquía indiana* (1615), among many others (see Fabié; Hanke and Giménez Fernández; Wagner and Parish).[1] During the Middle Ages and the Renaissance, textual appropriations were common and demonstrated trust in and deference to the precursory author; the borrowings of Las Casas's texts show that copies were available to and freely used by specific communities of readers. In the nineteenth century, Edward King, Viscount Kingsborough, included selections of the *Apologética* in his *Antiquities of Mexico* (1830).

The two most thorough and widely used editions of the *Apologética historia sumaria* have been that of Pérez de Tudela Bueso (*Obras escogidas*, vols. 3–4) and Edmundo O'Gorman's carefully annotated version (1967). We recommend O'Gorman's and the most recent edition (*Obras completas*, vols. 6–8 [1992]) prepared by a team of Lascasistas under the leadership of Vidal Abril Castelló.

In *De unico vocationis modo*, Las Casas develops his theories on religious conversion by peaceful means. A treatise on Christian rhetoric and on New World spirituality, it invokes scholastic tradition and uses classical and Renaissance rhetoric to prove the intellectual aptitude of Amerindians for learning the Christian dogma. The best edition in Spanish was prepared by Agustín Millares Carlo and translated from Latin by Atenógenes Santamaría, with an introduction by Lewis Hanke (*Del único* [1942]). Alianza's edition (*Obras completas*, vol. 2 [1990]) is remarkable but is indebted to the depth and complexity of Millares Carlo's and Hanke's scholarship. In English, there is an excellent edition prepared by Helen Rand Parish, with a translation by Francis Patrick Sullivan (*The Only Way* [1992]). Sullivan has also edited and translated Las Casas's tracts on Amerindian rights, *Indian Freedom: The Cause of Bartolomé de las Casas, 1484–1566* (1995).

The *Apología* (1550) is the most important legal document presented by Las Casas during his life and has been the last of Las Casas's major writings to be recuperated. Written originally in Latin, two outstanding critical editions in Spanish are available: Ángel Losada's (*Obras completas*, vol. 9 [1988]) and *Apología, o Declaración universal de los derechos del hombre y de los pueblos*, prepared by a team led by Vidal Abril Castelló (2000). In English, Stafford Poole's translation of the *Apología* under the title *In Defense of the Indians* was published in 1974 and is now widely available in paperback.

Although the *Obras completas* does not differ significantly from the *Obras escogidas* in its text selection and in some instances, especially of well-known texts, does not add much to existing critical editions, it sheds new light on less-known treatises, and on some virtually unexplored manuscripts. The "Tratado de las doce dudas," edited by J. B. Lassegue and introduced by J. Denglos, is one such text: for the first time a Lascasian letter addressed to Philip II and the version of the treatise housed at the John Carter Brown Library are rigorously considered. In the *Obras completas*, the letter is fully transcribed and the manuscript of the treatise is compared with other versions, revealing a deficiency in previous editions and offering a full picture of the type of political critique Las Casas was constructing at the end of his life (11.2: xix–xx, xxxiv–xxxv, xliii). Other volumes in the collection recover texts that have remained unpublished until the last decade (see, e.g., "Quaestio theologalis").

Our survey indicated that the *Brevísima relación de la destrucción de las Indias* is the Lascasian text most extensively assigned across the disciplines. It was included in the series of treatises first published by Sebastián Trujillo in Seville between 1552 and 1553 (*Brevissima relación*). The third of eight treatises Las Casas wrote to prepare new friars for religious conversion efforts, the *Brevísima relación* is the most edited, reprinted, and translated. In 1598, a Latin edition, famously illustrated by Theodor de Bry and his sons, was published in Frankfurt (*Narratio regionum*).

According to our survey, the most popular contemporary Spanish edition is André Saint-Lu's (Cátedra, 1982).[2] Other inexpensive editions worth considering are Consuelo Varela's (Castalia, 1999) and Trinidad Barrera's (Alianza, 2005). Barrera's edition, which can be used at the undergraduate and graduate levels, provides a good introduction, ample explanatory notes, and an updated bibliography. Another useful and accessible Spanish edition is Jean-Paul Duviols's, which includes de Bry's engravings. In addition, for graduate students and scholars we recommend Isacio Pérez Fernández's 2000 edition of the *Brevísima relación* (published by the Centro de Estudios de los Dominicos del Caribe). Over a thousand pages long, the edition offers the most comprehensive critical study of the intention and the legal and cultural contexts of the production, publication, and circulation of the text. Noteworthy for its seriousness is José Miguel Martínez Torrejón's edition, which evaluates previous editions of the *Brevísima relación*—including the contributions by Pérez Fernández—while offering a synthesis of insightful information on several centuries of Lascasian scholarship and reception (Martínez Torrejón, "Estudio introductorio").

Our survey reveals no consensus on an English-language edition. The most popular is the Penguin Classics edition, *A Short Account of the Destruction of the Indies* (1992), introduced by Anthony Pagden, translated by Nigel Griffin, and including some of the illustrations by de Bry—a good classroom choice overall. In order of preference, Herma Briffault's version of *The Devastation of the Indies* (Johns Hopkins UP, 1992) comes second, although it has been harshly criticized by Rolena Adorno ("Politics"). Adorno points out that Bill M. Donovan's introduction repeats clichés about Las Casas while Briffault's translation (originally from 1974) is inaccurate and faulty in important respects. We recommend instead Franklin Knight's edition, *An Account, Much Abbreviated, of the Destruction of the Indies* (Hackett, 2003). Knight's introduction is comprehensive and alluring, although the *Apología* and the *Apologética* are mistakenly treated as the same text (xxxiii). The translation by Andrew Hurley is superb and takes the reader through the perils and difficult choices embedded in the act of translation. Hurley preserves Las Casas's repetitive style, the antiquated flavor, and ultimately what he calls "the otherness" of the text (li–lv). The edition has meaningful footnotes, a few reproductions of de Bry's engravings, and an appendix of related texts including a fragment of the Laws of Burgos (1512–13), the New Laws (1542), selections from Bernal Díaz del Castillo and Hernán Cortés, and a small glossary of relevant terms. For the literary and cultural history of the translations in English and other languages, see the essays by Angelica Duran, Jonathan Hart, Elizabeth Sauer, and Gustavo Verdesio in this volume, which address the success of the *Brevísima relación* in the early modern period and subsequent centuries.

Selections of the *Historia de las Indias*, the *Apologética historia sumaria*, and the *Brevísima relación* are taught frequently in survey courses in many disciplines. In Spanish, they are featured in anthologies of Latin American literature such as *Momentos cumbres de la literatura hispánica* (Rodríguez), *Voces de Hispanoamérica* (Chang-Rodríguez and Filer), and *Huellas de las literaturas hispanoamericanas* (Garganigo et al.). In English, we can find selections of Las Casas's writings in *The Literatures of Colonial America: An Anthology* (Castillo and Schweitzer), *Early American Writings* (Mulford et al.), *American Literature* (Cain), and the eighth edition of the *Norton Anthology of Western Literature* (Lawall), which includes—and has included since its fifth edition in 1994—a short selection from *Brevísima relación*. Ralph Bauer is currently editing volume 1 of the *Thomson Anthology of American Literature, The Colonial Americas, 1492–1820*, which will include a more diverse selection of Las Casas's writings.

Las Casas in Literature

Bartolomé de Las Casas is the subject of several plays, novels, and short stories and is an important character or briefly alluded to in a variety of literary works, including poetry. Two pioneering articles in the important compilation *Bartolomé de las Casas in History* (Friede and Keen) make a good place to start investigating Las Casas in literature: Valeri Afanasiev documents the literary lives of Lascasian texts as they were reproduced, preserved, translated, and republished; and Raymond Marcus provides a limited catalog of literary appropriations of Las Casas's personae and texts in Europe, the United States, and Latin America. A more complete catalog and better analysis of this "literarization" of Las Casas appears in a recently published French volume, Nicole Giroud's *Une mosaïque de Fr. Bartolomé de las Casas (1484–1566)*, which traces the reception of Las Casas in history, theology, society, art, and literature. Specifically, the final section of the book (259–315) elaborates on Marcus's list and enumerates important literary works from Romanticism onward that have found inspiration in Las Casas. The list is not comprehensive but highly selective for the relevance of the following interrelated topics: the myth of the noble savage, the heroic figure of Las Casas, and the relevance of the Valladolid debate.

Las Casas Online

Biblioteca Virtual Miguel de Cervantes, the comprehensive digital library for Hispanic literature and cultures, has the most complete Web site on Las Casas (www.cervantesvirtual.com/bib_author/bartolomedelascasas). This Internet project, organized by José Miguel Martínez Torrejón, includes a detailed biography, portraits of the Dominican, maps of the period, Theodore De Bry's illustrations, and primary sources, as well as critical essays. Access is provided to a number of Las Casas's writings, including *De las antiguas gentes del Perú, Fray Bartolomé de las Casas, disputa o controversia con Ginés de Sepúlveda contendiendo acerca de la licitud de las conquistas de las Indias* (Casas, Aquí), Servando Teresa de Mier's 1821 edition of the *Brevísima relación* (Casas, *Breve relación*), and the 1875 edition of the *Historia de las Indias*. Students should be advised to stay away from any sites that still place Las Casas's birth date in 1474 (most encyclopedias have not corrected this erroneous information). Other useful Web sites include the following:

Bartolomé de Las Casas (www.lascasas.org): Established and updated by Lawrence A. Clayton, this is a helpful site about Las Casas, although it overemphasizes his religious doctrine. It features brief and engaging biographical information and introduces fundamental primary texts and English translations. In addition, it provides the full text of recent scholarship: Luis Rivera-Pagán's "A Prophetic Challenge to the Church" and Paolo Carozza's "From Conquest to Constitutions: Retrieving a Latin American Tradition of the Idea of Human Rights," for example, emphasize Las Casas's relevance today. Clayton offers links to the Las Casas Project sponsored by Dominicans who dealt with Native Americans in Oklahoma, to the important Centro

Bartolomé de las Casas in Cuzco, and to human rights centers in Madrid and Chiapas—all inspired by the legacy of Las Casas. The site also provides a gallery of portraits and a digital collection of Las Casas stamps issued in Guatemala, Mexico, Nicaragua, and Cuba.

Théodore De Bry's Illustrations for Bartolomé de las Casas's Short Account of the Destruction of the Indies (www.lehigh.edu/~ejg1/doc/lascasas/casas .htm): Included here are Theodor de Bry's well-known engravings from the 1598 Latin edition of Las Casas's *Brevísima relación.*

Fray Bartolomé de las Casas (www.staff.uni-mainz.de/lustig/texte/antologia/ lascasas.htm): This site provides a collection of brief selections in Spanish of the *Apologética, Memorial de remedios*, and the *Brevísima relación.*

Apologetic History of the Indies (www.columbia.edu/acis/ets/CCREAD/lascasas .htm): A good English-language selection from the *Apologética* appears on this page, including the four types of barbarians, a topic often assigned in classes dealing with early modern political culture.

The Instructor's Library

The overwhelming body of scholarship on Las Casas as a historian or as advocate of Amerindian rights makes the process of narrowing it down extremely difficult. In addition to the key secondary sources listed here, the reader may want to consult earlier bibliographies on Las Casas such as Lewis Hanke and Manuel Giménez Fernández's *Bartolomé de las Casas* (1954) and, more recently, Isacio Pérez Fernández's *Inventario documentado de los escritos de Fray Bartolomé de las Casas* (1981).

Books and Articles

Any discussion about Las Casas should refer to his place in literary, religious, social, and cultural studies in different historical periods. For critical assessments of his life and writings in the colonial period, one must turn to the essential first biographies by the Dominicans historians Agustín Dávila Padilla (*Historia de la fundación y discurso de la provincia de Santiago de México de la Orden de Predicadores* [1596]) and Antonio de Remesal (*Historia general de las Indias Occidentales y particular de la gobernación de Chiapa y Guatemala* [1619]). Important references are also found in Antonio de León Pinelo's *Epítome de la biblioteca oriental y occidental, naútica y geográfica* (1629), Juan de Solórzano Pereira's *De Indiarum Iure* (1629–72), and Juan José Eguiara y Eguren's *Bib-*

lioteca mexicana (1755). Las Casas's tangential entrance in the famous textual "dispute of the New World" (as Antonello Gerbi names it in his book's title) during the eighteenth century is discussed in detail by David Slade and Karen Stolley in this volume.

The editorial work of Juan Antonio Llorente (*Colección de las obras del venerable Obispo de Chiapas* [1822]) and Antonio María Fabié (*Vida y escritos de don fray Bartolomé de las Casas* [1879]) is crucial in discussions of the scholarly assumptions and procedures of nineteenth-century editors in Europe. Their literary editing demonstrates how Spanish thinkers perceived Las Casas's role in the development of Spain's intellectual history: for example, Llorente's *Colección* was for more than two centuries the most complete anthology of Las Casas's writings available to the reading public in Europe. Published in Spanish and French, it was read in educated circles, particularly because it included essays by the prominent French intellectual Henri Grégoire and other essays by the Mexican Fray Servando Teresa de Mier, the Argentinean political leader Dean Gregorio Funes, and Llorente himself. Mier's, Funes's, and Llorente's comments serve as a critical reading of Grégoire's essay on the misunderstandings of Las Casas's actions regarding the African slave trade, and the collection is an intricate part of Enlightenment debate concerning equality, freedom, and reason. References to Llorente's volume are found in the work of many nineteenth-century intellectuals, including José Martí, Ramón Emeterio Betances, and Eugenio María de Hostos.

A number of fundamental works on Las Casas emerged in the second half of the twentieth century. The prominent Latin American historian Lewis Hanke devoted his scholarly efforts to recovering and studying the friar's writings; he and others who worked with him, including Manuel Giménez Fernández (*Bartolomé de las Casas*), Venancio Carro, Manuel María Martínez, Agustín Millares Carlo, and Edmundo O'Gorman, created an international team of Lascasistas. The most important biography in English to date, Henry Raup Wagner and Helen Rand Parish's *The Life and Writings of Bartolomé de las Casas* (1967), is in part the result of this worldwide attention. Besides the critical and editorial work done in Spain, Latin America, and the United States, Marcel Bataillon (*Estudios, Etudes*), Philippe I. André-Vincent (*Bartolomé de las Casas, Las Casas*), André Saint-Lu (*Las Casas indigeniste*), Alain Milhou ("El concepto," "Las Casas"), Marianne Mahn-Lot, and others have greatly advanced the scholarship on Las Casas in the French-speaking world (note also Bataillon and Saint-Lu's *El padre Las Casas* and *Las Casas et la défense*).

During his lifetime, Las Casas had a number of enemies who wrote to the emperor and the king with their complaints. Others established a polemical relation with his writings and spent many pages attacking his religious, political, and ideological positions. Juan Comas's "Historical Reality and the Detractors of Father Las Casas" takes the reader through all the major accusations voiced against him, but if one book can be called the sum of all possible negative reception of Las Casas, it is the now discredited pseudobiography of the friar by the philologist Ramón Menéndez Pidal, *El Padre Las Casas, su doble personalidad* (1963). Menéndez Pidal constructed Las Casas as a psychopathological personality who was fully responsible for defiling the Spanish colonization of America.

The 1990s saw a gathering interest in Las Casas and a reexamination of his works. In Latin America, Gustavo Gutiérrez published *En busca de los pobres de Jesucristo* (1992; published in English as *Las Casas: In Search of the Poor of Jesus Christ* [1993]), his most important theological and political reflection on the cleric. Also of that decade are Juan Durán Luzio's *Bartolomé de las Casas ante la conquista de América* (1992) and Mauricio Beuchot's *Los fundamentos de los derechos humanos en Bartolomé de las Casas* (1994) and *Bartolomé de las Casas, 1484–1566* (1995). In Europe, it is worth noting the German scholarship produced by Thomas Eggensperger (*Bartolomé de las Casas, Der Einfluss*), Mariano Delgado ("Las Casas," "Moralische Unruhe"), and Matthias Gillner.

More recent studies include Paul S. Vickery's *Bartolomé de las Casas: Great Prophet of the Americas* (2006); Hidefuji Someda's *Apología e historia* (2005); José Alves de Freitas Neto's *Bartolomé de las Casas: Narrativa trágica, o amor cristão e a memória americana* (2003); Eyda M. Merediz's *Refracted Images* (2004); Nicole Giroud's *Une mosaïque de Fr. Bartholomé de las Casas* (2002); Felipe Castañeda's *El indio: Entre el bárbaro y el cristianismo* (2002); Santa Arias's *Retórica, historia y polémica: Bartolomé de las Casas y la tradición intelectual renacentista* (2001); Carlos Josaphat's *Las Casas: Todos os direitos para todos* (2000); and Daniel Castro's *Another Face of Empire: Bartolomé de Las Casas, Human Rights, and Ecclesiastical Imperialism* (2007). Lawrence A. Clayton's new biography of the Dominican friar is forthcoming.

The most important and useful volume of essays to date continues to be Friede and Keen's *Bartolomé de las Casas in History: Toward an Understanding of the Man and His Work* (1971). (Both scholars have independently produced important work on Las Casas: Friede, *Bartolomé de Las Casas*; Keen, "Legacy.") The commemorations of Las Casas's birth held in 1974 and 1984 in Spain and Mexico yielded essential collections of scholarship: *Estudios sobre fray Bartolomé de las Casas* (Saint-Lu, Marcus, et al. [1974]), *Actualidad de Bartolmé de las Casas* (1975), *Symposium Fray Bartolomé de las Casas* (1985), and *En el quinto centenario de Bartolomé de las Casas* (1986). Later compilations include *Las Casas entre dos mundos: Congreso teológico internacional* (1993), *El pensamiento lascasiano en la conciencia de América y Europa* (1994), and *V centenario del primer viaje a América de Bartolomé de las Casas, 1502–2002* (2003).

MLA sessions that we organized in 2004 and 2005 ("Teaching Bartolomé de Las Casas," "Teaching Bartolomé de Las Casas beyond the *Brevísima relación*") revealed that Las Casas is increasingly discussed in the context of English and comparative literature. The questionnaires we mailed to instructors in preparing this volume raised the significance of Las Casas in the sixteenth and seventeenth centuries, particularly for an English Protestant audience. Some major studies listed were William S. Maltby's *The Black Legend in England: The*

Development of Anti-Spanish Sentiment, 1558–1660 (1971); Anthony Pagden's *Spanish Imperialism and the Political Imagination* (1990) and his *Lords of All the World: Ideologies of Empire in Spain, Britain and France c.1500–c.1800* (1995); J. Martin Evans's *Milton's Imperial Epic:* Paradise Lost *and the Discourse of Colonization* (1996); and Christopher Hodgkins's article "The Uses of Atrocity: Satanic Spaniards, Hispanic Satans, and the 'Black Legend' from Las Casas to Milton" (2002). Las Casas is also important in the new reconfiguration of Atlantic history that seeks more comparative approaches.[3]

Of the large number of relevant articles, we would like to emphasize those that made an important contribution to the dissemination of knowledge about Las Casas either in terms of archival research or meaningful intellectual engagement. An essay by the Cuban intellectual José Antonio Saco was influential in the remarkable decision by the Real Academia de la Historia in Madrid to approve the publication of the complete text of the *Historia de las Indias* in 1875: Saco's "La *Historia de las Indias* por fray Bartolomé de las Casas y la Real Academia de la Historia," which appeared on 12 February 1865 in the *Revista Hispano-americana*, fueled the controversial publication of this foundational chronicle and can serve as the central text for discussion. Other essential readings are Fernando Ortiz's "La leyenda negra contra Bartolomé de las Casas" and a whole section on the subject in his *Contrapunteo cubano del tabaco y el azúcar* (*Cuban Counterpoint* [1940]), as well as José Juan Arrom's "Bartolomé de las Casas, iniciador de la narrativa de protesta" (1991). Antonio Benítez Rojo has also inscribed Las Casas in a selective and controversial Caribbean corpus by projecting him as an antecedent of postmodernism in "Bartolomé de Las Casas: Entre el infierno y la ficción," which debuted as an article in 1988 in *Modern Language Notes* and then became a chapter in his *La isla que se repite* ("The Repeating Island").

Among the texts that have contributed to a modern reevaluation of Las Casas, his writings, and his legacy, we recommend Lewis Hanke's work (*Aristotle, All Mankind, Bartolomé de las Casas*) and Juan Friede's *Bartolomé de las Casas* (1974), on Las Casas and the *indigenista* movement. Relevant also are Enrique Dussel's philosophical assessment, "Núcleo simbólico lascasiano" (1976); Helen Rand Parish and Harold Weidman's study about his tenure as bishop of Chiapas (*Las Casas*); and Tom Conley's "De Bry's Las Casas" (1992). From the field of Hispanic literary studies, Rolena Adorno (e.g., "Intellectual Life," "Discourses," "El arte," *Polemics*), Margarita Zamora ("Todas son palabras"), and José Rabasa ("Utopian Ethnology," *Inventing, Writing*) have provided important insights not only into Las Casas but into his relation to other foundational writers and critical issues in colonial studies. A view that does not reflect the consensus of Lascasian and colonial scholars is Alberto Moreiras's "Ten Notes on Primitive Imperial Accumulation," which attempts to denaturalize Las Casas's defense of Amerindians and suggests that his project serves the design of a more perfect imperial domination, rather than an anticolonial agenda.

Finally, two significant discoveries changed forever some essential information about Las Casas. Parish and Weidman, in "The Correct Birthdate of

Bartolomé de las Casas" (1976), amended the assumed year of his birth from 1474 to 1484 with new documentary evidence. Pérez Fernández, in his "Hallazgo de un retrato auténtico del P. Las Casas" (1992), revealed a recently found portrait of Las Casas and offered reasonable arguments in favor of its authenticity, although he only had access to photographs of the original painting, which is now lost (274).

When teaching Las Casas, instructors should be aware that the intellectual and methodological constraints of individual disciplines risk undermining some of Las Casas's most important arguments. Las Casas needs to be taught within an interdisciplinary framework to properly situate the significance of his writings.

NOTES

[1] See also Adorno ("Censorship") for an in-depth treatment of Román y Zamora's appropriations of Las Casas in the context of Perú.

[2] Other editions were released in 1984, 1987, 1991, 1992, 1993, 1995, 1996, 1999, 2001, 2003, and 2005.

[3] See Pagden ("Ius," *Fall, Lords*), Elliott (*Old World, Empires*), and Brading's now classic *First America*.

Part Two

APPROACHES

The Intellectual Life of Bartolomé de Las Casas: Framing the Literature Classroom

Rolena Adorno

Teaching Las Casas's works is the most paradoxical pedagogical experience I have ever had. At one extreme, I recall a distinguished colleague and former president of the American Council of Learned Societies, with whom I once cotaught a course, who told me that as a freshman student at Harvard in the 1950s he had read Las Casas's *Brevísima relación de la destrucción de las Indias* and that the experience has stayed with him, in a positive way, ever since. At the other extreme, a graduate student told me that he simply could not complete the seminar assignment that I had given, of writing a brief (even *brevísima!*) essay on Las Casas's work, because, emotionally, he could not face the text. In between these poles are hundreds of students, some of whom read Las Casas as a (belated) call to arms against Spanish colonialism and who have thoroughly assimilated the Anglo-American version of the Black Legend of Spanish history. Others take the approach of undoing the Spanish conquests in America by claiming that the Dominican friar must have exaggerated his demographic estimates of native destruction in the Indies and that, therefore, the deeds he described could not really have occurred—that is, that the conquests could not have been devastating (a typical denial-of-war-atrocities argument). Yet even these opposing views position themselves as extremes. Black Legend proponents and conquest-deniers alike tend to stake their claims on Las Casas himself, whom they interpret in opposing ways: he is seen either as an honest, creditable witness or as a flamboyant, flagrant liar. I know of almost no other author for whom readers' first approximations collapse under the weight of dead-certain speculations about the character and quality of the subject's historical personality.

Given this situation in the classroom, which has prevailed over my thirty-plus years of university teaching, I find it helpful to frame the reading of Las Casas's works with the most pervasive of the "dead certainties"—namely, the commonplace error that he was responsible for the introduction of black African slavery in the Americas. There is no charge heavier than this one, and it explains the popular focus on Las Casas the man rather than his works. Overcoming this obstacle first makes it possible to pursue subsequently my larger goal, which is to examine the landmarks of his juridical, historical, and ethnographic writings. I follow the same sequence here, beginning with a brief overview of Las Casas's life and his career as a reformist and counselor to kings (see also Adorno, "Intellectual Life"; Parish, Introduction; Wagner and Parish).

My aim is to survey the areas of his intellectual work while, at the same time, elucidating certain juridical principles (specifically, the canon law concept of *dominium*) that can help students interpret the sweep of Las Casas's intellectual production. This approach does not tell the whole story of Las Casas's intellectual life, but it effectively and appropriately anchors classroom treatment of an otherwise unmanageable literary corpus. Since Las Casas is as much a protagonist in his works as the author of them, the examples I take to examine his historical and ethnographic writings are familiar historical figures who appear in them: Christopher Columbus and Álvar Núñez Cabeza de Vaca.

Las Casas's Life and the Landmarks of His Reformist Career

Las Casas was born in Seville on 11 November 1484 (Parish and Weidman, "Correct Birthdate"; cf. Pérez Fernández, *Cronología documentada*). He went to the Antilles in 1502, when he joined his merchant father's provisions business on the island of Hispaniola and also managed there the lands in *encomienda* (native labor and tribute rendered to a Spanish trustee, or *encomendero*) that had been granted by Columbus to Las Casas's father, who had accompanied the admiral on his second voyage, in 1493. Las Casas returned to Spain and became a deacon in Seville in 1506; he was ordained a priest in Rome on 3 March 1507, in his twenty-third year. Upon his return to America, and while serving as chaplain to Pánfilo de Narváez in the conquest of Cuba, he witnessed in 1514 (at the age of thirty) an unprovoked massacre of Taíno Indians, which, by his own account, was the source of his conversion to the cause of protecting the natives of America from wanton destruction (*Historia de las Indias* 2: 533–41; bk. 3, ch. 20).

Las Casas's reformist career began immediately thereafter. Spanning a period of a full fifty years, it must be understood in its sequence and for its evolution. Perhaps the most important concept to convey to students is that historical experience is not "flat" but rather characterized by change over time; this is certainly true for Las Casas's half century of activism and active reflection on the Indies. Three key moments define this arc: Las Casas's 1516 recommendation to grant to Castilian settlers in the Indies the licenses to import black and white African slaves and his first attempts, in 1518, to challenge the Indians' subjection to slavery and the *encomienda* system; his 1542 proposal for the abolition of Indian slavery and the *encomienda* (which resulted in the passage of the New Laws in Spain but their rejection by governmental and private interests in America); and his 1563 and 1564 recommendations that Spanish imperial rule in the Americas cease altogether and that sovereignty over lands, possessions, and persons be returned to the native peoples.

Three pairs of texts correspond to these respective moments: (1) The "Memorial de remedios para las Indias" of 1516—the infamous memorandum that recommended licensing Castilians resident in the Indies to import black and white slaves from Africa to provide labor for mining—and the "Memorial de remedios para las Indias" of 1518, which proposed transferring administrative control over the Indians from the *encomenderos* to the Spanish king. (2) Las Casas's 1542 proposal of twenty reasons why Indians should not be granted in *encomienda*, published in 1552 under the title "Entre los remedios" alongside his *Brevísima relación de la destrucción de las Indias*. The two expositions functioned in tandem at court in 1542 when Las Casas presented them viva voce; in "Entre los remedios," he proposed remedies for the devastations caused by conquest and hard labor that he dramatically portrayed in the *Brevísima relación*. (3) *De thesauris qui reperiuntur in sepulchris indorum* 'On the Tomb Treasures of Perú' (*Los tesoros* [1563]) and the "Tratado de las doce dudas" 'Treatise of the Twelve Doubts' (1564). These great juridical works were provoked, first, by Philip II's attempt to sell Perú to its private Spanish landholders and *encomenderos* and, second, by the subsequent discovery of pre-Columbian tomb treasures in northern coastal Perú: to whom did they belong? In these two final treatises Las Casas expounded the principles of the rights of all peoples to sovereignty over their own lands and possessions.

This sequence of reformist activity was broken for some eight years, from the time Las Casas entered the Dominican order, in September 1522, through the end of 1530, after which a letter that he wrote to the Council of the Indies evidenced his return to the cause of seeking justice for the Indians (Pérez Fernández, *Cronología* 318, 340). In his last will and testament, written two years before his death, Las Casas bequeathed his voluminous papers, as well as the "multitude of letters" and accounts that he received from all parts of the Indies, to the Colegio de San Gregorio de Valladolid. He requested that a student of the college be appointed to catalog them as testimony of the truth that he "always and for many years" had defended and as explanation, should the kingdoms of Spain come to ruin, for their divine punishment ("Cláusula" 540).[1] Las Casas died in his eighty-second year on 18 July 1566, in the Dominican convent of Nuestra Señora de Atocha in Madrid.

Las Casas on African Slavery

The erroneous portrayal of Las Casas as the instigator of black African slavery in the Americas has been a theme coloring the evaluation of his life and work since the eighteenth century. Addressing the African slavery attribution is probably the most effective preamble to any classroom presentation of Las Casas's works. It gets students' attention (the issue is likely to be already on their minds), and it provides an immediate, hands-on exercise in textual interpretation that can reveal how historical fact and literary interpretation are generated, repeated, and transformed (and how historical errors are perpetuated). Three points can be made: when black slavery began in the Americas, when the notion of Las Casas's responsibility for it came into being, and what Las Casas himself had to say on the subject.

Las Casas was not the originator of African slavery in the Indies. It had begun within the first decade of Columbus's arrival in America. Slave traffic was already under way when King Ferdinand issued royal instructions on 16 September 1501 to the newly appointed governor of Hispaniola, Nicolás de Ovando, on whose expedition the eighteen-year-old Las Casas made his first voyage to the Indies in 1502. These instructions set forth provisions for the governance of the "islands and mainland of the Ocean Sea" that included the importation of black slaves from Africa, as long as they had been born "under the tutelage of Christians":

> [N]on consentyreis nin dareis logar que allá vayan moros nin xudíos, nin erexes nin rreconcyliados, nin personas nuevamente convertidas a Nuestra Fée, salvo si fueren esclavos negros u otros esclavos que fayan nascido en poder de cristhianos, Nuestros súbditos y naturales.
> (*Colección de documentos inéditos* 31:23)

> You are not to consent or allow to go [to the Indies] Muslims, Jews, heretics, former apostates reconciled to the church, or those persons who are newly converted to Our Faith, except for those who are black slaves or other slaves, born under the tutelage of Christians, our subjects and native peoples.

The royal instructions suggest that members of the aforementioned groups had already found their way to the Indies, and Ovando as new governor was charged with stemming the tide of this undesirable migration, carefully excepting slaves—black Africans or others—who had been born in the power of Christians, which likely would have been meant in Seville and its environs, where black African slaves, imported by the Portuguese, were common. Ovando's request to the king in 1503, asking that the flow of black slaves to the Indies be stopped because of the impossibility of controlling them, suggests that their numbers were already considerable in the Antilles by the previous year, when Las Casas had arrived in Hispaniola with Ovando.

When, then, did the idea of Las Casas as the author of black African slavery in America appear, and from where? It seems to have begun with Enlightenment thinkers of the eighteenth century, specifically in the works of the French Jesuit Pierre-François-Xavier de Charlevoix (1730–31), the Dutch cleric Cornelius de Pauw (1768–69), and Guillaume-Thomas, the abbé de Raynal (1770), interpreting wrongly a passage in Antonio de Herrera y Tordesillas's *Historia general de los hechos de los castellanos en las islas y tierra firme del Mar Océano* (1601–15). (The passage appears in Herrera's decade 2, book 2, chapter 2 [see Llorente 2: 335, 375–76, 440], and it quotes the statement found in Las Casas's 1517 "Memorial de remedios" [17]). The notion became solidified in the English-language tradition when the Scottish historian William Robertson wrote, in his classic *History of America* (1777):

> Las Casas proposed to purchase a sufficient number of negroes from the Portuguese settlements on the coast of Africa, and to transport them to America, in order that they might be employed as slaves in working the mines and cultivating the ground. . . . While he contended earnestly for the liberty of the people born in one quarter of the globe, he laboured to enslave the inhabitants of another region; and in the warmth of his zeal to save the Americans from the yoke, pronounced it to be lawful and expedient to impose one still heavier upon the Africans.
>
> (1: 320–21; bk. 3, year 1517)

While eighteenth-century misreadings of Herrera attributed to Las Casas the introduction of black African slavery to the Spanish Indies, twentieth-century readers have had at their disposal Las Casas's own statements on the subject. Published for the first time in 1875–76 but more widely available after the editions of 1951 and 1957, Las Casas's *Historia de las Indias* contains his expressions of regret at having proposed selling licenses to Castilian settlers in the Indies for the purchase of black African slaves, based on the misunderstanding, common in Europe at the time, that the Africans imported as slaves by the Portuguese had been captured in a just war—that is, in the defensive war against the Ottoman Empire that all European Christendom was waging at the time. (The Turks reached Vienna, overran parts of Italy, and received their first serious blow from Christian Europe only upon their naval defeat at the 1571 Battle of Lepanto, which occurred five years after Las Casas's death.) Las Casas acknowledges responsibility and regret for the role he unwittingly played, referring to himself, as he does customarily in the *Historia*, in the third person:

> Deste aviso que dió el clérigo, no poco después se halló arrepiso, juzgándose culpado por inadvertente, porque como después vido y averiguó, según parecerá, ser tan injusto el cautiverio de los negros como el de los indios, no fue discreto remedio el que aconsejó que trujesen negros para que se libertasen los indios, aunque él suponía que eran justamente captivos, aunque

no estuvo cierto que la ignorancia que en esto tuvo y buena voluntad lo
excusase delante el juicio divino.   (*Historia* 3: 275; bk. 3, ch. 129)

Of this advice that the cleric gave, he found himself afterward repentant,
judging himself guilty through ignorance, because as he subsequently saw
and came to understand, as will be shown, the captivity of the blacks was
as unjust as that of the Indians. The remedy he proposed, that blacks be
brought in order to free the Indians from toil, was not an appropriate one.
Even though he had understood at the time that they had been taken captive justly, he was not sure that his ignorance in this matter and his good
intentions would excuse him in the face of divine judgment.

The notion that the Africans "had been taken captive justly" refers to the common misunderstanding that they had been taken legitimately as war captives
in the struggle against the Ottoman Empire. Instead, as Las Casas (and the
world) later learned, they had been the victims of assault and capture, plucked
from the homes in which they lived securely and in peace (*Historia* 1: 134; bk.
1, ch. 25).

Las Casas, Licenciado

Las Casas's work, whether as activist reformer, missionary, historian, or theorist
of culture and ethnographer, was grounded on the authority of textual traditions:
Greco-Roman, biblical, patristic, theological, philosophical, and juridical—that
is, civil and particularly canon law. These intellectual frameworks constituted
his library and the laboratory of his thought. He famously remarked in a letter
written to his Dominican brethren, circa 1563, that he had been studying the
law and trying to draw sound conclusions about justice for forty-eight years,
and, if not mistaken, he had finally penetrated its basic principles: "y a cuarenta
y ocho años que trabajo de idquirir é estudiar y sacar en limpio el derecho; creo,
si no estoy engañado, aver ahondado esta materia hasta llegar al agua de su
principio" (Llorente 2: 577–78). He added that he had written more than two
thousand folios in Latin and Castilian, many of which had been read by learned
theologians, by the great professors of the universities of Salamanca and Alcalá
de Henares, and by the members of the Dominican house of San Gregorio in
Valladolid. His contemporaries, whether friends, admirers, or enemies, referred
to him as "licenciado" or "licenciado en leyes" (licentiate in law), and he did not
reject the title but repeated it when citing others' references to him. Although
no positive evidence of formal degrees has been brought forward, Las Casas's
considerable knowledge of the law—especially canon law—is increasingly well
attested by modern scholars who have documented its use in his works (Losada,
Introducción 38–42; Parish and Weidman, *Las Casas en México* 133–34, 141–
45, 372; Pennington).

While Las Casas is commonly considered to be Thomistic in his thought, following the Aristotelian-Thomist school of neoscholastic philosophy, particularly regarding natural law, it is also true that, as Kenneth Pennington observes, "Las Casas was a jurist whose ideas were based on medieval juridical theory [and that] he developed a central tradition of medieval legal thought in original and interesting ways." Not unusual in this respect, Las Casas was "part of a general movement of adapting ecclesiological and canon law concepts to political theory." Pennington adds:

> The basic premise in Las Casas's position on the rights of the Indians is that legitimate secular power does exist outside the church. Las Casas insisted throughout his life that the Indians' *dominium* was legitimate and just, and that the Spaniards did not have the right to usurp the Indians' just title. From this basic principle sprang all the rest of Las Casas's ideas.   (151)

Las Casas followed juridical tradition and augmented it with theological sources, but theology was not his primary expertise and was not as clear-cut on the principle of *dominium* as was canon law (155, 156). The basic canon law tenet Las Casas used was the principle of *Quod omnes tangit debet ab omnibus approbari*, "What touches all must be approved by all." Developed to regulate the affairs of a bishopric, the principle was applied by Las Casas to a wholly new situation. As it would be dangerous to assign a prince or a bishop to an unwilling people, so too a foreign king should not be imposed on a free people; "consequently, Las Casas concluded, the pope could not give infidels a new king without their consent" (157). Applying this definition of *dominium*, Las Casas was able to conceptualize the rights of the Indians to sovereignty in their own lands on the authority and logic of the law. In the classroom, this concept can serve as the anchor on or lens through which to examine the main arguments and interpretations of Las Casas's writings, from the *Brevísima relación* to the *Apologética historia sumaria*.

Common Misunderstandings Corrected

Las Casas's juridical perspective is essential to understanding his two interventions in the Indies debates that long have been the subject of misleading commonplaces: the purpose of his *Brevísima relación de la destrucción de las Indias* and the question formally debated by him and Juan Ginés de Sepúlveda in Valladolid in 1550–51. The *Brevísima relación*'s rhetoric, which uses biblical metaphor, portraying the Indians as docile sheep and the Spaniards as devouring wolves, is commonly the basis for the claim that Las Casas held a simplistic view of the Indians. In an equally uninformed and stereotyping manner, the Valladolid debate is often characterized as being centered on the question as to whether the Indians were human—that is, whether they had souls. Both of these misconceptions should quickly be dispatched.

The *Brevísima relación*'s objective was to persuade the king's council to reform colonial law by abolishing the *encomienda* system and Indian slavery. In other words, the 1542 speech (and the 1552 published pamphlet) aimed to provoke a fundamental change in the laws governing the Indies. Using the biblical sheep-and-wolves metaphor, Las Casas attempted to persuade the prince and his councilors of the need for such legislation, not to characterize or define the nature of the Indians. Convened by the emperor Charles V, the Valladolid debate likewise turned on the question of governance, specifically in relation to Christian indoctrination (see Abril Castelló). The task before Las Casas and Sepúlveda was to determine, as stated by Domingo de Soto in his detailed summary of the proceedings,

> si es lícito a Su Majestad hacer guerra a aquellos indios antes que se les prediquе la fe, para subjectallos a su Imperio, y que después de subjectados puedan más fácil y cómodamente ser enseñados y alumbrados por la doctrina evangélica del conoscimiento de sus errores y de la verdad cristiana.   ("Traslado" 295)

> whether it is legitimate for His Majesty to make war on those Indians before preaching the faith to them, in order to subject them to his Empire, so that, once subjugated, they more easily can be instructed and enlightened by the evangelical doctrine of the knowledge of their errors and the Christian truth.

Sepúlveda answered in the affirmative, arguing that it was not only legitimate but also expedient to do so. Las Casas responded in the negative, arguing that such a position failed on the criteria of both legitimacy and expediency and that it was contrary to the teachings of the Christian faith. From his canonist outlook, Las Casas maintained the right to sovereignty of the American peoples, both before and after their acceptance of the Christian religion. Sepúlveda did indeed introduce the issue of the Indians' rational capacity into the debate, justifying the "war first" argument by pointing to their (supposed) "natural" ineptitude. The Indians' mental abilities were not, however, the issue under consideration but rather a claim that Sepúlveda brought into the debate to support his side. Las Casas rejected such arguments; his canonist perspective focused not on the character of the Indians but on their legal right to freedom and sovereignty.

Las Casas, Historian

Las Casas's repentant recognition of the role he played in 1516 in supporting the African slavery under way for more than a decade and a half reveals that he saw himself as a significant actor or agent in the early history of the Indies. This sense of personal responsibility is a key to understanding his *Historia de las Indias*, in which his focus is always on the actors, including himself. Taking a long view of that history, he summed it up as consisting of an unprecedented diminution of the human race for which royal governance of more than a half century's duration could not be held blameless before God: "Y destos estragos y ofensas gravísimas de Dios y jactura y diminución tan nunca oída del linaje humano, no tiene ninguna excusa el Consejo ante Dios, porque no se hicieron en un día, ni en año, ni en diez, ni en veinte, sino en sesenta y más años" (*Historia* 3: 179; bk. 3, ch. 102).

Las Casas's aim in the *Historia* was to write the history of Spain's first sixty years in America, but he did not reach even as far as the 1519–21 conquest of Mexico. His close scrutiny of Columbus's maritime and administrative career takes up approximately half the work, ending with the admiral's death on 20 May 1506 (*Historia* 2: 329; bk. 2, ch. 38). The historical and philosophical question that Las Casas asked in his work, written over a period of some thirty years, was: how did things come to turn out as they did at the end of sixty years of Spain's rule in the Indies?

As Las Casas struggled to identify and explain all the factors that accounted for this destruction and loss, he strove to include all pertinent events. In his analysis, divine providence did not simplistically ensure victory in battle, as it did in the narratives of conquistador writers such as Hernán Cortés or Bernal Díaz del Castillo. For Las Casas, divine agency challenged humankind to exercise ethical conscience and to avoid succumbing to human frailty: there are no easy answers in his history of the Indies. He narrates events but does not offer a facile interpretation; he instead displays in great (sometimes excruciating) detail the complexities, leaving the reader to determine the causes and consequences of specific actions or patterns of behavior.

Las Casas's narrative about Christopher Columbus in the *Historia de las Indias* reveals that the Dominican examined history not with the certitude of his moral harangues but with perplexity at the great conundrums of Columbian history. Although Las Casas describes Columbus as a "good Christian," he shows him to have been caught in a web of conflicting goals and motivations. I recommend the reading of a single chapter (bk. 1, ch. 105) from the *Historia* to illustrate the point with students. Here is one of its most revealing passages:

> Pero el Almirante, con el gran deseo que tenía de dar provecho a los Reyes de Castilla para recompensar los grandes gastos que hasta entonces habían hecho y hacían, . . . y como hombre extranjero y solo (como él decía, desfavorecido), . . . juntamente con su gran ceguedad e ignorancia del derecho que tuvo, creyendo que por solo haberlas descubierto y los Reyes de Castilla enviarlo a los traer a la fe y religión cristiana, eran privados de su libertad todos, le causó darse más priesa y exceder en la desorden que tuvo, que quizá tuviera; porque ciertamente él era cristiano y virtuoso y de muy buenos deseos. . . .   (*Historia* 1: 418; bk. 1, ch. 105)

But the Admiral, with his great desire to offer the king and queen wealth
in order to compensate the great expenses that they had incurred, . . .
and as a foreigner and alone (as he said, disfavored), . . . together with
his great blindness and ignorance of the law or right that he had, believ-
ing that merely by having discovered the Indies and by having been sent
by the king and queen to propagate the faith and Christian religion, that
they—the Indians—were all deprived of their freedom, he was impelled
to rush and even surpass the disorder that he already created, or might
have created; because certainly he was a Christian and virtuous and of
very good intentions. . . .

This passage, which consists of fragments of a sentence nearly a page long, demonstrates how Las Casas shifts the reader's attention from one consideration to
another. Just when we think we have located Las Casas's target of culpability,
another factor is brought into play and redirects our consideration. Christopher
Columbus turns out to be neither Las Casas's hero nor the villain of his history but rather the exemplary case of a man who, like almost any other, fails to
understand the gravity of the stakes of the enterprise in which he is engaged
or to anticipate the larger consequences and implications of his most mundane
decisions. Columbus was an appropriate subject for reflection because his most
casual decisions contributed to chains of events and patterns of behavior that
ultimately brought about, in Las Casas's view, the ruin of the Indies and its
peoples, that "never-before-heard-of diminution of the human race" (*Historia
de las Indias* 3: 179; bk. 3, ch. 102).

Las Casas, Ethnographer

Another essential dimension in teaching Las Casas is to consider his writings on
the theory of culture and cultural differences and to appreciate his theoretical
arguments about the worthiness of Amerindian humanity. The discussions of culture in the *Apologética historia sumaria* helpfully override the common misunderstanding that he considered the native inhabitants of the New World as an
undifferentiated mass. (This misapprehension is usually based, as we have seen,
on Las Casas's political and juridical works, in which he refers to the natives of the
New World as "gentle folk" and "sheep among wolves," representing them, quite
literally, as parties [defendants] in a lawsuit in which he takes the role of attorney
for the defense [*Tratados* 1: 15, 19].) His theorizing of the Indians' universal humanity shows that his thinking far exceeded the rhetoric of the *Brevísima relación*
and that he drew, with precision and clarity, on the fields of ancient and medieval
environmental and social theory. Yet the *Apologética* is an immense work, and for
that reason the textual fragments highlighted here can be used as reading selections to set forth Las Casas's arguments about the essential, universal qualities of
Amerindian humanity and his acute interest in cultural variety and difference.

The heart of Las Casas's analysis in the *Apologética historia sumaria* is natural history: he takes classical and medieval environmental theories and applies them to the Antilles, demonstrating that this place was most propitious for fostering the development of a benign human nature (1: 178–79, 190–91; chs. 34, 36). Moving on to moral history, he uses the model of the city derived from Aristotle and Saint Augustine to theorize civil life and ultimately to show, through hundreds of chapters, that the diverse native societies of the New World had established civil orders. Las Casas follows Aristotle's *Politics* when defining the city as a social unit that is self-sufficient, inasmuch as it provides for the temporal and corporal needs of its inhabitants (protecting citizens from internal and external threats of harm and maintaining peace) as well as their moral ones (1: 237–38; ch. 45). Las Casas combined this view with that of Saint Augustine, for whom the city was the life of a community, carried out in concordance, harmony, and peace (1: 239; ch. 45). Las Casas argued that the inhabitants of the New World satisfied these criteria for social order, even if their cities were constituted by "algún número de barrios y de parentelas o linajes que se hacen de casas juntas, puesto que sean de paja o de otra cualquiera material" 'some number of districts and kinship groups or lineages made up of houses set together, be they made of straw or any other material' (1: 241; ch. 45). He then applied the principles expounded in Aristotle's social philosophy and Augustine's theology to Amerindian societies and argued, against the opinions of Juan Ginés de Sepúlveda and others, that the natives of the Americas had achieved the creation of civil order.

The *Apologética*'s historical and geographic discussions of America's native societies leave no doubt that Las Casas commanded a broad and extraordinarily detailed knowledge of the differences among them. In the more than forty-five years that he spent going back and forth between Spain and America, he came to know Bermuda, Cuba, Jamaica, Hispaniola (the island he knew and loved most), the kingdoms of New Spain (including the environs of the Mexican capital), the provinces of Jalisco and Nicaragua, Tierra Firme or the Spanish Main, the northern coast of South America to Cumaná, the kingdom of Yucatan, and Chiapas and Guatemala. He explicitly pointed out that he did not know from personal experience the immense territories of Perú, La Florida, or Cíbola (the latter two occupied today by the United States [1: 178; ch. 34]). Altogether, Las Casas gathered his data not only from personal experience but also—and importantly—from the writings of many other persons, which he acknowledged with care, including, he notes admiringly, the friars who knew Indian languages.

A good classroom example is Las Casas's treatment of the Indians of La Florida, which was the 1520s designation not only for the cape of today's state of Florida but for the entire, vast unknown territories to the north of New Spain—in effect, continental North America. An illuminating exercise is to read Las Casas's *Apologética* account alongside his source, Álvar Núñez Cabeza de Vaca's 1542 *Relación*, known since its 1555 edition by the familiar title *Naufragios*. I recommend specifically Cabeza de Vaca's chapters 32–36 (although Las Casas read the 1542 edition, which had no chapter divisions) and Las Casas's *Apologética*, chapters 124, 168, and 205–06. Such a juxtaposition demonstrates how Las Casas worked with his ethnographic sources and underscores, once again, the difference between his highly rhetorical and homogenizing image of the Indians in the *Brevísima relación* and the actual information about them he amassed. Students will also see how Las Casas relied on the authority of firsthand testimony and how the material takes on a new purpose in the hands of its "second author." That new purpose, in the *Apologética*, was to demonstrate the "universal principle" of humanity's natural inclination toward seeking and serving its maker (1: 213; bk. 3, ch. 40) and to elucidate the natives' readiness to receive Christianity, thus supporting Las Casas's advocacy of peaceful colonization.

The Persistent Image of Las Casas as Legal Advocate

As many as fifty years after his death, Las Casas was still being referred to as a licentiate—a lawyer or legal advocate—and his juridical works in manuscript continued to be circulated and cited. In *Comentarios reales de los Incas* (1609, 1617) El Inca Garcilaso de la Vega, for example, referred to Las Casas by the title *licenciado* and called him the "official solicitor and inventor" of the New Laws, which were intended to abolish the *encomienda* system in the Indies (*Comentarios reales* 3: 225; pt. 2, bk. 4, ch. 3). Quite remarkably, in *El primer nueva corónica y buen gobierno* (1615), Garcilaso's Andean contemporary Felipe Guaman Poma de Ayala quoted assiduously from Las Casas's "Tratado de las doce dudas" to advocate the return of sovereignty over the Andes to Andeans (929–30; see Adorno, *Guaman Poma* 21–27). Such references confirm the unifying principles of Las Casas's writings, be they devoted to the interpretation of the rights and limits of imperial rule, to Spanish history, or to New World ethnology. With this framework of Las Casas–as–legal advocate in mind, his most timeless work, the *Brevísima relación*, becomes more intelligible. Las Casas's fundamental perspective, based on time-honored juridical principles applied to a new situation, can be an effective lens through which to view the various facets of his intellectual life. That he combined those pursuits with reformist activism—or, rather, that he put scholarly inquiry into the service of practical goals—defines his modernity and his pertinence to readers today.

NOTES

All citations of Las Casas's *Historia de las Indias* refer to the version edited by Agustín Millares Carlo (Fondo de Cultura Económica, 1951), and citations of the *Apologética historia sumaria* refer to the version edited by Edmundo O'Gorman (U Nacional Autónoma de México, 1967). Citations of El Inca Garcilaso de la Vega's *Comentarios reales* refer to the version edited by Carmelo Sáenz de Santa Maria (Atlas, 1960–65).

[1] All translations of Spanish-language texts are mine.

Teaching Las Casas
through the Lens of the Historian
Lawrence A. Clayton

> Y con certificación esto afirmo: que no hay hoy vivo
> hombre, sino solo yo, que pueda como ellas pasaron y
> tan por menudo referillas [las noticias de la historia de
> la conquista]; y de otras también munchas que pocos las
> han escripto y no con aquella fidelidad que debían, quizá
> porque no las alcanzaron o porque no las vieron o con
> demasiada temeridad de la que debieran o informados de
> los que las corrompieron [y] fueron causa [de] que hoy en
> sus escriptos se hallen munchos e intolerables defectos.

> And I can affirm this with certainty: there is no other man
> alive other than me who can write of what happened in
> such detail [on the history of the conquest of the Indies];
> and of the many others, few have been written with faith-
> fulness they owed [to the truth], perhaps because they
> never reached the Indies or did not see them or were too
> imprudent or were corrupted by those who went there,
> so that today in their writings one finds many intolerable
> defects.   —Bartolomé de Las Casas

Most historians feel quite comfortable when approaching the works of Bartolomé de Las Casas: he was, and remains in some ways, one of us. One of the
earliest and most complete chronicles of the Indies, his three-volume *Historia
de las Indias* is among the most detailed resources for the early presence of
Spain in the Indies, beginning with Christopher Columbus's first voyage and
reaching about 1520. As one probes deeper into Las Casas's life and works,
however, the picture grows more complex and takes on more dimensions than
that of the mere historian or collector and chronicler: Las Casas is a commentator, interpreter, polemicist, and advocate, even while he putatively attempts
to remain true to the muse of history. He wants to "set the record straight,"
which is still the reason many historians with a particular perspective or ideology write contemporary history. They aim to produce a record of what "really"
happened—the truth, as opposed to fabrications and distortions produced by
others. In doing so, they tend to reveal powerful personalities with a sense of
mission. Perhaps the greatest drawback to chroniclers' writing about their own
times is also paradoxically the greatest strength: their closeness to—or even, as
was often true of Las Casas, presence at—the subject and events recorded. Eyewitness testimony produces a powerful narrative whose ring of authenticity no
secondary account can match. On the other hand, such immediacy also clouds

the issue with a myopic nearness whose only remedy is the passage of time. In Las Casas, chronicler and historian become one to produce a text for posterity, the *Historia de las Indias*, that he requested not be published until forty years after his death but that, in fact, was not published until the nineteenth century.

His prologue to the magisterial *Historia de las Indias*, a fairly brief text worth assigning to the history student, outlines his relation to history (*Obras completas* 3: 327–49). Las Casas devotes more than twenty pages to what any class of graduate students would easily recognize as historiography, or the history of history. Why is history written? How is it written? These questions are Las Casas's primary concerns in his prologue. He presents a theoretical frame for historiography, drawing on a long line of distinguished predecessors—pagan, Jewish, and Christian. While his frequent detours and digressions often frustrate modern readers, he is particularly clear and cogent in this introduction, which begins characteristically, with a prologue to his prologue,

> en el cual tracta el auctor difusamente de los diversos motivos y fines que los que historias escriben suelen tener. Toca la utilidad grande que trae la noticia de las cosas pasadas. Alega munchos auctores y escriptores antiguos. Pone muy largo la causa final e intención suya que movió a escribir esta corónica de las Indias. Asigna los grandes errores que en munchos casos cerca destas naciones indianas ha habido y las causas de donde procedieron. Señala también las otras causas, formal y material y eficiente, que en toda obra suelen concurrir.   (327)

> in which the author deals with the differing motives and goals that historians usually touch on. He touches on the great usefulness of dealing with things past. He refers to many ancient authors and writers. He deals with the rationale that prompted him to write this chronicle of the Indies. He defines the great errors committed against these Indian nations and how and why they occurred. He also points to other causes, formal, material, and efficient, which usually appear in all works of this kind.[1]

Las Casas identifies four principal reasons why historians write and then categorizes ancient historians such as Marcus Cato (Cato the Elder, 234–149 BC), Pliny the Elder (AD 23–79), Herodotus (c. 484–425 BC), Plutarch (AD c. 46–127), and Josephus (AD c. 37–100) according to these categories. Historians who fall in the first two categories—those who write for fame and glory and are carried away by their clever rhetoric and those who write to please rulers—are dismissed rather summarily. The final two categories are those historians who write to preserve the truth and those who preserve the past for posterity: Las Casas includes himself in both. Among the figures he admired were Herodotus, often thought of as the "father" of history; Josephus, the first-century Jew who witnessed and recorded the fall of Jerusalem to the Romans in AD 70, who also set the record straight regarding the much misrepresented Jewish nation; and a number of Christian historians, such as Justin Martyr (AD 100–165), one of the first Christian apologists in the second century.

Diodorus Siculus (90–30 BC), a Greek historian much admired by Las Casas, is presented as a model. Las Casas quotes him—as others he admires—at length, in Latin and in Castilian to reach a wider audience. The quotations are windows into Las Casas's mind as a historian—for example:

> Con justa razón deben los hombres grandes gracias a los que se ocupan en escrebir las cosas pasadas, porque aprovecharon siempre munchos con sus trabajos a la vida de los mortales. Enseñan a los leyentes con ejemplos de las cosas pasadas lo que los hombres han de desear y lo que deben de huir. Porque leyendo las cosas que con varios trabajos y peligros los pasados lexos de nosotros experimentaron, nosotros, sin trabajo y sin peligro, para utilidad y amonestación de nuestras vidas leemos.   (qtd. on 332)

> It is with good reason that great men owe thanks to those occupied in writing of things past, since they [great men] learn much of life from those who came before them. Readers learn from past examples what to desire and what to flee. We benefit from reading of all the work and danger people experienced in the past, because we can put that knowledge to work in our own lives.

Las Casas quotes Diodorus to emphasize that the lessons of history need to be recorded so they can teach; otherwise, they are lost, and nations are doomed or destined to repeat what they have forgotten.

Moving from the general to the specific, Las Casas's prologue then broaches the evolving history of the Indies—what was erroneous with it and why he chose to write the "true" history correcting all the falseness, lies, and ignorance of other chroniclers. Here Las Casas—the honest broker, as it were, of history—moves subtly but inexorably into the role of advocate. Although several of his historical works have often been targeted for the exaggerated and polemical style whose strident voice so offends modern readers, this voice was consistent with chroniclers and historians of his epoch and those who preceded him by hundreds or, in some instances, over a thousand years.

The shortcomings of other chroniclers of the Indies are many, according to Las Casas, who summarizes them in two broad categories: errors in exegesis and errors on the nature of the American Indians. Two examples: first, he pillories most chroniclers for their lack of experience in the Indies, although he excuses Peter Martyr d'Anghiera (1457–1526), whose *Decades* relied on the letters and reports of the discoverers and actors themselves, such as Columbus. But even Martyr does not escape the quick flick of Las Casas's lash: the Dominican adds parenthetically, "en las otras cosas que pertenecen al discurso y progreso destas Indias hartas falsedades sus *Décadas* contienen" 'but on other matters pertaining to these Indies, his *Decades* contain a lot of errors' (348).

Second, since Indians were being depicted as barbarians, Las Casas delves into the past of Iberia and discovers the same "barbarians." Quoting extensively from Cicero, Las Casas lays down the premise that all nations and people began as barbarous savages. But God endowed them with an innate sense of rationality and an industrious nature, which, when combined with the Christian religion and Catholic faith, transformed them into a civil people. Las Casas then moves beyond Cicero and applies this model of progressive improvement to his own nation, Spain:

> Notorio es a los que son expertos en nuestras y ajenas historias la barbárica simplicidad, y ferocidad no menos, de la gente española, mayormente la del Andalucía y de otras provincias de España; cuánta era cuando vinieron los primeros griegos a poblar a Monviedro, y Alceo, capitán de corsarios, y los fenices a Cádiz; todos astutísimas gentes, en cuya comparación toda la gente de aquellos reinos eran como animales.   (342)

> It is well known among those who write history that the Spanish people— those from Andalucía more than others—were simple, ferocious barbarians when the first Greeks came to settle in Monviedro and when Alceo, a captain of corsairs, and the Phoenicians came to Cádiz. These were all astute people compared with those in these kingdoms who were like animals.

From this historical antecedent Las Casas draws the lesson that the Indies and Indians too have been passing through these stages to civility and in some instances have already reached it, although Spanish chroniclers have failed to relate it truthfully. Las Casas also points out the natural "irracionalidad y vicios que habia en toda España" 'irrationality and vices that existed throughout Spain' and made Christianizing the nation difficult (343).

After this fascinating discourse on the nature and practice of history, in which he weaves together elements spanning more than two millennia (a long look not common today), he narrows his focus to the history of the Indies. His subsection "Dañosos inconvenientes o efectos que se han seguido de tales defectos de noticias acerca de las naciones indianas y cada dia se siguen" 'Damaging effects arising from defective reports concerning the Indian nations, and which continue today' moves him from historian to polemicist (343). His arguments emerge from discussions of divine and natural law, from scripture, patristic literature, and Aristotelian works and commentaries: the true nature of the Indians, he asserts, has been misrepresented and distorted to justify the conquest. From here we see the Black Legend spin off, eventually to take on a life of its own.

Las Casas finishes his prologue by detailing his objectives in a historical framework. Regardless of how he has been portrayed by his peers and scholars today, his image of himself as a chronicler and historian with a mission is clear in his section "Objectivos que persigue el auctor al ofrecer complida noticia de las cosas destas Indias" 'The objectives sought by the author on offering this finished account of the things of these Indies' (346). He lists eight objectives in writing his history, from the general "for the honor and glory of God" to more specific goals about describing the indigenous peoples as they were, as opposed to the barbarians and primitives portrayed by others. Like any good historian, Las Casas was cognizant of his predecessors, listing one by one the historians, chroniclers, and philosophers who inspired him.

Las Casas the historian thus represents himself as a complex figure. His primary motive is to rectify the errors and deceptions written about the colonization of the Indies and about its inhabitants and explain the true state of affairs. He writes his history to elevate readers' image of the Indians from depraved and ignorant savages incapable of entering the Kingdom of God to worthy recipients of the Gospel. Here the historian, advocate, and polemicist assumes the role of Christian evangelist and expects Spanish rulers and magistrates to act on his version of the truth.

His historic appeals to the Crown to rectify the great wrongs and injustices committed by Spaniards on Indians were in keeping with the conventions of his time. Luis Cabrera de Córdoba's 1611 treatise on the writing of history states that the importance of history rests on its didacticism and claims that reading it is essential for kings striving for prudence in the art of governance (11). Cabrera later describes truth in history as a primarily moral issue, calling truth but a stepping-stone to justice; Las Casas follows similar conventions and pursues both truth and justice with a passion, but in his devotion to living out his role as appointed universal "Protector [*Procurador*] of the Indians" (a title bestowed on him by Cardinal Ximénez de Cisneros in 1516, then regent of Spain), he himself mangles the truth. Teachers and historians are thus faced with a double-edged sword: Las Casas is one of the great resources of information for the European encounter with the New World, but his advocacy puts his credibility into question.

Historians depend on two basic resources: documentary evidence and, especially important in Las Casas's case, the testimony of eyewitnesses (not mutually exclusive, for eyewitnesses often leave written records). Las Casas witnessed much of what he wrote about, investing his narratives with a powerful and credible voice (that he often exaggerates, denigrates his opponents, trims the truth, and sometimes makes a feast of thin gruel does not reduce the potency of his voice), but his firsthand knowledge does not set him apart from contemporary historians. Another of the great chroniclers, Gonzalo Fernández de Oviedo (1478–1557), who sparred with Las Casas over an almost equally long career, also had much experience in the Indies, and his chronicle *Historia general y natural de las Indias* rings with the same veracity as Las Casas's works.

Las Casas gives historians a window into a fascinating set of questions about the practice of history. Perhaps the central challenge is how to separate the threads of truth from exaggeration and just plain invention. A younger contemporary of Las Casas, the Inca Garcilaso de la Vega (1539–1616), poses much the same problem: many have tried to squeeze him into convenient boxes—historian, commentator, epic writer, translator, literary genius—but without success. His great epic history of the Incas, the *Comentarios reales,* is both history and polemic, and his *La Florida del Inca,* the compelling narrative of Hernando de Soto's expedition of the American Southeast (1539–43), almost defies categorization, made up of strands of authentic history but interwoven with much that was imagined by Garcilaso. When I use Las Casas in my classes, I cannot wholly separate his role as historian from his polemical side. He has to be compared carefully against other documents from the period and chroniclers who wrote with equal freedom. Nonetheless, Las Casas remains the most useful figure to probe central historiographic issues of the age of exploration, discovery, and conquest.

For historians, truth is part of a longer strand that never exists in a chronological vacuum. They rely on the inevitable relation of cause and effect, seeing a parade of events, usually a progression to something better (Christian cosmology, for example, interprets the passage of time as positive progress) or to something worse (the end of the Roman Empire). Hayden White's "Rhetoric and History," an important contribution to the study of historical and cultural texts that concerns the disciplinary boundaries of history itself, warns that a process of emplotment always dominates the production of historical discourse and that the writing of fact and fiction are more intertwined than historians want to admit. Las Casas's text, then, becomes a perfect site for historical as well as rhetorical explorations (see also Cortijo Ocaña).

Las Casas found no ambiguity in his double role as historian and principal defender of the Indians. Good historians—the ones he admired, from Herodotus to sixteenth-century contemporaries—were all activists. He did not have to reconcile his objective with his subjective persona. In our own time, Las Casas is championed as one of the first voices of the other, a man who could see the world through the eyes of the Indians, no matter how imperfectly he understood or interpreted that world; thus, Las Casas became central to the struggle for human rights. This side of him has inspired the work of modern historians such as Lewis Hanke, a twentieth-century pioneer of Lascasian studies who explores in depth the works and legacy of the friar (e.g., *Spanish Struggle, All Mankind*). It has also generated much research in the field of theology, the most prominent example being the works of Gustavo Gutiérrez, who wrote (among other books) a massive, highly personalized biography that clearly delineates the role of advocate and identifies many echoes of Lascasian thinking in twentieth-century liberation theology (*Las Casas*). More recently, the theologian Luis Rivera-Pagán, in *A Violent Evangelism: The Political and Religious Conquest of the Americas*, presents Las Casas as the "voice of prophecy, reason, and truth" that continues to resonate (Schwaller 108).

Today, Las Casas is often viewed as a pocket imperialist who did not really recognize the havoc caused by the ascendant Spanish empire. The historian Daniel Castro brings this dimension to the fore: his *Another Face of Empire* reinterprets Las Casas as the benevolent, paternalistic, best-known representative of compassionate Spanish imperialism in the Americas rather than the unblemished larger-than-life hero depicted by his followers. Castro writes that for Las Casas to be fully understood, he must be seen not only as a defender of the Amerindians but also as a full, active, and willing participant in Spain's imperialist domination of the New World. Such contradictory readings of Las Casas are but representative examples of how the friar remains immensely controversial, the voice of both reason and intransigence, of empire and liberty, of benevolent despotism and freedom. His position at the center of a dynamic situation changing rapidly throughout the sixteenth century—and still challenging modern scholars and students to come to some consensus—makes him a powerful tool for teaching history.

As a historian, I find Las Casas, and use him, at just about every turn when studying the sixteenth century. He becomes a prism into a complicated world being transformed not only by the discoveries of Columbus (Las Casas and Fernando Colón were the principal historians of Columbus's first voyage) but also by the growing impact of the Reformation, set in motion by Las Casas's contemporary Martin Luther. Powerful forces were reshaping the world of geography, of ideas, of the basis of knowledge as it was understood by Europeans. And at the center of much of the recording of these events is Las Casas (Phillips and Phillips). His histories take my students and me back to Columbus and beyond, to the medieval and ancient world, for throughout his writings he draws allusions from the classics, the patristic fathers, and medieval philosophers and theologians, all in defense of Indian natural rights and sovereignty. Ultimately, the works of Las Casas give the historian a rich and complex entry into the roots of modern human rights, the origins of modern international law, and the interface between philosophers and kings at a time when rulers paid attention to philosophers.

In the process of teaching Las Casas through the lens of history, I specifically challenge my students to come to an understanding of one of the discipline's great debates: do human beings make history, or are they simply pawns of great movements (social, military, religious, economic, natural, etc.) that push them into making inexorable decisions that really only validate the forces of history? Did Las Casas make history, or was he just a bishop (he actually became the bishop of Chiapas [spelled "Chiapa" at the time]) on the chessboard? He was certainly more important than a pawn, but was he able to control the board any more than other players? The case for the "great man" versus the "great moments" in history weighs heavily toward the man when we look at Las Casas. He moved easily and often from polemicist to activist throughout his life. His career is well documented, and students can trace it from the epiphany of 1514, when he turned from settler to defender of American Indians, all the way to his final battles with the Peruvian *encomenderos* in the 1550s and 1560s. In between, he led a long life of activism and intense lobbying that produced results. The papal bulls of 1537 (defining the Indians as wholly capable of accepting and understanding Christianity) and the New Laws of 1542 (attacking Indian slavery and the *encomienda*) are but two examples of legislative signposts that bear the deep imprint of Las Casas.

I also bring up the humanist utopian perspective Las Casas shared with his contemporaries, a providential view of history that connected the New World with the salvation of the Old. Curiously, Las Casas's first treatise on reforms for the Indies, the *Memorial para el remedio de las Indias* 'Remedy for the Indies' (*Obras completas* 13: 23–48) composed in late 1515, resembled another, more famous, venture set in the New World: *Utopia,* by Thomas More (1478–1535), in which the ideal society exists on an island surprisingly similar to Cuba. From the size of and distance between the villages to the length of the working day and other aspects, the coincidences are so striking that some have suggested that More might have had access to a copy of Las Casas's *Memorial* while writing his famous text (Gutiérrez, *Las Casas* 77–78; Baptiste). Even if not, the acknowledgment that both participated in a current of European self-critique and reformation is enough to assure Las Casas's place as a major voice in the debates of his time. The *Memorial* is not as ironic or entertaining as *Utopia* but is, in its own way, immensely more compelling. More writes a fictional classic about a place so perfect it cannot exist, while Las Casas suggests a concrete utopian experiment designed to help Indians and Spaniards cohabit in peace and harmony. Las Casas launched several experiments over the course of his life: they all were spectacular failures, especially the one on the coast of Tierra Firme between 1519 and 1521 (near modern Cumaná in eastern Venezuela), but, in each instance, Las Casas the activist reformer trumped Las Casas the historian for periods of time.

I have used Las Casas in the classroom to open fruitfully an area that very much concerns the discipline of history: "just wars" and, concomitantly, the legality or justice of using force to evangelize. Here we invariably return to Saint Augustine and, before him, to the apostle Paul and even to the parables of Jesus as we search for the roots of this odd segment of Christianity that allows force to be used to teach the language of peace, love, and redemption. The theory of just wars is central to Las Casas's historical defense of the Indians. The friar followed the Thomists of the age in underscoring the natural rights inherent in all human beings, Christian or not. We can follow the evolution of natural rights from classical times through to Francisco de Vitoria (*Political Writings*), the Dominican most closely associated with the theory in the sixteenth century and himself a defender of Indian rights. From these bases flowed the various theories of law that defined legitimate sovereignty and dominion. And if one carries Vitoria and Las Casas to their logical conclusions, we even see the development of constitutional law in its modern format, which limits the powers and authority of the rulers and endows those ruled with rights that eventually lead to John Locke, Thomas Jefferson, and the ideas underlying the American Revolution.

Teaching Las Casas as historian and activist is a truly multidimensional, multidisciplinary activity, but he has to be invoked with care—there is no neutral, objective Las Casas. As one of the Hieronymite fathers in Santo Domingo said of him in 1517, "He is like a candle that lights everything in sight!" (*Obras completas* 1: 93). I have to balance his views, his championship of the Indians, and his excesses with other more temperate interpretations. Much of these come from sister disciplines (such as anthropology and literature) that have viewed Las Casas through different lenses and with different agendas.

Even with the immense outpouring of writing over a career that spanned more than half a century, he remains an elusive figure. Each Las Casas—the friar, the Indian apologist, the protoanthropologist, the historian, the scholar, the activist, the biographer, the imperialist—calls for a different approach, but one must never lose sight of the whole. There is no one or paramount Las Casas. For the historian, however, there are two principal roles that determine his place in our classrooms: as a chronicler-historian, he opens the path of historiography for students of all ages as we grapple with documentary evidence and truth; and, as an activist, he leads us down many roads, from cultural imperialist to utopian reformer, always armed with the great tracts of history, Christianity, and the classics in defense of the Indians. The most successful and most controversial historian of the Indies during the colonial period, he uses the past to interpret New World experience and translates his own New World experience to chronicle the great events of his time.

NOTES

The epigraph to this essay comes from Las Casas's prologue to his *Historia de las Indias* (*Obras completas* 3: 346); my translation.

[1] All translations are mine unless otherwise noted.

Pedagogical Uses of
Las Casas's Texts for Anthropologists

Laura A. Lewis

As an ethnohistorian and ethnographer, and a teacher of both colonial and contemporary Latin America, I find Bartolomé de Las Casas important to my research and instruction in a number of courses, including Peoples and Cultures of Latin America and Political Culture, Indians, and Nation-States in Latin America. My perspective is a critical historiographic one that addresses the "facts" as we can know them and the writing techniques and cultural influences of the sixteenth-century writers who presented those facts. The courses I teach using Las Casas are small, discussion-oriented seminars, in which I use the Penguin English-language version of the *Brevísima relación*, *A Short Account of the Destruction of the Indies*. I also assign sections of my book *Hall of Mirrors: Power, Witchcraft, and Caste in Colonial Mexico*, which covers the Sepúlveda–Las Casas debate and addresses Las Casas's and more general Spanish colonial views of Indians and blacks. Although I teach at a master's-level mid-Atlantic public university with a large, mostly upper-middle-class and white undergraduate student body, many students are activists. With little exposure to diversity issues at the university, they look for ways to expand their knowledge and to become involved. The writings of Las Casas, in dialogue with anthropological concerns, provide a platform for students to find intellectual venues for their activism.

I assign the Penguin version of the *Short Account* in my teaching in part because of Anthony Pagden's introduction, which locates Las Casas's works and life in the context of sixteenth-century theology and politics. Only rarely do I include excerpts from Las Casas's longer works, such as the *Apologética historia sumaria*, which Pagden identifies as a "comparative ethnology" (xvii), or the *Historia de las Indias* (which could be read in part as an amplification of the *Brevísima relación*), because the survey nature of the courses does not allow me to spend as much time as I would like on sixteenth-century European writers. However, the *Apologética* is one of the most relevant texts to deal with ethnography in the period, and it constitutes an irreplaceable source for more specialized or graduate seminars on the subject.[1]

When students read the *Short Account*, several interrelated issues arise. First, as Las Casas is a sixteenth-century Spanish figure, we have to treat him like any "native" whose cultural and historical distance from us we must learn to traverse. Second, we have to attend to the political and theological contexts in which he was writing and learn to read his texts as emerging from the world that contained them. Third, we have to ask who his writings tell us about. Fourth, we have to go beyond those writings to address Spain's and Las Casas's influences on the wider colonial world. Las Casas can thus teach us about culture, voice, relativism, interpretation, and global history.

The *Short Account* is useful for undergraduates because it is brief and one of Las Casas's most famous works. Indeed, before the end of the sixteenth century it had been translated into six languages. As Pagden notes, it is "an epitome, suitably reworded for a popular audience, of the records of Spanish brutality" (Introduction xxx, xxxvi). It is important to understand the historical context of the *Short Account* and of Las Casas's other works to address the central questions posed above. But the immediate reaction of students to Las Casas's brutal overview of the decimation of the Indians is outrage and a grimace, for while they know the general history, Las Casas's passionate words and themes bring out their own senses of justice. As we read the text for its rhetorical flourishes as well as for its historical "accuracy," the words and themes also strike a certain amount of confusion in students, for in the *Brevísima relación* and in his other works Las Casas is brutally condemning his own people—Spaniards—while glorifying those whom Spaniards have set out to conquer. Indeed, Las Casas's use of literary inversion turns conquistadors into the barbarians while indigenous people become gentle monks. Thus, the first task is to interrogate the twin questions of historical content and literary style. The point is not to ask whether or not indigenous peoples were decimated—many sources tell us that they were, although the numbers vary—it is rather to ask how the *Short Account* documents that decimation using a particular literary "poetics" (Comaroff and Comaroff 36).[2]

As students learn a part of early modern history and historiography, they also thus learn that objectivity is an elusive goal. In particular, the historical or literary conventions of an age, along with the author's voice—how he or she writes and is placed in the narrative—"affects the ways cultural phenomena are registered," as James Clifford asserts (4). Such an approach to the texts, especially given Las Casas's impact, can reinforce what I teach about writing: how students express themselves is just as important as what they have to say. Jean Comaroff and John Comaroff's insistence on poetics and Clifford's emphasis on writing also illustrate a transformation in the discipline of anthropology, including how it dialogues with other disciplines, particularly literature (Geertz).

As our discussion moves to the political and social contexts of Las Casas's arguments, we ask a number of questions: When were the *Short Account* and other major pieces written? In what sequence? Why? What was Las Casas's life work about? What was he responding to? What were his objectives? I like to address these questions by looking at a variety of missionary philosophies and styles. Doing so allows entry to Las Casas's world made up of different mendicant orders and theological viewpoints regarding the relationship between Indians and Europeans. Thus, as Inga Clendinnen writes, missionaries become as much "subjects for wonder and analyses" as the indigenous peoples on whom ethnohistorians traditionally focus ("Disciplining" 27; see also Comaroff and

Comaroff). This point is important for anthropology students, as older anthropological models tend to see only non-European "others" as having culture.

Comparing Las Casas, who became a Dominican friar in 1522, with members of other mendicant orders demonstrates the different ways in which the central questions raised during the period—particularly the association between Indians and Christianity—were approached. As we look at the example of New Spain and the work of Dominicans in comparison with, say, Franciscans, we learn that the "culture" of the conquistadors, especially their views of who these Indians were, was just as diverse as the culture of the people they were trying to convert. John Leddy Phelan characterizes the Franciscans as empirical and eclectic (10), while Tzvetan Todorov calls them "realists" (206). These mendicants believed that the objective of evangelization was to restore the primitive church in its original and uncorrupted form (Maravall 207–08). For them, therefore, New Spain presented an opportunity for friars and Indians together to (re)build the City of God (Phelan 91).

In contrast, the Dominican goal was to locate an uncorrupted natural substance beneath outward manifestations of the devil's work. Thus, unlike for Franciscans, for Dominicans New Spain did not present an opportunity for a new beginning. It was instead a New World extension of Old World Christian history. In his major works, including the *Apologética*, the *Historia*, and the *Short Account*, Las Casas therefore emphasizes a pure Indian Christian substratum hidden by idolatry but amenable to reason as knowledge of God's perfection.

But Dominicans did not believe in transforming Indians into mature Christians through violence. As we turn in the classroom to how Dominican beliefs were put into practice, we note that while conquistadors were clamoring for consistent Indian labor in the Caribbean (which facilitated the genocide of Indians), Dominicans were defending the Indians. Las Casas first became what my students can identify as an activist in Cuba in 1514, and it was in the Caribbean that Dominicans first called into question whether Indians could be considered legal slaves taken in "just war," as they had never actively impeded the spread of Christianity. Such doubts eventually led Dominicans to question "the very legality of the Spanish New World enterprise" (Robert Williams 86), and Las Casas himself came to believe that "Indians had just cause for war against the Spaniards" (Friede, "Las Casas and Indigenism" 164–65). As a result, Dominicans refused to hear confession from or give communion to the *encomenderos* they held most responsible for slaughtering and illegally enslaving Indians (Ulloa; Robert Williams 85–86; Zavala, *Encomienda indiana* 20–36).

Examining the worldviews of various missionary orders helps break down students' beliefs about missionaries as an undifferentiated group (and many students have their own modern Protestant evangelical understandings and experiences). As students develop a more complex understanding of "the missionary project" by learning about the range of approaches and beliefs, missionaries cease to be a monolithic unit and instead become groups whose viewpoints emerge from diverse Western intellectual traditions. These traditions speak to the contradictions at the heart of early modern Spanish views of the other and thus to the complexities of "culture," which we tend to think of as a unified entity shared by all members of a society. Understanding the contradictions in early modern Spanish culture in turn helps students understand the ways in which the colonial Spanish project played out "on the ground."

Las Casas traveled back and forth between the Old World and the New during the decades following his early stay in the Caribbean. On a trip back to Spain, he convinced the Council of the Indies to pass the 1542 New Laws, which explicitly made Indian enslavement illegal, declared that *encomiendas* could not be held in perpetuity, and eliminated labor as a tribute obligation of Indians. Early drafts of the *Short Account* influenced the ratification of these laws, and Las Casas published the work in 1552 because the Crown moved too slowly toward enforcing them.

In response to Las Casas's activism, the Spanish scholar Juan Ginés de Sepúlveda denounced Las Casas to the Inquisition for his defiance of papal authority. Invited to debate Sepúlveda in Spain in 1550, Las Casas argued that Indians, now suffering catastrophic demographic decline in Mexico and other parts of Latin America, should not be subject to enslavement, because they were taken captive in a war that unjustly denied them their sovereignty. While Las Casas argued that in a theological and in a Dominican sense Indians were capable of achieving reason, Sepúlveda, relying on a more literal reading of Aristotle, argued that Spanish domination of Indians was just, as Indians were incapable of reason and therefore inferior, "natural slaves." To this end, Sepúlveda made analogies between women, Indians, and children (Lewis 59–60).

While who "won" the Sepúlveda–Las Casas debate has not been adequately answered, the Crown was more sympathetic to Las Casas's position, perhaps because it took its religious mandate seriously, saw itself as paternalistic and Indians as "minors" in need of protection, and believed Spain's economic interests were at risk if New World *encomenderos* held too much power. Yet Spanish settlers, who had an important stake in continued access to inexpensive Indian labor, favored Sepúlveda's position (Pagden, Introduction xxxii). The debate thus underscores contradictions in Spanish colonialism, for both protecting Indians and exploiting them were part of the Spanish colonial project. Further discussion can show students how such contradictions led to policies that did both of these things, with consequences for social relations among all colonial subjects. Indeed, while the philosophical issues have been addressed by intellectual historians, few social scientists have looked at the effect of Crown policies on the day-to-day discourse of "regular" people that is, after all, what anthropologists typically study.

Yet, while we might be more sympathetic to Las Casas's position, it is also crucial for students to grasp one of Todorov's main arguments, also a lesson for today's world: that difference and equality are often incommensurable. Las Casas might have rejected Sepúlveda's position on Indian inferiority and seen

Indians as good rather than evil. However, the only way he could make Indians acceptable citizens was to find in them something resembling his own Christian beliefs (Todorov 163–67). This need to find likeness makes an important point about the difficulties of cultural relativism, not just in Las Casas's day but also in our own. How do we, after all, leave our own cultural baggage aside to write objectively about others?

Furthermore, Las Casas had recommended to the Crown as early as 1516 that the particularly arduous labor requirement of mining be carried out by black and white (Muslim) slaves (Adorno, "Intellectual Life" 7). Students can get incensed by this double standard: how can Las Casas defend Indians against slavery while sanctioning the enslavement of other peoples? At this point, students are further immersed in early modern political and theological worldviews surrounding the intertwined concepts of just war and conversion. They come to understand that Las Casas was not against slavery per se but only opposed it when there was no evidence that such slaves had resisted Christian conversion. They see, too, that Las Casas has to be read not just in contrast with other missionary writings but also for the seeming contradictions in his own words, for his early views of blacks versus his views of Indians are troublesome. While early on, Las Casas was supportive of just war against Turks and other Muslims, he was ignorant of the ways in which black slaves were taken by the Portuguese (Friede, "Las Casas and Indigenism" 165–66; Bataillon, "Clérigo Casas" 415–16). He later came to realize that blacks were no less deserving of freedom than Indians, and he even feared for his own absolution at his death (Friede, "Las Casas and Indigenism" 166). Moreover, Las Casas was not the only European to speak out. The archbishop of Mexico Alonso de Montúfar, likely influenced by Las Casas, wrote to the Crown that "we do not know what reason exists that blacks be captives more than Indians, because they willingly receive the holy spirit and do not wage war against Christians" (my trans.; Friede, "Las Casas and Indigenism" 166). Black enslavement remains one of the thorniest questions about early modern Spanish notions of difference. In the classroom it leads to important discussions about caste and the early history of racial thinking (Lewis 20–33).

My final point is that, despite the alleged controversy about blacks, Las Casas's defense of the Indians became fodder for later colonial powers in their constructions of the Black Legend of Spanish overseas colonialism (Pagden, Introduction xiv). In the classroom, we can situate Spanish practices in a wider global practice that spanned centuries and included many European nations. This contextualization allows students to understand that colonial powers did not act in isolation but influenced each other. As Lauren Benton shows, for instance, colonial powers drew on one another's experiences, legal regimes, and writings as they created their own colonial legal systems.

Later colonial powers also familiarized themselves with the Spanish experience as they forged their projects. Winthrop Jordan's discussion of early Anglo perspectives on Spanish slavery suggests a familiarity with Spanish experiences

(56–63), as does Ann Laura Stoler's contention that nineteenth-century Dutch officials drew on Spanish models to solve their own race problems ("Developing" 167). While Stoler argues that the Dutch consciously rejected what they perceived as the cruelties of the Spanish colonial project ("'In Cold Blood'" 160), she also hints that aspects of Spanish models, which were, after all, contradictory, might have been embraced. There might thus be covert references to Las Casas in a letter written by a Dutch official from Sumatra in 1876, which details the brutalities of his fellow Europeans, whom he refers to as the "so-called pioneers of civilization" (qtd. in Stoler, "'In Cold Blood'" 154). The imagery of inversion used in the letter is so similar to that used by Las Casas that one cannot help wondering whether the Dutch official had read Las Casas's work.

In conclusion, using Las Casas in anthropology classes introduces students to a range of relevant issues as they come to understand the sixteenth-century world. Some of these issues are the various intellectual paradigms and views that made up at least a slice of Spanish culture during that era, the problems of cultural relativism and ethnographic writing, the contradictions of colonial regimes, and the ways in which those regimes were intertwined.

NOTES

[1] On the era's ethnography, see Hodgen; Klor de Alva; and Rowe.

[2] See, for example, the popular *1491* by Charles C. Mann and its discussion "Numbers from Nowhere?" (31–133).

The Place of Las Casas in Religious Studies

Kristy Nabhan-Warren

Teaching Bartolomé de Las Casas's writings in the religious studies classroom reveals contestations of religion, self, and society that not only were real in medieval and Renaissance Spain but are still real in the modern world. Religious studies is a multidisciplinary field that looks at the interplay of religion, society, literature, anthropology, psychology, and history. In the undergraduate course in which I teach Las Casas, I use him as a springboard into understanding the modern Christian. I want students to learn that American religious history does not start with the Puritans but goes back even further. A major thrust of the course is that we need to know early modern Spain and its missionary and evangelizing impulse in order to understand the modern Christian, as well as themes in modern Christianity. I want students to comprehend that Christianity is transcontinental and socially and historically situated and that what they think of as distinctly, uniquely "American" is deeply rooted in the past.

I have found that the multidimensional Las Casas is an excellent author to use in the classroom, particularly when discussing religion and reform in medieval Europe and colonial to antebellum America. In my course Conquest, Colonization, and Reform, which is also part of my institution's general education program, students are introduced to a variety of Christian reformers from the sixteenth through the early twentieth centuries. The overarching goal of my course is for students to realize the overlap of discourse and thought in seemingly wide-ranging Christians, including sixteenth-century Catholics (e.g., Las Casas, Hernán Cortés, and Columbus) and Protestant reformers (Martin Luther and John Calvin); eighteenth-century Protestants (Solomon Stoddard, Gilbert Tennent, and Jonathan Edwards); and nineteenth-century Christians (Charles Finney, John Nevin). We explore how the eighteenth- and nineteenth-century theologians were caught up in the First and Second Great Awakenings, and by the time we look to the turn of the twentieth century, students can see that those Christians involved in the Social Gospel movement were as preoccupied with what it meant to be a good Christian and to uphold true Christianity as Las Casas was.[1] In addition to selected Lascasian writings, as well as others from the late medieval and Reformation era, the primary source accounts we read come primarily from Jill Lepore's *Encounters in the New World*; Robert Marcus, David Burner, and Anthony Marcus's *America Firsthand: Readings from Settlement to Reconstruction*; Albert Hurtado and Peter Iverson's *Major Problems in American Indian History*; and Michael P. Johnson's *Reading the American Past*.

We avoid the danger of making Las Casas historically unique when we look at how the seventeenth-century Puritans and eighteenth- and nineteenth-century Protestant Christians encountered the other—whether the other was the Church of England, Native Americans living in the eastern seaboard, or urban European Catholic immigrants in the nineteenth and twentieth centuries. As students discover, the religious, social, and cultural other was as much a pre-occupation for medieval Spain as it has been for modern Christians. Students need to understand that American Christian concerns are not unique: reading Las Casas and other medieval Christians introduces us to modern Christian thought and cultural and social preoccupations. Las Casas's writings become a lens through which we can better understand American Christianity and, per-haps, ourselves.

Contextualizing Las Casas with other Christian reformers, Catholic and Prot-estant, helps students gain a solid grasp of how the majority of European and American Christians imagined and interpreted cultural difference, how they constructed their own sense of moral and theological superiority, and how they struggled with their Christian identities. In class, we read Las Casas as repre-sentative of modern Christians' goal to reshape society in the name of true Chris-tianity, and part of that molding involves an encounter with an other—native peoples, Protestant Christians, or Catholics. When students read Las Casas's works alongside those of his contemporaries and those of more recent Chris-tians, they see the dialectics of culture and history and learn how Christianity is ultimately shaped by that discourse.

Las Casas touches on the main themes of my course: contact and colonization and the creation of an other; missionization and its emissaries; Christian reform; and theocracy—the notion of a city on a hill. When we read primary sources in the various sections, students see the continuity of Christian cosmology and how nineteenth-century Christians, experiencing "awakenings" in America, were not so unlike sixteenth-century ones in that their goals were to convert the population of the Americas in the name of Christ and to establish a godly king-dom on earth. Moreover, students can relate to the struggles that Christians have had over the centuries, and they understand that their issues are not so new after all. We also use Las Casas as a point of entry into discussions of the ethics of missionization and ask what we can learn from his own struggles with faith. (Although Las Casas believed in missionization, he rejected violent ways of carrying it out. In my class we question whether or not missionization ever was or is acceptable, even when nonviolent. When we compare Las Casas's stance with that of other modern Christians, namely American Christians, we also ask ourselves whether missionization is itself a form of violence.)

We start the course by looking at other medieval and Renaissance works, including texts by Thomas Aquinas, Alexander VI's papal bull *Inter caetera* (1493), and Paul III's papal bull *Sublimis Deus* (1537). Students also read Mar-tin Luther's seminal piece "Freedom of a Christian" (1520) as well as his earlier *Ninety-Five Theses* (1517), to gain an understanding of the issues at stake in the Protestant Reformation and the Protestant critique of the Catholic church. We discuss the differences between medieval Catholicism (ultramontane, trium-phalist, top-down theology) and the emerging Protestantism, which emphasized Luther's concepts of grace, the idea of justification through faith, and the priest-hood of all believers. Students are quick to note Luther's conciliatory tone in

"Freedom" (especially when compared with the *Ninety-Five Theses*) and the ways in which the Lutheran faith adhered to its Catholic roots.

We contextualize Las Casas's life and writings with the Reformation and Catholic Counter-Reformation (the 1545 Council of Trent), and we focus on how Las Casas was profoundly loyal to his faith, yet also deeply critical of the way he saw it being enacted in the colonies. It is important for students to understand that when Las Casas mentions Christians in his writings, he is referring only to Catholics. His definition of Christian was part of the Catholic Counter-Reformation, which sought to solidify Catholic doctrine and belief in the midst of the Protestant Reformation. And when we turn to seventeenth- through early-twentieth-century Christians in class, students see that Christians in each century had a particular understanding of what constituted Christian identity.

The two key papal bulls, Pope Alexander VI's *Inter caetera* and Pope Paul's *Sublimis Deus,* further contextualize Las Casas's Catholicism and theology in sixteenth-century Spain. In addition, we read an abbreviated English version of the 1513 *Requerimiento* (Palacios Rubios). *Inter caetera* shows students the religious and political justifications for conquest, colonization, and enslavement of Indians. The language is flowery and grand, and colonizers are praised for carrying "forward your holy and praiseworthy purpose so pleasing to immortal God" and are granted exclusive rights to what they "find": "And we make, appoint, and depute you and your said heirs and successors lords of them with full and free power, authority, and jurisdiction of every kind." The document generates a class discussion of the interconnectedness of cross and Crown and the hubris of colonial Catholicism. We talk about how Las Casas was not arguing against the pope's desire to spread Catholicism in the New World: what he objected to was the way his contemporaries interpreted *Inter caetera* as a mandate to brutally conquer native peoples.

Students then read the *Requerimiento* to see how the bull is carried out by Spanish explorers, who demand that the native peoples they encounter submit to them and to their Catholic faith. If the natives refuse to submit, they are greeted with the foretelling of their enslavement:

> [W]ith the help of God, we shall powerfully enter into your country, and shall make war against you in all ways and manners that we can . . . ; we shall take you and your wives and your children and shall make slaves of them, and as such shall sell and dispose of them . . . and shall do you all the mischief and damage that we can, as to vassals who do not obey, and refuse to receive their lord, and resist and contradict him. . . .

Moreover, the explorers tell the Indians that the death and destruction that will befall them will be their fault: "we protest that the deaths and losses which shall accrue from this are your fault, and not that of their Highnesses, or ours, nor of these cavaliers who come with us" (par. 7). While Las Casas shared Pope

Alexander's desire to see the "Savior . . . carried into those regions" and "holy baptism" administered, he opposed his contemporaries' violent methods.

In contrast, the 1537 papal bull *Sublimis Deus* exhorts Christian explorers to be an example "of good and holy living" and rejects the prevailing method of colonization and evangelization that treats Indians as "dumb brutes created for our service, pretending that they are incapable of receiving the Catholic Faith" (*Sublimis Dei,* par. 3). Pope Paul III supports the idea championed by the Dominicans and notably by Las Casas that Indians are capable of reason, have intellect, and are worthy candidates for receiving the sacraments. He insists that the right conditions must be present for the reception of Catholic doctrines and that those who receive the "doctrines of the faith" must be nurtured by those instructing them. *Sublimis Deus* is a strongly worded piece about the proper methods of evangelization and on the ability of Indians to receive the word of Jesus Christ. Deeply influenced by Las Casas, Paul minces no words when he asserts:

> Indians . . . are by no means to be deprived of their liberty or the possession of their property, even though they be outside the faith of Jesus Christ; and . . . they may and should, freely and legitimately, enjoy their liberty and the possession of their property; nor should they be in any way enslaved; should the contrary happen, it shall be null and have no effect.
>
> (par. 3)

We also discuss Las Casas's literary imagination and the edenic language he uses to describe Indians, as opposed to the brutal, angry language employed to describe the Spanish. Las Casas consistently posits Indians as "innocent," "pure in mind," "perceptive to learning and understanding the truths of our Catholic faith," and embodying a kind of "natural goodness." Yet it is important for students to note that, despite his appreciation of the Indians' morality and intelligence, he sees them as unfinished products in need of the Christian religion: "These would be the most blessed people on earth if only they were given the chance to convert to Christianity" (*Short Account* 10). The conversion Las Casas has in mind is not forced but is chosen by the Indians themselves—and here he challenges the Spanish Crown and the prevailing approaches. He points to the inherit deficiency of methods of conversion that result in indigenous peoples' choosing to go to hell over heaven because of the hyprocrisy of the religion and its representatives: the native lord Hatuey, for example, "chose to go to Hell to ensure that he would never again have to clap his eyes on those cruel brutes [i.e., Christians]" (28).

In *History of the Indies,* Las Casas discusses the horrors of enslavement at length, providing historical details of the starvation, brutality, and desperation that Indians experienced at the hands of the Spanish. He notes acidly, "And this was the freedom, the good treatment and the Christianity that Indians received under the commander's execution of this point of the warrant" (114). Throughout the

Brevísima relación, he provides numerous examples of the ways in which the Spanish conquistadors and the missionaries, Christians, flaunt true Christianity and place in its stead a greedy, self-centered, brutal kind of faith that is predicated on the acquisition of wealth at the expense of Indian lives. At the hands of the Spanish, Indians were treated as "brute animals" or more vividly as "piles of dung in the middle of the road." Las Casas decries the lack of concern the Spanish had for Indians' bodies and souls, "all the millions that have perished having gone to their deaths with no knowledge of God and without the benefit of the Sacraments" (*Short Account* 13). The Dominican saw real merit and beauty in Indians' cosmologies, but as a Catholic missionary priest, he strongly believed that these "gentle Indians" were in dire need of the "Word of Christ" because they were "ignorant of the truth" and were "in mortal danger of being denied the Life Everlasting" (88).

Las Casas the theologian makes explicit parallels between the Indians and the early Christian desert fathers, strongly suggesting that indigenous peoples have the capacity for Christian religious life and should be considered as Spaniards' equals:

> Their diet is every bit as poor and as monotonous in quantity and in kind, as that enjoyed by the Desert Fathers. Most of them go naked, save for a loincloth to cover their modesty. . . . They are innocent and pure in mind and have a lively intelligence, all of which makes them particularly receptive to learning and understanding the truths of our Catholic faith and to being instructed in virtue; indeed God has invested them with fewer impediments in this regard than any other people on earth.   (10)

At this point, I ask students to look for clues that tell us what Las Casas thinks about the cosmology of the indigenous peoples and to ponder whether or not he believes that Indians need Christianity to be saved. Students read passages aloud, paying special attention to the discursive language of "Christian" and "Indian" and analyzing their multiple meanings in the context of the sixteenth century. Indians, as we see in the quotation above, are the real or true Christians who share common traits with the early Christian fathers. They are uncorrupted by greed and materialism—unlike the Spaniards, who may be Christian but who are not properly living out their faith. Las Casas portrays indigenous peoples as living authentic Christian lives, and he fills the *Brevísima relación* with examples of Spaniards whose actions contradict their Christian identities. Spaniards are not living out an authentic Christianity, and Las Casas sees their collective redemption in the other—Indians, who are portrayed as more capable of grasping the "truth" of Christianity because of their noble savagery and closeness to original man. Students also read Montaigne's "Of Cannibals" and draw parallels between the two authors' use of irony and historical and literary inversion.

As a Catholic priest, Las Casas believes that the sacraments of the Catholic church are necessary to obtain salvation, but he advocates indoctrinating adult Indians before baptizing them instead of merely baptizing them en masse, a common practice of Franciscans like Motolinía (Wagner and Parish 98–102). The Dominicans, Las Casas claims, were "mortified at the wickedness shown by the Spanish" and "would have died rather than countenance such treachery," especially because they realized that brutality was not an effective method of conversion. In a chapter on the Pearl Coast, Paria, and Trinidad, he notes the complicity of missionaries (with the exception of Dominicans and a group of Franciscans) in the brutal *encomienda* slave system: "the magistrates there had no intention of investigating the case because they had themselves received a number of slaves taken in this evil and criminal fashion" (*Short Account* 89–90). I point out that Las Casas ultimately believed that the only true method of evangelization is based solely on love and kindness, as documented in his treatise *The Only Way*. In class, when we later turn to early-twentieth-century documents by the Protestant Social Gospel proponents Walter Rauschenbusch and Washington Gladden, students can track continuities of peaceful missionization and evangelization in America—noting, for example, how being a Christian means being socially engaged in the redemption of others (Ferm 242–62).

Reading translated verses from Las Casas's "Confesionario" (the title by which it is commonly known [*Rules for Confessors*]) introduces students to his refusal to perform the priestly task of absolving the sins of conquistadors, *encomenderos*, and slaveholders. As David Thomas Orique writes:

> In his mind there was no separation between making restitution for the sake of justice and the practice of Christianity. Las Casas believed that Christianity was a religion of deeds, one that demanded making compensation for injuries committed against one's neighbor.   (13)

Orique observes that Las Casas "initiates his argument for restitution by saying on the first page of the tract that confessors are obligated to demand that penitents make a legally binding pledge to make restitution before receiving absolution" (14). As we read in class a translated version of the "Confesionario," I contextualize it with the debate it generated. When students read about the confiscation of the book and the subsequent accusations Las Casas faced, they understand more clearly the overlapping roles of the Spanish cross and Crown and the blurring of the lines between church and state (Wagner and Parish 166–74).

It would be easy for one to assume that Las Casas was a lifelong champion of the Indians, especially since many secondary sources, serving more as hagiographies of Las Casas than as objective histories, downplay or make no mention of his conversion or of the immense influence that fellow antislavery Dominican priests had on his theology. Students need to read about the Dominican influence and Las Casas's evolution from a colonialist priest who had an *encomienda* to a vociferous opponent of Indian slavery, because it is crucial they understand that his defense of the Indians and his refusal to absolve slaveholders required a change of heart. The change took place as early as 1514 (before he became a member of the Dominican order, in 1522), when he renounced his *encomienda* to Diego Velázquez, the governor of Cuba.

Las Casas's colonialist perspective was changed by Dominicans who initiated an aggressive critique of the treatment of the Indians. However, it took time: Las Casas did not immediately give up his life as a Cuban *encomendero*, and he justified his position of authority over Indians by citing his kindness toward them. Here I have students read Ecclesiasticus, a second-century BC apocryphal work that offers moral guidance and advice. We read chapter 34, verses 21–22, the same chapters Las Casas read before his conversion, which persuaded him that the *encomienda* was morally wrong and that all *encomenderos* were profiting off blood labor ("Ecclesiasticus"). It is important, too, for students to realize that Las Casas's position as priest did not inoculate him from proslavery arguments. Many priests supported the system of slavery and justified it on theological grounds, selectively quoting and citing scripture in their sermons, notably from the letters of Paul. According to the New Testament scholar Ritva Williams, "the pseudo-Pauline letters do address slaves directly, enjoining them to obedience (Col. 3: 22–25; Eph. 5: 21–22) in a context where masters are also exhorted to treat their slaves justly and fairly." Students respond with special interest when we discuss the ways biblical Scripture has been used to justify slavery, and they inevitably draw parallels with the ways in which men of the cloth and other religious reformers defended it in antebellum America.

Students in my course also read selections from other Dominicans, especially Thomas Aquinas, to learn that Las Casas's arguments against slavery and for Indian rights were building on preexisting theological concepts. Instructors will want to look closely at Dominican writings to avoid romanticizing Las Casas and positing him as theologically unique. In the sixteenth century, Las Casas and his fellow Dominican Francisco Vitoria were part of a neo-Thomist revival and were drawing heavily on Thomas Aquinas's writings, especially his famous *Summa theologica* (2: 1008–13), as part of their assertion that Indians had natural rights. As Thomas O'Meara has noted:

> Aquinas viewed human and political rights as coming from nature and not from religion; this was employed through the sixteenth century to challenge the Spanish conquests advanced with the excuse that the peoples had not accepted baptism and so had no legitimate life now or in the hereafter. (241)

As a neo-Thomist, Las Casas did not condemn the practitioners of human sacrifice, much as Montaigne did not condemn those of cannibalism in his "Of Cannibals." Additional excerpts from the *Summa theologica* (1: 417–21) introduce students to the context of and the basis for Las Casas's moral theology. As we take another look at passages from the *Brevísima relación*, we see how Aquinas's understanding of the love of God, love of neighbor, and mystical union with God helps explain Las Casas's hope for Indians' embrace of the sacraments, especially baptism and communion, the necessary rites to become part of the larger body of Christ. I have students read *Summa* question 76, "Of the Causes of Sin, in Particular" (2: 930–33), which shows that Aquinas did not view ignorance as sin—an assertion Las Casas drew on during the Valladolid debates against Juan Sepúlveda, where he argued that Indians' ignorance of the sacraments and of Christianity did not justify brutal conquest and forced evangelization.

Luis Rivera-Pagán claims that Las Casas had a prophetic self-awareness:

> [He was] possessed by one obsessive passion: to be the prophet of Spain, a man called by God to be the scourge of the conscience of his nation and to be the defender of the autochthonous communities, in whose misery he perceived "Jesus Christ . . . not once, but thousand times whipped, insulted, beaten, and crucified. . . ."   ("Prophetic Challenge")

Rivera-Pagán further notes that Las Casas saw the encounter between Christian Spaniards and Native Americans as a "crucial act in the eschatological redemption of all nations, and as such it was a manifestation of divine grace." Like the Old Testament Israel, Spain risked forfeiting its divine sanction because of the brutality it oversaw and legitimated. Having students read the *Brevísima relación*, preferably in its entirety, allows them to grasp the enormity of European colonization and conquest and the significance of Las Casas's protest, rendered through the Dominican's riveting details of Spanish "Christian" colonization and his agony over the way in which his beloved faith was being enacted by fellow Catholics. To show that Las Casas was not the only Catholic priest wrestling with issues of missionization and colonization, I have the class read select writings of the seventeenth-century French Jesuit Father Paul Le Jeune, who wrote admiringly of native peoples in New France (Lepore 32–35). We also watch the movie *Black Robe* to further compare and contrast Spanish and French colonization and views of the native other. Students watch Las Casas, Le Jeune, and the film's Father Laforgue wrestle with triumphalism, empathy, and a colonial mindset, and as a result, they have a greater empathy for and see themselves in the complex historical figures (understanding historical continuity is an underlying goal of the class).

When students look at the scope of American religious history, they see Las Casas's theological and moral passion echoed by later Christians, Catholic and Protestant alike. Students read John Winthrop's 1630 Arabella sermon ("A Model of Christian Charity") and documents from the infamous Salem witch trials and are quick to see that, like the Spanish and French missionaries in New Spain and France, Puritans were also consumed with establishing a city on a hill and in perfecting Christianity. Like the Catholic Las Casas, the Protestant Christian reformers charged themselves with redeeming a people and a nation.

In his sermon, Winthrop speaks passionately about Christian perfection and love as the bond of perfection, and he claims that his people were chosen by God to set an example for the rest of the world (Johnson 43–48). And like Las Casas, Winthrop and other New England Puritans were deeply critical of their church but were nonseparatists—they sought to reform their institution while remaining loyal to it.

Introducing Las Casas in the religious studies classroom thus ideally involves asking students to read from a variety of texts, with the goal of contextualizing the sixteenth-century Dominican priest in larger theological and historical debates. When Las Casas's works are read alongside those of his contemporaries as well as later Christians, students learn that Christian thought and identity is historical, that it is socially constructed, and that themes of continuity prevail.

NOTE

[1] When we study early-twentieth-century Social Gospel reformers in my course, we read excerpts from Walter Rauschenbusch (*Christianity*, *Theology*) and Washington Gladden (*Recollections*, *Social Salvation*), Protestant reformers who emphasized that urban others were not so other after all and that it was the moral and social responsibility of Christians to responsibly evangelize. Gladden's and Rauschenbusch's messages parallel Las Casas's in many ways, and students are surprised to see such historical continuity of religious thought.

TEACHING LAS CASAS'S *BREVÍSIMA RELACIÓN DE LA DESTRUCCIÓN DE LAS INDIAS*

Hearing Las Casas Write: Rhetoric and the Facade of Orality in the *Brevísima relación*

Ruth Hill

My approach to teaching *Brevísima relación de la destrucción de las Indias* stresses that the rhetorical and the ideological (including the religious) were inseparable for Bartolomé de Las Casas. Even what appears to be conversational, off-the-cuff, or dialogical in the text is carefully scripted political theater. To hear Las Casas write, then, is to break through the facade of orality and reveal his rhetorical strategies for changing imperial policy toward the conquest and servitude of the New World native populations.

Las Casas's engagement with rhetoric was explicit and long-standing. In *De unico vocationis modo* (*Del único modo de atraer a todos los pueblos a la verdadera religión*) written in Latin in approximately 1536–37 (Hanke, Introducción xviii), the Dominican treated rhetoric as the sine qua non of both public discourse and evangelization:

> El predicador o maestro que tiene el encargo de instruir y atraer a los hombres a la fe y religión verdaderas, debe estudiar la naturaleza y principios de la retórica, y debe observar diligentemente sus preceptos en la predicación, para conmover y atraer el ánimo de los oyentes, con no menor empeño que el retórico u orador que estudia este arte y observa en su oración sus preceptos, para conmover y llevar a sus oyentes al punto que se propone. (47)

A preacher or teacher charged with teaching men and bringing them into the true faith and religion must study the nature and principles of rhetoric and strictly follow its precepts in his preaching, in order to stir and attract the soul of his listeners with no less effort than the rhetor or orator, who studies this art and follows its precepts in his speaking in order to stir and lead his listeners to the point that he is arguing.[1]

In an exemplum that implicitly argues for conversion and against conquest of the New World natives, Las Casas alludes to an ancient philosopher whose command of rhetoric reduced savage men in the Old World to living in cities:

> Con palabras llenas de dulzura, con la persuasión cariñosa y lenta, oportuna y delicada, pudo aquel hombre prudente convertir bestias en hombres, incitando con razones su entendimiento, y conmoviendo y atrayendo su depravada voluntad. No, por cierto, con el ímpetu o violencia de las armas, sino con la fuerza de la misma razón natural, que pudo obrar aun contra la segunda naturaleza misma, esto es, contra la costumbre inveterada. Logró su intento, moviendo, induciendo, persuadiendo afectuosamente a aquellos hombres de costumbres depravadas y de vida errante como la de las fieras, primero, a escuchar y entender las cosas provechosas de que les hablaba; en seguida [a pasar] de una vida salvaje a otra de costumbres apacibles; después, a reunirse en un mismo lugar y formar agrupaciones que posteriormente se llamaron ciudades; a amar la justicia, la equidad y la virtud; y, finalmente, a reverenciar la fe, esto es, a Dios.
>
> (*Del único modo* 101)

> With words full of sweetness, with tender and gentle, opportune and delicate persuasion, that prudent man was able to transform beasts into men, sparking their intellect with his reasoning and stirring and bending their depraved will. Not, to be sure, through the use of force or assaults with arms but, rather, with the force of natural reason alone, which was able to prevail even against second nature itself, i.e., against stubborn habit. He achieved this goal by emotionally stirring, inducing, [and] persuading those men of depraved customs and a nomadic way of life like that of wild beasts, first, to listen and understand the profitable things that he was talking to them about; and, next, to shift from a savage life to one of peaceful customs; then, to come together in one place and form communities that later were called cities; to love justice, equality and virtue; and, finally, to revere the faith, that is, God.

Las Casas's articulation of rhetoric as the foundation of evangelization and of society itself impinges on the *Brevísima relación* in ways that are often ignored in the classroom. To begin such a discussion, undergraduate and graduate students alike need a primer on classical and Renaissance rhetoric and on sacred oratory. The shortest path to gaining a working knowledge of all three is to read selections from Fray Luis de Granada's *Los seis libros de la retórica eclesiástica* ("Ecclesiastical Rhetoric in Six Books"). This handbook for aspiring preachers was published after the *Brevísima relación*, but the title and contents of *De unico vocationis modo* reveal that Las Casas and Fray Luis had drunk from the same rhetorical wells: Aristotle (*Rhetoric*), Cicero, Quintilian, and Augustine (*On Christian Doctrine*).[2]

In Spanish undergraduate and graduate courses, I give an overview of the three branches of classical rhetoric and where the *Brevísima relación* fits in this division. Unlike Las Casas's other writings, the text makes clear from the onset that his primary purpose was not to argue about past actions (as it was in his legal briefs, which belong to the judicial branch of rhetoric) or to qualify present ones as good or bad (as in his *Historia de las Indias* [*History of the Indies*], which belongs to the demonstrative branch). His text is a summary or compendium—an *epítome*—that shows its rhetorical cards in "Purpose of the Present Summary" ("Argumento del presente epítome" [*Brevísima relación* 69–70]). His purpose in writing the *Brevísima relación* was an ideological or political one: to persuade the Crown to abolish forced Indian labor (*la encomienda*), which places this influential work in the deliberative branch of rhetoric concerned with future actions, rather than past or present ones.

Though subordinate to the deliberative branch because of the author's ideological purpose, elements of judicial rhetoric nonetheless abound in the *Brevísima relación*. Particularly helpful to graduate students are James Muldoon's works that emphasize the legal and social interfaces of the reconquest of Spain and the conquest of America, the significance of legal studies to Hispanic institutions and culture, and the concepts of natural law and empire (*Americas* and "Medieval Canon Law"). I always remind my undergraduate and graduate students how Hernán Cortés used the law and legal formulas in his *Letters from Mexico* and how the Inca Garcilaso would later deftly employ natural, human, and divine laws in his *Royal Commentaries*. Demonstrative rhetoric—praise and blame—also has a significant presence in the *Brevísima relación*. Students will pick up on this right away, especially in the depictions of Indians and Spaniards. To a great degree, these representations are type-characters built from topoi, rather than individualized portraits. Working in groups to identify the tropes and figures that appear in descriptions of different Spaniards and Indians is a useful exercise for undergraduate and beginning graduate students. When students complain that Las Casas repeats the same things over and over, that he exaggerates in his praise and blame, one can reframe the debate around rhetoric. The instructor might ask students: Why litotes here, why hyperbole there, why repetition throughout? How do these make his case against conquest of native lands and servitude for native peoples?

No matter their level, students need to be reminded repeatedly of the Dominican's "Purpose of the Present Summary" and given the tools to analyze how he pursues that ideological purpose. I explain to them that written speeches (and, later, narrations) were typically divided into four or five parts: exordium; proposition; narration; confirmation (sometimes treated as part of the narration); and peroration (or epilogue). Graduates may read selections from Cicero or Aristotle before division of a speech is discussed in class; undergraduates profit if they are told what the divisions are and asked to work directly with the *Brevísima relación*. These four or five parts are readily identifiable and allow an instructor to divide up the text over two or three classes for undergraduates.

"Purpose of the Present Summary" and the prologue for Prince Philip (*Brevísima relación* 71–73) contain the exordium and proposition: Las Casas alludes to a legal filing on a similar topic and encourages Prince Philip to persuade Charles V to enforce the 1542–43 ordinances that curtailed the institution of forced native labor on behalf of Spanish conquerors. Praise for Prince Philip in the prologue is in keeping with the purpose of the exordium, for "uno de los primeros preceptos de la retórica enseña que, por medio del exordio, el orador debe ganarse insensiblemente la benevolencia de sus oyentes a fin de tenerlos de su parte" 'one of the first precepts of rhetoric teaches that by means of the exordium an orator must imperceptibly gain the benevolence of his listeners in order to get them on his side' (*Del único modo* 49). The narration, which contains the arguments that support the proposition, shows how the actions of the conquerors (*encomenderos*) against the conquered (*encomendados*) violate natural, human, and divine laws. It stretches from the division of said actions into conquest and servitude (*Brevísima relación* 75–79) until nearly the end of the work:

> Y porque sea verdadera la regla que al principio dije, que siempre fue creciendo la tiranía y violencias e injusticias de los españoles contra aquellas ovejas mansas, en crudeza, inhumanidad y maldad, lo que agora en las dichas provincias se hace entre otras cosas dignísimas de todo fuego y tormento, es lo siguiente. . . .   (172)

> And to prove the rule true that I stated at the beginning—that the tyranny and assaults and injustices of the Spaniards against those gentle sheep were always increasing in cruelty, inhumanity, and evil—what is now done in said provinces, among other things most worthy of fire and brimstone, is the following. . . .

I have students take apart the powerful epilogue, which uses figures of amplification found in Aristotle, Cicero, and Quintilian, plus others that Fray Luis's treatment of amplification defines as key figures that stir the emotions (551–53). Undergraduates and graduates alike should analyze segments such as the following, which appeals to the religious and political beliefs that aristocratic Spaniards held about themselves:

> Considérese agora por Dios, por los que esto leyeren, qué obra es ésta y si excede a toda crueldad e injusticia que puede ser pensada, y si les cuadra

bien a los tales cristianos llamallos diablos, y si sería más encomendar los indios a los diablos del infierno que es encomendarlos a los cristianos de las Indias. . . . Sepan todos los que son verdaderos cristianos, y aun los que no lo son, si se oyó en el mundo tal obra. . . . Todas estas cosas y otras diabólicas vienen agora probadas en procesos que han hecho unos tiranos contra otros. ¿Qué puede ser más fea ni fiera ni inhumana cosa?   (172–73)

Now let God and those who come to read this judge what an undertaking this is and whether it surpasses every cruelty and injustice that one could think of, and if it's fitting to call such Christians devils, and if assigning Indians to work for the devils in hell could be any worse than assigning them to Christians in the Indies. . . . Let all of those who are true Christians, and even those who are not, declare if they have ever heard of such an undertaking before. . . . All these things and devilish others have recently been proven in lawsuits that tyrants have filed against each other. What could be uglier, more beastly and inhumane?

Students should be asked to identify here the figures of adjuration (*adjuración*), hyperbole (*hipérbole*) and rhetorical question (*interrogación* [Luis de Granada 551–52]). Analyzing rhetoric is a lot like learning it—you must practice—and often it's helpful to explicitly shift classroom discussion from how students feel to how the text creates their emotions. Another example from Las Casas's epilogue is a pathetic and fawning appeal:

Fue inducido yo . . . que por la misericordia de Dios ando en esta corte de España, procurando echar el infierno de las Indias, y que aquellas infinitas muchedumbres de ánimas redimidas por la sangre de Jesucristo no perezcan sin remedio para siempre, sino que conozcan a su criador y se salven; y por compasión que he de mi patria, que es Castilla, no la destruya Dios por tan grandes pecados contra su fe y honra cometidos y en los prójimos. . . . Tengo grande esperanza que porque el emperador y rey de España, nuestro señor Don Carlos, quinto deste nombre, va entendiendo las maldades y traiciones que en aquellas gentes y tierras, contra la voluntad de Dios y suya, se hacen y han hecho (porque hasta agora se ha encubierto siempre la verdad industriosamente), que ha de extirpar tantos males y ha de remediar aquel Nuevo Mundo que Dios le ha dado, como amador y cultor que es de justicia. . . .   (174–75)

Compelled was I . . . , who through God's mercy am in this court of Spain [i.e., Madrid], seeking to throw hell out of the Indies and that those countless crowds of souls redeemed by the blood of Jesus Christ shall not perish for always but, instead, shall know their Creator and be saved; and out of compassion for my homeland, which is Castile, may God not destroy it because of the great sins committed against their faith and good name, and against their fellow men. . . . Since the emperor and king of Spain, our lord King Charles V, is beginning to understand the evils and acts of treason that are being done and have been done against those peoples and lands, against God's will and his Majesty's (because up until now the truth has always been carefully concealed), I have great hope that he will root out the many evils, and he will save that New World God has given him, being the lover and promoter of justice that he is. . . .

Students can be asked why this would be an effective way to close: how does it appeal to religion, statesmanship, patriotism, and so on? Again, the instructor should insist that students be specific in identifying tropes and figures in the passage. Having students read such passages aloud often helps them get a better sense of how this word or that shapes the passage as a whole. One can ask them to imagine the emotional response of someone—Prince Philip, Charles V, a twenty-first-century Native American or Spaniard—after hearing the passage read to him or her.

If the *Brevísima relación* is not assigned in its entirety, I explain the tripartite division of rhetoric and why the text fits into the deliberative branch; I then skip the division of a speech and its applications to the *Brevísima relación* and, instead, discuss how each rhetorical discourse was a combination of exposition, argumentation, and amplification that varied according to the needs of the speaker (or writer). I point out that amplification (*amplificatio*) did not mean simply going on and on or blowing things out of proportion: it meant moving the emotions. Fray Luis made this clear in his *Retórica eclesiástica*, as Aristotle, Cicero, and Quintilian had done in non-Christian rhetorics. Las Casas claims, in his peroration, that he has not made things bigger than they are in either quality or quantity (173). Yet, his strategies of amplification depend precisely on quality and quantity. Undergraduate students in particular should practice identifying the means and ends of amplification in the *Brevísima relación* by working in groups, then presenting examples to the entire class.

A common means of amplification especially effective in describing people was *sermocinatio* (*sermocinación*, *habla fingida*, or *razonamiento fingido* in Spanish), a figure that attributes speech to someone in a way that is true to character (Luis de Granada 544). Feigned (or re-created) speech was believed to make a discourse more dynamic and believable. Fray Luis suggests that no figure is better suited to the preacher (544) and notes further that *sermocinatio* is "Ni sólo . . . lo que dicen las personas, sino también lo que con razón debieran decir" 'not only . . . what people say, but also what they with good reason should say' (545). Las Casas must have highly valued this figure, because he resorts to it frequently in the *Brevísima relación* (97, 101, 108, and elsewhere). I'll limit myself here to a single example, one that is followed by two other figures of amplification—exclamation and epiphrase (i.e., moral reflection)—and reminds readers of the *Brevísima relación*'s ideological purpose:

Suelen decir los indios en aquella tierra, cuando los fatigan llevándo-
los con cargas por las sierras, si caen y desmayan de flaqueza y trabajo,
porque allí les dan de coces y palos, y les quiebran los dientes con los
pomos de las espadas porque se levanten y anden sin resollar: "Anda, que
sois malos, no puedo más, mátame aquí, que aquí quiero quedar muerto."
Y esto dícenlo con grandes sospiros y apretamiento del pecho, mostrando
grande augustia y dolor. ¡Oh, quién pudiese dar a entender de cient partes
una de las afliciones y calamidades que aquellas inocentes gentes por los
infelices españoles padecen! Dios sea aquél que lo dé a entender a los que
lo pueden y deben remediar.   (136)

When Spaniards wear Indians out by making them carry goods through
the highlands, if they fall down or grow faint due to weakness or duress
(because then they are kicked and clubbed, and the Spaniards punch their
teeth out with sword handles so that the Indians will get up and keep going without complaining), Indians in that land commonly say: "Go ahead,
you bad men, I can't take any more, so just kill me now, I want to die right
here." And they say this, gasping for breath and heartbroken, showing
great sorrow and pain. Would that someone could communicate even one
percent of the afflictions and calamities that those innocent people suffer
on account of the ill-fated Spaniards! May God be the one who communi-
cates it to those who can and must remedy it.

This passage does not contain a direct quotation, nor should Las Casas's pen-
chant for feigned speech be mistaken for orality or a burning desire to let the
indigenous and Europeans speak for themselves. He never intended to record
exactly what Indians or Spaniards had said, nor would his readers have expected
this. Even the supposed direct quotations in the *Brevísima relación* originated
in the written word: his written word, his mastery of the principles of rhetoric.

Rhetorical analysis of the *Brevísima relación* should always foster classroom
discussion of big-picture issues, for the rhetorical, as I have suggested, over-
laps with the ideological. When students ask (and they will), "How could he
have written down those speeches? He's just making them up," we discuss how
definitions of "truth" and "history" vary across time and place. It is also useful
to remind students that religion is part of ideology and that it is impossible
to think of pre-nineteenth-century imperialism without taking religion into account. Here, Fray Luis's parting comments on *sermocinatio* shed light on Las
Casas's predilection: "También nos servimos de esta figura muy cómodamente
en amplificar las gloriosas batallas de los mártires, cuando explicamos las palabras con que respondían a los jueces, o con que se animaban a sí mismos a la
constancia en la fe, y a la paciencia" 'We also make use of this figure most appropriately in amplifying the glorious battles of martyrs, when we explain the words
with which they responded to their judges or with which they kept themselves

steady in their faith and in their patience' (545). The deployment of *sermoci-nario* in the *Brevísima relación* tells Prince Philip that Indians are martyrs and Spaniards, savages (in their own words, so to speak), thereby supporting the ideological purpose stated in "Purpose of the Present Summary" and dramatiz-ing Las Casas's larger argument in favor of the conversion of the native peoples and against conquest and servitude.

NOTES

Quotations from the *Brevísima relación* are taken from André Saint-Lu's edition (Cá-tedra, 2005).

[1] All translations from the Spanish are mine unless otherwise indicated.

[2] Modern treatments of rhetoric in Spanish such as Marchese and Forradellas; Azaus-tre and Casas; and Mortara Garavelli are also helpful for undergraduates and graduates. Instructors in English-language courses should lead students to modern guides in En-glish (Barilli and esp. Kennedy). On Las Casas's rhetoric in particular, see Abbott; and S. Arias, "Bartolomé de las Casas's Sacred Place."

Confronting Stereotypes:
The *Brevísima relación* as Homily, Not History

Cynthia L. Stone

A unifying theme of Survey of Spanish American Literature 1, a third-year course for undergraduate Spanish majors, is the presentation of colonial-era chronicles not simply as historical sources but as texts structured by specific goals, which, in turn, influence the selection of particular topoi, narrative genres, and rhetorical strategies. Over the course of the semester, we cover major texts from pre-Hispanic times through the early nineteenth century, three hours of which (two seventy-five minute sessions) are dedicated to the works of Bartolomé de Las Casas.

An important goal of the course is to encourage students to critically evaluate common stereotypes about Indians and Spaniards, including the "noble savage" and the "cruel conquistador." Las Casas presents an interesting quandary from this perspective, since a pivotal metaphor from his most famous and most accessible work, the *Brevísima relación de la destrucción de las Indias*, involves the characterization of the Amerindians as defenseless lambs at the mercy of Spanish wolves. Readers commonly react to these stereotypes by either accepting them uncritically or dismissing Las Casas's denunciations as exaggerations and slanderous inventions directly responsible for the Spanish Black Legend. Yet, for those of us who specialize in this period of immense cultural ferment whose repercussions are still evident today, neither extreme does justice to the complexity and richness of Las Casas's writings and his enduring legacy in Spanish American letters.

A solution to this quandary is to avoid treating the *Brevísima relación* in a survey format. The reasons I prefer not to exercise that option are several. First, most Holy Cross students are Catholic, and close to a third of Spanish majors in my classes are heritage speakers. Nevertheless, they, like most United States students, have internalized anti-Catholic and anti-Hispanic prejudices. Teaching the *Brevísima relación* tends to bring these unquestioned assumptions to the surface, where they can be critically evaluated. Second, the *Brevísima relación's* combination of rhetorical strategies is amazingly effective at provoking outrage, and, to my mind, anything that stirs undergraduates from a general sense of disconnection regarding colonial-era texts is to be cherished.

Still, I postpone discussion regarding the above polemic until the end of the second class. Otherwise, the most vocal students tend to divide unreflexively into two camps—those all too ready to blame the Spaniards for the problems currently faced by the nations of Spanish America and those who feel the need to dismiss Las Casas for lack of historical accuracy in his denunciation of Spanish abuses.

My pedagogical strategy hinges on a comparison between excerpts from the *Historia de las Indias* and the *Brevísima relación*. We begin, accordingly, by returning to the Renaissance definition of history that was introduced during the preceding week's discussion of Bernal Díaz del Castillo's *Historia verdadera de la conquista de la Nueva España*: in the words of Luis Cabrera de Córdoba, "es la historia narración de verdades por hombre sabio, para enseñar a bien vivir" 'history is a true account by a man of wisdom with the purpose of instructing in righteous living (24).[1] The first point is that Las Casas, as a learned man of the cloth, corresponds to the Renaissance model of the historian as philosophical moralist better than Bernal Díaz. Second, Las Casas is no less qualified than Bernal Díaz to provide eyewitness testimony, as the Dominican amply demonstrates in his writings. Relatively speaking, however, the requirement that history provide moral and religious truth gives added weight to the evidentiary truth of Las Casas's account.

The first selections from Las Casas's *Historia* are introduced through part of a chapter from José Juan Arrom's *Imaginación del Nuevo Mundo*, which presents Las Casas as "iniciador de la narrativa de protesta" in Hispanic literature ("Bartolomé de las Casas"). Several brief excerpts that Arrom reproduces and analyzes include the anecdotes of the mastiff Becerillo (*Historia* 2: 389; bk. 2, ch. 55), the lies of Indians and Spaniards (3: 331; bk. 3, ch. 145), and the Indian messenger (1: 445; bk. 1, ch. 115). A supplementary online reading on the use of killer dogs in the wars of conquest that references Becerillo serves implicitly to call into question the charge of fabrication used against Las Casas (Grodsinsky).

The primary antithesis in the Becerillo story revolves around the personification of the dog—who is given a share in the booty equal to that of a crossbowman and addressed as "Señor perro" 'Sir Dog'—versus the dehumanization of the nameless "mujer vieja" 'old Indian woman' whom Becerillo ultimately mistakes for a wall and urinates on. The use of dramatic irony implicates us as readers in the cruel joke Becerillo's owner plays on the unsuspecting old woman. (We know that she is given a letter only to provide better sport by allowing the mastiff to chase her down before tearing her to pieces, but she thinks she is being given an important mission.) The surprising, happy ending, in which the Spaniards grant the old woman her freedom "por no ser más crueles que el perro" 'so as to not exceed the dog in cruelty' (2: 389), manages to illustrate succinctly the conquistadors' loss of humanity while also foregrounding Las Casas's characteristic blending of irony and black humor. Rather than exaggeration, the predominant tone here is understatement, which is highly effective in suggesting the matter-of-fact attitude of the seasoned torturer and also provides a good counterpoint to our later reading of excerpts from the *Brevísima relación*. The ironic definition of the experienced "cristiano" (Christian) as someone who knows how to lie convincingly and the inversion of stereotypes about the relative intelligence and prudence of the "indios" (Indians) as opposed to their supposedly more civilized masters are the highlights of the other brief selections discussed in class.

In preparation for the second day on Las Casas, students preview the story of the 1518–35 rebellion of the Taíno chief Enriquillo, in what is now the Dominican Republic (for a good summary, see Wagner and Parish 74–78; an alternate

Spanish version is Losada, *Fray Bartolomé de las Casas* 162–65), as well as a general profile of missionaries in the Spanish Indies (Rosati).[2] Depending on time constraints, the last few minutes of class are devoted to reviewing these materials.

The reading assignments for the next class session include Raquel Chang-Rodríguez and Malva Filer's selections on Enriquillo in the anthology *Voces de Hispanoamérica* (from the *Historia* 3: 259–70; bk. 3, chs. 125–27), two excerpts from the *Brevísima relación* (the prologue and the chapter on the conquest of the island of Hispaniola [71–73, 80–82]), plus a reproduction of the famous 1511 Hispaniola sermon by the Dominican friar Antón de Montesinos as remembered by Las Casas (*Historia* 2: 441–42; bk. 3, ch. 4).[3] I also provide an interview with Gustavo Gutiérrez on the topic of Lascasian influences on theology of liberation as optional reading (Gutiérrez, *Fray Bartolomé de las Casas*).

To focus attention on the generic conventions that shape the Lascasian texts, I supply students with a list of rhetorical figures and tropes classified by Quintilian under the Greek term *enargeia* and ask them to identify corresponding passages from the *Historia* and the *Brevísima relación* with a view to comparing the uses made of them in the two works. Among the main components of *enargeia* are *descriptio* (vivid description, including ocular demonstration, invented dialogue, and personification), *accumulatio* (the piling up of words and concepts, through climax, synonymy, asyndeton, exemplum, congeries, etc.), hyperbole (a species of amplification that can either exaggerate or attenuate), irony (encompassing antiphrasis, paralipsis, *contentio*, etc.), and antonomasia (the substitution of a descriptive phrase for a proper name or of a representative individual for a class of persons).

The personal motivation informing Las Casas's most polemical writings is aptly summarized in the *Brevísima relación* as the awareness that to remain silent in the face of the atrocities the friar has witnessed is tantamount to becoming an accomplice: "deliberé, por no ser reo, callando, de las perdiciones de ánimas y cuerpos infinitas que los tales perpetraran, poner en molde algunas" 'I therefore concluded that it would constitute a criminal neglect of my duty to remain silent about the enormous loss of life as well as the infinite numbers of souls dispatched to Hell in the course of such "conquests," and so resolved to publish an account of a few such outrages' (80–82; *Short Account* 6). Indeed, Las Casas's first draft was composed in 1542 for oral delivery to the court councils in an attempt to convince the emperor to halt the ongoing wars of conquest (*Brevísima relación* 21–22).

Las Casas's concomitant rhetorical challenge is to excite in his readers a similar sense of outrage, by bringing the subject matter so vividly before their minds' eyes that they imagine themselves to be witnesses to the events described and, as such, likewise compelled to moral action. In this sense, enargetic rhetoric is well suited to the biblical imperative to provide visible testimony of God's presence. Here the topos of the eyewitness is more prophetically charged than in Bernal Díaz, collapsing, as Santa Arias observes, the spatiotemporal distance between the reader and the events portrayed (*Retórica* 75–76). Las Casas's verbal pictures not only create the illusion of immediacy but also convey a deeper understanding of what is represented, the invisible significance of divinely sanctioned authenticity.

When stressing the major points of comparison between Las Casas's style of presentation in the *Historia* versus the *Brevísima relación*, note five rhetorical figures especially: antonomasia, *contentio*, irony, hyperbole, and *descriptio*.

First, the use of antonomasia: In the *Historia*, Las Casas provides proper names for historical figures, using baptismal ones for the cacique Enriquillo and his wife, Doña Lucía; surnames for the Spanish *encomendero* Valenzuela and the lieutenant governor, Pedro de Vadillo; and Taíno names for those Indian rebels who reject Christianity, such as Ciguayo. In contrast, in the *Brevísima relación*, Las Casas pointedly excludes names in the chapter on Hispaniola, referring simply to "los cristianos" (the Christians) and "los indios" (the Indians). Moreover, while the *Historia* includes a brief verbal portrait of the protagonist, Enriquillo,[4] the predominant descriptive mode in the *Brevísima relación* is an intensification and accumulation of associations through the reduction of individuals to occupational titles such as "capitán" (captain) or "alguazil" (law enforcement officer) and through the use of epithets like "tiranos" (tyrants), "inhumanos" (inhumane), "extirpadores" (extirpators), and "capitales enemigos del linaje humano" (principal enemies of the human race [80–82]).

The *Brevísima relación*'s lack of individualization and in-depth characterization is one of its most problematic aspects for modern readers. My goal is to help students perceive it as a rhetorical strategy Las Casas uses in some, but by no means all, of his writings. The rationale here is to underscore that, no matter the specific circumstances, the same dynamics repeat themselves throughout the wars of conquest. In the *Brevísima relación*, Las Casas focuses on the universal dynamics of human interaction in times of war, how those who commit acts of violence (unless in self-defense) are complicit in their own dehumanization.

Although Las Casas is frequently cited as an originator of the topos of the "noble savage," this attribution is only partially accurate. In the *Historia*, for instance, it is Enriquillo (despite the childlike diminutive conferred on him by the Franciscan friars) who exemplifies the virtues of prudence, articulateness, and self-control associated with the Renaissance ideal of the fully autonomous adult male. Indeed, the exposition of the rights of the Amerindians to self government due to their exemplary political and moral development (as perfectly as Las Casas considered humanly possible without the guidance of divine grace) is more central to his writings overall than the qualities of docility, humility, obedience, and peacefulness highlighted in the *Brevísima relación*.

The second point to underscore for students is the use of *contentio* (comparison through contraries): In the *Historia*, the main contrast is between Enriquillo and Valenzuela, but there are also significant secondary distinctions made within the separate categories of Indians and Spaniards. Enriquillo, for instance, is contrasted with other Indian rebels, such as Ciguayo, who stage unprovoked attacks on populations of Spanish civilians, while Valenzuela is contrasted with the members of the Audiencia of Santo Domingo (who give Enriquillo a favorable disposition to his legal case, albeit without the means of enforcing it), with captain Hernando de San Miguel (who negotiates a peace treaty with the cacique, though ultimately inconclusively), and with friars such as the Franciscans (who teach Enriquillo Christian doctrine and how to read and write in Castilian), as well as with Las Casas himself. These secondary contrasts are notably absent from the *Brevísima relación*, where the full force of pathos is brought to bear on the binary opposition between Indians and Christians: the Indians represented as "corderos metidos en sus apriscos" 'lambs in the fold'; the Christians, sardonically, as "feroces bestias" 'ferocious beasts' (81, 82). The generosity and humble lifestyle of the Indians, moreover, is contrasted with the covetousness, wastefulness, and ecological devastation wrought by the Spaniards: "lo que basta para tres casas de a diez personas cada una para un mes, come un cristiano y destruye en un día." 'What a European will consume in a single day normally supports three native households of ten persons each for a whole month' (80; *Short Account* 14).

A key distinction between the literary genres of history and homily involves just such a flattening out of particulars in the interest of emphasizing universal truths. In the category of homiletics, the *Brevísima relación* corresponds to the ministerial sermon delivered to believers, as opposed to the missionary sermon addressed to nonbelievers. Along these lines, it resembles Fray Antón de Montesinos's 1511 prophetic exhortation to the Spaniards of Hispaniola to bestir themselves from the stupor into which they have fallen and recognize the mortal sin in which they are living: "yo que soy voz de Cristo en el desierto desta isla [os aviso que] todos estáis en pecado mortal y en él vivís y morís" 'I, the voice of Christ in the desert of this island, [I declare unto you that] you are all living and dying in a state of mortal sin' (*Historia* 2: 441; bk. 3, ch. 4; see note 3 of this essay).

Accordingly, I draw students' attention to the division of the *Brevísima relación* into a prologue and a series of chapters set in diverse locales where the ravages of conquest are shown to repeat themselves over and over. Both the prologue (where the *thema* to be expounded on is first presented) and the final chapter on New Granada end with the word *amen*. As André Saint-Lu suggests (Introduction 17), the chapters are expository variations on the scriptural passage in the book of Luke in which Jesus's disciples are likened to lambs among wolves. The underlying theological proposition implies a world radically divided between the forces of good and of evil, in which God and Satan vie for the souls of unrepentant sinners (for more on this oppositional rhetoric, see Avalle-Arce). In other words, the rhetorical appeal of the *Brevísima relación* is more to the emotions than to the intellect, while the *Historia* presents a relatively balanced appeal to pathos and logos.

The third point of comparison concerns other characteristic uses of irony: once again there is a certain economy of expression and controlled understatement in the *Historia*, as when Enriquillo tells the *encomendero* who has assaulted his wife, impoverished his people, and abused him both verbally and physically, "Agradeced, Valenzuela, que no os mato; andad, id y no volváis más acá; guardáos" 'Be grateful I spare your life, Valenzuela. Go now, leave and return no more to these parts. Take heed,' or when the act of taking up arms in self-defense is pithily summarized as "alzarse y ser rebelde," rising up and rebelling (3: 261; bk. 3, ch. 125).

The *Brevísima relación*'s irony is more graphic and heavy-handed. In addition to the antiphrastic "Christian," which appears in most every sentence, the brief passages we analyze in class include ironic references to sacrilegious methods of torture ("de trece en trece, a honor y reverencia de Nuestro Redemptor e de los doce apóstoles, poniéndoles leña y fuego" '[Stringing their victims up] and burn[ing] them alive thirteen at a time, in honour of our Savior and the twelve Apostles' ([81; *Short Account* 15]) and to the great benefits conferred on the Indians by European letters ("otros . . . cortábanles ambas manos y dellas llevaban colgando, y decíanles: 'Andad con cartas', conviene a saber, lleva las nuevas a las gentes que estaban huidas por los montes" 'Some they chose to . . . cut their wrists, leaving their hands dangling, saying to them: "Take this letter"—meaning that their sorry condition would act as a warning to those hiding in the hills' [81; 15]). Class discussion tends to revolve around Las Casas's inversion of religious preconceptions—most Indian converts are better Christians than those who boast the name Christians; the *buen cristiano* is defined by acts, not heredity—and also his development of the Aristotelian conception of civil society along with the Thomistic conception of natural law into a theory of natural rights (Hanke, *Aristotle*; Pagden, *Fall*; and García).

Instructors will also want to track the use of hyperbole: the ironic understatement of the *Historia* contrasts with the unremittingly emphatic tone of the *Brevísima relación*, achieved through the prolific use of grammatical superlatives ("sumario brevísimo," "vastísimo y nuevo mundo," "tierras grandísimas," "gravísimos pecados mortals," "cosa . . . convenientísima," "perros bravísimos"; 'briefest of summaries,' 'most vast and newfound world,' 'exceedingly great lands,' 'gravest of mortal sins,' 'a matter of utmost convenience,' 'most ferocious dogs'), extreme descriptors ("destruición," "terribles y eternos suplicios," "inmensa copia de sangre humana," "cosas arriba dichas y otras infinitas"; 'destruction,' 'terrible and eternal torments,' 'copious amounts of human blood,' 'aforesaid matters and infinite others'), and quantitative and qualitative amplifications ("mil cuentos de gentes," "cincuenta años y más de experiencia," "tantos y tan grandes y tales reinos," "tan sin piedad y tan feroces bestias"; 'peoples by the scores of thousands,' 'experience of fifty years and more,' 'so many kingdoms, each and every one of such greatness,' 'so merciless and of such bestial ferocity' [72–82]). When the charged language is combined with the abundant use of congeries, as when Las Casas refers to the conquests as "inicuas, tiránicas, y por toda ley natural, divina y humana condenadas, detestadas y malditas" 'iniquitous, tyrannical, and condemned, detested, and accursed by every natural, divine, and human law' (72), the overall impression created in the reader is one of sustained verbal assault.

It is important to distinguish between the use of exaggeration for dramatic effect, without intent to deceive, and the deliberate misrepresentation of historically verifiable figures and events. Las Casas's rhetorical excesses are consistently of the first type, not the second. Indeed, taken individually, the above examples do not differ substantially from the use of hyperbole by Las Casas's contemporaries, as when the historian Francisco López de Gómara refers to the discovery of the Spanish Indies as "la mayor cosa después de la creación del mundo, sacando la encarnación y muerte del que lo crió" 'the greatest event since the creation of the world (excluding the incarnation and death of Him who created it)' (qtd. in Elliott, *Old World* 10). Rather, it is the cumulative effect of so many in such a condensed narration that contributes to the impression of "aglomeración saturada" 'saturated conglomeration' (Veres 5). Which leads to the question of why Las Casas overplays his hand, so to speak, in the *Brevísima relación*—why he is not more circumspect in his use of this trope. No less an authority than the classical rhetorician Quintilian suggests a possible rationale:

> Hyperbole only has positive value when the thing about which we have to speak transcends the ordinary limits of nature. We are then allowed to amplify, because the real size of the thing cannot be expressed, and it is better to go too far than not to go far enough.   (469; bk. 8, ch. 6)

The task Las Casas sets for himself in the *Brevísima relación* is not only to convince his readers of the validity of his moral and theological arguments but also to persuade them of the unprecedented nature of what is happening in the Spanish Indies, so they feel compelled either to join with him in putting an end to the abuses or to cover their ears and decry the shamelessness of such allegations. In giving voice to the unspeakable—the incomprehensibility of extreme violence—Las Casas crosses the boundary of decorum into the realm of absolutes.

Finally, there is Las Casas's use of *descriptio* (vivid description). The concise characterization in the *Historia* of individuals (e.g., Becerillo, Enriquillo), of places (e.g., Hispaniola as a *locus amoenus* before the conquest), and of events (e.g., the rapid sketching of action through sequences of verbs such as "tornóse . . . suénase . . . provéese . . . juntáronse"; 'returned . . . proclaimed . . . provided . . . set forth' [3: 261; bk. 3, ch. 125]) contrasts with the excruciating enumeration of the physicality of torture in the *Brevísima relación*: the detailing of body parts (smashed or severed heads, disemboweled entrails, amputated hands, roasting feet, screaming mouths), of types of people slaughtered (the aged, pregnant women, infants, caciques), of particular techniques favored by diverse executioners (stabbing, dismembering, drowning, burning on gallows or lashed to grids of rods).

The figure of ocular demonstration (Cicero's *sub oculos subjectio*) involves not just the recounting of events but the actual showing of them before the eyes of the mind. It thus constitutes a reality of its own making, which becomes self-evident and readily reproducible. In this sense, Theodor de Bry's images illustrating the 1598 Latin edition of the *Brevísima relación* simply take Las Casas's verbal pictures to the next logical stage of rhetorical intensification. (The de Bry engraving we tend to concentrate on in class is that of the thirteen naked men and women hanging from a gallows and slowly burning, along with the infant whose brains are about to be dashed against a wall [*Narratio regionum* 10]; for more on this topic, see Conley.)

The virtue of the preceding point-by-point comparison between Las Casas as historian and as preacher-prophet is that, when the class finally gets around to discussing the Black Legend, we can concentrate on the crux of the matter: namely, whether the publication of the *Brevísima relación* in 1552 was Las Casas's greatest mistake (in accordance with the thesis of Rómulo Carbia, among others); or whether, considered retrospectively, its positive contributions (to the development of protest and testimonial literature, to the theology of liberation, to the doctrine of natural human rights) outweigh the negatives of its propagandistic use by Spain's enemies to defame the Spanish national character. An alternate approach, for those who prefer to put a somewhat different spin on the debate, is whether those who disagree with their government's policies do well in openly voicing their objections so as to influence the course of foreign policy, both in the short and long term, or whether to do so is intrinsically unpatriotic.

NOTES

I follow André Saint-Lu's editions of the *Brevísima relación* (Cátedra, 2005) and the *Historia de las Indias* (Ayacucho, 1986). All translations from the Spanish are my own unless otherwise indicated.

[1] This summation is from a retrospectively oriented historiographic treatise by Luis Cabrera de Córdoba, first published in 1611.

[2] For more information on the life of Las Casas, see the essay by Rolena Adorno in this volume. The best full-length study is still the 1967 biography by Wagner and Parish.

[3] Available online at www.puc.cl/sw_educ/historia/conquista/parte3/html/index.html, path: sermón de Montecinos.

[4] Enriquillo is described as "a tall, impressive man, finely proportioned, his face neither handsome nor homely. It was the face of a serious and stern man" (Casas, *Indian Freedom* 189).

Images and War: The Representation of Violence in Colonial Times and Today

Gustavo Verdesio

The importance of the illustrations that accompany Theodor de Bry's editions of Bartolomé de Las Casas's *Brevísima relación* (*Narratio regionum indicarum*) is undeniable. As some scholars (notably Tom Conley and José Rabasa [*Writing Violence*]) have pointed out, their dialogue with the text alters the message contained in the original Spanish version. Also, as Conley has suggested, many European audiences' primary images of the colonial encounter came from the editions produced by de Bry and his sons. The drawings of indigenous bodies and foreign, exotic landscapes lent the texts they accompanied an aura of authenticity and gave readers a sense of firsthand contact with unknown peoples and places (103). These images were, for many readers, not only the first ones they had seen depicting colonialism and the distant lands where it took place but also the most authoritative ones.

The illustrations in the texts reproduced by the de Bry publishers were part of an apparatus of propaganda that advanced the cause of the Dutch Protestants (who had been in conflict with the Spanish since 1566)[1] by showing pictures of the crimes and barbarous acts performed by the Spaniards, their Catholic enemies. Among other functions, the images sometimes exaggerated the facts described by the original text or reorganized the information in ways that would make the Spaniards look even worse to unsympathetic European eyes. Therefore, images play a didactic role in the presentation and representation of the role of the Spanish forces in the colonization of the Americas. This essay focuses both on the political uses of the images included in the de Brys' editions (especially the 1598 Latin edition) and of those that inspired them (the watercolors that illustrate a 1582 French manuscript version of the *Brevísima relación* [*Tyrannies . . . perpetrées es Indes*]) and on the way in which images of violence are used today in the mass media.

In a seminal chapter of *Writing Violence*, Rabasa compares the different ways in which the watercolors from 1582 and the engravings from 1598 (*Narratio regionum indicarum*) depict the massacres perpetrated by Spanish subjects in the Americas. After a careful analysis of both sets of images, he concludes that neither seems to show an interest in portraying the massacres as the original text describes them. Instead, both try to offer a picture that "feels right" to the audience to whom they are addressed (236). The pictures "feel right" because they present the Spaniards as more cruel than what the written text depicts, thus becoming part of a concerted effort among Protestants to promote an anti-Spanish sentiment and therefore delegitimize the Spanish conquest.

At this point, it is useful to ask oneself what constituted cruelty at that time or, better yet, what sort of moral economy served as background for the French Protestant portrayal of Spanish barbarism (242). That is to say, the question is about the ethical rules that determine what is a massacre and what is not, what is allowed and what is not, what is right and what is wrong in human conflicts. These questions are especially difficult because massacres are not detached from their representation: they reach most of us only through some type of representation. As Rabasa correctly notes, the criteria for representation in the sixteenth century were different from those predominant today (243). Sixteenth-century standards allowed for the detailed depictions of violence in the watercolors of the 1582 manuscript and the engravings of the 1598 edition: mutilated bodies, people burned alive, pregnant women killed by soldiers, children hit violently against the wall, and other unspeakable atrocities (see illus.).

Today, discourse about a massacre always issues from the victims or a neutral (or not) third-party observer. Only rarely do members of the society that perpetrated the massacre go public and celebrate or repudiate it. However, in the sixteenth century, Catholic texts and images celebrating massacres perpetrated by Catholics were not uncommon: the massacre of Saint Bartholomew, which victimized French Protestants, was lauded in works by painters such as Giorgio Vasari (*The Night of St. Bartholomew* [c. 1572]) and in various Span-

Illustration from Bartolomé de Las Casas, *Tyrannies et cruautez des Espagnols perpetrées es Indes Occidentales quon dit le Nouveau Monde: Brievement descrites en lettre castillane par l'evesque Don Frere Bartelemy De Las Casas . . . fidelement traduites par Jackques De Miggrode* (1582). Courtesy of the Clements Library, University of Michigan

ish texts (Rabasa 263). The *Brevísima relación* must be appraised against this background. In the text, Las Casas does what brave journalists of our era have done: he denounces the crimes committed by his own people. Unfortunately, this practice is not the rule but the exception in journalism today.

The French versions of the text and the illustrations that are part of the de Bry editions do not condemn, according to Rabasa, the massacres qua massacres. That is to say, they are not against massacres in general but against specific ones: those committed by the Catholic Spaniards against the French Protestants (255). Amerindians are, then, a signifier that stands for a referent: they stand for other bodies and other historical events. They are used, in Hayden White's view, as a tool to criticize other European practices and nations—here, the violence perpetrated by political and religious enemies ("Noble Savage"). This rhetorical move resembles Michel de Montaigne's in his paradigmatic essay "Des cannibales" ("Of Cannibals"): Montaigne uses the image of the noble Amerindian (the "noble savage," which has become a frequent trope of colonial discourse) to criticize the society in which he lived. In the French versions of the *Brevísima relación*, the noble Amerindians suffer unspeakable (but overtly, or so it seems) violence at the hands of their enemies, the Spaniards. According to Rabasa, the images in the French versions displace the Amerindian as a central subject in the original text, seeking not to depict events accurately but to provoke moral outrage (255).

This very old strategy continues to have currency even as I write these lines. For example, the images of bleeding bodies, of people crying or in pain that covered most American news magazines after the terrorist attacks in Madrid on 11 March 2004 were circulated to create a feeling of solidarity but also of anger or outrage. Showing violent acts performed by the enemy is still a common political strategy. However, this approach is not universal: the same United States press that in 2004 showed the pictures of the Madrid attack does not show images of American soldiers wounded or killed in the war in the Middle East. It does not even show certain footage of American POWs held prisoner by clandestine Iraqi insurgent forces. It is not immediately clear why the American press has this contrasting approach to images recording the violence committed against themselves and their allies, but one thing is certain: the reasons are political. The American military has ordered the press not to show what, according to the generals, is not convenient to show in times of war, responding not to a strategic military logic but to a political one.

In the film *Control Room*, a documentary about the war on Iraq, one can watch such logic at work in the conflict between the American government and the Arabic-language media network Al Jazeera. One sees the Arab network, based in Qatar, showing several kinds of images that were not released by American media: among them, images of American prisoners of war, which provoked outrage from the American government. Al Jazeera also aired pictures of Iraqi civilian casualties that the American media did not. The almost invariably gory and heartbreaking images included wounded children, dead people lying in the streets, women crying over the bodies of family members, children expressing their hatred for the occupation army, and many other kinds of disturbing footage. Al Jazeera was doing, then, something similar to what the French did to the Spaniards: they gave detailed visual representation of the violence committed by other people.

Interestingly, Al Jazeera was not even a supporter of Saddam Hussein's regime. On the contrary, the network's policy is to criticize Arab or Muslim despots and to promote the importance and value of tolerance, democracy, and free speech for all societies but for the Arab and Muslim worlds in particular. This position has led several totalitarian regimes to ban Al Jazeera from their airwaves altogether. So, if Al Jazeera shares many of the values that democratic nations of the developed West hold dear, why did it show its target audience—the Arabic-speaking world—the effect of the violence performed by American troops? While one cannot know for sure, the answer seems to point in a direction different from the one that led the French Protestants to visually expose Spanish violent acts.

Perhaps easier to understand is why it is impossible for United States audiences to see any raids or searches American or English soldiers conducted in civilian houses. I believe the reason behind this strategy can be found in the Vietnam War. Images of American military violence in Vietnam had devastating effects on American audiences: hence, the war on Iraq has been always displayed as a clean, precise operation and not the messy affair that any war invariably is.

There is a comprehensive political rationale behind any policy regarding the depiction of violence. In sixteenth-century Spain, showing violence inflicted by the Spanish themselves was not only acceptable but also desirable, because it glorified their military victories and portrayed their enemies' humiliation. The French, however, preferred to show the violence they themselves endured at the hands of their enemies. Today, the most powerful country in the world, the United States, chooses not to show the violence either perpetrated or suffered by its troops.

The detrimental effect of the circulation of images of destruction during the Vietnam War is only one possible explanation for the United States' policy: there are also strong ideological, not completely conscious foundations of said policy. In *Precarious Life*, a text worthy of inclusion in a class on Las Casas, Judith Butler suggests that the public acts of contrition and mourning of American casualties are the counterpart of the erasure or omission of images and names of the Iraqi victims of the violence intrinsic to any military action. In this framework, the loss of some lives can be lamented while the loss of other lives cannot. The decision of what lives to lament is made at a level that does not depend exclusively on our conscious acts (Butler 20). It depends on the regimes that determine who is human and who is not, or who is more human than who (xiv–xv). Those who do not qualify as human (or who are less human than our own people) do not get a personalized representation. That is, their faces are not shown, and therefore, something that is profoundly human (their identity) is not part of our cognitive universe. Others get a visual representation: the villains, the symbols of pure evil, the Osama bin Ladens, and the Saddam Husseins of the world. These faces of evil, which are the only ones that reach American audiences, authorize us to become senseless before those lives (the lives of the faceless) that American and allied troops have eradicated (xviii).

To the Spaniards of the sixteenth century, the lives of French Protestants were not as valuable as their own, and the lives of the Amerindians were expendable as well. Las Casas was involved for years in a debate about whether the Amerindians should be included among those condemned to "natural servitude": his polemic with Ginés de Sepúlveda involved this issue and others, such as the rights Amerindians had under the Spanish colonial regime. However, the most important aspect of Las Casas and Sepúlveda's exchange is the underlying assumption in Spanish society that those people called Indians were either inhuman or at least an inferior kind of human being. Given this assumption, civilization was then the crucial concept to define if one was to argue for or against Amerindian rights.

Before we move to a discussion of civilization, it seems appropriate to clarify first the notion of human. The issue here is not that discourses that deny human status to other peoples are unaware that they are members of the same species but that the human is not a biological or a natural entity: it is a construct. The way in which the human is represented in Western culture varies historically, but it is always a tool for the organization of the living world, and Western society has been insistent on classifying the living through the use of categories such as the human and the nonhuman. Giorgio Agamben, an Italian philosopher who has studied the historical distinction between humanity (he uses the term *man*) and human animality, believes that there are mechanisms, notions, and social practices that define what is human. The combination of them is what he has called "the anthropological machine"—the machine that governs our conception of the human (*Open* 83). Understanding how this machine works is crucial because, according to Agamben, the distinction between what is human and what is not relies on the most important of political conflicts: the biopolitical domination of human populations (80). In Agamben's analysis, the life that is viewed as not human, that has no form-of-life (i.e., that is conceived as bare life), that is not invested of humanity within the legal and civil frameworks, cannot be defended or appreciated in the same way as the lives of those considered citizens or humans (*Homo Sacer* 1–12).[2]

The Spaniards defined civilization by their own form of social organization, which resembled those of the other European colonial powers. The model was Aristotle's, in which those who did not fit into the civilizational standards developed by Greece in the classical period did not enjoy the same rights that Greek citizens had. Powerful nations have attempted throughout history to justify their domination of other societies by considering the subjugated population inferior, and it is a short step from there to the harder and tougher position of considering one's enemy inhuman. Butler believes that the term *civilization* conspires against an expansive conception of the human, because it offers a limited norm for the determination of what is human and what is not. The term, in her view, "provides the measure by which the human is defined."

A question to raise with students is how the West has defined itself as a civilization against the background of populations understood as "illegitimate or dubiously human" (91). According to Butler, the determination of the other as a nonhuman entity is useful because it makes managing those populations easier (98). Although it is more common to find European nations characterizing Amerindians or non-Europeans as the nonhuman enemy or other, Europeans have been—and still are—known to dehumanize each other. The hatred professed among different nations and ethnic groups in the Balkans, for example, reminds us of the way in which fascist regimes treated some segments of the populations they were trying to control.

The mechanisms that determine what can be represented and what cannot, that distinguish between what is human and what is not, are complex and vary historically and geographically. Not all empires or powerful nations behave the same way, and a nation does not follow the same patterns of conduct throughout its own history. Butler believes that multiple strategies operate simultaneously, in paradoxical relation with one another. The choice of faces represented visually in the United States is an example—Osama bin Laden's face is frequently displayed, being at the service of war and patriotism because it instigates Americans to see him as an incarnate evil, while the faces of civilian casualties in Iraq are not shown. The faces that call us to destroy them play an important role in the strategy of the West: they distract our attention from the other thousands of faces that, if shown, would offer our eyes the image of suffering itself—would show the effects of war, of violence, in a way that would undermine the plans of the powers that be. This differing treatment of faces involves two complex matters that Butler indicates she hopes to elucidate in the future: the relation between representation and humanization and between ethics and violence (140). One thing is clear, according to her: those who have the opportunity to represent themselves have more chances to be considered human than those who cannot represent themselves (141).

This imbalance was analyzed as early as 1978 by Edward Said, who described how orientalism (the discursive representation of oriental subjects by the West) is made possible by the differential of power between dominating and dominated cultures: that is, the West produces a discourse on the Orient because the West holds the power. If the situation had been the opposite, we would have had something that could be called occidentalism: the representation of the West by oriental subjects. Butler's opinion about the importance of having the capacity to represent oneself is enlightening here: the lack of power to represent themselves puts subjugated populations in the awkward position of depending on others' discourses. The French Protestants who suffered the massacre of Saint Bartholomew, for example, lost the power to represent that violence, and the best recourse they found was a text by Las Casas, a member of the society that inflicted the violence on them. The Protestants seize on a self-critique from the opposite camp and embellish it with illustrations that emphasize the cruelty of their enemies. And in this story of unequal access of representation, those who get the worst part (as has been the pattern since 1492) are the Amerindians, who are voiceless despite being represented by the Lascasian text and de Bry's engravings. They are, like the objects of the discourse of orientalism, powerless to produce their version of history.

Not unlike the current state of international affairs, which is dominated by media that deprive Western audiences of the face of the other by showing only the face of what one is supposed to interpret as evil, the sixteenth-century French Protestant representations of Amerindians deprive us of the possibility of hearing their version of the events. The Amerindians are proxies, a sign for something else, an image that stands for another image; they are merely a tool for the French to use against European enemies. We get Amerindian images but not their voices, and those images are not even realistic. The de Bry editions favored a Europeanized image of indigenous peoples—their bodies and facial features are indistinguishable from those of the Spaniards, and what makes them Amerindians is the clothing they wear. For example, in the 1582 watercolor depicting an Amerindian being burned alive, there is an Amerindian who seems to sport a beard of a European style (*Tyrannies . . . perpetrées es Indies* 15). This beard, which is brown in the watercolor, is absent in the engraving published by de Bry in 1598 (*Narratio regionum indicarum* 12), but the woman who hangs from the gallows in the engraving, completely naked, seems to have light if not blond hair, and her body is represented in the manner of European Renaissance painting. The Amerindians in the watercolors bear additional European traits: for example, the color of their skin is as pink as that of the European soldiers included in the illustrations.

The similarities between the representational strategies of the Spaniards and the French in the sixteenth century and those of the American media in the twenty-first century are remarkable—much more remarkable than their differences. The strategies have in common the power to represent the defeated other and the tendency to dehumanize enemies (more often than not considered other), either by showing the violence they are capable of or by denying them the right to represent their own version of events. In sum, the 1582 watercolors and the engravings from de Bry's editions offer us an early example of how violence and ethics, representation and humanization, are constant presences in the struggles for power that characterize human history. They are also a good genealogical point of departure for understanding the roots of the violence we witness today—or, better said, the violence that happens today, which we may or may not be allowed to see. The early images remind us that without the face and the voice of the defeated and the oppressed, we, by making them less human, dehumanize ourselves.

NOTES

[1] As Isacio Pérez Fernández points out in his introduction to Las Casas's *Brevísima relación*, the Low Countries were occupied by Spanish troops at the command of the Duke of Alba. Theodor de Bry, escaping the repressive Spanish government, moved to Frankfurt, where he developed a successful career as a printer ("Estudio preliminar" 11).

[2] Agamben reminds us of the Greek distinction between a life that is simple and natural and one that is qualified—that is, a particular kind of life (*Homo Sacer* 1).

The Textual Conversation of Las Casas's *Brevísima relación* and Its 1656 British Translation

Angelica Duran

Bartolomé de Las Casas's *Brevísima relación de la destrucción de las Indias* is an important text whose inclusion in history or introduction to humanities courses requires much careful deliberation but little justification. Moreover, while the *Brevísima relación* is a mainstay in Hispanophone anthologies of Spanish literature and is beginning to make its way into Anglophone anthologies of American literature, it does not appear in the major anthologies of British literature and is generally absent from undergraduate British literature courses and British components of comparative literature courses. There are some obvious, practical reasons for such a state of affairs: the original adheres to neither the language nor forms generally associated with English literary studies; there are so many other decidedly literary texts to include in a syllabus; and primary texts addressing the Black Legend of Spanish atrocities are often considered the provenance of American studies or American literature because the atrocities were committed in the Americas. My own research and pedagogical beliefs, however, prompted me to design successful ways to include this important Spanish (language and nation) text in a number of undergraduate and graduate English (language) and British (nation) literature classes.

I generally include at least one translated, non-British text in my British literature courses to expose students to the influence of non-Anglophone literatures as well as to introduce them to comparative literature as a discipline and to translation theory and practice as a subdiscipline. John Phillips's early modern English translation of the *Brevísima relación*, *Tears of the Indians* (1656), has provided some of the most exciting and fruitful moments of such ventures, especially in introductory undergraduate and graduate courses required for the English literature major or graduate degree. There is no second-language requirement for these courses, and generally only one to three of the twelve to twenty-five students have a Spanish-language or Latino-heritage background.

It takes careful preparation to minimize student reluctance toward any translated work in a specifically British course; and even more so with *Tears of the Indians*, with its definitively disheartening subject matter. But the important benefits of using translated texts in required introductory courses are well worth the effort. Foremost is that such courses are composed of the general English-major population rather than the self-selected student subpopulations often found in specialized courses. English literature majors, who otherwise might never encounter the *Brevísima relación*, profit greatly from good and early exposure to the work: it informs a large portion of students' academic careers, increases the likelihood that they will revisit the text for individual class assignments in future courses, and might even encourage them to incorporate the text into an even wider range of classes throughout their professional careers.

Course and Text Selection

While my emphasis here is on concepts rather than techniques, it is helpful to begin with a short account—so to speak—of the itinerary for a particularly successful introductory undergraduate course to provide an example of situating those important concepts. I assign the *Brevísima relación* in English translation over three class periods, in the last section of the three-part undergraduate methodologies course. The first part of the course introduces students to the resources that we use throughout the semester: Jonathan Culler's *A Very Short Introduction to Theory*, the *MLA Handbook* (Gibaldi), a glossary of literary terms, the campus library, a special-collections library, the writing lab, and their fellow students. During the library and special-collections tour, students receive training on *Early English Books Online* (*EEBO* is the electronic version of the microfiches of the *Short-Title Catalogs* by Donald Wing and by A. W. Pollard and G. R. Redgrave) and work briefly with original sixteenth- and seventeenth-century texts. The second part of the course is mainly student-driven, with group presentations, discussions, and in-class workshops. In the third part of the course, we expressly transition from general literary studies to comparative literature studies. Situated in week 11 of a sixteen-week semester, Las Casas is positioned strategically. First, his work is at the forefront of students' thoughts as they are settling on topics for their final papers and therefore is more likely to be included in those papers. Second, by this time in the semester, students have gained confidence in their abilities to work with a variety of textual media. While I use modern editions of all the other major course texts, I provide *Tears of the Indians* downloaded from *EEBO* in my course reader. A facsimile copy gives students invaluable experience in adapting to the textual layout, learning about unfamiliar fonts and catchwords, and determining meaning without the aid of modern footnotes, so that they acquire philological skills that enhance their ability to read manuscripts on any topic.

The choice of which English edition of the *Brevísima relación* to use is as important as its placement on the syllabus because I ask it to serve three main purposes: to create a bridge between reading the Anglophone John Milton's *Paradise Lost* in weeks 7–10 and the Hispanophone Miguel de Cervantes Saavedra's *Don Quixote* in weeks 12–13; to serve as a touchstone for discussion of translation theory and practice; and to explore the notion of "literariness" by working with a text that refuses easy categorization into genre.

Tears of the Indians accomplishes all three. Phillips's translation serves as a bridge between the Milton and Cervantes because of Phillips's personal and textual relationships with both. Phillips was Milton's nephew and onetime student, and the translator's kinship with the author of *Paradise Lost* piques the interest of students who might otherwise be reluctant to study Las Casas, a name usually unfamiliar to them. Also, in 1687 Phillips produced his era's most popular English translation of *Don Quixote*. Additionally, the text's status as nonliterary by conservative definitions provides the class with the opportunity to explore the nature of the literary. This exploration is, on the one hand, recursive, because of our early library tour and our reading of Culler's chapter 2, "What Is Literature and Does It Matter?" It is also new, however, in that we address Culler's chapter 8, "Identity, Identification, and the Subject," which opens discussion of how translated texts establish individual and cultural identities and how those identities affect readers' understandings of those texts' literary or nonliterary status.

These aims are large indeed, especially given that we dedicate roughly only one week to the text. But this class is only introductory: students will not emerge experts in comparative literature, Las Casas, or translation. However, a short introduction is better than complete omission, and if I do my job right, students will emerge enthusiasts about all three.

Introducing Las Casas

Before we start in on *Tears of the Indians*, I explain to students that I will be introducing them to the nature of comparative literature for the same reason I have introduced them to all the practices and resources in the course: to prepare them for full participation in the future developments of literary studies. As with all our texts and topics, this setup is vital to students' reception of this text and its topics as simultaneously *ours* and *other*. While comparative literature has been an important way of looking at texts—even before it received its formal nomenclature at the beginning of the twentieth century—it has become crucial in a globalized world where knowledge of or about a multiplicity of languages, literatures, and cultures is useful and in some arenas required. I tell students that, indeed, we have already been practicing comparative literature in our earlier reading of, for example, an Anglophone edition of Ovid's originally Latin *Metamorphoses*; now, we will focus expressly on such aspects as the motives for translating texts at specific historical moments, as well as techniques of translation (tone, word choice, and more) that affect reception of texts. I end the class by turning to the opening pages of Phillips's translation. I call attention to the Spaniards' violence toward the natives depicted in the woodcuts (see fig. 1), which were absent from the original, and the proposed British violence on the Spaniards implied by the epigraph from Deuteronomy: "Therefore thine eye shall have no compassion; but life for life, tooth for tooth, hand for hand, foot for foot" (see fig. 2). Having generated interest in the dynamics of the violence described in the edition, I then instruct students to mark their texts where numbers and types of deaths are described, to prepare for a subsequent discussion on the nature of the literary and the historical.

Day 1: Translating and Transforming

I start off identifying Las Casas's original and Phillips's translated texts as social acts directed to specific audiences and founded on specific discursive and educational choices. The focus is first on our spectral text of the *Brevísima relación*. As practical aid and as illustration of the theoretical concept of the spectral

Fig. 1. Frontispiece of Bartolomé de Las Casas, *Tears of the Indians* (trans. John Phillips, London: Nath. Brook, 1656)

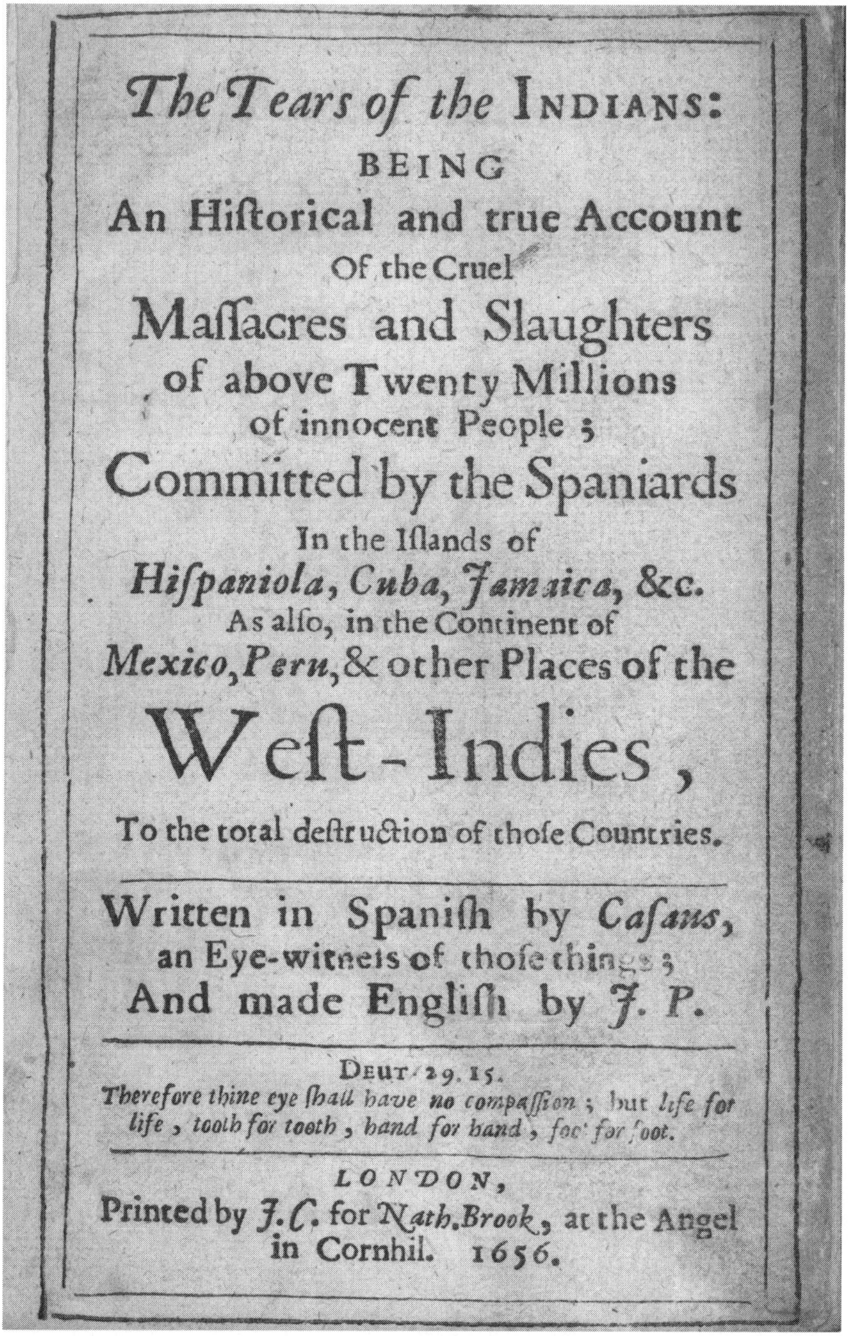

The *Tears of the* INDIANS:

BEING

An Hiftorical and true Account

Of the Cruel

Maffacres and Slaughters

of above Twenty Millions
of innocent People ;

Committed by the Spaniards

In the Iflands of
Hifpaniola, Cuba, Jamaica, &c.

As alfo, in the Continent of

Mexico, Peru, & other Places of the

Weſt-Indies ,

To the total deſtruction of thofe Countries.

Written in Spanifh by *Cafaus,*
an Eye-witnefs of thofe things ;
And made Englifh by *J. P.*

DEUT 29. 15.
Therefore thine eye fhall have no compaffion ; but life for life , tooth for tooth , hand for hand , foot for foot.

LONDON,
Printed by *J. C.* for *Nath. Brook,* at the Angel
in Cornhil. 1656.

Fig. 2. Title page of Bartolomé de Las Casas, *Tears of the Indians* (trans. John Phillips, London: Nath. Brook, 1656)

original text behind translated texts, I project an overhead of a facsimile copy of Las Casas's Spanish prologue as I address his construction of his text as a moral and ethical instructional tool for his fellow countrymen. (I use the 1552 version, available online at the Sabin Americana, 1500–1926 digital collection [http://gale.cengage.com/Sabin/].) We consider the elements of his authorial role: his firsthand experience in the Americas decades earlier and his position as a Roman Catholic bishop at the time of the writing of the text (Friede and Keen; Losada, *Fray Bartolomé de las Casas*). Las Casas's construction of the work as a "short account" speaks to its immediate historical use. The prologue identifies both its brevity and genre as expressing its urgent aim to have Prince Philip of Spain "put a stop once and for all to [the] infernal clamour" of the Spanish colonists (*Short Account* 7). Its hyperbolic language to describe the New World as "wonderful" and "marvelous," on the other hand, appropriates the discourse of the much longer genre of the epic, a genre imbricated in empire building (Quint; Greenblatt, *New World Encounters*).

The focus then shifts to the adjoining issues in Phillips's translation. Comparing the opening paratext and the concluding text of the *Brevísima relación* and *Tears of the Indians* is particularly illuminating for demonstrating how much Phillips mediates Las Casas's authorial role for readers of the English translation. Phillips's version is meaningfully if verbosely entitled *Tears of the Indians: Being an Historical and True Account of the Cruel Massacres and Slaughters of above Twenty Millions of Innocent People Committed by the Spaniards in the Islands of Hispaniola, Cuba, Jamaica, &c. As also, in the Continent of Mexico, Peru and Other Places of the West Indies, to the Total Destruction of Those Countries*. Phillips replaces Las Casas's title with his own; and his elongation polarizes the Native Americans as tearful and "Innocent People" and the Spaniards as the perpetuators of "Cruel Massacres and Slaughters." While elsewhere, British writers rhetorically transformed native Americans into dehumanized entities, here they are more fully humanized as "People," in contrast to the distancing term "Spaniards" (Abbott). The title encapsulates the fact that to be "made English" (the term the title page uses to describe the act of translation) refers to both linguistic translation and ideological transformation (Bermann and Wood).

The differences in the conclusion of Las Casas's original and Phillips's translation reinforce the major role of translators in constructing "meaning" (Culler 65). I hand out a copy of the conclusion in the Penguin Anglophone translation of the *Brevísima relación*—*A Short Account of the Destruction of the Indies*—and I project an electronic version of the original Spanish. Students readily note that, while *Tears of the Indians* ends with Las Casas's famous "*Amen*" to his prayer that King Charles V of Spain reform colonization (*Tears* 134; *Short Account* 128; *Brevíssima relación* 94), *Short Account* continues, as does the original, describing the famous "New Laws" directed to Spanish colonists (*Short Account* 128–30; *Brevíssima relación* 95–96). We interrogate students' often irritated responses to Phillips's elimination of a passage that would leave British readers with a sense of the positive aims of Spain's New Laws. Their irritation stands in sharp contrast to their easy acceptance of other textual modifications—for example, Phillips's replacement of Spanish "castilians" with British "Crowns" to refer to the monetary value of the treasures described (*Tears* 88; *Short Account* 94).

We then discuss the function of the educational choices that stand behind Phillips's editorial choices. We have historical clues that Milton might have known Spanish and taught the language to his students (including John and his brother Edward Phillips) in addition to the more traditional languages taught in early modern English schools—Latin, Greek, Hebrew, and French—thereby providing Phillips with the linguistic tool needed to commit his social act of translation. Equally interesting are early modern methodologies for language acquisition, including translation, reverse translation, recitation, and full language immersion. Milton has much to say about reforming language studies in his pamphlet *Of Education* (see Fletcher). His nephews John and Edward Phillips are themselves evidence that he was able to put into effect "the most rationall and most profitable way of learning languages" that he describes in that pamphlet (Milton 981). Edward, in his short biography of Milton, writes that his uncle had an "excellent judgment and way of Teaching, far above the Pedantry of common publick Schools" in their home-school, which he lovingly calls a "House of Muses" (E. Phillips 60, 67). John Shawcross lists John Phillip's many publications, including numerous translations from Latin, Greek, French, Spanish, and Italian, and concludes from them that "[t]he success of Milton's teaching and the abilities of John Phillips should not be ignored" (107).

Students' knowledge of these facts, combined with their knowledge (from reading *Paradise Lost*) of teacher-Milton's exceptional poetical and rhetorical skills, leads us to a discussion of how their own educational and discursive choices reflect and inform their social acts. The conversation often includes their experiences of successful and unsuccessful foreign language courses, rationales for selecting specific languages over others, and conscious use of various vocabularies in different social settings. Such a discussion is a recursive component of the class, because earlier we concentrated on language acquisition and manipulation in reading Culler's chapter 4, "Language, Meaning, and Interpretation," and on educational moments in *Paradise Lost*. I end this class session with my usual practice of asking students to do some preparatory work for the next meeting, in this case writing down some preliminary answers to two questions focused on "implied readers" and "interpretive communities" (Abrams 266, 268): Why would Phillips publish *Tears of the Indians* in 1656 in London, England? How do Phillips's regular moments of elevated style, or "purple patches" (Abrams 263), help account for its popularity?

Day 2: The Black Legend and Purple Patches

At the start of the next class, students share their findings, usually garnered from the Web and encyclopedias. The 1650s were known as England's Interregnum, the period after the beheading of King Charles I in 1649 and before the restoration of King Charles II in 1660. During that period, the new Cromwellian government sought to wrest control of some of the islands off the American coasts from Spain as part of its "Western Design" (Cromwell; Maltby 12–28). Reviving past class notes, some students attribute Phillips's interest in texts about international relations to the influence of his uncle, who held the visible post of Secretary of Foreign Tongues in the Cromwellian government. Students are usually quick to point to the prominence attributed to Oliver Cromwell through the use of capitals in "The Epistle Dedicatory" of *Tears of the Indians* ("To His Highness OLIVER, LORD PROTECTOR of the Commonwealth of England, Scotland & Ireland, *With the Dominions thereto belonging*") and to the equally incendiary, prefatory "To all English-men" (i, ix). Amid stirring biblical characterizations associating Cromwell with the "holy Warriour *David*" and "*Joshua* [leading] his Armies forth to Battel" and linking Englishmen with "*the Prophet* Jeremiah" lamenting "*the Effusion of so much Innocent Blood*," the prefatory materials demonize and generalize "the Popish Nation of the Spaniards, whose Superstitions have exceeded those of *Canaan* and whose Abominations have excel'd those of *Ahab*" (iii, iv).

It is also important to note that Phillips's translation was undertaken in the context of numerous anti-Catholic and especially anti-Irish pamphlets published between 1640 and 1660 in England. Kevin A. Creed observes that, in the wake of the Irish rebellion of 1641, directed against the Protestants of Ireland, "[s]treams of pamphlets, some highly fictionalized, concerning the revolt poured forth and it is obvious that many people accepted them wholly as truth. . . . While the gross exaggerations of Irish ruthlessness seem almost comical today, this sort of propaganda was common and its effects on naive readers should not be discounted." The Irish Rebellion was put down in 1650 by Oliver Cromwell, the "Protestant Champion," whom Phillips asks in the dedicatory epistle of 1656 to avenge the Indians for the Spanish explorers' "bloudy Massacres, far surpassing the Popish Cruelties in *Ireland*" (vi). Creed suggests that the work of Milton's nephew "was surely encouraged, if not authorized by the government": having invoked comparison with the dreaded Irish, Phillips's "timely translation and dedication were used to help rouse up support for the coming war with Spain."

We explore the way prose style constructs implied readers by comparing Phillips's prefatory materials and a handout of Las Casas's prologue from the Penguin *Short Account*, the Spanish original of which I project as an overhead in class. The prologue is omitted in Phillips's *Tears of the Indians*. Directed to the future King Philip II of Spain, Las Casas's prologue stirs readerly passion but primarily compassion for the natives, from "kings, who are (as Homer would have it) fathers and shepherds to their people" (*Short Account* 5), as opposed to provoking rancor toward a generalized "*Proud, Deceitful, Cruel, Treacherous Nation*" from English readers seeking to wrest American territories from Spain (*Tears* xxi). Incorporating the less politically infused Penguin edition as a new classroom resource, I ask students to share purple patches they have found in *Tears of the Indians*. A section that regularly comes up is the description of the pearl divers, equally and distinctly heart-wrenching in both Anglophone editions, as it is in the Hispanophone original. *Tears of the Indians* weaves a mysterious (literary) tale of New World pearl divers who are "devoured by certain sea monsters, that are frequent in those seas" (82). *Short Account*, on the other hand, represents the scene using more factual (historical) language: "the poor wretches are easy prey to all manner of sharks, those most ferocious of marine creatures, capable of swallowing a man whole" (94).

To forefront the complex role of translated texts to literature, history, and identity, I define some key differences between poesy (fiction and literature) and history, as understood in the Renaissance. In 1595—that is, between the publication of Las Casas's *Brevísima relación* in the 1550s and Phillips's *Tears of the Indians* in 1650s—*A Defence of Poetry* was published, in which the British statesman and poet Philip Sidney (who, interestingly, was named after his god-father, King Philip II of Spain) concluded that poetry was better than history: poetry, "disdaining to be tied to any . . . subjection, lifted up with the vigour of his own invention, doth grow in effect into another nature, in making things either better than nature bringeth forth, or, quite anew," while history, on the other hand, "bringeth you images of true matters, such as indeed were done, and not such as fantastically or falsely may be suggested to have been done[, and,] being captived to the truth of a foolish world, is many times a terror from well-doing, and an encouragement to unbridled wickedness," and therefore poetry "excelleth history, not only in furnishing the mind with knowledge, but in setting it forward to that which deserveth to be called and accounted good" (23, 35, 38).

These definitions inform the day's concluding assignment, in which students divide into small groups to add up the numbers and types of deaths described in differing sections of the text and then find a map on which to highlight the geographic locations described in their group's section. I define such data—namely, what the text represents as "true matters"—as historical research, and I ask students to find other methods by which the text implicitly or explicitly defines itself as history.

Day 3: Disciplined Characters

As students filter into the classroom for our last class dedicated to *Tears of the Indians*, they put their findings and maps on the board. I also provide an overhead with definitions of the literary terms "Character and Characterization" (Abrams 33) that will help us develop our sense of the traditional similarities and differences between literature and history and reassess the permeable border that divides them. Students are usually eager to share their shocked responses to the atrocities described in *Tears of the Indians*. The assignment of counting the dead and listing the types of atrocities enables them to discover for themselves that literary techniques, such as hyperbole, metaphor, and simile, are deployed in the historical mode or components of the work.

I end the last class with two final overheads that enable us to transition to the subsequent week's reading of *Don Quixote*. The first is the title page of

Phillips's British translation of *The History of the Most Renowned Don Quixote of Mancha, and His Trusty Squire Sancho Pancha*, perhaps the most popular Anglophone translation of his day (fig. 3). Students' puzzled expressions and comments demonstrate how much Phillips's translation of perhaps the most enduring literary advertisement for the greatness of Spanish literature worldwide and by extension Spain (*Don Quixote*) retrospectively modifies their too-easy construction of the translator of a text that so effectively vilifies Spaniards (*Tears of the Indians*). Students gain a deep appreciation of the complexity of the task of the translator, to echo Walter Benjamin's famous essay. And what to do with a text like *Don Quixote*, which so boldly, playfully, and misleadingly identifies itself as a "History" in Spanish and English editions? (Wardropper).

The second overhead is a particularly interesting section of Phillips's translation of *Don Quixote* (fig. 4). I call students' attention to the last line, where Phillips slyly adds an anachronistic reference to his uncle's *Paradise Lost* (1667), published sixty-two years after *Don Quixote* (1605). Phillips's playful and intentional modification, in imitation of Cervantes's playfulness with his readers, does much to nuance students' understanding of the "reliable translator" and emphasizes the value of knowing multiple languages and historical contexts, so that they can be critical readers who not only detect political motivations but also enjoy inside jokes. I also ensure that we think of our classroom as a reading

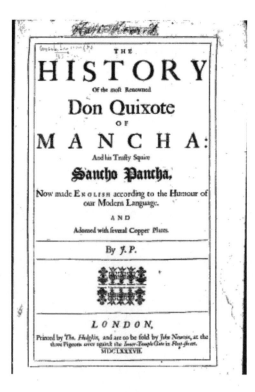

Fig. 3. Frontispiece of John Phillips's translation of Miguel Cervantes-Saavedra's *Don Quixote* (London: Thomas Hodgkin, 1687)

> *Sancho* faid no more, but having thus pleas'd his humour, return'd to co-
> ver his Pack-faddle, not without tickling his Mafters's Spleen; who not-
> withftanding all his Flegm, could not forbear laughing out-right at the
> Simplicity of his Squire.   But his mirth being foon over, he went on with
> his difcourfe, and ask'd the Gentleman how many Children he had? ad-
> ding withal, how he had ever obferv'd that the Ancient Philofophers plac'd
> their chief happinefs as well in the Advantages of Nature, as thofe of For-
> tune; in number of Children and Friends.   I have but one only Son, re-
> ply'd the Gentleman, and perhaps if I had not him, I fhould not think my
> felf the lefs unhappy.   Not that he is leudly inclin'd, but only becaufe he is
> not fo good as I could wifh him.   He is a Lad of about Eighteen years of
> Age, and has been fix years at the Univerfity to perfect himfelf in his
> *Greek* and *Latin*; of both which he is a competent Mafter.   But when I
> prefs'd him to improve himfelf in the profound Myfteries of true Learning,
> I found him fo addicted to Poetry, that he defpifes all the other Sciences;
> fo that I cannot get him fo much as to look upon a Law Book, and but ve-
> ry little to mind Divinity; to either of which I would have had him apply'd
> his Studies, to fit him for the Service of his Prince: efpecially living in
> an Age wherein Wife and Learned Men are fo highly efteem'd by His Maje-
> fty.   He fpends whole days in his *Criticifms*, whether *Homer* faid well or ill,
> in repeating Ton'd Apomeibomenos fo often?— whether fuch an Epigram
> in *Martial* ought not to be expung'd for its Obfcoenity— whether *Virgil* had
> he liv'd, could ha' better'd his *Eneads*— He is a great admirer of *Horace, Ju-
> venal* and *Perfius*— but as for the Modern Poets, he allows very few to be
> worth a Straw; among the reft, he has a particular Peek againft *Du Bartas,*
> and *Paradife loft*, which he fays has neither Rhime nor Reafon.   Neverthe-
> A a a   lefs

Fig. 4. Overhead of a passage from John Phillips's translation of Miguel de Cervantes-Saavedra's *Don Quixote* (361)

community, where I and projected images of Spanish originals (which are, for the most part, linguistically inaccessible to the students) have served as authorization for the Penguin edition's English translator, Nigel Griffin.

My aim in this essay has been to explain the conceptual bases and classroom practices for including a specific English (language and nation) translation of Las Casas's *Brevísima relación* in an introductory undergraduate course. In such courses we need our (oh, too few) texts to accomplish much, in order to provide students with a strong foundation for their intellectual development. *Tears of the Indians* familiarizes students with and enables them to analyze an important world text, Las Casas's *Brevísima relación*, and helps them reconstruct their demarcations of and comfort with British, American, Spanish, and comparative literature. Its classroom use enacts the very world conversation that literary studies makes available.

NOTE

I dedicate this essay to Jonathan Culler for his generosity in reviewing it and to the good-natured students in my first English 301 / FLL 230 course, in autumn 2005.

On the *Brevísima relación's* "Black Legends": Eighteenth-Century Texts and Contexts

David F. Slade and Karen Stolley

In his essay "The American Enlightenment and Endless Emancipation," Frank Shuffleton begins by acknowledging the wariness with which his students typically react to any mention of the Enlightenment (155). The eighteenth century's faith in reason and progress strikes them as overly optimistic, and eighteenth-century writing—scientific essays, travel journals, autobiography—seems dull or insufficiently "literary." If this is true for students of Anglo-American cultural history, it is even more so for those in Spanish American literature classes, in which the eighteenth century tends to drop out between the chronicles of the discovery and conquest and postindependence Romanticism. As many have noted, Latin America in the eighteenth century cannot be easily classified as either colonial or fully modern. In the wake of the changes in global awareness set in motion by the European explorations of the sixteenth and seventeenth centuries, the eighteenth century was a time of transition, a period of administrative consolidation and the encyclopedic systematization of knowledge. As cosmopolitan thinkers theorized about how to develop global commerce and expand European political supremacy, Spain's legacy of colonialism in the New World was both condemned and defended.

In the process, Bartolomé de Las Casas's writings became a focal point for arguments waged in the transatlantic republic of letters about the history and future direction of the Americas. Two hundred years after the *Brevísima relación de la destrucción de las Indias* (*Brief Account of the Destruction of the Indies*) was first published, Las Casas himself can be seen as a monumental figure in these spirited debates, viewed either as a self-aggrandizing polemicist who lacked the necessary objectivity of a historian or as a champion of the noble savage, courageously renouncing both church and country in defending humanity. Guillaume-Thomas Raynal is representative of the positive view when he praises Las Casas in his *Histoire philosophique et politique des établissements et du commerce des Européens dans les deux Indes* (first published in 1770 and quoted here in a 1783 translation): "O! Las-Casas! Thou wast greater by thy humanity, than all thy countrymen were by their conquests" (*Philosophical and Political History* 4: 267).

Our own experience has been that reading Las Casas in an eighteenth-century cultural studies context offers a number of interesting pedagogical opportunities. Readings can be organized around several contexts and topics—the Black Legend, the dispute of the New World, the noble savage—included as a unit in an upper-level undergraduate or graduate seminar devoted to Las Casas or in a comparative seminar on the transatlantic eighteenth century. By studying how Las Casas was read (and misread) in Spain, Spanish America, and Europe, students gain greater insight into how the articulation of these topics evolved over time. The Spanish- and English-speaking colonial Americas (too often separated in the curriculum) can be linked through discussion of common themes, such as the figure of the noble savage or the alleged inferiority of New World species (supposedly due to climactic determinism). Students gain an increased appreciation for the highly charged nature of eighteenth-century transatlantic debates—at the same time deeply speculative and intensely pragmatic—and for the broad range of participants in these debates. Finally, the eighteenth century's role in the evolution from colonial encounters to nineteenth-century nation building in the Americas can be more fully explored and discussed in undergraduate and graduate courses than it has been to date.

Eighteenth-Century Texts

Teaching editions of the *Brevísima relación* published in the eighteenth century means dealing primarily with texts published in English, French, and German (though if one accepts a definition of the long eighteenth century that extends into the first two decades of the nineteenth, then several Spanish-language editions could be included as part of the eighteenth-century *Brevísima relación* corpus). In the early 1700s, seventeenth-century editions of the text were reprinted, reflecting how Las Casas's rhetoric spoke to specific public polemics being debated in the republic of letters. Editorial license was often taken with editions of the *Brevísima relación*, so that Las Casas's text was sometimes interwoven with related accounts of Catholic barbarism or bungled colonial endeavors. The titles of a series of English-language tomes published in the late seventeenth and early eighteenth centuries provide a striking example of this type of compilation. Sections of the *Brevísima relación* were published in 1689 as an anti-Jacobin narrative that recounted the evils of Catholicism, entitled *Popery Truly Display'd in Its Bloody Colours*. A text similar to the 1689 translation was published in several eighteenth-century editions such as *Popery and Slavery Display'd*, which sought to guard British national discourse against "the demands of the Pope and Pretender" (Casas and Harris, title page). Here politics and religion converge to identify Spain with Catholicism and Spanish Catholicism with the pope. Las Casas's account is read by English editors as evidence of the cruel effects of Catholic governance, a view in direct opposition to what the Dominican hoped to achieve with the *Brevísima relación*.[1] A volume published in Paris in 1697, *La decouverte des Indes Occidentales par les Espagnols*, included translations by J. B. M. de Bellegarde of the *Brevísima relación* and several other brief writings by Las Casas (Hanke and Giménez Fernández 241).[2] Other editions of the *Brevísima relación* were published in Germany in 1710, 1757, and 1790.

As evidenced by the lack of Spanish-language editions, the *Brevísima relación* was debated in the eighteenth century much more than it was printed.

In the early decades of the nineteenth century, the work was published in London (1812); Santafé de Bogotá, Colombia (1813); Philadelphia (1821, 1822); Puebla, Mexico (1812); Guadalajara, México (1822); Mexico City (1822, 1826); and Paris (1822, 1826). Studying this moment in Las Casas's trajectory is a useful way to learn how the eighteenth century reconsidered, rewrote, and recast past narratives. Nineteenth-century renderings and readings of Las Casas are treated in Santa Arias's essay in this volume, but it is important to point out to students that the pre-Independence production of Las Casas's work was a continuation of eighteenth-century debates.

Besides the *Brevísima relación*, other texts by Las Casas entered the public sphere as several key eighteenth-century authors draw from lesser-known historical works. Studying these authors in an upper-level undergraduate or graduate seminar can open up questions of archival reading in Bourbon Spain and Spanish America, the evolving historiographical practices of the late eighteenth century, and the way in which the broader corpus of Las Casas's writings gradually made its way to a lettered public.

For example, Juan Bautista Muñoz, the official Spanish cosmographer of the Indies and founder of the Archive of the Indies, played a significant role by reading and citing Las Casas as an archival source for his *Historia del Nuevo Mundo* (1793). In 1784, Muñoz penned a brief report to José de Gálvez, minister of the Indies, entitled *Relación de documentos de fray Bartolomé de las Casas*, in which he describes five volumes of Las Casas's manuscripts held by the secretariat of Indies.[3] Included in the report are the first two books of the *Historia de las Indias* (*History of the Indies*), several texts written in both Latin and Spanish, and a small fragment of the *Apologética historia sumaria*. Muñoz extensively transcribed both histories and drew heavily from them for his own *Historia*.[4] The first volume of the *Historia del Nuevo Mundo*—the only one that Muñoz would publish before his untimely death—is virtually a biography of Christopher Columbus. Thus, in a parallel dynamic to the one linking Las Casas and Columbus, Muñoz becomes the eighteenth-century editor of the Lascasian archive just as the Dominican played a fundamental editorial role in the preservation and dissemination of Columbus's writings.

One could argue that nearly any eighteenth-century text dealing with the Americas engages on some level Las Casas's descriptions of Spanish conquest and Amerindian culture. In addition to Muñoz's *Historia*, a course reading list that reflects how Las Casas was perceived and represented during the Enlightenment might include *Bibliotheca mexicana* (1755), by Juan José de Eguiara y Eguren; *Memorias históricas, físicas, apologéticas de la América Meridional* (1761), by José Eusebio de Llano Zapata; *Historia de Nueva España* (1770), by Francisco Antonio Lorenzana; *Historia antigua de México* (1780–81), by Francisco Javier Clavijero; and *Reflexiones imparciales sobre la humanidad de los españoles en las Indias contra los pretendidos filósofos y políticos* (1783), by Juan Nuix, among many other possibilities.

In addition to the *Portal de Archivos Españoles* project (see note 3 in this essay), *Eighteenth Century Collections Online* (available by institutional subscription from Gale) offers many English-language texts that could easily be incorporated into a syllabus that reads Las Casas in the eighteenth century: for example, an English translation of the German playwright August von Kotzebue's *Pizarro in Peru; or, The Death of Rolla*, which was performed and published in London in 1799. "Las Casas" appears as a character in the play who attempts to "intoxicate" youths against Pizarro's plans for conquest. Thomas Clarkson published in 1786 *An Essay on the Slavery and Commerce of the Human Species*, in which he names Las Casas as the first of many advocates against slavery. Other suggested texts available through *Eighteenth Century Collections Online* include *The Fall of Mexico: A Poem* (1775) by Edward Jerningham; *The History of America* (1777) by William Robertson; *A Philosophical and Political History of the Settlements and Trade of the Europeans in the East and West Indies* (1783) by Raynal; and Voltaire's *An Essay on Universal History* (1759) and his tragic drama *Alzira* (1736). Finally, Françoise de Graffigny's *Letters from a Peruvian Woman* is available in French and in English translation as part of the MLA Texts and Translations series.

Eighteenth-Century Contexts

It has been long acknowledged that Las Casas was largely responsible for the creation of the "Black Legend"—the widespread notion among Spain's political enemies in seventeenth- and eighteenth-century Europe of unbridled Spanish cruelty during the conquest and colonization of a paradisiacal Americas. Spain made some attempts to respond defensively. Both the Archivo General de Indias and the Archivo Histórico Nacional contain documents pertaining to the confiscation of works by Las Casas in the mid–eighteenth century, testament to the continuing polemic surrounding the Dominican (Hanke and Giménez Fernández 249). In 1748, the Council of the Indies took the unusual step of reaffirming a decision by the Audiencia de la Contratación to seize Las Casas's *Narratio regionum indicarum*, noting that its content was detrimental to Spain: "su contenido se dirige a infamar los celebres conquistadores del nuevo orbe, tratando de cruelísimos, para hacer odiosa la nación Española" 'its content was intended to dishonor the celebrated conquistadors of the New World, treating them as the cruelest of people, to make the Spanish nation hated' (qtd. in Hanke and Giménez Fernández 247; our trans.). Some writers argued in Las Casas's defense that perhaps the friar had not penned the most virulent critiques attributed to him (246, 248). Others, such as Juan Nuix, a Catalan Jesuit exiled from Spain in 1767, sought to defend Spain's colonial project by advancing a "white legend" counterdiscourse that undermined Las Casas's credibility as a true and loyal Spaniard and insisted he was of Flemish origin (Cañizares-Esguerra 183;

Gerbi, *Dispute* 192n). The erudite Peruvian historian José Eusebio de Llano Zapata offered a more balanced assessment in the preface to his *Memorias históricas, físicas, apologéticas de la América Meridional*. He lamented the use Spain's enemies had made of Las Casas's impassioned accusations and called for an enlightened mix of sensibility and reason in evaluating the Black Legend: "Hasta hoy con sus escritos, renuevan los unos la llaga, y avivan los otros la ofensa. Siempre, que se añadiese pábula al incendio de la enemistad, crecerá la llama de la discordia. Esto ha hecho el Ilustrísimo Casas" 'Even today some of his writings reopen the wound, and others aggravate the offense. Always, when one adds fuel to the fire of enmity, the flame of discord will grow. This is what the illustrious Las Casas has done' (qtd. in Hanke and Giménez Fernández 248; our trans.).

In the eighteenth-century European political imagination, the Dominican is seen, not as part of an ongoing ideological debate about the nature of the Amerindians and Spanish claims to sovereignty in the Americas, but rather as a lone voice crying out in a wilderness of oppression and cruelty. The comment made by the translator of the 1699 edition is typical: "Este Obispo escribe con tal aire de Honestidad, Sinceridad y Caridad, que bien podría haber sido Obispo de una religión mayor que aquella en la cual tuvo la desgracia de ser educado . . . 'This bishop writes with such an air of honesty, sincerity, and charity that he might well have been bishop of a greater religion than that in which he had the misfortune to be educated' (qtd. in Hanke and Giménez Fernández 242; our trans.). This prevailing view demonstrates a fundamental misunderstanding of Las Casas's position in the context of the ongoing debates in Spain during the mid–sixteenth century. Eighteenth-century readers rarely recognized the Crown's official response to Las Casas's campaign, which included the promulgation of the New Laws of 1542, or acknowledged that Las Casas was generally considered to have prevailed in the Valladolid debates. Ironically, during succeeding centuries, "in the rest of Europe, Sepúlveda's ideas were held to represent Spanish official views, largely because of the wide publicity accorded in Protestant countries to Las Casas's description of Spanish colonization in the New World" (Cañizares-Esguerra 173–74). Spanish apologists were therefore caught in a bind and in response chose generally to distance themselves from Las Casas and his writings.

In a separate but related arena, many of the central issues of the sixteenth-century debates of Valladolid between Las Casas and Sepúlveda are reframed as what Antonello Gerbi has termed "the dispute of the New World" (in his book of the same name) over the alleged inferiority of New World flora and fauna. In his exhaustive study of the origins and evolution of this dispute, Gerbi traces a genealogy beginning with Georges-Louis Leclerc, Comte de Buffon, and with Cornelius de Pauw, who both argued that the Amerindian's primitivism and physical weakness are the inevitable result of his geographic and climactic environment, and continuing through the abbé Raynal and William Robertson. Las Casas had emphasized Amerindian weakness (mainly in the *Brevísima relación*) not as a criticism but rather to highlight their vulnerability in contrast to cruel conquistadors. However, his detailed critique of the theory of natural slavery as a means of justifying Amerindian enslavement is misread in the eighteenth century as a wholesale opposition to Spanish colonization and as an argument for American inferiority. Gerbi speculates then that "the good Las Casas could hardly have expected that his ardent defense of the wretched, weak, languid, and innocent Indian would within two centuries be turned into proof of the corrupt and degenerate nature of the Americans" (*Dispute* 71).

This double misreading helps explain the ambivalence many eighteenth-century *criollos* felt toward Las Casas. In *Historia antigua de México*, Clavijero outlines his vehement refutation of de Pauw, Buffon, Raynal, and Robertson in nine dissertations on Mexican animals, plants, and ancient civilization. Clavijero's defense of the moral constitution, religious practices, and intellectual abilities of the ancient Mexicans relies in many instances on Las Casas's writings.[5] However, as David Brading observes:

> It is testimony to the perennial ambiguity of creole patriotism that Clavijero should have adopted a decidedly cool attitude to Las Casas. . . . Although he praised the great Dominican's defense of the rationality of the Indians, he criticized his denunciation of the conquerors' cruelties as too passionate and exaggerated.   (*First America* 459)

While Las Casas's writings undoubtedly fueled the fires of the proponents of American degeneracy, they also helped lay the foundation for the myth of the noble savage, which is integral to the European Enlightenment's understanding of the other.[6] Like the Inca Garcilaso, Las Casas describes Amerindian society in both the *Brevísima relación* and the *Apologética historia sumaria* in terms of classical analogies, giving Europeans a conceptual structure for understanding political and cultural difference and for articulating a history of human origins (Pagden, *European Encounters* 13–14). The noble savage, or *bon sauvage*, was a contradictory and compelling figure, and during the eighteenth century, the genre of the dialogue or conversation between a European and his Amerindian interlocutor became enormously popular, as evidenced by the success of the Baron de Lahontan's *Dialogues curieux entre l'auteur et un sauvage de bon sens*. These dialogues give voice to an enlightened exploration of the difference between the natural and the socially constructed world and owe much to Las Casas's portrayal of Amerindian society, as do the various utopian formulations set forth by Diderot, Rousseau, Voltaire, and others (Pagden, *European Encounters* 121; Outram 63–79).[7] Students might also be assigned selections from Alonso Carrió de la Vandera's *El lazarillo de ciegos caminantes*, in which the discussions between Concolorcorvo and El Visitador function as an ironic recasting of these enlightened dialogues.

Raynal's vision of Las Casas as the monumental figure of human liberation and justice would be revived as independence movements began to evolve across the Americas toward the end of the eighteenth century (*Histoire philosophique* 4: 267). The Dominican's stature as a kind of founding father of Latin American cultural and ethical identity was consolidated—albeit in radically different terms than those the friar might have wished—in the century's many debates. By focusing on the ways in which the sixteenth-century *Procurador de los Indios* (defender of the Indians) and his texts were read, edited, archived, and monumentalized in the eighteenth century, students gain a more nuanced appreciation of Las Casas's role throughout history.

NOTES

[1] The *Brevísima relación* was published in English as *An Account of the First Voyages and Discoveries Made by the Spaniards in America* in 1699.

[2] Other editions of this French-language text were published in Amsterdam (1698) and again in Paris (1709).

[3] The report is housed in the Archivo Histórico Nacional in Madrid and is available online for registered users at the Spanish Ministry of Culture's archival Web site, *Portal de Archivos Españoles*. The PARES is an excellent resource for instructors who wish to incorporate archival resources as class materials (http://pares.mcu.es). Also note that Hanke and Giménez Fernández discuss Muñoz's report (249–50).

[4] Muñoz's original transcriptions of Las Casas's works survive as a part of the Colección Muñoz, housed in the Spanish Royal Academy of History in Madrid, copies of which (compiled by Maxine Emert) can be found in the nineteenth-century Obadiah Rich Collection of the New York Public Library (Real Academia de la Historia, *Catálogo de la colección*).

[5] See Gerbi, *Dispute* 195–217; Brading, *First America* 459; Pagden, *Spanish Imperialism* 91–116.

[6] Dorinda Outram suggests that eighteenth-century thinking on the exotic other focuses on the following questions: "the debate generated by the idea of a 'universal' human nature; the associated debate on the meaning of human history; and the debate generated over the worth and nature of 'civilisation'" (65).

[7] See Wertheimer for a discussion of how the eighteenth-century North American imaginary appropriates Aztec and Inca figures.

Learning by Doing:
Applying Language Classroom Techniques to the Study of Las Casas's *Brevísima relación*

Sara L. Lehman

Since the latter decades of the twentieth century, colonial Spanish American literature has been gaining respect and popularity as an interdisciplinary field with innumerable resonances in the modern world. New editions, many bilingual, of colonial historical accounts and literature have been released in Latin America, Spain, and the United States. Most institutions of higher education offer colonial literature (as well as colonial history, religion, anthropology, and arts), yet students frequently report feelings of distance and irrelevance when faced with a colonial text, complaining that the language is too difficult and archaic, the time frame is too distant, or that the style is too affected and rhetorical. In short, for undergraduate students, colonial literature seems unapproachable.

Despite its relatively accessible length, the *Brevísima relación de la destrucción de las Indias* by Bartolomé de las Casas often provokes such negative reactions in students. Those unaccustomed to political treatises may be repelled by the tone and shockingly violent content of the text. The author's intellectual and persuasive rhetoric may sound exaggerated and repetitive to modern ears. The sixteenth-century orthography, vocabulary, and syntax do little to endear the work to twenty-first-century students.

Some of the comments described above may remind one of complaints regarding foreign language education in the past, when class often consisted of reading and constructing mechanical sentences solely about the textbook's fictional "Juan and María" and students seldom practiced recombining the language in meaningful ways to communicate and express their own reality. However, the gradual incorporation of the techniques of active, cooperative, and collaborative learning suggested by decades of pedagogical research has done much to surmount this irrelevance of foreign language study. Indeed, most instructors regularly create space for students to work with the language, to express themselves, to make connections between theirs and the target cultures, and to discuss issues relevant to their own lives. I suggest that the extrapolation of such language-classroom methods into the undergraduate literature forum helps dissolve the barriers that students experience between their own reality and that of colonial texts—and of the *Brevísima relación* in particular.

Before considering the application of these techniques in the literature classroom, a brief overview of each of them is necessary. Active learning (AL), championed by T. A. Angelo, K. P. Cross, and W. J. McKeachie, stems from the belief that students best internalize, comprehend, and retain material through active engagement in their learning process (Sutherland and Bonwell, "Active Learning" 3). Functions of AL range from enhancing lectures by creating space for students' participation to introducing interactive reading and writing methods; and its techniques include solving problems, formulating and answering questions, discussing, explaining, debating, and brainstorming.

A subset of AL is cooperative learning (CoopL), which is defined by Karl Smith as "the instructional use of small groups so that students work together to maximize their own and each others' learning" (71). In CoopL, students work in teams on problems and projects that are structured to ensure positive interdependence, as well as individual accountability. The flexibility of AL and CoopL makes them easy to incorporate into any teaching style; professors can choose any place on the continuum from enhanced lecture style to total group learning, depending on their preferred level of control.

"Cooperative learning" is a term often used interchangeably with collaborative learning (CL), yet the philosophical differences between the two are notable. CoopL typically assumes a traditional view of the learning process—that is, that teachers are experts who guide students through varying degrees of group interaction toward the "right" or "best" answers in the discipline. In contrast, collaborative learning takes a less teacher-centered perspective, one in which students and faculty members work together to create knowledge through discussion and consensus (Barkley, Cross, and Major 6). As such, CL intrinsically helps develop autonomous, articulate, critically thinking students, which is consistently one of the stated missions of higher education. As with AL and CoopL, professors incorporate CL techniques in accordance with their comfort levels; some choose to establish short-term learning groups, while others structure an entire course around permanently established teams.

The differences among these three pedagogies and their implementations are philosophical and somewhat subtle. In practical application, it is not necessary to become a proponent of one over another. Rather, just as language professors structure varied activities to capitalize on diverse student learning styles, professors of literature can enhance their teaching with elements borrowed from one or all of these pedagogies. The challenge, particularly in undergraduate colonial courses, is to adapt comfortable, traditional approaches in order to more effectively engage students in the study of literature while improving comprehension, retention, capacity for critical thinking and deep analysis, and (most important, from their perspective) the approachability of the material. To help achieve this goal as it relates to the *Brevísima relación*, I present here some of its most notable characteristics alongside tested techniques from AL, CoopL, and CL, which will break the ice between undergraduates and Las Casas's text.

"Lobos y Corderos": Approaching the *Brevísima relación*

Because the *Brevísima relación* presents several special linguistic, rhetoric, and content-based challenges to students, it is best suited to a collaborative approach that places students at the center of the learning process. Since they are generally unaccustomed to working cooperatively in literature courses, it is essential to consciously establish the collaborative tone that will accompany their reading of the text. A low-pressure opening activity, perhaps using a visual cue and assuming no prior knowledge of the text or the author, is an effective means of achieving this goal. For example, display a picture of the planet Mars with an alien figure, and ask students to envision an encounter with such a creature: imagine that we have just arrived on this planet and have seen these creatures, which evidently have great skill and ability, judging from the cities and structures they have built. Since we intend to live here, perhaps they could be of service to us. They do not speak our languages, they cannot communicate with us, and we need their labor to build our own city. Should we harness their skills for our projects? Do we have a responsibility to treat them a certain way? Why? Where should they live? Will we own them? Are they "people" like us? Questions of this nature encourage creative discussion and sharing of opinions from the outset, while providing the instructor with a seamless introduction to some of the ethical issues present in the *Brevísima relación*. To extend the Martian metaphor further, consider a five-minute creative writing task in which students write a letter to the president of the United States, telling of the Martian discovery and the imperialistic plans. This imaginative exercise removes to some extent the perceived distance between students and the thematic material of the text.

During this introductory stage, students require a certain amount of acclimation to the *Brevísima relación* and its often horrifying content. The text's preliminary documents and first chapter lend themselves well to this prereading purpose. In addition to exposing students to the setting, themes, and linguistic challenges of the text, these documents present ample opportunities to draw connections to other moments of conquest, human rights violations, and imperialism throughout history. Activating students' background knowledge of other disciplines in a lively discussion increases interest and rapport with the text, while establishing mental connections that aid in synthesis of the unfamiliar material that students will encounter. Drawing on comparisons from other imperial experiences also serves as a good deconstructive exercise that frames the Manichean metaphor of *lobos y corderos* (wolves and lambs).

Lobos y corderos is the *Brevísima relación*'s key metaphoric opposition, and this prereading stage is an appropriate time to begin considering it. Using the AL technique of prediction, one can invite students to discuss or write their initial interpretation of this phrase and to predict the ways in which this dichotomy will manifest in the text. Similarly, making oral or written predictions on the theme after briefly reading the "Argumento del presente epítome" (*Brevísima relación* 69–70) allows students to incorporate their knowledge about the Spanish conquest into a class discussion or simply to react to the material. Thus, they become accustomed to participating actively with the text and learn to read more critically and reflectively.

"Porque Su Alteza la Leyese con Más Facilidad": Techniques for Active Reading

Once the principal dichotomy of the text is introduced, students will be able to track its full realization during the course of independent study and reading. The main challenge faced by students at this point is comprehending the extent of the *Brevísima relación*'s apostolic context, an understanding essential to their successful independent reading of the work. From Las Casas's perspective, supported by the papal bulls, the purpose of the conquest of the New World was to spread the divine word across the sea. By acting with greed and cruelty, the Spaniards—that is, the *lobos*—were blatantly defying God's word and will.

This apostolic context appears in a variety of iterations throughout the text. Indeed, the whole work is an uninterrupted succession of acts of violence with few memorable differences among them. Spanish destruction is multifaceted, encompassing physical, moral, cultural, and spiritual abuses in each named territory. To separate and distinguish between the events Las Casas narrates, students should create graphic organizers, which will aid in comprehension and identification of key textual points. Word-webbing, which categorizes quotations and phrases gleaned from the text around broader terms such as *actions, descriptions of the land*, or *presentation of the people* is one useful note-taking technique to suggest (Barkley, Cross, and Major 206). Similarly, invite students to take textual notes on a map of the region described in each section of the text; the spatial organizer helps associate narrated events with the appropriate locale.

On a lexical level, the *Brevísima relación*'s rich vocabulary not only reveals Las Casas's strongest opinions and judgments but also provides a useful survey of some of the rhetorical techniques most used at the time. It is in establishing the diametrical opposition of *lobos y corderos* that Las Casas employs his most favored techniques, such as using powerfully emotive adjectives to describe the Europeans and their actions ("los inhumanos hombres," "extraño y pestilencial cuchillo," "infelices españoles" 'these other inhumane men,' 'foreign and pestilential knife,' 'wretched Spaniards' [154, 148, 136; 70, 65, 56]), the superlative to oppose the peaceful indigenous world with the cruel Spanish colonization ("felicísimas y admirables provincias," "gentes obedientísimas," "tiranía infernal" 'exceedingly fertile and admirable provinces,' 'people excellent in obedience,' 'infernal tyranny' [165, 75, 78; 78, 5, 7]), and hyperbolic expressions of quantity to emphasize the extent of the destruction ("infinitas gentes," "treinta mil ríos y arroyos" 'infinite numbers of people,' 'thirty thousand rivers and streams' [165, 83; 78, 12]). He frequently employs the rhetorical technique of synonymic repetition to add further emphasis ("han muerto y destruído," "matanzas y crueldades," "tiranías y opresiones" 'have slain and destroyed,' 'slaughters and singular cruelties,' 'tyrannies and oppressions' [78, 81, 89; 8, 9, 17]). Additionally, incidents of direct discourse ("¿Por qué me quemáis? ¿Qué os he hecho?" 'Why are you burning me? What have I done to you?' [160; 74]) and apostrophe ("¡Oh, cuántos huérfanos hizo, cuántos robó de sus hijos, cuántos privó de sus mujeres. . . " 'Oh!

How many orphans did he make, how many fathers did he rob of their children, how many men strip of their wives. . .' [120; 43]) abound in the most passionate moments of the work. To draw students' attention to these linguistic characteristics, encourage the use of textual annotation, a technique by which students mark up their exemplars with notes to themselves, underline passages that contain particular rhetorical techniques, and so on. In this way, students create a personalized copy of the text to aid in their analysis and class discussion, as well as in any later review of the reading, such as before a final examination.

Double-entry journaling can also help students follow the text's systematic juxtaposition of good versus bad (i.e., *lobos* versus *corderos*, native population versus Spanish). This practice begins with note-taking on the topic from readings and class discussion, using the right-hand pages of a notebook. The left pages are used reflectively for comments *about* the right-hand notes; they provide a space for summarizing, revising, associating, questioning, and reacting to the items written on the right. The dialogue created between the left and right pages encourages students to challenge their own and others' reactions to the basic dichotomy presented by Las Casas, at the same time that they become more effective critical readers (Cain, DeCiccio, and Rossi 39).

E-mail journaling is an effective form of online collaboration that serves the same purpose as double-entry journaling. Here, students send a weekly message to the professor or to another student, the recipient reacts to the content of the e-mail, and a dialogue journal begins. This exchange encourages continued reflection and conscious participation of each student in a lower-pressure online environment. Online discussion boards can serve a similar purpose, providing a forum for students to offer opinions, ask questions, and respond to others' contributions. When they feel comfortable expressing themselves, their skills and confidence grow, and the results resonate in their classroom participation and in their written production.

Focused free writings, for which the *Brevísima relación*'s ethical content provides rich fodder, may also accompany the reflective reading process. Continuing with the central opposition of the text, assign students to write a persuasive letter from the perspective of the cacique Hatuey to the Spanish colonists or government. If cross-cultural and cross-disciplinary connections are the focus of the course, assign a reaction paper in which students compare the treatment of the indigenous people as presented by Las Casas with experiences of the African slaves in the United States. These activities encourage continuing reflective, creative, and critical thinking and can also be paired or group tasks in which students' collaborative writing is informed by the unique perspective of each group member.

"Pues, Otra Cosa Diré": Techniques to Enhance Lecture

Lecture remains an efficient means of assuring a common knowledge base, particularly regarding factual information (biography, bibliography, critical theories, and so on). However, studies demonstrate that retention and comprehension are significantly increased if techniques to break the expository format are implemented. Following are several elements of the *Brevísima relación* that invite in-class examination, with a brief suggestion for incorporating AL and CoopL methods of enhancing lectures into each minilecture.

The use of irony: ironic phrases such as "este piadoso capitán" 'this pious captain' (116; 39) are not infrequent in the text and present a more complex reading layer than the literal level on which one typically reads the *Brevísima relación*. When presenting this concept in class, invite a student to be the "model note-taker," publicly taking lecture notes on an overhead projection, guiding the class and illustrating for the professor any areas needing clarification.

Stylistic and rhetorical devices: after a lecture on Las Casas's style elements, such as those presented in the essays by Ruth Hill and Cynthia Stone in this volume, invite a student or group to orally recount the main points of the presentation in the form of a lecture summary.

The religious and historical context of the *Brevísima relación*: to confront the anonymity of the perpetrators whose acts Las Casas depicts, have students discover their identities through online research or by consulting other Lascasian texts (e.g., *Historia de las Indias*) and present them in class. Associating the accusations with the accused lends a relevance to the text. During this student-led presentation, and also when explaining the Las Casas–Juan Ginés de Sepúlveda polemic, pause the lecture to allow students to share their notes with a neighbor. This exchange enables them to check comprehension of tricky issues and to raise any resulting questions.

Social context: to situate the *Brevísima relación* in its sixteenth-century social context and to aid in retention of factual material, incorporate days in which students research and briefly present material on contextually relevant topics such as the *encomiendas*, the New Laws of 1542, life in the Americas before Spanish colonization, Spanish policies in the Low Countries, and so forth. Such student lecture days allow the class to participate actively in the teaching and learning process.

Critical response: after presenting an overview of critical perspectives on the text, pause to allow students to summarize the main point of the lecture and indicate any questions during approximately four minutes of reflective writing. Reading these paragraphs alerts the instructor to any area needing further emphasis.

All these techniques keep students in continual dialogue with the text, with the professor, and with one another during the reading process, while presenting the key points of the *Brevísima relación* more formally.

"Yo Vide el Tirano": Collaborative Writing and Research to Question Authority

One other element of the *Brevísima relación* requires special attention for students: Las Casas's persistent assertion of truthfulness. Throughout the text, the Dominican calls on his own experiences as eyewitness and those of others as authorities to corroborate his accusations. He relates his own moments of intervention (140; 59) and cites his sources when he was not personally present (166; 78). Yet in some cases, he admits that he cannot provide any examples but asserts nonetheless that the same atrocities surely happened there that occurred elsewhere (156; 71)—in other words, by that advanced point in the text, Las Casas is asking the reader to have confidence in his truthfulness. This ambiguity invites the assignment of a position paper, in which students argue for or against Las Casas's veracity. Here, CL writing techniques help students build confidence in their position, enable them to benefit from others' insights and knowledge, and provide opportunities for refining writing that are not easily achieved working in isolation.

To lay the groundwork for collaborative writing on this topic, the professor can pose a question when assigning the reading selection from the text, such as, How does Las Casas make his stories of destruction believable? Ask students to list proper names, dates, witnesses, sources, and rhetorical techniques the Dominican draws on to achieve this goal. Using any of the tools outlined in the section on active reading will produce a useful organizer that can be shared and compared in class, employed to stimulate whole-class or small-group discussion, or brought to a collaborative writing group as a first step in addressing the issue of veracity.

Brevísima relación writing groups can function collaboratively from this point or throughout the semester by preparing and delivering brief presentations on student lecture days, reading and studying together, and producing a term paper. Students cooperatively develop and hone their topics, brainstorming and using double-entry journals, notes, and word webs before research and writing begin. All stages of production involve group work: peer-editing, reading sections of writing aloud to evaluate flow and logic, and developing a presentation. Through these ongoing techniques, students confront the question of verisimilitude in Las Casas's narrative with a collective authority. They typically respond favorably to the group projects, remarking on the benefits of the shared workload, greater collective knowledge and creativity, and inventive presentations including poster sessions, Web sites, and PowerPoint, which derive from improved student confidence.

The colleagues to whom I mentioned this project at its outset almost invariably expressed surprise and doubt at the idea of teaching Las Casas in the language classroom. This mistaken response—that is, the assumption that active techniques pertain only to language acquisition courses—illustrates the reluctance of academia to incorporate interactive, collaborative work in "serious" literature classrooms. By challenging this notion and borrowing from methods used successfully in second-language courses, professors construct strong scholars of literature while deconstructing perceived barriers between them and the *Brevísima relación*.

NOTE

I follow André Saint-Lu's Spanish-language edition of the *Brevísima relación* (Catédra, 2005). Translations are by Andrew Hurley (Casas, *An Account, Much Abbreviated*).

Imperial Reason, War Theory, and Human Rights in Las Casas's *Apología* and the Valladolid Debate

Carlos A. Jáuregui and Luis Fernando Restrepo

> War is essentially an evil thing. Its consequences are not confined to the belligerent States alone, but affect the whole world.
>
> To initiate a war of aggression, therefore, is not only an international crime; it is the supreme international crime differing only from other war crimes in that it contains within itself the accumulated evil of the whole.
>
> —International Military Tribunal, Nuremberg, *Trial of the Major War Criminals*

The *Apología*, an edited part of the manuscript that Bartolomé de las Casas read at the renowned debate at Valladolid in 1550, is a lengthy and complex text that poses several difficulties. It is nonetheless a rich work that sheds light on the fundamental principles of the sixteenth-century Spanish conquest and colonization of the New World and provides valuable insights into the development of the modern notions of sovereignty, imperialism, and human rights. Even though it is inseparable from its early modern historical context, the *Apología* touches on key issues in today's world, including the establishment of a legal order above that of the state and the legality of war.

The first thing that we would like to stress about the task of teaching the *Apología* is that there is a symbiotic relation between this text and the Valladolid debate, a sort of pedagogical tautology: the debate cannot be taught without reading the *Apología* or selections thereof. At the same time, the *Apología* turns out to be almost unintelligible without the context of the debate.

Contextualization

The Debate at Valladolid

The *Apología*, as we know it, is an edited version of the first part of the text that Las Casas read for several days during the "Great Debate at Valladolid" (Hanke, *Aristotle* 38). The famous debate is a standard point of reference in colonial and early American studies. However, key texts of the debate such as Las Casas's *Apología* are seldom taught. Most often used by instructors are the *Brevísima relación de la destrucción de las Indias* and the *Historia de las Indias*, texts that are not strictly part of the historical debate. This substitution is problematic (as we will argue later).

From a pedagogical point of view, it is important to define the nature and objectives of the Valladolid dispute between Las Casas and Juan Ginés de Sepúlveda and to place it in a wider historical context. There is an ample corpus of events and documents that are often referred as part of "the debate," using this term in a broad sense, which leads to some confusion. Lewis Hanke offers a clearer definition, using the term "controversy" to refer to the historical antecedents of the debate and other related documents that are not strictly part of it. The debate itself was ordered by Charles V, after he placed a moratorium on all new conquests. The emperor's decision was in part due to intense lobbying by Las Casas in court and at the Council of Indies. The newly established junta was instructed—as stated by Fray Domingo de Soto in his summary of the deliberations—first, "inquerir e constituir la forma y leyes cómo nuestra sancta fe católica se pueda predicar e promulgar en aquel nuevo orbe que Dios nos ha descubierto" 'to inquire into and develop the forms and laws to preach and promote our Holy Catholic Faith in the New World that God has discovered to us' and, second, "examinar qué forma puede haber cómo quedasen aquellas gentes subjectas a la majestad del Emperador nuestro señor, sin lesión de su real conciencia, conforme a la bulla de Alejandro" 'to examine how those peoples may be subjected to his majesty the emperor, our lord, without damage to his royal conscience, according to the [*Inter caetera*] bull of [Pope] Alexander [VI].'[1] Therefore, this was initially a deliberation about just methods of evangelization and the exercise of imperial sovereignty in the Indies. However, thanks to Las Casas's *Apología*, the debate went beyond its initial purpose, and it became a discussion of

> si es lícito a Su Magestad hacer Guerra a aquellos indios antes que se les predique la fe, para subjectallos a su Imperio, y que después de subjectados puedan más fácil y cómodamente ser enseñados y alumbrados por la doctrina evangélica del conocimiento de sus errores y de la verdad cristiana.
>
> (Soto, *Aquí* 229)

whether it is lawful for His Majesty to make war on those Indians before preaching the faith to them, in order to subject them to his Empire, so that, once subjugated, they can be more effectively and easily instructed and enlightened by the evangelical doctrine, becoming aware of their errors as well as of the Christian truth.

The debate was not about the *encomienda* system, the royal title to the Spanish empire, or the nature of the Indians, although these topics were addressed in the course of it. It was fundamentally a dispute about the justice or injustice of war as a way to fulfill the evangelical mission dictated by pontifical decrees (the *Inter caetera* and *Eximiae devotionis* bulls of 1493) and to exercise imperial sovereignty. The debate was symptomatic of the new Spanish imperialism that emerged in the course of the sixteenth century, replacing its military conquering telos with an evangelical telos: the empire fashioned itself not as a conquering power but as a loving father figure (Rabasa, *Writing Violence*). But the debate was also, in a way, the epilogue of a long controversy concerning imperial reason (*ratio imperii*) and Spanish sovereignty over the New World, a controversy that could be traced back to the time of Columbus (Jáuregui).

The Question of the Indies

The Valladolid debate revisited some of the issues regarding the legitimacy of the conquest and colonization of the Indies that had been discussed at various times since Columbus's first voyages to the New World. An early instance of the controversy occurred in 1495, when Columbus sent some enslaved Indians to the Catholic monarchs. The sovereigns initially wanted to sell them but decided to consult legal experts and theologians to determine "if in good conscience" it was appropriate or not to sell the Indians. The imperial concern for "good conscience" would become a recurring political motif of the Spanish crown when seeking advice.[2] Almost two decades later, a sermon denouncing the maltreatment of the Indians, given in 1511 by Antón de Montesinos, a Dominican priest in Hispaniola, prompted the Crown to examine its colonial policies and seek counsel from a group of theologians and jurists. Las Casas gives a succinct summary of those deliberations in his *Historia de las Indias* (bk. 3, chs. 9–22). Based on the recommendations by the junta, in 1512–13 the Crown issued the Laws of Burgos, regulating Indian labor and indoctrination. Another important document issued at that same time concerned the Indians not yet subject to the Crown: it was an infamous protocol for conquest, drafted in 1513 by Juan López de Palacios Rubios, known as the *Requerimiento*. Based on Alexander VI's bull of donation of the Indies to the Spanish Crown, the *Requerimiento* demanded peaceful submission to the Crown and the church. If the Indians resisted, the Spaniards could lawfully wage war against them, seizing and enslaving those captured in such wars (Seed, *Ceremonies*).

Over the next two decades, the controversy would develop around the topic of the rationality of the Indians, understood as their juridical capacity for self-government and possession of property (Pagden, "Dispossessing" 81). In this context, the sixteenth-century usage of terms such as *barbarian* and *natural serf* and *servitude* (*servidumbre natural*) had specific juridical value in relation to Indian sovereignty and property rights. An example comes from the discussion that took place between Las Casas and Friar Juan de Quevedo at the royal court in Barcelona in 1519. Based on the philosophy of John Maior and on Aristotle's *Politics*, Quevedo discussed the conditions determining legitimate subjection of the Indians to natural servitude (Zavala, *Filosofía política* 57).

In the following decade, we find several other important precedents to the Valladolid debate and the rise of a prominent figure in the controversy over the legitimacy of the Spanish conquest of the Indies: the Dominican Francisco de Vitoria, a professor of theology at the University of Salamanca. In "De temperantia" (c. 1537) and "De indis" (c. 1539)—two lectures later published in his *Relectiones Theologicae XII* (1557)—Vitoria examined the Spanish title over the Indies, identifying just and unjust causes of the war against the Indians. In sum, the matter of his treatises was *jus ad bellum* (a just war theory). According to Vitoria, it was not lawful to wage war based on the papal donation (since it was not a valid title), the irrationality of the Indians, or their infidelity. However, the Salamancan scholar presented several causes for just and lawful wars, among which were: the impediments to the right to move freely; the indigenous obstacles to the right to communicate and socialize and to do commerce freely; self-defense against attacks from the Indians; the obstruction of the right to preach the faith freely as ordered by God; to meet obligations with allies; and for the protection of the innocents. Vitoria refrains from judging the Indians' alleged barbarism and the corresponding legal implications (what Las Casas will call the "vitorian doubt" [Casas, *In Defense* 340–41]), but he affirms an emerging international legal order that supersedes national sovereignty (including Indian autonomy) and that ultimately justifies war.

In 1542, Las Casas finished writing his *Brevísima relación de la destrucción de las Indias*, in which he denounced Spanish massacres and abuse of the Indians. Las Casas had already sent three letters to the Council of the Indies. His efforts were instrumental in the passing of the New Laws of 1542, which prohibited Indian slavery and limited the creation, sale, inheritance, and other transferring of *encomiendas*. Through the New Laws, the Crown sought to limit the growing local power of the *encomenderos*. These laws were strongly opposed in the New World and incited such events as the rebellion by Gonzalo Pizarro in Perú. In 1545, the Crown responded to the unrest in the Indies by revoking the provisions of the New Laws that restricted the establishment and transmission of the *encomiendas*. Las Casas returned to Spain once again to lobby in defense of the Indians in 1547. During that period, Sepúlveda attempted to publish his *Democrates II* (*Tratado sobre las justas causas de la guerra contra los indios*).

When he was denied license to publish it and received unfavorable reviews from scholars at Salamanca and Alcalá de Henares, he decided to publish an *Apología* or defense of his *Democrates II* in Rome (1550). Las Casas read a summary of Sepúlveda's *Apología* and soon started working on his own. The groundwork for the Valladolid debate had been laid.

Issues of the Debate

Even though many critics (e.g., Hanke) and instructors envision the debate as a passionate series of interchanges, it resembled not a heated courtroom drama but a tedious litigation procedure in which each participant came separately to give his deposition. At Valladolid, Sepúlveda spoke for three hours on the first day. In the next five or six days, Las Casas read his own *Apología* page by page, until the reading was completed, or until the members of the junta, as Sepúlveda suggested, could bear no more. The most significant piece of the debate corresponds then to a lengthy and fatiguing reading in Latin by Las Casas of a text written against Sepúlveda apropos of a published defense of an unpublished book (more on the texts' publication histories below). The debate developed around Sepúlveda's arguments in his *Democrates II*, in the following order, according to the summary by de Soto. For Sepúlveda, the wars against the Indians were lawful for four reasons: because of the gravity of the sins the Indians had committed, especially their idolatries and their sins against nature; on account of the rudeness of their natures, which obliged them to serve persons having a more refined nature, such as the Spaniards; in order to spread the faith, a task more easily accomplished by the subjugation of the natives; and to protect the innocents among the natives themselves from unjust injuries and sacrifices.

To the first argument by Sepúlveda, Las Casas responded that even if the Indians were committing crimes, it was not lawful for the Spaniards to punish them, since the Spaniards had no jurisdiction over them. The bishop's argument was based on the distinction between the different kinds of unbelievers: in particular, between pagans and heretics. Pagans were not under the jurisdiction of the church or the Crown. On this point, Las Casas coincided with Vitoria. In contrast, heretics were under the jurisdiction of the Crown and therefore could justly be subdued by force. The radical discursive difference between Sepúlveda and Las Casas, then, was limited to the first stage of colonialism: at the end, both assumed that the Indians would become Christians.

Sepúlveda's second argument was that war against the Indians was lawful because they were barbarians whose natural condition was such that they should obey those more civilized than themselves. Losada (*Introducción*) and Adorno ("Los debates") point out that Las Casas distorted Sepúlveda's argument about the natural inferiority of the Indians. Sepúlveda did not question the humanity of the Indians, nor did he claim that the Indians were inherently and hopelessly inferior. Las Casas's "distortion" was a contentious, selective, and highly strategic reading of Sepúlveda's argument. Las Casas refuted Sepúlveda by providing a more precise use of the term *barbarian* that could not possibly be applied to all the Indians. According to Las Casas, there are four uses of the term and only one that could really be defined as a true barbarian in the Aristotelian sense: there were cruel people; linguistic barbarians (as in its original meaning, a non-Greek speaker); barbarians in the strict sense of the word (i.e., those incapable of governing themselves, considered by Aristotle natural serfs); and religious barbarians (non-Christians). For Las Casas, the Indians could only be considered barbarians linguistically and religiously; neither of which justified war.

Las Casas refuted Sepúlveda's third argument by affirming that war was not conducive to evangelization, because it would make the Indians hate Spaniards. Sepúlveda had claimed that war would allow the Spaniards to preach the faith: as Christians, it was their obligation to evangelize the Indians, and the war was justified against those who intentionally and with malice prevented the Christians from fulfilling their pope-mandated duty.

The fourth Sepúlvedan reason for the just war—to prevent the natives from unjustly injuring one another—is paradoxically modern and imperial, in that it advocates for the imposition, by force if necessary, of an international legal order for the benefit of all (*bonum commune totius orbis*) that supersedes national sovereignty. Las Casas, in contrast, defended the sovereignty of the Indians, stating that the church has no secular jurisdiction over nonsubjected unbelievers.

What was the outcome of the debate? After the marathonlike reading by Las Casas, the junta asked de Soto to summarize the arguments of both parties in Spanish. Then, Sepúlveda requested the *sumario* by de Soto and later presented his twelve objections. Las Casas, subsequently, refuted these objections one by one. De Soto's *sumario* clearly demonstrates that the *Apología* could not and cannot be read as a stand-alone work. There is no known formal verdict of the debate,[3] but even if the debate did not result in any concrete, immediate decision, it is significant for several reasons. First, it summarizes the main juridical and theological issues that the conquest of the Indies had generated up to 1550. Second, in the debate we already find the use of the new imperial language of peaceful colonization that will be key in Philip II's 1573 "Ordenanzas," which, for example, ordered colonizers not to "conquer" but instead to "pacify" the Indians (495). Third, the debate transcends the sixteenth-century Iberian context. In their exchanges, Las Casas and Sepúlveda touched on some of the fundamental political issues of the modern world, such as sovereignty and universal human rights.

The historic Valladolid debate has generated interest throughout the centuries, including the seventeenth-century response by Bernardo de Vargas Machuca (*Apología*) and the attention of nineteenth-century Hispanists like Menéndez Pelayo. In 1603, Samuel Purchas made the debate known in English. Twentieth-century scholars such as Silvio Zavala (*La filosofía*), Edmundo O'Gorman, Ángel Losada, Lewis Hanke, and Marcel Bataillon have produced solid scholarship and valuable editions and translations. The debate continues to generate significant scholarship, including the more recent contributions by Anthony Pagden ("Dispossessing" and *Fall*), Helen Rand Parish (*Las Casas as Bishop*), Rolena Adorno

("Los debates" and *Polemics*), José Rabasa (*Writing Violence*), and others. We hope the following recommendations for teaching Las Casas's *Apología* will generate new interest in a complex but illuminating intellectual exchange that has great relevance today despite having taken place almost five centuries ago.

Teaching Las Casas's Apología: Problems and Strategies

The Tacit Substitution (the Brevísima relación for the Apología)

The *Apología*, a key text of the debate, is often alluded to in scholarship and in the classroom but seldom studied, although it is available in Spanish, as *Apología* (trans. Ángel Losada), and in English, as *In Defense of the Indians* (trans. Stafford Poole). The unexpected effect of the pedagogical substitution of the *Apología* is that Las Casas's arguments in the debate are presented and understood through the *Brevísima relación*, even though the document was written a decade before the Valladolid dispute (but not published until 1552). Certainly, the *Apología* and the *Brevísima relación* share common images, tropes, ideas, and arguments, but the texts are complementary, not equivalent. It is important to reconsider this implicit pedagogical simile. If we decide to continue such substitution, we should make it clear in our classes, at least pointing out the discursive, historic, and teleological differences between the texts.

A compare-and-contrast approach to the *Brevísima relación* and the *Apología* is a productive pedagogical exercise: the *Brevísima relación* draws from the genre of the conquest account (*relación*), but it is a counterdiscourse where the deeds of conquest (*conquista*) are replaced by an account of massacres and evil acts of destruction (*destruycion*).[4] In contrast, the *Apología* belongs to a genre of texts vindicating or debating something or someone. There are two apologies in the Valladolid debate, as we will explain below. The *Brevísima relación* is a brief lobbying for what would become the New Laws. The *Apología*, on the other hand, is a treatise that originates from the failure of such laws. The *Brevísima relación* is a report that addresses Prince Philip, whereas the *Apología* is a text in a debate between jurists and theologians. The *Brevísima relación*, with its inventory of injustices and cruelties, calls for the abolition of the *encomienda*. The *Apología*, in contrast, is primarily a juridical argument against using claims of cultural superiority as a basis for waging war on and conquering the Indians and in favor of peaceful means of evangelical colonization.

The Textual Corpus of the Debate

The *Apología* is almost inseparable from other main texts related to the debate. To teach the *Apología* would require at least a partial reading of the arguments of Las Casas's opponent, Sepúlveda, as well as a selection of the large and complex corpus of texts that constitute the debate, of which the following is a brief inventory.

1. *Democrates II* (*Tratado sobre las justas causas*) by Sepúlveda: a text that is both present and absent in the debate and in Las Casas's *Apología*, since its publication was not allowed. As we noted above, what Las Casas read was not the *Democrates II* but a summary of Sepúlveda's defense of his unpublished manuscript. In a related way, *Democrates II* can be considered the application to the New World of Sepúlveda's earlier work from 1531: *Democrates* (I), a treatise about the compatibility of the military and Christianity.

2. The *Apología Ioanis Genesii Sepulvedae pro libro De justis belli causus* (1550) by Sepúlveda: irritated by scholars' rejections and not getting a license to publish his *Democrates II*, Sepúlveda published a defense of his vetoed manuscript in Rome.

3. The *Apología* by Las Casas: a response to Sepúlveda's just war theory at large. Las Casas did not directly respond to Sepúlveda's *Apología* or even its summary, but as de Soto noted, the bishop attempted to answer to everything his opponent had written (*Aquí* 229). Las Casas's *Apología* opposes Sepúlveda's thought (the complete title in Latin specifies that the work is *adversus Genesium Sepulvedam*). It was presented by Las Casas to the Valladolid junta but would remain unpublished until 1974. Las Casas's *Apología* had two parts, as is customary in legal action. The first part delineated the supporting juridical and doctrinal framework, and the second cited the facts that would allow its application. We have only the first part, written originally in Latin. What about the second part? Taking into consideration the content of the *Apologética historia sumaria* and Las Casas's references in the *Apología* to a second part aimed at refuting the historian Gonzalo Fernández de Oviedo's assertion that "los indios eran indómitos e incorregibles es más falsa que falsa . . ." 'the Indians are unable to learn and incorrigible' (643), it seems logical to assume a certain connection between the unknown second part of the *Apología* and the *Apologética*.

4. The *Tratado tercero* by Las Casas (1552 [Soto, *Aquí*]): a summary of the debate, prepared by Domingo de Soto (president of the junta). It includes twelve responses by Sepúlveda and the corresponding replies by Las Casas.

Besides the corpus of the debate, the *Apología* would have to be taught taking into consideration the other texts by Las Casas, the legislation of the Indies, and Spanish juridical thought. Given the voluminous size of most of the texts in question, there is a great need for English and Spanish anthologies and critical editions appropriate for classroom use.

The Anthology Option

How to teach the *Apología*? Should we try a comprehensive reading of the text or make some selections accompanied by supporting materials? The answer largely depends on the discipline, topic, level, and goals of the course.

We would like to recommend some key passages and related texts useful in any course and to point out some of the important issues that the *Apología* allows us to bring into the classroom.

1. The *Tratado tercero* (Soto, *Aquí*): as noted earlier, this text provides a concise and illustrative summary of the debate as it developed. It also includes the responses by Sepúlveda and Las Casas.

2. The *argumento, sumario,* and *prefacio* of the *Apología*: the Lascasian framework of the debate. The *Apología* contains an initial section that presents the topic to be discussed ("Argumentum apologiae"), followed by the opposing thesis ("Summarium Sepulvedae"), and a third part that anticipates the argument of the *Apología* ("Praefatio Apologiae"). These short fragments illustrate the rhetorical strategies used in the *Apología* to undermine and reframe Sepúlveda's arguments.

3. Definitions of the barbarian and their juridical implications: as mentioned above, Las Casas describes four kinds of barbarians in the first chapters of the *Apología*, asserting that the Indians are only linguistically and religiously barbarians. The other two classes were those cruel and ferocious (which included the Spaniard) and the barbarians *sensu stricto*—that is, those completely uncivilized, without any government, laws, city, or institutions. This last form of barbarism was, according to Las Casas, a rare phenomenon in the realm of teratology. Although barbarianism was not the main issue of the debate, Sepúlveda brought in Aristotle's notion of the barbarian to justify imposing imperial sovereignty and waging war if the Indians offered resistance. For us, the main issue here is the argument of cultural superiority and its colonial consequences (military or pacific) and the place of such argument as an axiom of the narrative of Western colonial modernity (Dussel, *Underside*). Some possible discussion themes are: key semiotic elements defining the different kinds of barbarians, juridical implications of the use of such terms, and the colonial implications of the argument of cultural superiority. Besides the first four chapters of the *Apología*, complementary readings for this exercise would be the so-called "Epilogue: The Different Kinds of Barbarians" from the *Apologética historia sumaria* and selections from Hanke (*Aristotle*), Pagden (*Fall*), and Aristotle's *Politics* (bks. 1 and 3).

4. The religious question and the church's jurisdiction over unbelievers: the religious question is a central topic in the *Apología*. Las Casas defines four kinds of unbelievers to restrict the lawful use of war to those already under the church's jurisdiction: Jews and Moors under Christian rule, apostates and heretics, Turks and Moors "fighting against us" (503), and infidels practicing idolatry in remote provinces (such as the Indians). Special attention should be placed on Las Casas's exceptions to his pacifist stance against war. The bishop argued that heretics and apostates can be ultimately brought back to the faith by force, an argument that presents an opportunity to apprise students of an important distinction: Las Casas's proposal of a peaceful evange-

lization method should not be confused with a universal defense of religious freedom. Las Casas's doctrine was adopted by the Crown and became a defining element of the discourse of "softer" imperialism, an imperialism that conceived itself as carrying out not a punitive but a paternal evangelical mission. Key chapters of the *Apología* to assign about this topic would be 6, 7, 25, 49, and 50;[5] also useful would be selections from Sepúlveda's *Democrates II* and Vitoria's "On the Evangelization of the Unbelievers" (1534–35).

5. Las Casas and Vitoria: our final suggestion is to examine how Las Casas selectively and strategically reads Vitoria in the *Apología* (against Sepúlveda's reading). An initial contrast between Vitoria's just war theory ("De temperantia" [c. 1537], and "De indis" [c. 1539]) and Las Casas's early pacifist treatise *De unico vocationis modo omnium gentium ad veram religionem* ("The Only Way of Attracting All People to the True Religion" [c. 1537]) will illustrate the indirect role of Vitoria's doctrine in the debate. This exercise sheds light on the often-ignored differences between the two intellectuals regarding the conquest, the just causes of war, and imperial reason. Here, for example, we find that, paradoxically, Las Casas's defense of the papal titles (because of the evangelical mission they impose to the empire) seems more conservative than Vitoria's seminal vision of an international economic and legal order. However, Las Casas's position is quite modern from a human rights perspective. The bishop was seeking a legal framework for the protection of the Indians; his positions were not mere academic exercises of intelligence but acts of involved politics. Basic readings for this unit would be corresponding chapters of the *Apología* (24, 31, and 56), *De unico vocationis modo*, and Vitoria's "De temperantia" and "De indis."

Teaching the *Apología* should not be only about reading an intricate juridical and theological dispute that occurred centuries ago to other people but also about our academic intervention in an open debate that is part of our present. The *Apología* invites us to discuss with our students issues that are still unresolved: for example, compared to the early modern imperial military campaigns, how are war and imperialism justified today? Why and how can a humanitarian or human rights position be alleged both against and for imperialism? The challenge and potential lie in our ability to teach the *Apología* as the basis for a critical and ethical discussion on war and imperialism today without obliterating its specific historical context, the early modern colonial world.

NOTES

The epigraph to this essay is taken from the section of the International Military Tribunal's judgment entitled "The Common Plan of Conspiracy and Aggressive War" (Nuremberg: Intl. Military Tribunal, 1947) 1: 186 (www.loc.gov/rr/frd/Military_Law/pdf/NT_Vol-I.pdf).

[1] Soto, *Aquí* 227, 229. All translations are ours, unless otherwise indicated.

[2] See the *Colección documental del descubrimiento* 783–90. The Crown's consultants determined that, except those captured in a just war, the Indians were free and could not be sold (Adorno, "Los debates" 48).

[3] There are only three known opinions by the members of the junta (Adorno, "Los debates" 50).

[4] The *relatio* or *narratio* is the required official report of an expedition by the Conquistadors (Mignolo 70).

[5] We follow here the chapter numeration as it appears in Losada's bilingual edition of the *Apología* (Latin and Spanish).

The Noble Savage as Utopian Figure?
Teaching the *Apologética historia sumaria*

José Rabasa

In teaching Bartolomé de las Casas at the graduate level, I often encounter two commonplaces: one, that Las Casas did not demonstrate the same solidarity toward Africans as he did toward Indians; and, two, that his representation of Amerindians as childlike noble savages (most particularly in the *Brevísima relación de la destrucción de las Indias*) is as detrimental to Indians as those representations that denied them full humanity. Las Casas's suggestion that African as well as European slaves should replace Amerindian labor would support the first thesis; however, the ubiquity of the claim is the product of a campaign by eighteenth-century French antislavery pamphleteers, as explained in several essays in this volume. To counteract it, I provide my students with readings from the *Brevísima relación de la destrucción de Africa*, a volume that collects chapters 17 through 27 of the *Historia de las Indias* with an introduction by Isacio Pérez Fernández ("Estudio preliminar"). In these chapters from the *Historia de las Indias*, Las Casas discusses the exploration of Africa and the Canary Islands and denounces the systematic African slave trade in the fourteenth and fifteenth centuries as a material and ideological preparation for the invasion of the Americas. About the second commonplace some argue that Las Casas's idealization of the Indians, in contrast to portrayals of them as fierce savages, neutralizes their resistance. To correct it, I lead my students through selections from his massive two-volume *Apologética historia sumaria*, the text I focus on here.

Las Casas's *Apologética* offers a utopian ethnology that articulates a cultural critique and a textual form of utopian practice (Rabasa, "Utopian Ethnology"). The concept of utopian practice does not refer to the common understanding of utopia as the proposal of an ideal social world but to utopia as a discursive practice. In outlining a utopian ethnology, my objective is to trace a prophetic dissolution of anthropology as the disciplinary formation in which the West studies the "rest" of the world. Following this alternative approach to anthropology and utopia, I examine the figures of the noble savage and the paradisiacal natural garden in the *Apologética*. The analysis of these two paradoxical figures ultimately renders the semantic field from which the "West" defines the "rest" and posits itself as a universal cultural model.[1]

These theoretical revisions reveal in the *Apologética* a dismantling of the grounds for historical-evolutionary schemas. Note that the noble savage and the natural garden are not empirical entities subject to verification but utopian rhetorical figures. Their paradoxical nature resides in that they combine the natural and the cultural in one term without incurring contradiction.

The *Apologética* is divided into three books and an epilogue. Book 1 is dedicated to the climate of the island of Hispaniola and gives a geographic foundation for book 2's demonstration of the Amerindian's physical fitness, which in turn supports claims made for New World cultures in book 3. While book 3 contains a series of ethnographies originally compiled by several authors in different areas of the Americas, the organization and interpretation of the ethnographic materials follow the chain of causality initiated in the first two books: climate produces bodies and intellects, which create culture. The descriptions of geography, physiology, and culture are determined by the initial demonstration of a temperate climate, and thus the Americas as a whole partake of the ideal climate, bodies, and cultures. In teaching the *Apologética*, I select sections from the three books and include the whole epilogue, though this practice varies depending on whether I am teaching undergraduates or graduate students. From book 1, I select the first nine chapters, which offer an approximation of Hispaniola by means of four *vueltas*, discursive turns that focus on different aspects of the climate and nature of the island. In book 2, I find particularly relevant the chapters in which Las Casas discusses the application of the *causas esenciales* (essential causes) that determine the intelligence of peoples in different latitudes. For book 3, I assign the initial chapter, in which Las Casas lays out his anthropology, and then select a chapter that corresponds to one region in the Americas; since I often teach courses on Mexico, I frequently assign chapters that correspond to New Spain.

I teach the epilogue in its integrity because it presents a difficult and complex argument that lends itself to a range of practical readings when quoted out of context. The epilogue offers a semantic critique of four possible meanings of the term *barbarism*. The first two definitions of barbarism that Las Casas discusses pertain to the semantics of the term—that is to say, they explain the derivation of the word and the varieties of barbarian peoples. The third definition discusses the concept of barbarism as denoting a degeneration of human customs. For Las Casas, the fourth modality of barbarism corresponds to all gentiles. These standard definitions of barbarism provide a discursive space for Las Casas to explain their contradictory meanings and dismantle their applicability to the peoples of the Americas.

In reading Las Casas, we must avoid taking the propositions in his enthymemes (incomplete syllogisms) as statements of fact. Palinode awaits us with a vengeance: in ignoring semantic play, we end up subjecting the same peoples we pretend to defend to a symbolic violence that utopian discursive practices generally warn us against. For instance, Las Casas characterizes the lack of letters as a type of barbarism, but the applicability of this definition to Amerindians is then analyzed and critiqued. In ignoring Las Casas's palinode that overturns the equation of barbarism with lack of letters (or writing more generally, since the argument against Las Casas's opening statement often underscores the fact that Amerindians did have forms of writing, even if not alphabetical), we risk claiming that writing, history, and other communal formations such as states constitute intrinsic characteristics of being human. We are left to wonder what to do when facing a culture that defines itself as willing to remain without writing, history, and state.

The objective of the epilogue is not to classify Amerindians as barbarians but to dismantle the transparency of the concept of barbarism. The most complex modality of the barbarian that Las Casas examines is the definition of all infidels as barbarians, a definition that amounts to a call to bring all peoples under the fold of Christianity—that is, of universal history. Given that Las Casas critiques this ideological cornerstone of Roman Catholicism, is it accurate to speak of his *Apologética* as exposing and undoing Catholic teleology? In effect, the figure of the noble savage conveys the impossible, paradoxical task of incorporating a people to Christianity *without* history.

The italics in *without* highlight an amphibology: the word signals the coexistence of an outside of history and an absence of history. This concept is paradoxical because it constitutes a critique of history as understood by the universal vocation of Roman Catholicism at the same time that it promotes that vocation. The *Apologética*'s main objective is to defend Amerindian cultures from the defamation they incurred in European discourses that justified the invasion of the Americas. Accordingly, Las Casas interprets the seemingly indefensible practices of human sacrifice and anthropophagy as proof of deep religiosity. While compiling the *Apologética historia sumaria*, he collects and reviews information pertaining to all known New World cultures. In a similar spirit to the one already manifest in the *Brevísima relación de la destrucción de las Indias*, Las Casas underscores that all native cultures participate in the same ideality. Thus, he dismantles the ever-recurring split between good and bad Indians, first instituted by Columbus's invention of the cannibal in his *Diario,* a text Las Casas knew well. The *Apologética*, then, does not provide a narrative, nor does it inscribe native cultures within a Christian historical paradigm; rather, it undoes all possible locations of native cultures within a historicist model. Las Casas expresses no desire to understand degrees of cultural sophistication as evidence of a preparation for the reception of the Gospel. In exemplifying savage Christian virtue, nomadic peoples partake of the same ideality as the representatives of urban centers in Mesoamerica and the Andes.

The following passage from the *Apologética* expresses a state of natural virtue in which physiology becomes a mirror of the soul:

> Así que, pues como todos los moradores destas Indias, . . . sean de buenos aspectos y acatamientos, de hermosas caras y proporcionados miembros y cuerpos, y esto desde su nacimiento . . . síguese haberles Dios y la naturaleza dotado y concedido nobles animas naturalmente, y así ser bien razonables y de buenos entendimientos.   (1: 179; ch. 34)

> Consequently, since all the inhabitants of this Indies . . . are of good appearance and composure, of beautiful faces and proportioned parts and bodies since birth . . . it follows that God and nature gave and endowed them with noble souls that make them very reasonable and of good understanding.[2]

The criteria listed in this passage are the same ones Las Casas chose to highlight when selecting direct quotations from Columbus for a summary of the explorer's *Diario*, but Las Casas generalizes Columbus's portrayal of the Lucayos to all the peoples in the Americas. The description of naturally virtuous peoples, gifted with reason and understanding, would lend further credibility to his argument in *De unico vocationis modo omnium gentium ad veram religionem* (c. 1534) that reason and love were the only acceptable modes of attracting people to Christianity.

Edmundo O'Gorman, in his *Fundamentos de la historia de América*, locates Las Casas's treatise as a transitional moment between medieval scholasticism and Descartes's *Metaphysical Meditations*. I do not have the space here to do justice to O'Gorman's argument, so I limit myself to underscoring O'Gorman's point that the task of converting infidels through the use of reason alone would be potentially endless, if not impossible; given the revealed nature of Christian truth, the exchanges between Indians and missionaries could lead to logical impasses and differends.[3] O'Gorman poses a similarity between the provisory ethics that Descartes assumes while doubting the existence of self and world and the cultural limbo that Las Casas would need to account for in the transit to Christianity (59–60). We must insist, however, on a radical difference between Las Casas and Descartes; whereas for Descartes it is the thinker himself who doubts and assumes a provisional morality, Las Casas never doubts that reason is the only mode of conversion. Indeed, since Amerindians live naturally virtuous lives, one cannot but assume that they would continue to live according to their cultural values and institutions. However, there is more to Las Casas's call for reason and to his concept of naturally moral noble savages: to be consistent, Las Casas must be dialogical—that is, open to a critique of forms of rationality in Western discourse—in his conversations with Native Americans. Contrary to what some misleadingly claim, Las Casas's use of reason does not mean that his main contribution in the history of human rights is the argument that Native Americans are educable races.[4] Las Casas's articulation of love and reason as the only acceptable forms of conversion presupposes that Native Americans have the full use of reason and do not merely partake of a proto-Western rationality.

While the primitivism of Las Casas's Amerindians suggests potential ideal Christian subjects, the *Apologética* does not define the figures of the noble savage and the paradisiacal natural garden in terms of a new Spanish social order. As discursive and rhetorical fictions, the noble savage and the natural garden dismantle the need of imposing a new order in the Americas. After all, how can one surpass a paradisiacal natural garden or, indeed, a noble savage that naturally embodies Christian ideals? Instead of evaluating the feasibility of political projects in Las Casas, we can explore with our students how to redefine the utopian dimension of these fictions in the *Apologética* with the following observation from Louis Marin's *Utopics: Spatial Play*:

When talking about the Perfect Island, the Lunar States, or the Austral Continent, utopia talks less about itself or the discourse it has on the island, moon, or lost continent than about the very possibility of uttering such discourse, of the status and contents of its enunciating position and the formal and material rules allowing it to produce some particular expression.   (10)

Let's add the noble savage and the natural garden to Marin's list of utopic practices and topoi: their inherent contradiction of terms (nature and culture coexist) encloses in their figural surface (thus, concealing and revealing at once) the rules and codes that produce them. Accordingly, the figures of the noble savage and the natural garden function as neutral terms that manifest the semantic field from which the opposition between nature and culture, civilization and savagery emerged in the first place—that is, the ideological underpinnings of a binary opposition.

If "noble" encompasses Christian and civilized ideals, which is certainly the meaning Las Casas intends when he applies the adjective to Amerindians (though we must not forget that apologists of conquests used this same term to characterize the natives as savages or barbarians), the figure of the noble savage cancels the opposition between nobility and savagery while prompting a fetishistic reification. Such a reification becomes evident if we consider that "noble" (insofar as *limpieza de sangre* [supposed "cleanliness of blood"] is a condition of "nobility"), in sixteenth-century Spain, refers to the *cristianos viejos* (the "old," nonsavage—i.e., not recently converted—Christians) in opposition to *conversos* (nonnoble—i.e., not old—Christians); thus, in this respect, the reference to Amerindians as noble savages retains the same values of the distinction it sets out to critique in the first place—the "savages," because of their recent conversion, are nonnoble. At face value, *noble savage* is a contradiction of terms and works against itself. It can also work in the other direction, with the assumption that "savages" in their poverty might truly incarnate the ideals of Christianity better than nominal (old) Christians. This last possible shift, however, lends itself to endless squabbles over the proper meaning of what is a true Christian. This antinomy—that is, the infinite polemics of the term *noble savage*—undoes authoritative univocal meanings, another characteristic of Marin's utopic practices.[5]

As I read him, Las Casas is not so much attempting to substitute the description of a barbarian with that of an empirical ideal primitive existing in some unproblematic way in the Americas. Rather, he seeks to show that even though the term *barbarian* does not have a corresponding referent, it proves a powerful device that produces juridical and anthropological statements and constitutes others in terms of political, economic, linguistic, and cultural deficiencies. The noble savage, then, would not be the opposite of a barbarian but rather would mark the passage away from a concept of civilization and barbarism as a binary opposition by including a double negation: "noncivilization" (savage) and "nonbarbarism" (noble). The figures of the noble savage and the natural garden are rhetorical devices that dismantle the possibility of predicating the need of imposing a new order on the Americas. In so doing, they expose the semantics with which the "West" presents itself as a universal cultural model and relegates other cultures to being merely "the rest."

In this essay, I have outlined the elements for guiding a reading of the *Apologética* as a utopian discourse that complicates the commonplace that considers Las Casas's idealizations of Amerindians to be as detrimental as those discourses that reduce them to savagery. My definition of the natural garden and the noble savage seeks to avoid readings that view these figures as if they were empirical descriptions. Nevertheless, the prevalence of these readings suggests that Las Casas falls prey to and is a powerful example of Marin's thesis: "Utopia is an ideological critique of ideology" (195). It is no wonder that we end up snarled in Las Casas's ideological fictions when we insist on taking them at face value. We may ask if we are ever free of ideology, especially when elaborating figures that, because of their imaginary nature, lend themselves to reductive meanings. The dream of an ideology-free version of the social sciences that Marin still entertained in the 1970s when he wrote *Utopics* might seem to us a scientific ideological contrivance that no longer seduces us. We should perhaps instead practice an ethos of historical difference, in the spirit of Michel de Certeau's heterologies. To my mind, this lesson is the most important one we can derive from Las Casas's practices of utopian discourse in the *Apologética*.

NOTES

Citations of Las Casas's *Apologetica historia sumaria* refer to the version edited by Edmundo O'Gorman (U Nacional Autónoma de Mexico, 1967).

[1] In reading the past, we are haunted by the fallacies of presentism and finalism. Whereas presentism assumes that a model or a concept has a parallel meaning in the past, finalism finds prefigurations of the present in the past. There is a difference between finding present meanings in the past (presentism) or tracing in the past the kernel of the present (finalism); and sustaining a mutually enlightening dialogue rather than using the past to reinforce existing beliefs retains historical difference and opens the future to new possibilities. In reading Las Casas, we should not further redefine his utopian ethnology by taking for granted the "truths" of modern anthropology and, consequently, projecting them into the past. Johannes Fabian has diagnosed an eventual dissolution of anthropology's colonial legacy that sums up well the critical position that Las Casas had already envisioned in the *Apologética* at the beginning of modernity: "Little more than technology and sheer exploitation seem to be left over for the purpose of 'explaining' Western superiority. It has become foreseeable that even those prerogatives may either disappear or no longer be claimed. There remains 'only' the all-pervading denial of co-evalness, which ultimately is expressive of a cosmological myth of frightening magnitude and persistency. It takes imagination and courage to picture what would happen to the

West (and to anthropology) if its temporal fortress were suddenly invaded by the Time of the Other" (35).

² All translations are mine unless otherwise indicated.

³ I posit the missionary-Indian exchanges as possibly ending in a differend because they involve an infinite process of translation in the going back and forth between languages and life structures with radically different backgrounds (namely, those of sixteenth-century Spain and Mesoamerica). By "background" I understand the absolute presupposition from which and against which a given culture makes sense of the world. I owe this definition of background to Ankersmit (164). On the concept of the differend, see Lyotard.

⁴ Anthony Pagden makes this claim about Las Casas in *The Fall of Natural Man*, stating that the Dominican believed that "[j]ust as the child is taught by his elders to understand the physical and moral world in which he is to live, so too entire races of men may be taught by those who have reached a higher level of civility than they" (143).

⁵ For an analysis of the noble savage theme as fetish, see Hayden White ("Noble Savage"). On antinomies and infinite polemics, see Marin 3–28.

Teaching *De unico vocationis modo*: The Maternal Discourse of Bartolomé de Las Casas

Song No

Students reading *De unico vocationis modo* (originally written in Latin) will first notice the striking contrast between its eloquent persuasions and the vehement denunciations in the *Brevísima relación de la destrucción de las Indias* and *Historia de las Indias*. *De unico vocationis modo* lays a theoretical foundation for the rest of Las Casas's works, and one may summarize its basic theme with Christ's words, "Go ye into all the world and preach the gospel to every creature" (*Holy Bible*, Mark 16.15). Faithfully following the words that guide the Christian dogma, the Dominican priest explains how to convert Indians to Catholicism: urge them gently, kindly, yet persistently.

Opposed as he was to the rampant violence used by Spanish conquistadors and colonialists, Las Casas uniquely and audaciously insists on a humane spiritual conquest. Even though the forceful occupation and the humanist evangelization worked toward the same result—namely, Spanish domination—it is important for students to understand different uses of hegemonic power: strict compulsory subjugation versus moderate voluntary assimilation. From this understanding, students learn that the Christianization of Latin America was a complex process and that the interaction between European missionaries and Amerindians was sometimes reciprocal, with less "coercive conversion" than "persuasive conversation" (Griffiths 7). Inga Clendinnen employs the term "paternalist metaphor of authority" to describe the sixteenth-century Franciscan missionaries' confidence in the use of physical coercion and austere chastisement ("Disciplining" 41), a model in which Indians were treated as children who needed caring fathers' guidance and discipline.[1] To highlight the difference in Las Casas's approach, I use the term "maternalist metaphor of nonviolence" to describe his advocacy in *De unico vocationis modo* of evangelization through insistent persuasion without the use of corporal punishment.

Rather than frame the study of *De unico vocationis modo* in strictly religious terms, I encourage a rhetorical and ideological reading that sprouts from a feminist or gendered angle. Since the text endorses only the nonviolent Christianization of Indians, students benefit by considering it alongside Sara Ruddick's arguments in *Maternal Thinking: Toward a Politics of Peace* (1989). Ruddick argues that maternal thinking originates from maternal practice that responds to three major demands—for "preservation, growth and social acceptability" (17)—and she demonstrates the practical and concrete usefulness of its strategies of maternal nonviolence (160–84).[2] She argues that mothers generally rely on nonviolent ideals and tactics (161–65) and that this can be a model for the development of "peace politics" as an alternative to the destructiveness of war (12).[3] In *De unico vocationis modo*, Las Casas's insistence on peaceful evangelization bears close resemblance to the nonviolent approach Ruddick describes. At the same time, Las Casas's use of the maternal discourse of nonviolence must be analyzed within the historical context of the Spanish conquest and colonization. In advocating that New World Indians be Christianized through maternal persistence and nonviolent persuasion alone, Las Casas merely modifies the imperialist hegemony of Spain over Latin America. His maternal discourse structures the parameters of parent-mother versus children—that is, Spanish evangelizers versus Indians—within the already established sociopolitical hierarchy of Spanish colonization[4] (a good example of the text's use of hegemonic discourses other than the authoritarian and militaristic imposition of power).

De unico vocationis modo stands out among all Las Casas's writings for its distinctive attempt to offer practical methods for communicating with the other—namely, non-European people. The text shows Las Casas developing his ideological basis, while the rest of his works elaborate his humanist thought and pacifist stance.

De unico vocationis modo is recognized as Las Casas's first writing, but one cannot know the exact dates he began and finished composing the text. Lascasian scholars have offered different speculations but share one conclusion: the book was not written before 1522, the year Las Casas entered the Dominican order. Lewis Hanke first proposes that it may have been written in 1536 and 1537 (Introducción 22),[5] but later, when he collaborates with Manuel Giménez Fernández, the two scholars argue that it must have been composed between 1522 and 1534 (Hanke and Giménez Fernández 50). Other historians have speculated on the dates as well: Marcel Bataillon thinks it was produced between 1535 and 1536 (*Estudios* 181); Manuel Martínez insists that Las Casas must have created it during his stay at the convent of Santo Domingo on the island of Hispaniola between 1522 and 1527 (154); José Vargas shares Martínez's speculation (144); Isacio Pérez Fernández disagrees slightly and suggests between 1522 and 1526 ("Sobre la fecha," *Cronología documentada* 142–43); André Saint-Lu loosely speculates that it was written in Hispaniola around 1530 ("Fray Bartolomé de las Casas" 118). From these conjectures one can make the following assertions: that Las Casas started composing *De unico vocationis modo* after officially becoming part of the Dominican order in 1522; that he completed it before 1537 and kept reediting it; and that it was never published in his lifetime. He makes numerous references to the book in *Historia de las Indias, Apologética historia sumaria*, and other works (Barreda ii).[6]

Unfortunately, we do not know what happened to Las Casas's manuscript of *De unico vocationis modo* after his death. In *Historia general de las Indias Occidentales*, Antonio Remesal states the precise title of the work and offers his own summary of the text. Remesal speaks of four existing copies of *De unico vocationis modo*: one in his own possession; one in Valladolid, at the Colegio de San Gregorio; one in New Spain (what is now Mexico); and one in Guatemala, belonging to Antonio Prieto de Villegas (2: 370).[7] Among these copies, only the one in New Spain has survived; it is currently located in the Public Library of Oaxaca (León 177). This copy was translated into Spanish by Antenógenes Santamaría in 1942 (Casas, *Del único modo*). In 1990, Marianne Mahn-Lot partially translated the Spanish version into French (Casas, *De l'unique manière*), and a bilingual version in Latin and Spanish is available as part of Las Casas's *Obras completas*. An English translation entitled *The Only Way* was published in 1992 with some textual rearrangements—additions and omissions of material. Its translator, Francis P. Sullivan, justifies his restructuring of the text, and while his English version reads coherently and succinctly and will help students understand the logical organization and content of the material, it dilutes the work's rhetorical richness and is not suitable for studying Las Casas's different uses of discourse.

Las Casas's text can be divided into three sections according to theme: the indigenous people's rational ability to accept Christianity (chs. 1 through 4); nonviolence as the only moral method of evangelization (ch. 5); the immoral way—using force—to preach the Gospel (chs. 6 and 7). Only three chapters of the first book—chapters 5, 6, and 7—remain in the Oaxacan manuscript. Chapter 5 contains thirty-six long paragraphs; chapter 6, eight paragraphs; and chapter 7, six paragraphs. What happened to the previous four chapters is unknown, and it is not certain that he ever wrote the second book. In the last chapter, Las Casas leaves the book number blank, implying that he may have written more than one book. At the very least, he plans to write a second book: five times in *De unico vocationis modo* he promises to develop certain topics further in "next book" or "the second book" (317, 475, 493, 513, and 567). The most significant statement about this second part appears in Las Casas's last book, *Los tesoros del Perú* (*De thesauris*, originally written in Latin), dated 1563. Commenting on the Spanish king's jurisdiction over the indigenous, Las Casas refers to the second book of *De unico vocationis modo* (*Los tesoros* 387). The second part of *De unico vocationis modo* has never been found, and thus the question of its existence remains unanswered.

Chapters 1 through 4

The four chapters missing in the Oaxacan manuscript of *De unico vocationis modo* are briefly summarized in the preamble of the fifth chapter. They are dedicated to explaining that all the peoples on the face of the earth have been called by God to receive the faith as "the free gift of divine grace"—that while human beings are different, one from another, in every part of the world, it is simply impossible that any race or nation lacks the rational capacity to accept the Christian faith (63–64).[8] This affirmation clearly includes the indigenous peoples of the New World, whose gift of exceptional understanding is evident in their achievements in "the liberal and allied arts" (65). Enrique Dussel deems this first example of Las Casas's humanism his "symbolic nucleus" and underlines the importance of the fact that the Dominican's idealism starts from respect and positive affirmation of the other, avoiding any sort of alienation or violation. ("Núcleo simbólico" 14).

Chapter 5

This chapter is the most extensive and significant part of *The Only Way* and displays Las Casas's erudition through numerous quotations from the Old and New Testament. Students may feel overwhelmed by his use of biblical authorities, so instructors may need to point them to paragraphs 15 through 21 and to the Saint Paul references in paragraphs 23 to 29, which are significant for analysis of the text; Las Casas uses these biblical examples repeatedly to insist on and justify peaceful evangelization in America. Using the Scriptures, Las Casas explains ten basic points for the first mission of the Apostles in paragraphs 15 to 18, and for the second and universal mission in paragraph 19. Saint Paul mentions five crucial elements that constitute the method of preaching the Gospel according to Christ's command and intention: first, preachers should not exert power over people (non-Christians); second, preachers should not go after people's wealth; third, preachers should treat people with modesty and respect; fourth, preachers should show people charity through gentleness, patience, and kindness (*The Only Way* 103–06; *De unico vocationis modo* 247–57). The fifth comprises paragraphs 25 to 28; the gist of this method is that preachers should live the life of Christ not by words but by deeds: "a life visibly virtuous, a life that harms no one, a life blameless from any quarter" (*The Only Way* 108–16; *De unico vocationis modo* 259–97).

In this chapter, Las Casas places great stress on the literal sense of the Bible, using solely theological proofs instead of figurative and allegorical comments. He assumes a prophetic voice and declares that only peaceful evangelization should be allowed in missions in America. First, he provides a comprehensive justification of such evangelization, building a step-by-step argument to prove it the one effective and righteous method of sharing the Gospel. As Don Paul Abbot puts it, Las Casas essentially underlines that "it was rhetoric, rather than force, which forged human civilization" (64). In other words, Las Casas advocates peaceful persuasion because its role was important not only in the creation of European civilization but also in the ministry of Christ. To further support his position, he cites the bull *Sublimis Deus* of Pope Paul III (1537), which too affirms that the New World Indians were capable of receiving the Christian faith (Casas, *The Only Way* 39, 114–16). Las Casas believes that, before having faith, one needs to understand truth. Understanding is a voluntary act. According to the first section of this chapter, God created all people to love truth, so that everyone has an innate desire to understand truth and have faith (68–69).

Then, Las Casas demonstrates the way to bring people to the Christian faith voluntarily. The only method to preach the Gospel is by persuasion, "in a gentle, coaxing, gracious way" (*The Only Way* 68), "delicada, dulce y suavemente" in

Spanish, "blande, dulciter atque suaviter" in Latin (*De unico vocationis modo* 15–16). I call special attention to this expression because the author continuously repeats it in this chapter—at times using synonyms but always conveying analogous meaning. In addition to reiterating this phrase, Las Casas compares the peaceful evangelization with "parental encouragement," ("exhortación paternal"), which is peaceful, gentle, and pleasant (*De unico vocationis modo* 109, 111, 113, 115). The author gradually uses more expressions of nurturing parents and tries to present his method of gentle and peaceful preaching as being similar to tender maternal insistence.

Here, I encourage students to analyze different gendered discourses—for example, to contrast Las Casas's nurturing method with the authoritarian Spanish discourse of the conquistador. Two of the best examples are Bernardo de Vargas Machuca's *Milicia y descripción de las Indias* (1599) and his *Apología y discursos de las conquistas occidentales* (published in 1879). If the Spanish colonizers are considered to assume a strict father's role in the conquest of America, Las Casas adopts a caring mother's role.[9] The main purpose of these analogies is to demonstrate to students that there are many forms of hegemony. As Raymond Williams in his *Keywords* defines, hegemony is not limited to political control but encompasses a way of seeing the world, human nature, and relationships: "it is expressed over a range of institutions to relationships and consciousness" (145). In the practice of religious conversion, hegemonic power is essentially established by the distinction between "an imposing 'us' from a 'them' whose inferiority is undoubted, and whose destiny lies in their subordination and radical rupture from older understandings" (Mills and Grafton x). Working from this foundation of inclusion ("us") and exclusion ("them"), hegemonic power can be exerted in various ways. I remind students again that hegemony is not always manifested through a forceful or stern approach. Hegemony can be more fluid and fragile and even expressed or exposed in a gentle, caring, pleasant way. Although Las Casas would ultimately denounce the illegal domination of Spain in the New World, the purpose of *De unico vocationis modo* is to further the evangelization of the entire New World. In his mind, Spanish domination is a fact, and what initially troubles him is the use of violence to assimilate Indians to the Spanish culture. What differentiates his discourse from the violent colonizers' is the use of discourse diametrically opposed to patriarchal male discourse, especially his refusal to endorse forceful domination as an ultimate solution, even if his persuasive method fails.

My emphasis on discourse takes me to *Sex and Conquest*, in which Richard C. Trexler asserts that conquerors have discursively feminized the conquered throughout human history (31–34). Trexler analyzes the use of violence and gendered subordination—subjugating Indians by feminizing them—during the Spanish conquest of Latin America (64–74). Having fashioned for themselves a notion of hegemonic masculinity (e.g., civilized men [Europeans] versus barbarians [Indians]), Spanish conquistadors and colonizers considered Indians inferior (thus feminine) and felt justified using violence to conquer them.[10] In this forceful venture, Las Casas stands out for his controversial role: appropriating a maternal discourse of nonviolence and promoting the practice of an alternative hegemonic power. Las Casas's peaceful evangelization is coherent with his self-image as the caring and nurturing defender of Indians. Like Ruddick's maternal practice—in which mothers provide "preservative love, nurturance, and training" to children (17)—Las Casas's evangelization attempts to offer God's unconditional love and spiritual nourishment as well as religious training (catechism) to the indigenous people. However, the Dominican works for the propagation of Christianity on behalf of the Spanish empire and the Catholic church, and that makes him after all an agent of hegemonic power.

Chapters 6 and 7

After passionately promoting peaceful evangelization in the previous chapter, Las Casas condemns antithetical examples of his method in these two chapters. Chapter 6 is an explanation of why Christ chose a peaceful method to preach, and chapter 7 reiterates that forceful conversion is a moral sin. These parts of the text would seem to be the perfect place for the Dominican priest to denounce the actions of the Spanish colonizers. Nonetheless, he hardly refers to the New World Indians. Instead, Las Casas chooses the Moors and their cruel conversion techniques as exemplary adversaries of the peaceful evangelization he advocates (*The Only Way* 144–151; *De unico vocationis modo* 441–55).

Students will easily recognize this choice as a remarkable difference between this text and Las Casas's other works, particularly his *Brevísima relación*. I encourage students to suggest their own explanations for this contrast. I remind them that Las Casas probably had access to the manuscript of *De unico vocationis modo* until his death—if he had wanted to, he could have easily added a denunciation of the Spaniards, yet he did not. One of the harshest comments he makes in this chapter is, "May the war the Christians wage—those who vaunt the name of Christ—be not more vicious than the wars of the Mohammedans!" (*The Only Way* 147). One plausible explanation may be his desire to maintain consistency in the text; unlike Las Casas's historical writings, *De unico vocationis modo* not only offers a new method of evangelization but is also written in the same gentle manner he suggests. Any fervent denunciation would contradict the thesis and theories of this evangelical text.

De unico vocationis modo was the only text whose theory Las Casas successfully put into practice, in his Verapaz experiment in Guatemala between 1537 and 1547 (Saint-Lu, *La Vera Paz* 13).[11] Before his evangelization, the area was called Tezulutlán ("Land of War") supposedly because the opposition of unconquered Indians rendered it impossible to enter. Yet without violent evangelization, Las Casas and other Dominicans were able to partially control the region and convert to Christianity indigenous settlements of the region currently known as Alta Verapaz (Saint-Lu, *La Vera Paz* 173–86; Galmés 117–18). In his comprehensive study *La Vera Paz, esprit évangélique et colonisation*, André Saint-Lu explains the current controversy over how successful Las Casas was in Verapaz, especially surrounding the rivalry between the friar and the bishop of Guatemala, Francisco Marroquín. For example, Marroquín denounced what he described as Las Casas's pretensions, vanity, and hypocrisy in a letter to the Spanish emperor Charles V, dated 17 August 1545 (Saint-Lu, *La Vera Paz* 177). (Prince Philip [who later became King Philip II] responded to the letter without commenting on Marroquín's accusations.) Saint-Lu ultimately suggests that the success of Las Casas's Verapaz project was recognized by the Spanish court (178–79), and he concludes that the results of Las Casas's evangelization in the area were modest yet positive (*La Vera Paz* 450). Thus, *De unico vocationis modo* is not a mere theoretical treatise but holds practical value; instructors must contextualize it with historical events—Las Casas's experience in Verapaz in particular but his other utopian projects as well.

While Las Casas's later writings put tremendous effort into defending the indigenous populations and condemning European conquistadors, *De unico vocationis modo* proposes alternative methods of conquest and colonization. Las Casas is firmly against the use of violence by the Spanish but does not doubt that the spread of Christianity must continue in the New World, and in this way, his hegemonic voice takes a Janus-like duality: on the one hand, it perpetuates a patriarchal discourse to assure its rational and moral superiority over the conquered; on the other, it problematically uses a feminine, maternal discourse to criticize the use of military and physical force. Instructors will find that *De unico vocationis modo* has great pedagogical potential; at the same time students learn to comparatively analyze the critical use of patriarchal and maternal impositions of hegemonic power over the other, they also gain a complex picture of discursive practices during the European colonization of Latin America.

NOTES

[1] Among the colonial texts Clendinnen analyzes, a document on the *junta eclesiástica* of 1539 stands out (Clendinnen 30; García Icazbalceta and Aguayo Spencer 149–84). The document officially approved the use of corporal punishment on Indians and justified this forceful treatment as "appropriate to the master with his apprentice or the teacher with the person in his charge" (qtd. in Clendinnen, "Disciplining" 30).

[2] Ruddick also regards Gandhi's philosophy of nonviolence as an effective model to work out an understanding of political action that gives consideration to peace, morality, and sexuality (160–84). To help students understand Ruddick's *Maternal Thinking* better, I draw from background readings of feminist interpretation on motherhood and maternal discourse as well, especially Adrienne Rich's *Of Woman Born* (1976), an invitation to consider the distinction between motherhood as universal experience of women and as patriarchal institution; Nancy Chodorow's *The Reproduction of Mothering* (1978), which explores the sociological and psychological concepts of gender identification;

Carol Gilligan's *In a Different Voice* (1982), an assessment of why women make moral decisions differently than do men (a man considers his own rights and noninterference with the rights of others to be most important, whereas a woman gives greater weight to interdependence and the balancing of conflicting responsibilities); and Nancy Hartsock's *Money, Sex, and Power* (1983), a philosophical exploration of power not as domination over others but as the ability to "act in concert" with others.

³ Ruddick avoids sweeping generalizations of maternal nonviolence, and she meticulously studies counterexamples of her claims (i.e., violent mothers [163]).

⁴ Here I have modified the ideas of Marcia Stephenson's *Gender and Modernity in Andean Bolivia* (1999). Stephenson studies "social maternity" in Bolivia in the 1930s and 1940s, a time when upper-class women, taking advantage of woman's "natural" condition of maternity, formed organizations on behalf of working-class women (28).

⁵ Hanke suggests the year of its completion as 1537 because the Spanish edition he uses includes references to Pope Paul III's *Sublimis Deus*, dated June 1537 (Introducción 22).

⁶ In his last known writing, "Petition to His Holiness" ("Petición a Su Santidad"), just before his death in 1566, Las Casas asks Pope Pius V permission to publish *De unico vocationis modo* (Hanke, Introducción 22). This attempt was not successful, but it reveals the persistence of his desire to publish the work, by then some 30 years old (Hanke, Introducción 22–23).

⁷ Agustín Dávila Padilla, author of *Historia de la fundación y discurso de la provincia de Santiago de México* in 1596, may be the first one who indicated that copies of *De unico vocationis modo* existed in both Latin and Spanish (387; bk. 1, ch. 98).

⁸ All translations of the text are mine unless otherwise noted. This particular section is omitted from Sullivan's translation. Other omissions are paragraphs 18, 23, and 26 through 33.

⁹ George Lakoff's *Moral Politics*, for example, makes this point clearer and relates *De unico vocationis modo* to our contemporary North American scene. From his extensive analysis of current United States politics, Lakoff concludes that Republicans and Democrats take advantage of completely distinctive discursive modes. Republicans tend to use "the Strict Father" role, whereas Democrats insist on "the Nurturing Parent/Mother" model (15).

¹⁰ Robert W. Connell explains that hegemonic masculinity is the strategy for global and transhistorical domination of women by men (*Gender and Power* 183). He elaborates on this definition as follows: "hegemonic masculinity can be defined as the configuration of gender practice which embodies the currently accepted answer to the problem of the legitimacy of patriarchy, which guarantees (or is taken to guarantee) the dominant position of men and the subordination of women" (*Masculinities* 77). Despite inconsistencies, hegemonic masculinity is "always constructed in relation to various subordinate masculinities as well as in relation to women. In this way, it generates dominance not only over women but also over subordinate masculinities (*Gender and Power* 183).

¹¹ Saint-Lu dates the starting point of Las Casas's Verapaz project as 1537 and the ending as 1547, when Las Casas returned to Spain permanently (*La Vera Paz* 15, 180). However, the Dominican remained well informed about the project and continuously worked to promote peace in the region until his death in 1566 (191–222). Las Casas formally resigned his position as bishop of Chiapas in 1550 (Pérez Fernández, *Cronología documentada* 788).

Teaching Restitution: Las Casas, the *Rules for Confessors*, and the Politics of Repayment

Regina Harrison

Bartolomé de Las Casas's *Rules for Confessors* (*Reglas para confesores*) pales next to the pixilated confessants threatening to tell all on *Jerry Springer*, is less than compelling when compared to the cleavage of the confessants on *Oprah*, and often loses out to the dramatic claustrophobic interrogation room show-cased on the gritty *Homicide* series. However, carefully inserted in my honors course, True Confessions: Literature, Film, Video, Las Casas's text provides a bridge from the origins of confession to its role today. The *Rules for Confessors*, discreetly written by Las Casas to guide Dominican priests who were entrusted with absolving penitents in the Indies, presents Las Casas's knowledge of theology and law within the domain of confession. This document published in 1552, although not easily skimmed, presents students with economic, legal, and feminist themes that extend well beyond the confines of the sixteenth century.

Confession and Restitution

As a sacrament, confession was key in denoting the conversion of the native peoples in the Americas to Christianity, just as much as it was seen to demonstrate the Christian faith of the converted peasants in Europe. For the Christian believers, the Fourth Lateran Council in 1215 decreed that all Christians must examine their conscience, appear before a priest, and orally declare their wrongdoings. The Easter season was the preferred time for this annual confession, although some penitents confessed more frequently throughout the year. For the last confession in one's life, the priest was summoned, and often the process of absolution was performed at the deathbed. Guided by the priest's trained interrogation into sin, the confessant was expected to contritely spin out a narrative that would lead to a purified state of the soul.

Just as important, at the moment of the last confession, another figure loomed at the bedside—the notary, who arrived for the dictation of the will, if there was not one previously written. Thus, theological doctrine was conjoined with economic principles when, in confession, the spiritual estate was assessed along with material possessions. So important was the act of creating a will that burial was denied to those who did not write out specific directives. Often, composing a will became an act of penance itself, a form of confession:

> At the end of one's life, even after one had departed from this world, when others read the will—or, more likely, had it read to them—one could confess one's faith, acknowledge one's sins, and attempt to redeem them by making certain statements and arranging for certain liturgies and public gestures. (Eire 23)

This selected narration of a life lived, sins accomplished or contemplated, also included memory of wrongs to be righted. The concept of restitution, a prerequisite to absolution of sin, is central to the sacrament of confession. Specifically, restitution is defined with moral purpose as "an act of commutative justice by which exact reparation as far as possible is made for an injury which has been done to another" (Slater). Whether in the annual confession or in the last rites of death, making amends was primary for forgiveness from sin. From the time of the Middle Ages, for instance, wealthy merchants commonly designated certain monies in their wills to alleviate possible injustice to injured parties, administered by priests (Friede, "Las Casas and Indigenism" 224).

Las Casas penned his own thoughts on confession in 1544–46. Not a confession manual, which is often based on permutations of the Ten Commandments, his *Rules for Confessors* is primarily a commentary on the topic of restitution. Originally in manuscript, the *Rules* circulated among a select few of the religious, yet caused great turmoil. The *Rules* were written in the era of the proclamation of the New Laws of 1542–43, which were drawn up to prohibit the practice of *encomienda* for more than two lives (the conquistador and his family). Hotly contested by the conquistadors, who believed that they had fought bravely for the right to inherit these benefits, the Crown yielded and revoked the Law of Inheritance (1545), the most controversial of the New Laws. Stirred to action by this "backslide" in legislation, Las Casas urged the religious to take a stronger stand—to be guided by his *Rules for Confessors* and refuse absolution to conquistadors, *encomenderos*, and merchants who had obtained and retained wealth based on unjust wars with the Amerindian native peoples.

Before plunging into the Las Casas text, my students read Peter Brooks's "Confession, Selfhood, and the Religious Tradition" (*Troubling Confessions* 88–113), which historicizes the sacrament of confession, explaining its role in the practice of educating the local populace through sermons, along with the writing of confession manuals to train the priests. The most useful text of the *Rules* is translated and abridged by Francis Patrick Sullivan (281–89). The more abbreviated selections by George Sanderlin also could be adapted to encourage student reading of primary sources (Casas, *Bartolomé de las Casas*). Both authors draw upon the Spanish texts in the Biblioteca de Autores Españoles 110 for their English versions ("Aquí se contienen"). Before students read the texts, necessary background has to be introduced: the nature of the grant of *encomienda*, an explanation of the debates regarding the "just" war of conquest, and the theory of slavery in the era of the Spanish conquests and settlement of the Americas.

Study sheets referring to Sullivan's translation of the *Rules* focus on the all-important role of the confessor:

> Which penitents are especially singled out for the confessor's examination? Why?
> For absolution of sins, is it enough to call a priest to the side of the dying penitent?

Who else must appear there? Who is granted power of attorney?
When does Las Casas stipulate that confession should begin?

Further discussion centers on the disposal of material goods accumulated in
the New World territories. Wills usually provide for the family of the deceased.
However, Las Casas specifies patterns of inheritance for poor as well as wealthy
confessants, as seen in the guided questions for the study sheet:

What budget does Las Casas prescribe?
What dowry provisions are made?
How are husband and wife's assets managed, if one spouse survives the
other?
In cases of slaveholders, what is suggested?

Sullivan's abbreviated translation offers a more spirited entry into what could
be a dull six pages. While primary sources are often tough going for undergraduates, my use of marginal numbering and question marks on the course pack
pages guides the reading. Students are expected to come to class with reasons
for my attention to the marked passages or further questions about them.

The text they read has interrogator indicators placed in the margins, with
these items: the conquistador as one of three categories of offending parties;
the call for a notary before confession; confessor has complete power over all
matters; admission that the conquistador took part in the conquest; admission
that all accumulated wealth comes from the natives; granting freedom to slaves
immediately; revoking any previous wills; a solemn oath that the confessor may
determine the future of all material goods, nothing excepted; signing the will
and then confessing.

The following issues regarding disposal of goods and restitution to those
harmed are noted in the remainder of the text: there was no authorization from
the king for what the Spaniards did, only insatiable greed; penitents' sons may
be left penniless or on a modest budget if the confessor so decides; even if the
confessant recovers and does not die, he still has to pay; the sixth rule: whether
rich or poor, if the confessant is living off the labor of Indians, he must be placed
on a modest budget, even in regard to dowries for his daughters; the eighth
rule: the confessant must not resist an order from the king; the ninth rule: if
the penitent owns Indian slaves, he must buy back any he has sold, must free
them all, and if he has no resources, he must become a slave; the tenth rule:
husband's assets and wife's assets and disposal of them; role of merchants in
the wars; acknowledgment that the penitent will not participate in future wars
against the natives.

The points above are nicely supplemented with discussion of the Spanish
legislation of the New Laws in 1542–43; the uproar that ensued, especially in
the viceroyalty of Perú when *encomenderos* rebelled against the Crown; the
Crown's decision to revoke the Law of Inheritance in 1545; and Las Casas's

upcoming debate with Juan Ginés de Sepúlveda over the concept of a "just war" (1550–51).

Of particular importance is discussion of the patterns of inheritance and property laws affecting women in the colonial period, alluded to in the tenth rule. Kimberly Gauderman's *Women's Lives in Colonial Quito* (2003) cautions against envisioning the Spanish colonies as an entirely patriarchal society. Based on Visigoth, Roman, and canonical precepts, Castilian private law upheld female property rights declared at the marriage: "At the beginning of the sixteenth century and throughout the seventeenth, Spanish women owned, bequeathed, and inherited property on their own account." The notarized value of the dowry and the *arras* (a gift given by the groom, limited to ten percent of his worth at the time of the marriage) remained part of the bride's private estate, although her husband administered it. In the event the marriage ended—through death, annulment, or divorce—the husband was obliged legally to return the dowry to his wife or to her heirs (33). Even community property, jointly acquired during marriage, was divided equally among the separate estates when the marriage ended (40). Las Casas's careful wording in the tenth rule respects the legal aspects of the woman's inheritance and estate decisions that may be separate from those of her husband.

Restitution and Restoration: Colonial and Contemporary Contexts

The *Rules for Confessors* is a major introduction to the problematic colonization of the Americas. The results of the Lascasian call to conscience, however, are documented in few testamentary sources. Some light on its Andean reception is shed by Thomas Abercrombie's and Guillermo Lohmann Villena's searches of the archived texts of the period following Las Casas's distribution and publication of his *Rules*. In one example, we find that Diego de Aguero's son decided that his father, the conquistador, was in arrears for four thousand pesos from excess tribute collected from his *encomienda* Indians. He thus ordered that four hundred pesos in gold be distributed to hospitals in Lima, Cuzco, and Trujillo in restitution (Lohmann Villena 60). Another conquistador, Lorenzo de Aldana, unmarried and childless, left all the benefits of his extensive holdings to the Indians of Arequipa (39). Abercrombie's search in the Andean archives reveals the numerous examples of restitution written in recognition of the Spanish ill-gotten gains (260).

The question of the *encomiendas*, confession, and restitution remain intertwined until the end of Las Casas's life. One of the most compelling tales of restitution is closely linked to Las Casas's project of restoration of the Indies to indigenous control. Scarce years after the publication of the *Rules* in 1552, the bishop of Chiapas acted to thwart the millions of gold ducats that Andean *encomenderos* offered to the Crown to obtain permanent rights to Andean *encomiendas*. Las Casas and an Andean-based Dominican (Domingo de Santo Tomás) were granted power of attorney in 1560 by Andean Indians and presented the Crown with a counteroffer of one hundred thousand Castilian ducats, more than the sum offered by the *encomenderos* (Casas, "Joint Memorial" 328). If this were not sufficient, the natives agreed to pay two million more over a period of four years. The joint "Memorial" (1560) to Philip II written by the two Dominicans revisits the unwise granting of perpetuity of holdings, urging instead that Indians would be better off held by the Crown, paying tribute directly to the royal coffers, with rights to regain those indigenous common fields usurped by the Spaniards (329–31).

Knowledge of indigenous (Inca) customs is evident in the 1560 "Memorial" document. Although Las Casas had never traveled in the Andes and had rejected the bishopric of Cuzco for that of Chiapas in the 1540s, he was well informed by the Quechua-speaking Domingo de Santo Tomás. The two Dominicans mention excessive tribute required by the *encomenderos* and advocate for adjustment of tribute in times of hardship, a realignment of lands back to the manner in which they were held under the Incas, consultation with Indian delegates regarding matters of governance, restoration of privileges to principal rulers, and prohibitions against the taking of land and water rights from a community of Indians or from Indian individuals (330–31).

Although the dream of restoration of the Incan empire did not come about in the Andes, Las Casas and Santo Tomás did manage to slow down the sale of the *encomiendas*. An investigatory commission, sent over from Spain and active in Perú in 1560–61, eventually recommended a three-part solution in contrast to the monetary offers from the Spanish landholders and the indigenous lords. Some perpetual *encomiendas* would be set aside for the first conquistadors, some would be designated for one lifetime only, and some holdings would revert to the Crown (Wagner and Parish 220).

It might appear that the issue had been settled and required no further comment, yet Las Casas in his eighties wrote definitive treatises on conscience and restitution. The opening commentary in his "Doce Dudas" ("Twelve Problems" [1564]) concerns "al bien de las conciencias de los reyes de Castilla y León y a las de los españoles que viven y vivirán en las Indias" 'the welfare of the consciences of the Kings of Castille and León and of the Spaniards living now and in the future in the Indies' ("Tratado de las doce dudas" 478; qtd. in Wagner and Parish 233). Indeed, the situation in the viceroyalty of Perú—the invasion and the subjugation of the native peoples—provoked an examination of conscience and a plea for guidance on these matters. Las Casas wrote the "Doce Dudas" in response to the Andean complexity, yet his reasoning was applicable to all the Spanish colonies. As might be expected, he reiterates his anti-*encomienda* perspective as well as his comments on the illegality of the conquest. As Rolena Adorno states, "Las Casas presented his Latin treatise and its Castilian sequel to Philip as his last will and codicil, in other words, as his enduring and final gift to the King" ("Colonial Reform" 350). Convincingly, in this document Las Casas also writes down his most extensive argument regarding restitution, according to Wagner and Parish "to a point almost entirely impossible of realization" (234).

In this tract of 1564, in response to twelve interrogatory cases of restitution, Las Casas still has faith in the power of the confessional. His solution to each query firmly assigns guilt to each person who stole Inca treasure, collected tribute, was paid for their services with ill-gotten *encomendero* tribute, derived riches from the mines, plundered ancient tombs and offering sites, or lived in Incan lands and houses. Every single guilty person was to offer restitution, including the Spanish sovereigns. Restitution could be accomplished gradually, but the envisaged result was the restoration of authority of the Inca rulers over their lands and peoples. Yet, in this grand scheme, even Las Casas admitted that full restitution would require the return of an overwhelming sum of gold and silver, a nearly impossible task:

> Pueden ser persuadidos por los religiosos que perdonen por su libre voluntad la hacienda que a los reyes de Castilla han traído y habido de las Indias, porque sería cosa dificultosa volver y restituir allá tantos navíos de oro y plata como han venido a España; y dándoles a entender cómo de aquí adelante será parte de la restitución lo poco que llevarán los dichos reyes de España, aunque lo que han de llevar ha de quedar señalado y concertado.   ("Tratado de las doce dudas" 535)

> The Indians can be persuaded by the religious not to ask back the treasure taken from the Andes and kept by the Kings of Castile, and it can be a free act on their part. The difficulty would be extreme of hauling back there and handing over all those boatloads of gold and silver that went to Spain. And the Indians can be given to understand that from this point onwards the small amount the Kings of Spain do return should be considered restitution and though small what they return, it is nonetheless significant and intended.   ("Twelve Problems" 351)

At the close of his life, Las Casas followed his own rules and conceived of a last will and testament that bleakly summarizes Spain's involvement in the Indies:

> [C]reo que por estas impías y celerosas e ignominiosas obras, tan injusta, tiránica y barbáricamente hechos en ellas y contra ellas, Dios ha de derramar sobre España su furor e ira, porque toda ella ha comunicado y participado poco que mucho en las sangrientas riquezas robadas y tan ursapadas y mal habidas, y con tantos estragos e acabamientos de aquellas gentes, si gran penitencia no hiciere, y temo que tarde o nunca la hará. . . .
> ("Cláusula" 540)

And I think that God shall have to pour out his fury and anger on Spain for these rotten, infamous deeds done so unjustly, so tyrannically, so barbarously to those people, against those people. For the whole of Spain has shared in the blood-soaked riches, some a little, some a lot, but all share in goods that were ill-gotten, wickedly taken with violence and genocide[1] . . . and all must pay unless Spain does a mighty penance.   ("Last Will" 359)

This module on Las Casas is a three-week assignment in the honors seminar, interspersed with Brooks's commentary on the confessional and leading to his discussion on confession and the law. As students begin to understand the role of the church, the priest's vow of silence, and the means by which penance reintegrates the sinner to society in Christian ritual, additional non-Western confession practices are introduced based on my studies of Incan and Spanish cultural confrontation. How are the concepts of sin, examination of conscience, and penance conveyed in Quechua, the indigenous Andean language? Which Andean Indian sources provide commentary on conversion? Felipe Guaman Poma's explanation of confession often gets mired in these definitions of faith, as seen in my studies in cultural translation (Harrison, "Cultural Translation," "Theology").

Further relevance of Las Casas's texts is seen in the global context of restitution, this time in a contemporary setting, given the tasks of the truth and reconciliation commissions assembled in response to human rights violations all over the world. In East Timor, South Africa, South Korea, Germany, Perú, Morocco, Chile, and Greensboro (North Carolina), victims who had been wronged clamored for restitution in front of the commissions (*Truth Commissions*). To understand better the ramifications of Lascasian ideology regarding restitution, students are assigned Internet research about a specific country. Their task is to write a one-page evaluative report on the usefulness of the Web sites, which helps sharpen their evaluation of numerous sites. So, for instance, researching a lawsuit for restitution brought against a multinational company that profited during the regime of the South African apartheid government, the students remembered Las Casas's scathing indictment of the merchants who profited from the conquest of the Americas. Although centuries later, the guidelines set by Las Casas still apply to the modern world.

Extensive search of the Internet is also assigned for broader, controversial topics of restitution, such as the origin of the phrase "forty acres and a mule," the Maine Indian Land Claims and Restitution, and Pumla Gobodo-Madikizela, a South African psychologist who introduces the concept of forgiveness as an alternative to restitution. The history of the phrase "forty acres and a mule" brings reparation for past injustice to the fore, referring to Major General Sherman's deeded allocation of forty acres on the southern coasts to each black family who desired it, along with a mule to till the land. In effect for less than a year, with additional legislation obstructing more land grants and access to education, these circumstances are cited as a failure of the United States to make reparations for slavery. In the case of the Maine Indians, restitution is decided legally in their favor with an $81.5 million settlement given for the reacquisition of their former lands. An interview with Gobodo-Madikizela enters the psychological realm of forgiveness (not monetary restitution) after confession, and in a similar vein, one student explored the rehabilitative and psychological support for public and private retelling (or confessing) of traumatic events.

Reading the original colonial texts in the energetic translations by Sullivan or the more stolid style of Sanderlin is difficult for undergraduate students and daunting even for graduate students. Constructs such as church hierarchy, transatlantic politics, the entity named *encomienda*, and attitudes toward slavery complicate the pleasure of reading the texts. These days, in late afternoon television broadcasts, we might tune in to follow the less complicated "cult of confession" popularized by Oprah. Her couch, not the confession box, is the site for examining what she calls "truthiness" of public admission of guilt and of public redemption. Las Casas, the sixteenth-century "superstar" given an opportunity today, would not have needed a teleprompter to guide his searing analysis of the current state of affairs and his vigorous quest for reparations.

NOTE

[1] Here Sullivan's translation uses the contemporary noun "genocide," which was actually coined in 1944, with reference to Nazi atrocities.

APPENDIX: SYLLABUS FOR AN HONORS COURSE

True Confessions: Literature, Film, Television

Week 1: Confession in Film: Hitchcock's *I Confess*
Week 2: Confession in Narrative: Alec Wilkinson's "Mr. Apology"
Week 3: Peter Brooks, "Storytelling without Fear? The Confessional Problem" (*Troubling Confessions* 8–35)
Week 4: Short Essay: Comparison of genre in confession
Peter Brooks, "Confession, Selfhood, and the Religious Tradition"
Week 5: Regina Harrison, "The Theology of Concupiscence" and "Cultural Translation in the Andes: The Case of the Pregnant Penitent"
Week 6: Bartolomé de Las Casas: *Rules for Confessors*, "Twelve Problems of Conscience"
Week 7: Bartolomé de Las Casas: "Joint Memorial to Philip" and "Last Will and Testament"
Web Assignment Summary: Evaluation of truth and reconciliation commissions and reparation for African Americans, Native Americans, Japanese, and Jews

Week 8:   Confession in the courts: Miranda rights, false confessions

Peter Brooks, "Confessor and Confessant" (*Troubling Confessions* 35–65)

Week 9:   *Homicide* TV series: "Three Men and Adena"

Week 10:   Court TV: *The System*: "The Interrogation of Michael Crowe"

Martin A. Conway, "Past and Present: Recovered Memories and False Memories"

Week 11:   Saint Augustine: Confession and memory (*Confessions*, bk. 10)

Web readings: <http://ccat.sas.upenn.edu/jod/augustine/Pusey/book10>

Week 12:   Performative confession

Guillermo Gómez Peña and Roberto Sifuentes's *Temple of Confessions* (book and audio)

Week 13:   Video confessions

Michael Renov: "Video Confessions"

Sadie Benning and her project of video confessions

Week 14:   Filming of class video confessions

Week 15:   Confessional documentary and truth assertions

Andrew Jarecki's *Capturing the Friedmans*

Week 16:   Presentation of class video, short story, blog, and term paper projects

Teaching Columbus
from the Margins of Las Casas

Margarita Zamora

Few pedagogical decisions have greater impact in the classroom than the choice of a text to begin a syllabus. For many years, I initiated my introductory courses on Spanish American literature at the advanced undergraduate and graduate levels with the *Diario* of Christopher Columbus's first voyage. In the introductory remarks, I dutifully explained to my students that the original version of the *Diario* was lost and that the text we would be reading was a summary transcription prepared by Bartolomé de Las Casas using a copy of the original, probably loaned to him by the Columbus family. To avoid confusion, I pointed out that the narrative voice alternated between first and third person, according to Las Casas's preference for citing verbatim or paraphrasing and summarizing portions of the text he transcribed. Our subsequent discussion soon lost sight of Las Casas, however, focusing on the images of the Amerindians, the lyricism of Columbus's descriptions of the landscape, the imaginative elements in the text in relation to medieval travel literature, and so on. If my former approach sounds familiar, it is undoubtedly because it faithfully reflected the didactic tradition of literary interpretation of the *Diario* found in the vast majority of histories of Spanish American literature in Spanish and English. Las Casas rarely is mentioned in relation to the Columbian texts, excepting the occasional casual acknowledgment that he transcribed the *Diario* as we know it. None of the literary histories I was familiar with explained the connection between Las Casas's own writing and the transcription, nor did they mention the editorial manipulations, emendations, interpolations, and extensive marginal commentary in the *Diario*.

Most modern Spanish editions and English translations of the *Diario* also suppress in varying degrees the substantial presence of Las Casas's hand in the text. One need look no further for evidence of this systematic suppression than the title: Las Casas referred to the text as the "Libro de la primera navegación y descubrimiento de las Indias." The popular Austral edition by Ignacio Anzoátegui makes no mention of Las Casas whatsoever and changes the title to "El primer viaje." A more recent and readily available pedagogical edition, published by Alianza and edited by Consuelo Varela, entitles the text "Diario del primer viaje," following the prevailing editorial custom. While Varela, an eminent Columbus scholar, acknowledges Las Casas's role in the transcription of the text in her introduction, she includes only a limited selection of the marginalia dealing with philological or geographic aspects, silently omitting the more substantive critical commentary altogether. Even the recently released softbound version of the diplomatic edition in bilingual format by Oliver Dunn and James E. Kelley (*The Diario of Christopher Columbus*) omits the marginal annotations in the English translation. The fact that the *Diario* was extracted, emended, and annotated by Las Casas to serve as an *aide-mémoire* and citation source for the composition of his own history of the discovery and biography of Columbus in the *Historia de las Indias* is another glaring, if not surprising, silence in the pedagogical literature.

Given the systematic suppression of Las Casas's hand in the transmission and canonization of the *Diario* on its way to becoming the founding text of the Spanish American letters, it would be tempting to see a plot among modern editors, publishers, and the academy to sanitize the Columbian text of the Lascasian contaminant. I have considered elsewhere the consequences for modern readers of the editorial purging of the marginalia and the silence surrounding Las Casas's interventions in the body of the text itself (e.g., the interpolations, the alternation between verbatim quotation and third-person paraphrase), practices that promote the editorial fiction that we have the pristine original words of Columbus (Zamora 68–73). Sexy conspiracy theories aside, it is a fact that Las Casas himself privileged the *ipsissima verba* of the admiral—not as a strategy for obscuring his own hand in the text, however. Quite the contrary, Las Casas authorized Columbus's words to render the text a worthy object of commentary. In the marginalia, he followed standard humanist commentating practices.[1] From Valla and Erasmus to Nebrija and Fray Luis de León, philological commentary served as the indispensable tool for correcting the corrupted texts of pagan and Christian antiquity and establishing the authoritative version. It was also a discursive strategy for the advocacy of religious, political, and cultural reforms. Many of Las Casas's annotations in the margins of the *Diario* are corrective in nature, directed at scribal error, at Columbus's geographic mistakes, and at his misinterpretations of Arawak terminology he heard from the natives of the Antilles during the first voyage. However, the more substantive critical commentary makes it evident that Las Casas's edition was undertaken in the larger context of his political agenda on behalf of the rights of the Amerindians and the critique of Spanish colonialism, to which he dedicated his life's work.

By establishing the "antigüedad" of the original text (Casas, *Historia* 1: 182), in humanist parlance its primacy and authority, Las Casas established a qualitative boundary between Columbus's words and his own writing. This criterion of differentiation is reflected in the manuscript in the graphic encircling of the marginal commentary (Colón, *Diario*) that sets it in relief and visually distinguishes it from the main text. The profound awareness of the primary text's otherness, its "antiquity" with respect to their own "modernity," allowed humanists to approach the original text's authority from a critical vantage point, thus rendering the commentary a secondary yet necessary kind of textuality. Such a critical disposition toward canonical texts is precisely what rendered humanists a dangerous heterodox element subject to vigilance, censorship, and discipline by the Inquisition in the increasingly conservative and intolerant intellectual culture of Counter-Reformation Spain, as Luis Gil Fernández has shown.

When I ask my students to consider Columbian writing from the vantage point of Las Casas's commentary, several important aspects come into view that would not have been evident otherwise. Among the most significant is the rhetorical canonization of the *Diario* that takes place in the *Historia de las Indias* (completed in 1566, published in 1875), thereby transforming Columbus into an *auctor* in the canon of New World historiography. By establishing the primacy and authority of Columbus's testimony, Las Casas restored its centrality in the narration of the discovery and secured the circulation of a text that had been zealously guarded in the royal and private archives of the Crown and the Columbus family. No small feat, considering that the admiral's reputation had been tarnished in the protracted legal battles between the Crown and Columbus's heirs over the contractual rights and privileges of the discoverer known as the *pleitos colombinos*. This may explain, at least in part, why Las Casas imposed a forty-year moratorium on the *Historia*'s publication, effectively bypassing his contemporaries in the text's transmission to future generations of readers. Ultimately, however, the virtual canonization of Columbus by Las Casas was a necessary first step in strengthening his own oppositional discourse. Establishing Columbus's *auctoritas* allowed Las Casas to situate his own writing in the critical space of commentary, defined and exploited so effectively by the European humanist reformers. From that position, the *Diario* comes into view as the authoritative words of Columbus supporting Las Casas's political critique of Spain's colonialist project. At the same time, the *Diario* functions as the object of Las Casas's critical commentary, aimed polemically at a founding text of Spanish colonialism. The rhetorical strategy at work here is an intensely ironic double inversion: Las Casas's commentary authorizes Columbus's testimony as a witness against the necessity of Spanish force in the Indies, only to turn Columbus into a witness against himself in the ethical commentary.

The passages quoted below illustrate the intertextual incorporation of the commentary from the *Diario* to the *Historia*:

> Domingo, 16 de diciembre [from the main text]: Crean vras al. Qstas trras son en tanta cantidad buenas y fertiles y en especial estas desta isla española:

q no ay p[er]sona q lo sepa dezir: y nadie lo puede creer si no lo viese. Y crean qsta Isla y todas las otras son asi suyas como Castilla: q aqui no falta salvo assiento y mandarles hazer lo q quisiere porq yo con esta gente q traygo q no son muchos : correria todas estas yslas sin afrenta . q ya e visto solos tres destos marineros desçendir en trra y aver multitud destos yndios y todos huyr sin q les quisiesen hazer mal. ellos no tiene armas y son todos desnudos y de nigu ingenio en letras y muy cobardes q mill no aguardaria tres . y asi son buenos p[ar]a les madar y les hazer trabajar sembrar y hazer todo lo otro q fuere menester : y q haga villas y se enseñen a andar vestidos y a nras costubres.   (Columbus, *Diario* 234, 236)

May Your Highnesses believe that these lands are so greatly good and fertile, and especially those of this island of Hispaniola, that there is no one who can tell it; and no one could believe it if he had not seen it. And may you believe that this island and all the others are as much yours as Castile; for nothing is lacking except settlement and ordering the Indians to do whatever Your Highnesses may wish. Because I with the people that I bring with me, who are not many, go about in all these islands without danger; for I have already seen three of these sailors go ashore where there was a crowd of these Indians, and all would flee without the Span- iards wanting to do harm. They do not have arms and they are all naked, and of no skill in arms, and so very cowardly that a thousand would not stand against three. And so they are fit to be ordered about and made to work, plant, and do everything else that may be needed, and build towns and be taught our customs, and to go about clothed.   (235, 237)[2]

Domingo, 16 de diciembre [marginal text adjacent to passage quoted above]:
nõ [nota]
algo mas parece aqui estenderse el almirate dlo q̃ devria   (236)

Here the admiral seems to expand on the point more than he should
                                            (my trans.)

Diario, 16 December [intertextualized in the *Historia*]: Es aquí de notar, que la mansedumbre natural, simple, benigna y humilde condición de los indios, y carecer de armas, con andar desnudos, dio atrevimiento a los españoles a tenerlos en poco, y ponerlos en tan acerbísimos trabajos en que le pusieron. Y cierto, aquí el Almirante más se extendió a hablar de lo que debiera. Y desto que aquí concibió y produjo por su boca, debía tomar origen el mal tratamiento que después en ellos hizo.
                                    (Casas, *Historia* 1: 269)

It should be noted here that, owing to the docile, simple, benign, and humble condition of the Indians, together with their lack of arms and their nudity, the Spaniards dared to hold them in disdain and to put them to such harsh labors. Surely, the admiral expanded more on this point than he should have. And what he conceived and uttered here likely gave rise to the abuses later perpetrated on them.   (my trans.)

The first excerpt consists of a verbatim quotation (in Las Casas's characteristic shorthand) of one of the numerous passages in the *Diario* where Columbus addresses Ferdinand and Isabella. This particular apostrophe is notable for the formulaic yet remarkably complete and precise application of the political, economic, and military ideology of "descubrimiento," understood as reconnaissance and control of territory and markets, stipulated in his contract with the Crown in the "Capitulaciones de Santa Fe." It also contains typical Columbian observations about the docility and vulnerability of the natives of Haiti-Hispaniola. The second passage contains Las Casas's understatedly ironic marginal commentary on the admiral's *ipssissima verba*. The third selection, from the *Historia*, exemplifies the intertextual transformation of the *Diario*'s main text and marginal commentary into an oppositional historical discourse. In this passage, Las Casas supports his representation of the Indians as gentle, humble, benevolent folk on the authority of Columbus's testimony that they were unarmed, naked, and fearful. He then takes up the critique of Spanish attitudes and actions (the scorn and abuse of the natives), concluding with the ethical chastisement of Columbus's loose tongue and the resulting consequences suffered by the Indians.

To summarize, the principal features of Las Casas's hand in the *Diario* include: editorial manipulation of Columbus's words, setting into relief parts of the text as the privileged *ipssissima verba* of the admiral; corrective marginalia establishing the authoritative version of the text and Columbus as *auctor;* and marginal commentary establishing the critical vantage point from which Las Casas reads the Columbian intertexts. All these features are still discernible in the politico-ethical discourse against the Spanish colonization of the Indies in the *Historia,* which tracks the Columbian narrative nearly day to day. It is not pedagogically cumbersome in the least, then, to perform a dramatic representation of Las Casas's dialogue with the Columbian text in the classroom. I will refer to this strategy as teaching Columbus from the margins of Las Casas. It consists, initially, of simple role playing. Students assume the various parts, corresponding to the diverse voices in the texts, and enact the critical dialogue as a prelude to discussion.

The pedagogical advantages of assuming the marginal vantage point on Columbus's *Diario* are too numerous to detail in a few pages, so I offer here some general comments on how locating class discussion at the boundary between Columbus and Las Casas can enhance the teaching of the *Diario*, the *Historia*, and colonial literary studies in general. First, the literary field comes into focus as a dynamic space formed in the multiple negotiations between production and reception that constitute the cultural life of texts. Second, the foundation of Spanish American letters in the *Diario* as the pristine original word of Columbus reveals itself as an editorial tour de force, facilitating the discussion of the power of institutional mediations in the constitution of canons. Third, Columbian writing, as we know it, comes into view as a cultural artifact shaped by a history of reception that, as John Beverley has noted in relation to the baroque of the Indies, "cuenta más, o a la par, que el acto de producción" 'is at least as important as the act of production' (*Una modernidad obsoleta* 119; my trans.). This provides a segue into the larger discussion of reading practices as important catalysts in cultural change. Finally, Las Casas's reading of Columbus enhances our understanding of the Spanish American literary canon's peripheral beginnings in the discourse of commentary—a secondary, supplemental yet necessary writing that derives its strength from its critical difference.

From the margins of Las Casas, as I discuss at greater length in a forthcoming study, the rise of colonial commentary (e.g., Garcilaso Inca's *Comentarios reales*, Espinosa Medrano's *Apologético en favor de don Luis de Góngora*, Sor Juana's "Carta atenagórica," Fray Servando Teresa de Mier's "Apología," etc.) can be appreciated as a decisive discursive move in the emergence of what we call the Spanish American literary field. The Lascasian commentary inscribed in the margins of the *Diario*, explicitly aware of its distance and difference from the original text, provides a critical angle on the discourse of discovery and privileges the revisionist potential in the act of reception. It is in this re-visioning, especially, that the *Diario* comes into view as a foundational text. From the Lascasian margins, it becomes possible for the first time in the history of transatlantic writing to envision the emerging cultural field of Spanish American writing. In that marginal space, and only from there, the field begins to take shape, not in an essentialist differentiation from the European tradition but rather through the articulation of a divergent criterion. Las Casas's tactical occupation of the marginal space of commentary to engage polemically with the discourses of Spanish imperialism is the decisive move toward defining new sites of critical difference.

NOTES

I follow André Saint-Lu's Spanish edition of Las Casas's *Historia de las Indias* (Caracas: Ayacucho, 1986).

[1] The complete marginalia can be found in the facsimile of the *Diario* edited by Carlos Sanz.

[2] All translations of the *Diario* are from Dunn and Kelley's *The Diario of Christopher Columbus's First Voyage to America 1492–1493*. The translations of Las Casas's text are my own.

Las Casas versus Oviedo:
The Polemic between the "Defender of the Indians" and the "Enemy of the Indians"

Kathleen Ann Myers

Se me ocurre una cosa que he mirado muchas veces en estos indios, y es que tienen el casco de la cabeza más grueso cuatro veces que los cristianos. E así cuando se les hace guerra y vienen con ellos a las manos, han de estar muy sobre avisos de no les dar cuchillada en la cabeza, porque se han visto quebrar muchas espadas.   (Fernández de Oviedo, "Proemio")

It has just occurred to me that one thing I have seen very often in these Indians is that their skulls are four times as thick as those of Christians. And so, when you are engaged in warfare with them and you engage in hand-to-hand combat, you must be very careful not to give them knife thrusts to the head, as many swords have been seen to shatter.

Undergraduate and graduate students respond well to the writings of colonial Latin America's most provocative personalities. When I give students descriptions of Native Americans from the lengthy, lively, and at times contentious *Historia general y natural de las Indias*, the first on-site official chronicle of the Indies, they are immediately curious about the policy and debates spawned by the Spanish conquest and colonization of the New World. Statements such as this essay's opening quotation illuminate why Bartolomé de las Casas dubbed the *Historia*'s author, Gonzalo Fernández de Oviedo (1478–1557), the "Enemy of the Indians." Oviedo argued that Native Americans were not able to be fully civilized. His life and text exemplify who and what Las Casas fought against during his years as "Defender of the Indians." As Oviedo was both an *encomendero* (a Spaniard who had the right to the labor and tribute of a certain number of Indians) and an official Crown historian, who helped legitimize the empire by promoting political and cultural hegemony, his interests were threatened by Las Casas's plan to outlaw the *encomienda* system. Moreover, the editorial success of Oviedo's first publications about the Indies and its inhabitants (the *Sumario*, 1527, and the *Historia*, 1535) greatly hindered Las Casas's efforts to portray Native Americans as civilized beings ready to become Christians. Indeed, in the important 1550–51 Valladolid debate, Las Casas's opponent, Juan Ginés de Sepúlveda, based much of his argument about the nature of the *indio* on Oviedo's *Historia*, which recently had been republished (1547).

The decades-long adversarial relationship between Las Casas and Oviedo was infamous in its time and serves today as a useful focal point for teaching Las Casas's ideas and texts to students. Lewis Hanke was the first to begin outlining these two men's contentious interaction. Studying Oviedo helps students understand that the stakes were high in the polemic between Oviedo and Las Casas.

I find that a course unit on Oviedo works better after students have read Las Casas's *Brevísima relación*. Once they are familiar with Las Casas's arguments and style, I set out the initial historical context for understanding Oviedo's and Las Casas's relationship. Next, students examine passages in which the two writers deal with similar topics. This reading strategy highlights the dialectic (the argumentation and rebuttal process) between the friar and the chronicler and the important role that Las Casas's opponents play in his texts.

Contexts

During Oviedo's initial trip to America (1514), the historian became the first Spaniard to read aloud the *Requerimiento* (Palacios Rubios), the document dictated to the Indians before waging war on them. Oviedo describes this scene in book 29, chapter 7. It is ironic that he read it to a deserted town. In a short time, he became an *encomendero*. By 1519, Oviedo and Las Casas had participated in the first public debate about how to deal with Native Americans. Both men petitioned the king for land grants in the main land of America (Tierra Firme) and for knights to help settle the region. While Oviedo requested a hundred aristocratic knights from an established order to pacify the Indians, Las Casas petitioned for the right to create a new order of knights, who would be farmers protecting the land from intrusion. Neither man's petition was granted in full, but in 1520 Las Casas received the rights to establish an experimental community, known as Cumaná, in which the Dominicans attempted to help Native Americans live without being subjugated to Spaniards. Within a handful of years, Oviedo was granted the governorship of Cartagena, with rights to an *encomienda*. However, both men failed to carry out their visions for forming new societies in America—the Spaniards in Cumaná were killed, and Oviedo declined the governorship because of native rebellions and lack of funding.

Nonetheless, Oviedo continued to encourage the Crown to maintain the *encomienda* system, based on the theory that Indians were fallen Christians and unable to adopt civilized European customs. Las Casas strongly objected to this position. He argued that the Indians were not barbaric but eminently teachable human beings. As social experiments in converting Native Americans to Christianity failed, debates intensified in Spain. In 1525, Oviedo was called before the newly formed Council of the Indies (the body created to help govern the new lands) to render an official opinion on the subject. He argued that the subjugation of the Indians to the Spaniards was the only way to bring about peace. He was then recalled before the council to make further depositions in 1530–31 and 1532. In the 1540s, as the comprehensive New Laws were instituted and then revoked, he continued to advise the Crown through official correspondence. By the end of the decade, Sepúlveda, the advocate for the *encomienda* system in the 1550 Valladolid debate, based many of his arguments on Oviedo's published writings about the nature of the Indian.

Las Casas and Oviedo were key informants to the Crown throughout many of these decades of policy making regarding Native Americans. While Las Casas worked diligently to abolish the *encomienda*, Oviedo wrote feverishly to document the general and natural history of the Indies. In his several-thousand-page *Historia* (1535, 1547) and in the Spanish courts, Oviedo discussed the legality of the *encomienda* and supported it through his portrayal of indigenous customs and beliefs.

Dialectic Texts

Two sets of readings help students realize the impact of Oviedo's and Las Casas's relationship on their texts. First, students read short selections in which the two authors criticize the policies each promoted. Chronicling the Dominicans' attempt to evangelize and settle Tierra Firme, Oviedo's book 19 vividly describes the missionaries' brutal martyrdoms. Oviedo blames Las Casas for the fiasco and characterizes the friar's 1519 proposal for evangelization as a fantasy that smacked of the passé knight-errantry (2: 194–99; bk. 19, chs. 3–5). (The accusation is ironic given Oviedo's request for a hundred knights when he was offered a governorship.) The chronicler reveals that Las Casas's Cumaná experiment ended in disaster, with the enslavement of the Indians (2: 201; bk. 19, chs. 5–6). According to Oviedo, the warlike nature of the Indians and the pretensions of some churchmen were responsible for the colonization that went awry. This version of the *History* was first published in 1535 and then republished in 1547, just as Las Casas and Sepúlveda began their debates. In another book, Oviedo elaborates his criticism of Las Casas's plan, saying that the friar gained the Crown's favor through false promises and lies while his, Oviedo's, more solid plan was rejected (3: 61; bk. 26, ch. 1). Once again, however, Oviedo's remarks about Las Casas should be read as part of the chronicler's self-serving picture. In these same chapters, Oviedo boasts of his own success in pacifying the Indians: he confiscated their bows and arrows and gave them axes, which, because of their inferior quality, had to be sharpened often by Spaniards. Oviedo's harangue continued well through the 1540s as Las Casas first won the case against the *encomienda* system (when the New Laws were instituted) and then lost it (when the laws were repealed). In one instance, for example, while recording a 1547 interview with Juan Cano about the conquest of Mexico, Oviedo takes the opportunity to make a sarcastic remark about how Santo Domingo was "raining" with young friars, followers of Las Casas (4: 257–64; bk. 33, ch. 53). For his part, Las Casas harshly condemns Oviedo. In the *Apología*, the Dominican complains bitterly about Oviedo's use of lurid descriptions of the Indians to gain fame for his publications (633). Las Casas's later work, the *Historia de Indias*, also paints a scathing portrait of Oviedo, first in the 1519–20 encounter between the two men at the royal court (3: 511–33) and then when critiquing Oviedo's text. In particular, Las Casas condemns Oviedo's greed and his false and dishonorable representation of the friar:

> Oviedo excedió en hablar tan falsamente del clérigo, atribuyendo el de-
> seo y fin que tuvo de mamparar estas desmamparadas gentes y quitar de
> su conversión y salvación tan eficaces impedimentos, a ambición y deseo
> de mandar, y también a codicia, todavía se sobrepujo en maldecir, detra-
> yendo de la honra del clérigo Bartolomé de Las Casas.   (588)

> Oviedo overdid his defamation of this priest, by attributing to greed and
> yearning for power both his desire and goal of protecting these defense-
> less people and of greatly facilitating their conversion and salvation; and
> he even exceeded in damning and detracting from the priest Bartolomé
> de Las Casas's reputation.

In sum, both men were ambitious, prolific authors and harsh critics of each
other. Oviedo saw colonization as providing free access to a native labor supply, while Las Casas viewed the colonization of new subjects as primarily the
domain of the church.

Moving beyond this personal display of animosity, the second set of readings
highlights how the two authors used the same data, philosophical traditions, and
rhetorical strategies to argue radically different positions. The success of their
views about colonization and the *encomienda* hinged, first, on their descriptions
of Native Americans and, second, on assigning blame for the brutality of the
conquest. Reading Las Casas and Oviedo together reveals that, while the friar
and the bureaucrat differed enormously about the nature of the Indian, as the
years passed they frequently borrowed material from each other—if only to use
it for different ends.

In the *Brevísima relación*, the *Historia de Indias*, and the *Apologética,* Las
Casas's descriptions of Indians focused on the unity of their physical beauty
and souls. The friar argued for the rationality of Native Americans, saying that
they followed the classical models for the natural causes of rationality and thus
had the potential to be civilized and Christianized. To underscore his argument,
Las Casas compared Indian customs and culture with the ancient Greeks and
Romans.

Whether using biblical metaphors, hyperbole, generalizations, or classical
comparisons, he portrays the majority of indigenous peoples as beautiful and
somewhat peaceful, observing civilized cultural practices, and, more important,
engaging in religions that prepared the way for Christianity. In the process, he
creates a composite portrait of the Indians as perfect subjects for church and
Crown, with no need for the interference of greedy conquistadors and colonizers. Notably, the friar's depictions, many written well after the publication of
Oviedo's first two works, rebutted the chronicler's extensive early representations of the inhabitants of Tierra Firme and the Islands. In general, Oviedo
portrayed them as physically inferior to Europeans, with thick bestial skulls, and
as inspired by satanic religions.

While in Spain in 1525, Oviedo wrote his brief natural history of the West
Indies, the *Sumario*. Destined first for the new emperor, Charles V, the text

provides a schematic view of the territories. Writing after his first two sojourns to America, Oviedo focuses on exotic New World phenomena. Only one chapter details the inhabitants of Tierra Firme (35; ch. 10). The author's opening sketches portray the specific details about the region's geography and the inhabitants' social organization. With what appears to be a humanistic concern for including linguistic terms and names, the first paragraphs seem to be an objective report. The chronicler soon turns, however, to a listing of the inhabitants' "idolatrías y errores": they practice polygamy, divorce, abortion, premarital sex; they eat human flesh; and they bury people alive (35). The source of these sins, argues Oviedo, is the "religion of the devil," worse than any practiced by pagans in ancient times (36). God punishes their crimes by sending devastating hurricanes and, ultimately, the Spaniards. The chronicler argues that although Spanish conquistadors committed grave crimes in Tierra Firme, it was all part of the divine plan. Having established a strongly negative moral interpretation of indigenous practices and having asserted the Spaniards' God-given obligation to conquer the Indies, the author turns again to a more detached description of native artifacts: houses, hammocks, and *henequín*. Yet these, too, are placed in a moral framework, albeit indirectly, by his repeating the description of the natives' heads as bestially thick. This passage serves as a bridge into a description of how inhabitants paint their bodies and prepare for war. Whereas the "idolatría y errores" emphasize the Native Americans' status as fallen Christians (Oviedo believed that the natives had been part of an ancient evangelization by the first Christians), the comment about "bestial" skulls and barbaric war practices underscores the Indians' place as natural slaves in the Aristotelian order. Both depictions rationalize the *encomienda* system (precisely at a time when Oviedo stood to gain significantly from policy that supported it).

Notably, in between the brief condemnation of the Spanish pacification as depopulation and his characterization of the Indians as the worst pagans in history, Oviedo inserts a reference to the monarch's policy and new formation of a governing body for the Indies, the Consejo de las Indias (Council of the Indies). The *Sumario* was written on the heels of Las Casas's failure in Cumaná (1522), of Oviedo's loss of his house and lands in Darién, now Central America (1524), and of Oviedo's deposition in 1525 to the Council of the Indies and was written contemporaneously with the 1524 law that allowed the enslavement of Indians in Tierra Firme. At the same time, Oviedo was offered the governorship of Cartagena. New policies were being tested, implemented, and revoked, and Oviedo worked ambitiously (and with some degree of success) to become an important royal official. He helped determine policy in the Indies and personally benefited from it. Seen from this perspective, the *Sumario* was yet another tool of Oviedo's ambition.

In the 1535 edition of the *Historia general de las Indias*, the author expands his description of Native Americans and elaborates on his attempts to legitimize Spanish rule of the Americas and label Indians as fallen Christians. First, he argues that the Indies were once part of the legendary Hesperides, where the Visigoth monarchs of Hispania had ruled (15; bk. 2, ch. 3);

second, that Christ's apostles had evangelized America (25; bk. 2, ch. 7). Having
established the Indies as part of the monarch's original territories and its natives as lapsed Christian subjects, Oviedo says that he will document the Indians' "criminales costumbres" 'evil costumes,' their warlike nature and inability
to live in a civilized manner, but not until later in the history, "en su lugar" 'in
their place' (35; bk. 2, ch. 8).

At times, however, a new ethnographic impulse temporarily displaces his
strong condemnation of Native Americans. Book 6, on miscellany (*depósitos*),
includes many ethnographic chapters on indigenous customs, languages, and
artifacts (canoes, fire drills, and houses). Within this narrative frame of exotic
curiosities, book 6's descriptions of indigenous life avoid the moral censure this
same material carried earlier in the history. In this new context, stories of such
practices as cannibalism are added to a list of novelties to pique the reader's interest: indigenous peoples are an extension of a land filled with exotic marvels.

This difference in representation suggests that Oviedo's portraits of Indians
had a great deal to do with the interpretive context. In book 5 and other sections of part 1, the descriptions are used as points of discussion, to illustrate the
underlying challenges of the governance of a new territory. In these same years,
the debates over the *encomienda* intensified: royal policy reversed itself three
times (1529, 1530, 1534), and the recent conquests of the urban civilizations of
the Aztecs and Incas once again challenged Spaniards' views of native populations. By contrast, in book 6 of part 1, the native subjects are independent
"miscellany"—curiosities—and therefore require less narrative framework for
the reader about the moral or administrative context.

The completed revision of part 1 and all of parts 2 and 3 of the *Historia general y natural de las Indias* (c. 1547) did not appear until nearly fifteen years
after the first edition of part 1. (The 1535 and 1547 editions only included the
first version of part 1.) During that time, Oviedo's historiographic methodology
evolved, as did the conquest itself. As a result, parts 2 and 3 have a more coherent narrative placement of information about Native Americans than part 1.
When Oviedo reports firsthand about Tierra Firme native populations in books
26 through 29 of part 2, for example, most of the information is carefully divided into general history (the role of Native Americans in the conquest) and
natural history (the "particularidades" 'specific details' of indigenous social and
ethnographic practices and organizations [e.g., 3: 321, 342]). After depicting
the general conquest and colonization of the area in book 29 (along with the
extensive litigation involved), Oviedo turns to ethnography and natural history.
Of the thirty-four chapters in this book, Oviedo devotes five chapters to various Native American groups in Tierra Firme (chs. 26–28, 31, 32). Each native
population, with its distinct language, customs, rites, and histories, is far more
"particularly" described than in the *Sumario* or the 1535 *Historia*. By comparing versions, students can see the maturing of Oviedo's ethnographic impulse.
The chronicler discusses indigenous dress (or lack of it), religious beliefs, hous-
ing, languages, bathing, food, social organization, marriage customs, and sexual

practices. Even when these customs fly in the face of Christian norms, Oviedo provides extensive and detailed information that is sensitive to regional differences. Unlike the descriptions in the *Sumario*, the sexual and religious practices are not a list of sins and idolatrous acts. In book 29, chapter 27, for example, the author refrains from condemning divorce, prostitution, polygamy, and abortion. On the whole, there is less moralizing and politicking and more ethnographic documentation—although Oviedo never accepted the practice of sodomy.

Only one chapter title includes negative labels ("viciosas" 'those given to vice' and "idolatrías" 'idolatries' [ch. 26, "De las costumbres e maneras de vivir viciosas de los indios de la provincia de Cueva y de sus idolatrías"]), while the other chapters, titled "Ceremonias e custumbres" 'ceremonies and customs' and "Particularidades de los indios" 'particular traits of the Indians,' provide information intended to assist in knowing the province (*gobernación*) of Castilla del Oro. More complete information about the new subjects, argues Oviedo, should lead to better government of them, to integrating Indians into a new economic and political system. In this framework, ethnographic information is collected to support good government.

Even the narrative passages on Tierra Firme cited verbatim from the *Sumario* in chapter 28 of part 2, such as the paragraph on the thickness of Indian skulls, lose some of their effect. Placed into a longer narrative without further discussion and wedged between a fairly objective description of warrior costumes and blood-letting practices, the observation still has the political implications it had in the *Sumario*, but it is now part of an extensive, complex description. There no longer seems to be an overriding emphasis on the barbarism of the Indians so prevalent in the first edition of part 1 (bk. 5). Although Oviedo continues to state that the Native Americans were "gente sin razón" 'people without reason' (3: 313), he grants narrative space and interest to elaborating their customs— some of which undermine his negative statement about the rationality of the natives of Tierra Firme. Several important factors help account for this shift in the portrait. In the dozen or so years separating the composition of these two versions, Oviedo's situation had changed. He no longer lived in Tierra Firme as an aspiring governor but in Santo Domingo as a royal chronicler. Moreover, Oviedo wrote from the perspective of the successful conquistador; by the 1530s, most of the West Indies had been conquered, and native inhabitants were no longer a threat. (In fact, they were on their way to extinction.) Spaniards had arrived at what Álvaro Félix Bolaños has called the "desired status quo," a state of affairs in which the rules of contact between colonizer and colonized reached a stable point for the Spaniards to pursue their business interests ("Place" 284). Indians were now "safe" to treat as subjects of ethnographic interest and as a New World novelty within the larger scheme of the *Historia*.

Elsewhere Oviedo spells out the multiple purposes this information served. Both anticipating and responding to criticism, such as Las Casas's, about his description of Indians, Oviedo claims a higher purpose for his history, as a tool for both God and Crown:

Para considerar que estos tractados se fundan principalmente en loor de
Dios, que de tantas novedades e diversidad de cosas es el Hacedor . . . y
lo segundo, porque la clemencia de César quiere que por su mandado
se sepan e comunique al mundo todo; y lo terecero, porque es un grand
contentamiento a los hombres, de cualquier estado que sean, oír cosas
nuevas.   (3: 322)

Consider that these treatises are founded principally on the praise of God,
as He is the maker of so many new and diverse things . . . and second,
because the mercy of the emperor wishes that at his command all this
be known and communicated to the entire world; and third, because it is
a great joy for all men, of whichever rank they might be, to hear of new
things.

In a chapter added in 1548 or 1549, Oviedo blames the church for the failure
of the conquest to convert the Indians (3: 337; bk. 29, ch. 31). It was in the
hands of the clergy to administer and evangelize the Indians, and they failed to
produce good Christians. Instead of completing the evangelization process, the
clergy lined their own pockets:

Muy reverendos obispos e perlados, que examinéis bien vuestros ministros, porque a veces os engañáis en la elección e os engañan. ¿Quereíslo
ver? Mirad las bolsas a algunos, e los negocios particulares, y el caudal con
que entraron en sus granjerías; e veréis cuán apartado anda el ejercicio del
oficio del sacerdocio.   (3: 338; bk. 29, ch. 31)

Most reverend bishops and prelates: Examine your ministers well, for at
times you are deluded in your choice, and they deceive you. Do you wish
to see this? Examine some of their purses and their private ventures and
the fortune with which they entered into their profits, and you will see
how far removed they are from the profession of the priesthood.

According to Oviedo, the Indians may be continuing their own religious practices, but they are not to blame as much as the clerics who were not doing their
job.

By the 1540s, another element probably influenced Oviedo's representation
of the Native Americans. By this time, the conquistadors' greed had sabotaged
the original visions of establishing new societies in America. Whole native populations had disappeared in the Antilles and Central America, and Spaniards
were murdering one another at alarming rates in rebellions and civil wars extending from Tierra Firme to Perú. By this time too, Las Casas's scathing portraits of the destruction of the Indies had circulated throughout Spain. Echoing
his opponent's condemnation of the devastation of the conquest, Oviedo depicts many royal officials and conquistadors as acting more barbarically than the

Indians. Critical portraits of most Spaniards contrast with largely sympathetic portrayals of native leaders, caciques. In the 1535 edition of part 1 there was a lone laudatory sketch of a native chief, Don Enrique, accompanied by a praiseworthy description of the Spanish captain Barrionuevo (1: 124–32; bk. 5, chs. 6–8). By the 1540s, in part 2, Oviedo depicted many wise Native American leaders who were betrayed time and again by treacherous Spaniards. Book 29 on Tierra Firme abounds with such stories. With the exception of only a handful of paragraphs out of the entire thirty-four chapters of book 29, Oviedo's description of the conquest and colonization under Governor Pedrarias Dávila's leadership echoes Las Casas's systematic rhetoric of the destruction of the Indies. Most of the central chapters argue that the Spaniards' greed led to diabolical and unchristian acts, while the natives were mostly friendly and civilized until provoked. In chapter 13, for example, Oviedo juxtaposes the portrait of the wise cacique Paris, who worked hard to protect his people, and Captain Espinosa, who in a greedy rage executed an Indian with a cannon shot. Oviedo coins phrases that one might think were Las Casas's: "comenzarse la distruición de la tierra, (a que ellos llamaban pacificación e conquistar)" 'so began the destruction of the land (what they called pacification and conquest)'; "no bastaría papel ni tiempo a expresar enteramente lo que los capitanes hicieron para asolar los indios e robarlos e destruir la tierra . . ." 'there is not enough paper or time to describe fully what the captains did to devastate the Indians and rob them and destroy the land' (3: 234, 243). Students can make their own judgment about the implications of Oviedo's more evenhanded tone in these passages.

Unlike Las Casas's hyperbolic descriptions and one-conquest-fits-all sketches in his *Brevísima relación* presented to Prince Philip in 1542, however, Oviedo's books on Tierra Firme provide careful, convincing historical detail: the Indian leaders are named, towns described, exact atrocities outlined, and dates given. With legalistic detail, the author describes how the men under Pedrarias systematically ignored the king's instructions for a fair conquest. Oviedo's account of Tierra Firme may have deflected Las Casas's charges that Oviedo was an enemy of the Indians, implicated in the destruction of the Indies and guilty by association with Pedrarias's administration. (For a short period of time Oviedo served as Pedrarias's lieutenant governor.) The author concludes that, in the end, it was left for him alone to fight Pedrarias and seek justice (3: 285; bk. 29, ch. 20). Books 26 and 29 provide a more permanent record of the governor's misdeeds and Oviedo's importance to the king, even as policy about the administration of the Indies shifted and justice was unevenly administered.

The chronicler's portrayal of Spaniards as barbarians and Indians as just rulers inverts the discourse of conquest and further underscores his overarching preoccupation with the effective administration of the Indies. Those who impede good government, not the Indians, are now the problem. As the native populations were decimated, Oviedo saw less need to portray them as enemies. He began to portray partially lost cultures with some degree of sympathy. Although the chronicler increasingly placed the blame for the destruction of the

Crown's property on greedy conquistadors, he never agreed with Las Casas that the *encomienda* was at the heart of the problem. The friar and the chronicler would live out their final days defending their positions, even as they adopted aspects of each other's arguments and discourse.

In the end, Oviedo's pro-*encomienda* stance prevailed: it was not until the 1570s that the *encomienda* system saw a significant change. To a degree, however, Las Casas triumphed over his archenemy: the label "Indian hater" endured for centuries when critics wrote about Oviedo. Yet, the friar's success may also be attributed to the fact that Oviedo's full history was not published until the 1850s. Oviedo's 1540s revisions of part 1 and sections of parts 2 and 3 show more nuance and ambivalence than his earlier publications when describing the Native Americans and the devastation caused by the conquest.

Course Options

By this point in the course unit, students have a solid sense of the content and rhetorical construction of Oviedo's and Las Casas's texts, allowing us to delve deeper into the theological and political issues that informed their writings. For an undergraduate class, this section of the course is more suggestive than substantial; for a graduate class, it can be expanded to include readings by Oviedo's and Las Casas's contemporaries, such as Sepúlveda and Motolinía, as well as more theoretical texts on colonialism (e.g., Homi Bhabha, Edward Said). I conclude the course unit by asking students (both undergraduates and graduates) to write short position papers on an aspect of the historical debate or a representational issue. The exercise provides the ideas and basis for conducting a mock debate on the topic. The debate is a particularly good place in the course to encourage students to express their reactions to the more jarring ideas of the period, such as Aristotle's theory of natural slaves and the theory that appearances were linked to intellectual and civilizing capabilities. To engage students more fully in thinking about race, power, and colonialism and as a variation on this exercise, I have the class discuss how these early modern situations may apply to the twentieth and twenty-first centuries. The addition of the often vivid arguments of Las Casas's opponents to a study of the friar's texts adds a dynamic element to the classroom. Students see more clearly the nature of the polemic about the conquest and the role of Native Americans. They also see how these issues evolved over the first half of the sixteenth century and have continued into the modern and postmodern eras.

NOTE

All citations of Oviedo's works are from Juan Pérez de Tudela Bueso's edition of the *Historia* (Atlas, 1992), except for citations of the 1535 edition of the *Historia*, which are from the Juan Cromberger edition. All translations are by Nina M. Scott. For Las Casas, I follow Isacio Pérez Fernández's edition of the *Historia de las Indias* (1994) and Ángel Losada's edition of the *Apología* (1998), both in the *Obras completas* (Alianza, 1988–98).

APPENDIX

SUGGESTED COURSE UNIT ON OVIEDO AND LAS CASAS

Contexts

Gonzalo Fernández de Oviedo (readings from Brading, *First America*; Bolaños, "The Historian" and "El líder"; Gerbi, *La naturaleza*; Merrim, "Apprehension," "Castle," and "Un Mare"; Myers; Pagden, *European Encounters*)

> Oviedo's role in the initial years of the conquest as a Crown administrator
> Oviedo's later role as Royal Chronicler

The fluctuation in Crown policy over the *encomienda* system and Oviedo's position (readings from Hanke, *The Struggle*, ch. 5; *All Mankind* 34–56)

Dialectic Texts

The "Enemy of the Indians" and the "Defender of the Indians"

> Oviedo on Las Casas: the Cumaná experiment, *Historia general*, bk. 19, chs. 4–6; Las Casas in general, *Historia general*, bk. 27, ch. 1
> Las Casas on Oviedo: Oviedo in 1519–20, *Historia de las Indias*, bk. 3, chs. 139–45; Oviedo's history, *Historia de las Indias*, bk. 3, ch. 160

Oviedo's descriptions of Indians over time

> 1525, devil worshipers, the *Sumario*, ch. 10, and *Historia general*, bk. 5, ch. 1
> 1535, the *Historia general*, pt. 1: reflecting policy debates, bks. 2–3; ethnographic impulse, bk. 6, various chapters
> c. 1540s, *Historia general*, pt. 2, bk. 29, chs. 26–28, 31, 32

Las Casas's ethnographic descriptions of the Indians, *Apologética historia sumaria*

The destruction of the Indies and assigning blame: *Historia de las Indias*, bk. 29; review selections from the *Brevísima relación*.

Theological, political, and theoretical issues about the conquest and colonialism

Contemporary theological and political stances on the conquest and Native Americans

> Primary sources: Sepúlveda, *Historia*; Motolinía (*Historia, Memoriales*); Betanzos
>
> Secondary sources: Gerbi, *La naturaleza*; Hanke (*Spanish Struggle, All Mankind*); Seed, *American Pentimento*

Theoretical issues dealing with colonialism: Homi Bhabha, Edward Said

Mock debates and discussions

Students write position papers.

Mock debate

Extension to the twentieth and twenty-first centuries: race, rights, and colonialism

Conclusions

On Barbarism, Demons, and Natural Reason: Las Casas's Rhetoric of Human Sacrifices in Pre-Hispanic Mexico

Viviana Díaz Balsera

Human sacrifice is one of the most controversial issues to be considered when teaching about the experience of European missionaries in sixteenth-century central Mexico. It was a salient practice of pre-Hispanic culture that missionaries had to contend with in their early evangelizing efforts or when accounting in their chronicles for the Amerindian subject they had come to transform. Because of its long history as a marker of otherness, Mesoamerican human sacrifice was invested by these missionaries—as well as by Crown officials, theologians, and conquerors—with a negative ideological charge unmatched by any other precontact social practice. A notable exception in the representation of Mesoamerican ritual killing was the writing of Bartolomé de las Casas. In his lifelong crusade to defend Indians from European abuse, Las Casas interpreted Mesoamerican human sacrifice as a rational act of heightened religious piety. In this essay, I examine how human sacrifice in Mexico was rhetorically constructed as a diabolic practice by one of the first missionary-ethnographers of Mexico, Toribio de Benavente, or Motolinía, and how Bartolomé de Las Casas rewrote Motolinía's text to prove otherwise. Las Casas's unique framing of the controversial practice of ritual killing allotted universal standing and agency to the pre-Hispanic Mexican subject, and this framing or rhetorical construction would play an important role in the Dominican friar's denunciation of the use of military force in the Spanish conquest of Mesoamerica during the sixteenth century. It was also intended to impinge on the legal configuration of the Amerindian subject under colonial rule. All these were central issues in the political thought and practice of Bartolomé de las Casas.

Historicizing the Practice of Human Sacrifice

Human sacrifice in Mesoamerica harked back to 5000 BC. There are human skeletons found dating from that time that bear marks of having been sacrificed (Davies, *Aztec Empire* 219). Although scholars today vary in their estimates of the number of victims, many, if not most, agree that at the peak of Mexica power in central Mexico in the fifteenth century, the scale of human sacrifice attained heights never reached before in human history (Nicholson 432). The Mexica usually sacrificed warriors, male and female slaves, or children during what the Spanish missionaries denominated calendrical feasts. The celebrations were held in honor of different deities every month of the eighteen months of twenty days in the Mesoamerican calendar. They also sacrificed victims on special occasions (such as the inauguration of the Templo Mayor in 1487) and in other ceremonial observances that fell on different days of the calendar every year. Depending on the feast and on the honored deity, there were different ways of putting to death the human offering. According to Henry Nicholson, the most common methods were

> gashing open the chest with a stone knife and ripping out the heart, de-
> capitation (especially for female victims), shooting with atlatl darts or ar-
> rows . . . burning nearly to death—the *coup de grace* delivered by heart
> extraction, drowning, hurling from a height, smashing against a hard sur-
> face, strangulation, shutting up and starving to death.   (432)

Since classic antiquity, historians and philosophers such as Herodotus, Socrates, Tacitus, Plinius, and Cicero had condemned human sacrifice as a mark of barbarism (Pagden, *Fall* 81; Davies, *Human Sacrifice* 43–59), but it was Christianity that finally eradicated the practice in Europe and in those lands to which it eventually expanded. The notion of human sacrifice and ingestion of the flesh was and is central to the Christian religion, but the actual human sacrifice for appeasing divine forces was forever displaced by the posited all-encompassing historical crucifixion of the incarnated deity itself.[1] This ultimate sacrifice is re-enacted over and over again in a quasi-symbolic supernatural way in the transubstantiated host in the mass. It can be said, then, that the principle of human sacrifice for the atonement of sin and transgressions is fundamental in Christianity, as in all religions where human sacrifice was practiced, but that its form was reified into a symbolic realm. With the expansion of Christianity, the practice of human sacrifice was downgraded to the category of crime, and the usually accompanying ingestion of the sacrificed flesh became the mark of a barbaric transgression of "natural law."

The concept of natural law as something universal, self-evident, and existing independent of human will was also first developed in a systematic way by ancient Greek poets and philosophers, particularly Aristotle (Brown 180). Although some fathers of the early church such as Saint Paul, Saint John Chrysostom, Saint Augustine, and Saint Isidore from Seville made reference to natural law, it was Saint Thomas Aquinas who refined the concept for Christianity (Brown 181). He conceived it as an "efficient cause which underpinned man's relationship with the world about him and governed every practice in human society" (Pagden, *Fall* 161). Natural law provided light for distinguishing between good and evil in those areas where no precedents had been established. One of the arguments expounded by recalcitrant defenders of the use of force in Spanish conquest and colonization, such as Juan Ginés de Sepúlveda, was that war was acceptable against the Amerindians because they had violated this principle (Pagden, *Fall* 86). Using Paracelsus's concept of *homunculi* (little men), Sepúlveda argued that anthropophagy had degraded Indians to a state of monstrosity that made them unworthy of being treated like men (Palencia-Roth 48). Another argument, propounded by the Dominican Francisco de Vitoria, was that in performing human sacrifice, the Amerindians had evinced a confused notion of reality. Although not outright unnatural, this practice showed that they had not been able to discern the priority of respecting the natural scale of being over the imperative of sacrificing to God what is most precious to humanity (Pagden, *Fall* 90).

Motolinía and Las Casas: A Contemptuous Dialogue

When Franciscan missionaries arrived in Mexico in 1524, one of the first things they did was to abolish the great public, ceremonial calendrical feasts in which human sacrifice was usually practiced. While there are testimonies of actual witnessed sacrifices in Hernán Cortés's third letter to Charles V ("Third Letter") and in Bernal Díaz del Castillo's *History of the Conquest of New Spain*, the first attempt at a systematic description of Nahua ritual killings appears in Motolinía's *Memoriales* and in his *History of the Indians of New Spain*, finished in 1541. Motolinía was one of those first missionaries arriving in Mexico. He was a great defender of Christianized Nahua Amerindians as the forerunners of a more spiritually elevated church that would culminate human history (Baudot). Nonetheless, Motolinía saw the pre-Hispanic past as dominated and ruled by Satan. His quasi-ethnographic descriptions of calendrical feasts and sacrifices are deeply informed by this view. What is of particular interest here is that the great Dominican friar Bartolomé de Las Casas will use extensive passages from Motolinía's ethnographic material on Mesoamerican human sacrifice in his monumental *Apologética historia sumaria*.

Originally conceived as part of the *Historia de Indias*, the *Apologética* grew into an independent voluminous treatise whose main project was to prove the Amerindians' rational capacity for self-government. This capacity was warranted by their physical environment, by the organization of their bodily nature, and by the products of their free will or culture (O'Gorman, "Estudio preliminar" xxxvii). It is revealing to examine Las Casas's rewriting of Motolinía's text, as it discloses a radically different rhetorical construct of pre-Hispanic Nahua human sacrifice while keeping significant proximity to the original in terms of the narrated events. As mentioned earlier, these rhetorical, historiographical constructs would have significantly different implications regarding the legitimate mode of Spanish intervention in the Mexican highlands and the political status of the Amerindian subjects in the colony.[2]

In his representation of the feast of Panquetzaliztli, dedicated to the gods of war Tezcatlipoca and Huitzilopochtli, Motolinía writes:

> Tenían una piedra larga. . . . En esta piedra tendían a los *desventurados* de espaldas para los sacrificar, y el pecho muy tenso, porque los tenían atados los pies y las manos, y el principal sacerdote *de los ídolos* . . . de presto con

una piedra de pedernal con que sacan lumbre . . . con aquel *cruel* navajón, como el pecho estaba tan tenso, con mucha fuerza abrían al *desventurado* y de presto sacábanle el corazón y el oficial de esta *maldad* daba con el corazón encima del umbral del altar de parte de fuera y allí dejaba hecha una mancha de sangre. . . . Cuanto a los corazones de los que sacrificaban, digo: que en sacando el corazón a el sacrificado, aquel *sacerdote del demonio* tomaba el corazón en la mano, y levantábale como quien le muestra a el sol. . . .   (*Historia* 32–33; emphasis mine)

They had a large stone. . . . Over this stone they stretched the *unfortunate* victims on their backs when sacrificing them. Their chest was very taut because both feet and hands were bound. . . . The executioner approached promptly with a flint stone, which was a knife that resembled a spearhead. . . . With this *atrocious* knife . . . they cut open with great force *the unfortunate victim* and promptly tore out his heart. Then the one who presided over this *inhuman ceremony* struck the heart on the lintel on the outside part of the altar and left there a blotch of blood. . . . Regarding the hearts of those whom they sacrificed, may I say that after tearing it out of the victim, *the minister of the demon* took the heart in his hands and held it aloft as if he were showing it to the sun. . . .
                               (*History* 114–15; emphasis mine)

Indeed, for Motolinía and his Franciscan brothers, Andrés de Olmos, Bernardino de Sahagún, and Gerónimo de Mendieta, and, a few decades later, for the Jesuit José de Acosta,[3] Nahua human sacrifice had a demonic origin. It was inspired by the devil in his ageless quest to disfigure and degrade humanity. Although Motolinía recognized that the conquest of Mexico was extremely bloody and came at a tremendous human cost (he compares it to one of the biblical plagues), he regarded it nonetheless as an act of providence. Spanish conquest had rescued Amerindian humanity from the sorry, debased condition to which it had been reduced by the devil, as manifested above all by the barbaric cruelty of the feasts celebrated in honor of their false gods. This belief in a holy purpose is why Motolinía uses highly charged adjectives in his description of the feast, such as "atrocious" and "inhuman," and finally refers to the priest as "minister of the demon." He wishes to emphasize the extreme cruelty with which the devil treated his Amerindian oppressed subjects. Remarkably, the diabolical in central Mexico did not come in the form of unbridled lust, sloth, greed, or other vices that diminished humanity by perversely gratifying the flesh at the expense of the spirit. In Mexico, the diabolical manifested itself in the inordinate extremes of physical suffering inflicted on others as well as on the self, which trampled on the bodily nature of humanity and mutilated its form. All this sacrifice was to no avail, since the devil subjected the Indians to unimaginable hardships "only to bring them in the end to eternal sufferings" (*History* 135). For Motolinía and many other missionaries, then, Christianity had delivered the Nahuas from a spiritual as well as from a horrendous physical bondage to the devil. The violence of the Spanish conquest was interpreted as divine punishment for the grave, serious sins of idolatry the Evil One had induced the Amerindians to commit against the majesty of God.

Bartolomé de Las Casas conceived Nahua precontact human sacrifice in a different way. His unique interpretation is weaved into the *Apologética historia sumaria* in his subtle rewriting of Motolinía's passage:

> Tenían enhiesta una piedra . . . hincada encima de las gradas del altar de los ídolos. En ésta tendían de espalda a la persona que habían de sacrificar, de manera que quedaba el pecho muy teso, y teníanlo atado de pies y manos. Entonces, uno de los sacerdotes o ministros de aquello . . . con una piedra de perdernal de hechura de un hierro de lanza jineta, como el pecho estaba muy teso, y con muncha fuerza y ligereza, como estaba ya muy experto en aquel oficio, abríalo fácilmente y sacábale el corazón y daba con él encima del umbral del altar, de partes de fuera, y dejaba hecha una mancha de sangre. . . . En otras solemnidades y días célebres tomaba el sacerdote el corazón en la mano, levantándolo hacia el Sol. . . .
>
> (2: 187)[4]

> They had an upright stone . . . on top of the steps of the altar for the idols. On this stone they stretched the person whom they were going to sacrifice over his back, in such a way that the chest was very taut, and they had his feet and arms bound. Then, one of the priests and principal ministers of all that . . . with a flint stone having the form of a spearhead, because the chest was so taut, with great alacrity and force, since he was so very expert in that trade, opened it with great ease and took out the heart and struck the heart on the lintel of the altar, of the outside parts, and left there a blotch of blood. . . . In other solemnities and holidays the priest took the heart in his hand, raising it toward the Sun. . . .

The reader will readily notice that Las Casas deletes from the original passage the phrase that refers to Nahua priests as agents of the devil. The Dominican friar also omits adjectives that indicate aberrant behavior. Consequently, no repulse or rejection is communicated by the narrative voice regarding the object of representation, human sacrifice by heart extraction. And, although in other passages about the calendrical feasts in the *Apologética* one may encounter similes such as "they looked like the devil himself" or "they looked like furious beasts" (2: 189, 191), these comparisons presuppose difference (A is or looks like B) rather than identity (A is B). Thus, they deny a direct intervention of the satanic supernatural and, at most, imply an occasional, not essential, degradation to the beastly. Although narrating exactly the same historical events, Las Casas's rewriting of Motolinía shows the Dominican's shift from a theological, supernatural interpretation of human sacrifices to an anthropological one.

The Anthropological Contribution of Las Casas

Bartolomé de Las Casas's perspective on the precontact Amerindian past in general and of human sacrifice in particular was strongly influenced by Thomas Aquinas's Aristotelian view that all human beings had been imbued with the capacity of fulfilling the telos or destiny of *man qua man*, even if they were not Christians. Las Casas claimed that, although pagans could not reach ultimate happiness and contentment, "they could achieve a state of 'active happiness,' adequate to the needs of most men" (Pagden, *Fall* 135). Clearly, one of the reasons why pagans could not reach the highest degree of happiness was the fact that they did not know the true God. All peoples of the world, however, had both the aptitude and tendency to worship something greater than mankind. This universal proclivity was part of the *lumbre natural*, or natural reason, that God had instilled in all human beings at the moment of their creation (Casas, *Apologética* 1: 369–70).

The origin of idolatry or the cult to false gods was not diabolic, then, but anthropological: it lay in the very fabric of humanity, always looking for a higher good. Thus, according to Las Casas, all civilized cultures that evinced the exercise of human reason but that had not received Christian revelation would invariably be idolatrous (Bernand and Gruzinski 46; F. Cervantes 31). For the Dominican friar, it was in this predicament where the devil found propitious opportunities to operate. He constantly sought "to perpetuate his perversities" in human cults to false gods arising from an obfuscated fallen nature not yet fortified by Christian grace (F. Cervantes 31). For, by following the dictates of unaided human reason, non-Christian people sinned in failing to keep the first commandment of loving God above all else.

And yet, the insistence on the essential goodness of human nature in spite of the errors of idolatry is what sets Las Casas aside from his contemporaries in the rhetorical construction of the Amerindian subject. Although acknowledging all the potential for demonic contamination in the worship of false gods, Las Casas waged a campaign for the merit of the human desire for God that lay behind idolatry. A significant part of his *Apologética historia sumaria* is dedicated to showing, first, how all Amerindian nations, particularly the Inca and Mexica, fully met Aristotelian criteria for the constitution of human polities with the power to civilize (Pagden, *Fall* 135; S. Arias, *Retórica* 69). Las Casas sought then to prove that the Inca and Mexican civilizations superseded all great pagan nations of antiquity, including Greeks and Romans, in their unaided understanding of the greatness and devotion owed to the divinity. It is at this juncture that the Dominican friar made his audacious claim that, far from being a violation of natural law, Amerindian massive human sacrifices were precisely the opposite. They were incontrovertible evidence that in comparison with all the nations of antiquity, the Mexicans "excedieron sin alguna comparación ni proporción, en usar muy mejor del juicio de la razón, teniendo en esto más desenvuelto y desenerrado, libre y claro entendimiento" 'had exceeded, without comparison or proportion, in a much better use of the judgment of reason, showing in this a more developed, less erroneous, free and clear understanding.' The complexity and scale of Mexica sacrifices, the devotion, punctuality, and "religious honesty" (*Apologética* 2: 292) with which they were carried out, the precious value of the offerings, the excruciating pain to which they subjected themselves and their victims to honor the gods, all this showed that the Mexica had an elevated conception of what humanity owed to God. With this optimistic fabrication regarding Mexica human sacrifice, Bartolomé de Las Casas cleansed the Amerindian precontact past from the opprobrium of being cast out from the human community of nations. But, as Santa Arias has observed, Las Casas's rhetorical, historiographical, and philosophical constructions in the *Apologética* were also a means of establishing actual power and authority ("Bartolomé de las Casas's Sacred Place" 122). The important political offshoots in Las Casas's argument were that, because Amerindians had shown an excellent and privileged use of natural reason regarding their religious practices in their precontact past, they were capable both of self-government and of readily accepting Christianity once they understood its truth by proper, doctrinal instruction and rational argumentation. The use of force defended by those who claimed that the Indians had transgressed natural law, or by those who, like the Franciscan Bernardino de Sahagún (*Florentine Codex*, *Historia*) and later the Jesuit José de Acosta, saw in human sacrifices and autosacrifices the heavy hand of a devil who would not easily give up his preeminence in Amerindian soil, was not warranted, according to Las Casas's rhetoric on the full rationality of human sacrifices.

But Las Casas's humanistic position regarding Amerindian human sacrifices did not prevail among contemporary theologians and missionaries (Pagden, *Fall* 90; Palencia-Roth 48). As the sixteenth century unfolded, other missionaries like Sahagún and the Dominican Diego Durán uncovered the fact that the Nahuas had accepted Christianity but did not abandon many of their precontact practices and beliefs. Las Casas's rhetoric of a full, rational, and voluntary acceptance of Christianity by the Amerindians became less and less ratified by the course of events. For many missionaries and clerics, evidence showed that the chilling practice of public ritual killings had been effectively abolished by Spanish colonial forces, but the "demonic" matrix on which it was founded had still to be fully eradicated by their vigilant, evangelizing efforts. Decades after Las Casas's death, the Mexican priests Hernando Ruiz de Alarcón and Jacinto de la Serna wrote treatises in which they denounced a wide range of ongoing practices that they considered idolatrous. These practices harked back to a pre-Hispanic conception of the world still very much alive in spite of one hundred years of Christian presence in Anáhuac.[5]

Indeed, the mindset of the Nahuas did not conform to the great Dominican friar's Western universal model, as they had other ways of constructing reality that had been in place for many centuries before the arrival of the Europeans. In this sense, when we teach Las Casas's *Apologética historia sumaria*, his hard labor spent bringing Mesoamerican human sacrifices under the mantle of an

Aristotelian universal reason may ironically be deemed another instance of colonial imposition on the Amerindian. Las Casas's representational efforts reveal a strong desire to suppress cultural difference, however vindicating they were in comparison with the subalterizing depictions of Nahua past and present by other missionaries and ecclesiastics. European conceptions of the subject were still the gold standard against which the Amerindians had to be measured. And yet, we should also remind students that, beyond the colonialist implications of his universalizing rhetorical constructions, the power of Las Casas's work as testimony of a resolute, ecumenical will not to leave pre-Hispanic antiquity behind the community of nations stands high among the great cultural legacies of all times.

NOTES

Citations of Las Casas's *Apologética historia sumaria* refer to the version edited by Edmundo O'Gorman (U Nacional Autónoma de Mexico, 1967).

[1] There is a penal element in Christ's Passion and Crucifixion: "The word *propitiation* reminds one that Christ's suffering and death were an expiation for an offense or an appeasement of an offended God" (Hennessy 702). Christ's sacrifice, "costly in human endurance, is 'the great price' (1 Cor. 6.20) of man's deliverance; by it man who was once afar off has been brought near through the blood of Christ" (703).

[2] It should be pointed out that Bartolomé de Las Casas and Motolinía had been enemies since Las Casas's first short stay in Mexico in 1536, where the Dominican stood up against the Franciscan practice of mass baptism. According to Helen Rand Parish and Harold E. Weidmann (*Las Casas en México*), Las Casas was instrumental in the promulgation of the bull *Altitudo divini consilii* (1537), in which Pope Paul III ordered that the Indians be properly instructed in Christian doctrine before being baptized. The enmity would continue throughout the years and is clearly documented in a letter of Motolinía to Charles V in 1555, where the Franciscan accuses Las Casas of defamation and of ignorance of native languages and of the pre-Hispanic past. Interestingly, or perhaps only coincidentally, it was also toward 1555 when, according to Edmundo O'Gorman, Las Casas started writing the text of what a few years later would become his *Apologética historia sumaria* ("Estudio preliminar" xxxv).

[3] José de Acosta is an important point of reference in all discussions regarding pre-Hispanic past because his *Historia natural y moral de las Indias* was one of the few such texts that saw light during the sixteenth and seventeenth centuries, after Philip II's 1577 prohibition of the publication of chronicles dealing with Amerindian past. Acosta's *Historia natural y moral* was published in Seville in 1590.

[4] All translations of Las Casas's *Apologética historia* are mine unless otherwise indicated.

[5] Hernando Ruiz de Alarcón, zealous ecclesiastical judge and parishioner in northern Guerrero, Mexico, wrote the notable *Tratado de las supersticiones y costumbres gentílicas que oy viuen entre los indios naturales desta Nueva España* in 1629 (Ruiz de Alarcón, *Aztec Sorcerers*). Jacinto de la Serna wrote his "Manual de ministros de indios para el conocimiento de sus idolatrías, y extirpación de ellas" (1656) based on Ruiz de Alarcón's work and on his own observations. He was a doctor of theology and three times rector of the University of Mexico.

Las Casas as Genealogical Keystone for Discourses on Political Independence

Santa Arias

In their attempts to reject Spanish geopolitical domination and economic ex-ploitation, intellectuals and leaders of the Latin American independence move-ments connected their political concerns not only with their indigenous past but also with the first voices of resistance to colonial power. In eighteenth- and nineteenth-century studies, these colonial intertexts are significant, since liberal intellectuals read, interpreted, and ideologically manipulated the experience of the conquest to justify their struggle against imperial rule.[1] Their handling of the past, particularly the writings and actions of Bartolomé de Las Casas, pro-vides one of the best examples of the use of early colonial documents during this extended age of revolutions.

Las Casas's aggressive defense of the Amerindian populations and critique of the conquest are themes that were frequently invoked and form a common thread in patriotic narratives. Here I offer some possibilities of exploring in a seminar this Lascasian historical interjection, which, by dealing with the ques-tion of war, provides clarity on the emergence of indigenism and Las Casas's role in the advancement of revolutionary principles such as abolition of slavery, civil liberty, and sovereignty of the people. To those principles that informed key debates of liberalism (natural rights, equality, freedom) one must add the roles of religion, cultural identity, and the pragmatic use of Las Casas's ideo-logical stance in the formulation of liberal nationalist projects. We must under-stand that early-nineteenth-century intellectuals were still under the influence of eighteenth-century ideas that formed the backbone of the Latin American independence movements.

Up to the late nineteenth century, Las Casas's actions and ideas not only formed the subject of literary texts, such as Manuel de Jesús Galván's *Enriquillo* (a foundational novel of the *indigenista* tradition) and neoclassical poems and plays (see Marcus), but, more important, those ideas and his personality ap-pealed to the intellectuals who fueled the struggle for independence. To exam-ine the uses and authority of Las Casas during this period, I propose a reading of key essays, such as the 1564 "Tratado de las doce dudas," one of Las Casas's last pleas to the Council of the Indies about the increasingly aggravating situ-ation in the Spanish colonies; Simón Bolívar's "Carta de Jamaica" (1815); Ser-vando Teresa de Mier's introduction to his edition of the *Brevísima relación de la destrucción de las Indias* ("Discurso preliminar" [1812]); Ramón Emeterio Betances's "Cuba" (1874); and José Martí's "El padre Las Casas" (1889). Bolívar (1783–1830), Mier (1765–1827), Martí (1853–95), and Betances (1827–98) wrote some of their most persuasive treatises on political resistance from exile. They empowered their compatriots and influenced other intellectuals while undermining and exposing colonial domination. Reminiscent of Las Casas's writings, their letters and essays represent the best of rhetorical force at the service of colonial emancipation and collective and individual rights.

The essays selected show the dialogic nature of nineteenth-century Latin American political writing. Bolívar, Mier, Betances, and Martí were linked to each other by their predicaments, conceptually and rhetorically. They engaged in conversation through direct communications with one another and references to one another in their writing. Examples include Bolívar's and Mier's correspondence and writings about each other, including Mier's portrait of Bolívar in several letters and essays. Betances, the most important Puerto Rican independence nineteenth-century leader, read Bolívar and corresponded with Martí while living in Paris. The letter "Betances," in which Martí requests the Puerto Rican leader's assistance in Paris to organize support for Cuban independence, is crucial to any discussion of the shared Cuban and Puerto Rican struggle for emancipation from Spain during the second half of the nineteenth century. Bolívar, Mier, Betances, and Martí read Las Casas's writings carefully, and their admiration is evident in letters and essays. Their reliance on Las Casas was a wholly original way of applying the lessons of the Enlightenment to their nineteenth-century reality. They also read Locke, Montesquieu, Rousseau, and Voltaire, but their political and intellectual imperatives were rooted in the Spanish American colonial experience, as their close reading of Las Casas demonstrates.

When studying Las Casas's nineteenth-century reception, it is important to highlight the heavy editing of the texts and their history of circulation. Most intellectuals depended on secondary sources until 1822, when Juan Antonio Llorente's first critical collection of Las Casas's writings was made available in French and Spanish and became the most important primary source of the Dominican's work (Llorente). (The only exception was Las Casas's *Brevísima relación*, which circulated widely before the publication of Llorente's edition.) Looking at this two-volume collection helps students appreciate the role of interpretative scholarship (editing, commentary, and authorial orientation) during the Enlightenment. Llorente's collection of Las Casas's writings also included four critical essays: by the editor himself; the Bishop of Blois, Henri Grégoire; the Argentinean Dean of Tucuman, Gregorio Funes; and Servando Teresa de Mier. Its editing and critical commentaries demonstrate the transatlantic dimension of the struggle for independence: Spanish, French, and Latin American intellectuals united in this book to reflect on Las Casas's life and ideas and apologize for his role in the African slave trade.

In Spanish America, Creole patriots narrativized the colonial past to engineer the future of the American territories. On a clear political and civic mission, they found in Las Casas's writings a historical authority and a rhetorical model. Lascasian texts provided not only firsthand accounts but also persuasive images that formed part of the symbolic capital exploited in the discourses of independence. Creole leaders, such as Mier, moved readers to support emancipation using Las Casas's master narrative of the destruction of the Indies, the one found not only in the *Brevísima relación* but also in the *Historia de las Indias* and in his letters, *memoriales,* and treatises. Las Casas's images of the Spanish as greedy and savage wolves and the Indians as lambs persisted and were reiterated by Mier and many others.

The process of historical and ideological reconstruction necessary to understand Las Casas's influence on the patriotic agenda begins with a discussion of his "Tratado de las doce dudas." This essential text, written in Madrid in 1564, offers a summary of Las Casas's legal and moral argument against Spanish colonialism. In the classroom, this point is as controversial as Las Casas's early roles as an *encomendero* and as a promoter of the African slave trade. The "Tratado" answers twelve doubts presented to Las Casas by another Dominican, Bartolomé de la Vega, who was concerned with the situation in Perú. Considered one of Las Casas's major texts, several copies of the "Tratado" circulated and a first printed edition appeared in Juan Antonio Llorente's collection.

As Las Casas states in the introduction, the "Tratado" is intimately related to his Latin treatise *De thesauris* (1563; translated into Spanish as *Los tesoros del Perú*]). Written between *De thesauris* and the lesser known "Memorial de despedida al Consejo de Indias" (1565), which was sent to the council fifteen days before his death, the "Tratado" represents his strongest objections against the conquest. In the "Memorial," Las Casas reveals that his *De thesauris* and "Tratado de las doce dudas" are the two treatises with which he accomplished his spiritual mission of offering a remedy for the many offences committed by *encomenderos* and Spanish officials in the New World territories.

A class on the "Tratado de las doce dudas" should begin with analysis of its format, its different parts, and their rhetorical function in the construction of an argument regarding the laws and ethics of the conquest. Those parts consist of the introduction, the argument, a list of Vega's twelve doubts, the eight principles that guide Las Casas's reply to each doubt, and Las Casas's conclusions. Some of Las Casas's most significant and convincing points are his brief history of and attack on the *encomiendas*, the obligation of Spanish colonizers to offer restitution to the Indians, and the rights of Indians to wage wars of self-defense. (While discussing the influence of Las Casas on nineteenth-century liberalism, instructors need to emphasize that when he advocated for peaceful conversion, he firmly believed in indigenous self-defense against aggression.) Las Casas begs Philip II one last time to bring the conquest to an end, an appeal to the king's Christian consciousness reiterated in many other treatises and letters. In the conclusions of the "Tratado," Las Casas returns to the theme of restitution, asks the Crown to return the land, kingdoms, gold, and pearls that were stolen from the native populations, and requests a ban on the tyrannical practice of the *encomiendas*.

Instead of introducing Las Casas with the *Brevísima relación*, the text usually used to teach his ideas, I prefer this legal document that clearly and succinctly presents the Dominican's most radical anticolonial perspective. Here, Las Casas does not voice a new ethical or political demand, since his earlier requests for restitution and banning of the *encomiendas* failed, but reasserts that his lack of success has not changed his mind. Reading the "Tratado" opens up a space for introducing Las Casas's influential ideas without the digressions caused by the shock students typically feel when reading the many horrific episodes depicted in the *Brevísima relación*. Comparing Las Casas's sixteenth-century requests of the Spanish Crown with the intellectual products of the most influential leaders of the Latin American independence efforts helps students understand the movements' responses to the long history of Spanish colonialism's political abuse and violations of individual rights.[2]

Bolívar's "Carta de Jamaica," written in Kingston in 1815, invokes the name of Las Casas among the many authorities who influenced his assessment of how his fellow Spanish Americans are to assume control of their own destiny. In this prophetic letter, Bolívar outlines his proposals within the ideological framework of Pan-Americanism, offers a critical account of the legacy of the colonial regime, and analyzes the political history that has culminated in the struggle for independence. He believes in the value of personal experience: as John Lynch puts it, for Bolívar "institutions are really agencies of survival and not expressions of abstracts principles" (*Simón Bolívar* 33). In this sense, Las Casas, with many years of fighting injustice, would carry more weight with Bolívar than the philosophers whose idea of liberty had no pragmatic experience behind it. Examining Bolívar's letter before assigning Mier's, Betances's, and Martí's essays can open a discussion of the significance of Las Casas's critique of Spanish domination and how it found its way into the patriotic discourse of freedom and citizenship that framed modernity in Latin America. In his letter, Bolívar refers to Las Casas as the most sublime historian of his period and declares, "Todos los imparciales han hecho justicia al celo, verdad y virtudes de aquel amigo de la humanidad, que con tanto fervor y firmeza denunció ante su gobierno y contemporáneos los actos más horrorosos de un frenesí sanguinario" 'All impartial accounts support the integrity and passion for truth of that friend of humanity, who so fervently and forcefully denounced before his own government and contemporaries the most depraved acts of that bloodfest' ("Carta" 56, "Jamaica" 13). Bolívar's treatises and letters, such as this one, his "Manifiesto de Cartagena" (1812), and "Discurso de Angostura" (1819), represent effective critiques of colonialism in their analysis of Latin America's fundamental problems and arguments for the political integration of the region.

The lives and intellectual legacies of the towering figures of the nineteenth-century Spanish American revolutions are still being rewritten and interpreted (e.g., Lynch's recently released major biography, *Simón Bolívar: A Life*). Las Casas's passionate denunciation of the Spanish conquest can be found restated in Mier's introduction to his editions of the *Brevísima relación*, which Mier published in London, Paris, Philadelphia, Mexico City, and Puebla.

Las Casas's ideology and accounts provided Bolívar and Mier a solid foundation in the quest for autonomy and the intellectual construction of nationhood.

Mier framed his anticolonial argument around the notion that Spain had no legal rights over the Americas. He supported his claims by asserting the existence of a valid constitution drafted after Las Casas's debate with Juan Ginés de Sepúlveda, where "se abolió el título de conquista, se declararon injustas y prohibieron las guerras á los Indios, se les volvió su libertad y su gobierno . . . y por decirlo asi, se le dio una Constitución" 'the title of conquest was abolished, wars against the Indians were declared unjust and prohibited, their freedom and government were returned . . . and, if you want to call it that, a constitution was given [to the Americas]' ("Discurso preliminar" viii).[3] (He elaborated this statement in the essay "Idea de una constitución dada a las Américas.") The question of an original constitution was also a political imperative for Bolívar, who referred to Mier's Lascasian ideas in his "Carta de Jamaica": "El emperador Carlos V formó un pacto con los descubridores, conquistadores y pobladores de América, que como dice Guerra es nuestro contrato social" 'The emperor Charles V entered into a pact with the discoverers, conquerors, and settlers of the America, which is, according to Guerra,[4] our social contract' (64; "Jamaica Letter" 20). For both leaders, Las Casas played a crucial political role by engineering an early constitution that they could adapt to fit their needs, including the abolition of monarchy and its privileges. Too, Las Casas served as the perfect model of the persuasive intellectual and civic servant who dedicated his life to helping his nation.

Ramón Emeterio Betances was Puerto Rico's most important intellectual figure in the struggle for emancipation. Betances, conscious of being mulatto, believed in the future of an Antillean federation based on principles of equality and freedom for all. His politics were reflected in his pseudonym, "El Antillano." He fought for Puerto Rico's and Cuba's independence and expressed concerned about Haiti's and the Dominican Republic's weak democracies. Accepting Martí's request for assistance in promoting the Cuban cause, Betances became a Cuban diplomatic agent in France, delegate of the Cuban Revolutionary Party, and president of the Cuban Committee in Paris (Estrade and Ojeda Reyes 15).

By introducing Betances's essay "Cuba," instructors can link Las Casas's writings to the late-nineteenth-century Caribbean struggle for emancipation. In his essay, Betances elaborates on three different chapters of Cuba's history (colonial, insurgent, and independent) and constructs parallels between early colonial episodes and present ones, using history to justify the war of independence. Betances demonstrates that Spanish abuses had not declined over time: a key moment in the essay is the comparison between the cacique Hatuey (whose portrait draws on Las Casas's representation of Amerindians) and the modern hero of the Cuban revolution, Carlos Manuel de Céspedes, a link that embeds anticolonial Amerindian defense in a Caribbean nationalist indigenist discourse (137–38). Provocatively, for Betances Amerindians were "indomables" 'unconquerable,' while the African slaves possessed "incanzable dulzura" 'untiring sweetness' (135). This contrast reveals the complexity of Betances essay, raising nationalist discourse to a literal and ideological level. Most research on Las Casas underlines his representation of the Indians as noble savages or docile lambs. Betances, however, echoes Las Casas's depiction of the Amerindians' courage, wit, and strength.

When discussing Betances's essay, instructors should devote attention to how Las Casas's ideas were used in the discourses of national identity. First, Spain's cruelty and its ingratitude to those who achieved great deeds on its behalf (Columbus, Vasco Nuñez, and Capitán Dulce) remain common themes. Second, as Betances underlines, Latin Americans had much to learn from African and Indian ancestors: "del uno [el africano] la paciencia que transige, perdona y espera; del otro [el indígena], la dignidad que, al sentirse ultrajada, sacude con desprecio el yugo imponente de la tiranía" 'from one [the African] the patience that respects, pardons, and waits; from the other [the Amerindian], the dignity that, when violated, shakes with scorn the imposing bondage of tyranny' (135). "Cuba" can be read alongside Betances's novel *Les deux Indiens: Episode de la conquête de Borinquen* ("The Two Indians: An Episode on the Conquest of Borinquen"), originally written in French and published in Toulouse in 1853 and eventually translated into Spanish in 1998 by Carmen Lugo Filippi (*Los dos indios*). This romantic, understudied novel presents the complexity and contradictions of colonial rule, its cruelty and differential histories of race, class, and gender. A Spanish woman falls in love with an Indian and gives birth to a mestizo who will survive and live among rebel Indians, sons of Borinquen. The novel shows the influence of the *Brevísima relación* in its depiction of Spaniards as gold-loving beasts who saw the Indians only as slaves; the narrator reiterates the horror of the work in the mines and of the 600,000 Indians killed, two facts found in the *Brevísima relación*'s chapters on the islands of San Juan and Jamaica (90).[5]

Reading any one of the historical essays included in José Martí's publication *La edad de oro*—"Las ruinas indias," "Tres heroes," or "El padre Las Casas"—complements the readings from Bolívar, Mier, and Betances and provides another perspective on the Spanish American patriots' use of Las Casas's ideas. These essays, beyond offering the opportunity to discuss the *modernistas'* aesthetics and politics, exemplify how Las Casas's texts, recovered and circulated by the *ilustrados* (Enlightenment social philosophers), were manipulated decades later in different ways, for different nationalist agendas, by different readers.

In his unique 1889 periodical *La edad de oro*, Martí maps out key ideas for the ethical education of the youth in Cuba and throughout the Americas and for helping them understand the need for emancipation.[6] He was inspired by similar North American publications aimed at educating the youth on principles of nineteenth-century liberalism, such as *Harper's Young People*, *The Youth's Companion*, and *St. Nicholas* (Vigne Pacheco 476). In *La edad de oro*, Martí undermines colonial power and advocates for freedom and honor that can only be found by getting rid of the colonial system and establishing an egalitarian, color-blind society (Fraser 225). The first reference to Las Casas in *La edad de oro* is in "Las ruinas indias," where students will find a humorous physical description of the friar. However, in the essay "El padre Las Casas," his representation is dominated by a *modernista* aesthetic:

> No se puede ver un lirio sin pensar en el Padre las Casas, porque con la bondad se le fue poniendo de lirio el color, y dicen que era hermoso verlo escribir, con su túnica blanca, sentado en su sillón de tachuelas, peleando con la pluma de ave porque no escribía de prisa.   (11)

> One cannot look at a lily without thinking about Father Las Casas, because with his kindness he became white like an iris, and people say that it was beautiful to see him write, with his white robe, seated in an armchair of tacks, struggling with the feather pen because he did not write quickly.

By portraying Las Casas sitting at his desk writing, Martí provides a poetic narrative of the well-known portrait by Tomás López Enguídanos, reproduced in Martí's main source on Las Casas, Juan Antonio Llorente's collection.

The modernist representation of Las Casas is based on the biography by the Enlightenment intellectual Llorente, which serves as an introduction to his collection. Two other intertexts, as Ana Cairo points out, are the novel *Enriquillo* (1882), sent to Martí by the author himself, Manuel Galván (58); and the Mexican Félix Parra's Romantic painting *Bartolomé de las Casas* (1875 [see illus.]). Considered one of Parra's major achievements, the painting places Las Casas at the scene of an anachronistic historical episode—one of the many massacres that took place before the Dominican's arrival to the region. Las Casas, holding a crucifix and looking upward, is the focal point of the image, at the footsteps of a destroyed Indian temple. The scene is completed by an Indian couple, the husband dead and the woman in silent appeal at his feet. In Parra's painting Las Casas can represent, on the one hand, the only hope of the surviving Indian and, on the other, "cultural assimilation through conversion" (Widdifield 129). Las Casas's figure is contrasted to the Aztec deity that stands behind him to his right. It is clear that the Indian prefers the Catholic friar: she holds onto him instead of the statue, which shows recent flower offerings. A series of oppositions speak to the nationalist revision of the Amerindian and colonial past: light and darkness, destruction and hope, and indigenous religions and Christianity. Martí included the illustration in the same issue of *La edad de oro* where his essay "El padre Las Casas" appeared.

All these elements work together in Martí's essay to symbolically represent Las Casas as the protector of the Indians, an image that feeds on the *modernistas'* use of color, plasticity, exoticism, and universalism. Paul Estrade states that Martí wanted to educate and shape new generations by emphasizing the "generous and combative spirit" of Las Casas (245): like Bolívar, Betances, and Mier, Martí was stirred by Las Casas's tenacity in his struggle to defend the native populations. He saw in the friar one of the best models youth could follow.

Félix Parra, *Friar Bartolomé de las Casas*

The citations and appropriations of Las Casas's writings during the nineteenth century shed new light on the colonial and independence periods. First, they demonstrate that intellectual and political leaders drew from some of the same colonial sources and saw in the first century of Spanish colonialism fundamental lessons to learn. Instructors will want to explore with students how modern national images, a poetic thread throughout nationalist discourses, crossed national boundaries (in letters and essays), providing the ideological foundation for political action. Mauricio Trillo outlines epic tropes such as "the path from darkness to light, from exploitation to freedom, from falsehood to authenticity" (66). To those images of national liberation we must add the Lascasian vision of sinful Spain that went against the most basic principles of Christianity and humanity to maintain control of its possessions. These visions and national images are tropes of ideological opposition found in Las Casas's discourse, along with the many other voices he attempted to represent.

Reading Las Casas's original treatises and looking at how and when they were edited, circulated, and received reveal to students a network of connections among Las Casas's struggle for Amerindian rights, its textual recovery by the *ilustrados*, and his influence on nineteenth-century intellectuals building the case for independence.[7] The Dominican left his imprint on the many forms of Pan-Americanism reflected in the thought of the movements' major political leaders, whose numerous references to him offer an exceptional opportunity to learn how his defense of native populations and anticolonial stance proved useful to them. The comparative study of the texts discussed above provides students with examples of history used and reinterpreted to address a later author's political concerns. In broader terms, students can see how the critical cultural practice of reading, an act always mediated by the writers' experience, knowledge, and context (see Reeser and Spalding's translation of a conversation between Roger Chartier and Pierre Bourdieu), was performed during the late eighteenth and nineteenth centuries. Moreover, they can also appreciate how colonial history, issues of cultural identity, and political action intersected and fed on each other during the long struggle for independence. The study of the social context of Las Casas's writings, their reception, and the circulation of his ideas through time and space can help students understand some of the most complex, rich, and crucial moments in the history of nation building in Spanish America.

NOTES

[1] Excellent references for students on this topic are John Lynch's *The Spanish American Revolutions (1808–1826)*; D. A. Brading's *Origins of Mexican Nationalism* and his classic *The First America*; David Bushnell and Neil Macaulay's *The Emergence of Latin America in the Nineteenth Century*; and the essay collection edited by Anthony McFarlane and Eduardo Posada-Carbó, *Independence and Revolution in Spanish America*.

[2] Hispanic studies tends to encapsulate the colonial period with texts produced between 1492 and 1810. This periodization is problematic as we consider the Spanish colonialism that dominated Cuba and Puerto Rico until the Spanish-American War and present-day forms of neocolonialism.

[3] All translations are mine, unless otherwise indicated.

[4] Mier was also known as José Guerra. He published his *Historia de la revolución de Nueva España* (1813) under that name.

[5] In my teaching, I use Cátedra's edition of the *Brevísima relación* (ed. André Saint-Lu [2005]), since it is widely available.

[6] Martí only published four issues of this intended monthly publication.

[7] My discussion has centered on four canonical figures of colonial emancipation, but any thorough reflection on how the colonial past framed a social contract and the struggle for individual rights must touch on the role of others, such as Francisco de Miranda, Simón Rodríguez, and Eugenio María de Hostos. This list should also include women, whose marginalized voices also critiqued the colonial past, in articles and essays in nineteenth-century women's journals and in private readings by women intellectuals such as Juana Maria Gorriti, whose *veladas literarias* (literary evenings), organized between 1876 and 1877 in Lima, remain one of the most understudied subjects of Latin American literary history. (Many of these readings were published in 1892, with an introduction by Ricardo Palma.)

Addressing the Atlantic Slave Trade:
Las Casas and the Legend of the Blacks

Eyda M. Merediz and Verónica Salles-Reese

The literature curriculum, which is increasingly interdisciplinary and organized in thematic clusters, can benefit from a unit that directly addresses Africa in the Americas. A class that fuses literary texts and other forms of cultural expression has a place for Bartolomé de las Casas and his well-known propositions about the African slave trade, both in undergraduate and graduate designs. Although Las Casas's primary texts that deal with the subject may occasionally be read in specialized upper-division or graduate seminars, they are rarely introduced or mentioned in basic survey courses. We believe that undergraduate students should be exposed to a selection of these texts early in their careers as Spanish or Latin American studies majors. Graduate students could be engaged in more theoretical panhistoric issues that point to the reception of Las Casas, especially in the Caribbean. A selection of such fragments can help contextualize subsequent readings on Las Casas and the origins of the slave trade, which have turned his stance on African slavery into a polemical and often misguided declaration in favor of the introduction of African slaves to alleviate or substitute for Indian forced labor.

Las Casas's pronouncements with respect to indigenous rights, the Crown's economic and social policies, and the church's approaches to evangelization were controversial, as they often constituted oppositional discourse. Yet they were never perceived as inconsistent—unlike his views on the Atlantic slave trade. Las Casas has been the subject of many scornful attacks and passionate defenses: he has often been singled out as a major promoter of the African slave trade while simultaneously being recognized as a powerful defender of Indian rights. To clarify such an apparent contradiction, it is crucial to introduce in the classroom two texts by Las Casas—"Memorial de remedios para las Indias" ("Petition for Remedies for the Indies") and his *Historia de las Indias (History of the Indies)*—framed by a brief discussion of the philosophical and historical background of slavery itself, not as a way of naturalizing the concept or the institution but as a matter of contextualization.

An introduction to the history of slavery might start by pointing out that the institution seems to be as old as human civilization itself. Provisions in the Hammurabi code referring to slaves are evidence that slavery existed two millennia before the Christian era. A trajectory of slavery since classical antiquity until the sixteenth century, when Las Casas wrote his texts, will put into perspective and enrich the interpretation of the two texts under scrutiny and will also allow a critical reading of the defenders and detractors of Las Casas's role in promoting or not promoting slavery in the New World. Two types of questions about slavery are basic for the discussion: those that are factual and those that are more philosophical or ideological.

What peoples were enslaved? In what kind of activities were slaves involved? How and where was the slave trade instituted? These are some of the possible questions that a historical background should address. Depending on what point in history and where, slaves belonged to different racial and ethic groups. They were Scythians, Carthaginians, Saxons, Slavs, Ethiopians, Germans, Poles, Moors, Spaniards, West Africans, and others. Egyptians, Greeks, and Romans used slaves in agriculture, mining, and as domestic servants, and they were of key importance in the development of these civilizations. Rome's prosperity at its height between the first century BC and the third AD was partly due to its slaves. In the Roman republic some slaves were even doctors or lawyers. Some of them were educated; Cicero's secretary, Tiro, was his slave (Thomas 26).

Originally slaves were obtained mainly in two ways: prisoners of war became slaves, and captives from razzias (raids on towns or islands) were then sold in markets. Captives were taken in Europe during its almost constant culture of warfare, giving rise to an active slave trade at different points in history and in various places. In classical antiquity, slave markets were found in Chios, Rhodes, Delos, and Ephesus; and in the Middle Ages in Verdum, Arles, and Lyon. Besides war and razzia captives, extreme poverty in Europe during the Middle Ages caused people to sell their children or even themselves in search of a better life. While in Northern Europe the slave markets practically disappeared around the eleventh century, in the Mediterranean region slave trade prospered because of the wars between Muslims and Christians. Slaves were so coveted by the Muslims that, at the beginning of the eighth century, there seem to have been close to thirty thousand slaves in Damascus taken at the fall of the Visigoths, and there were still about the same number in Granada in 1311. Razzias to capture Christian slaves were carried out frequently in the Mediterranean world from the ninth century onward. Russian slaves were also common until the fall of Constantinople, when they became scarce and were substituted by other groups (Thomas 41).

Toward the end of the Middle Ages there begin to appear more and more black African slaves, usually captured by one tribe and sold to the Europeans. By the middle of the fifteenth century, the Portuguese had a well-established trade of African slaves, mainly Azhanaghi (23).[1] This history brings us to the moment of the discovery and conquest of the New World, and class discussion should be centered on how, when, and by whom African slaves were brought to the Americas up to the first quarter of the sixteenth century, when Las Casas wrote his *memorial*.

The picture would not be complete if the issue of slavery in pre-Columbian America were not addressed, because it will shed light on how the indigenous peoples might have seen and engaged with Africans. Slavery was not unknown in the Americas. Among the Aztecs, for instance, the inability to pay one's debt might force one to become a slave, and in times of famine, people sometimes sold their children. Masters could not sell their slaves, and slaves could obtain their freedom on paying the debt (Krickeberg; Clendinnen, *Aztecs*). In a similar

fashion, in the late Inca empire there was a group of slaves called *pina* in Quechua (*pinacuna* in the plural), consisting of prisoners of war who had refused to
accept Inca rule. Although entire families and ayllus (kinship groups—the basic
unit of Inca social civilization) could become *pinacuna*, there were not that
many. These slaves worked in the coca fields; they belonged solely to the Sapa
Inca—the state—and were never sold (Espinosa Soriano 293–94).

A philosophical or ideological approach to slavery should address how the
practice was conceptualized and how it was justified. This discussion should also
bring into the forefront those who attacked or rejected slavery who can be seen
as Las Casas's ideological forefathers. Aristotle's theory of natural slavery (*Politics*, bk. 1), pivotal to the 1550s Valladolid debate, makes an excellent point of
contrast with Plato's assertion that slavery was what we would call now a cultural
construct (168). With the conceptualization of slavery came its regulation in the
different legal systems. Roman law considered slaves objects, without agency
to represent themselves legally. Influenced by Christianity, Romans later added
humanitarian laws in favor of slaves.

At the same time, Christians and Muslims justified slavery based on their sacred books. Many Christian writers attributed slavery to a moral flaw, a sin committed by the slave's ancestors. It was not uncommon to identify this "sin" as the
curse of Ham when he saw his father, Noah, naked. Saint Augustine, for instance,
in his *City of God*, viewed the root of slavery in sin (693; bk. 19, ch. 15). Most of
the critics of slavery attacked the cruelty of the masters and advocated for more
benign treatment without questioning the institution itself. Saint Ambrose believed that God had made all men equally free, yet he stated that masters had
obligations to their slaves (Thomas 30–31). Some of the popes also wrote bulls
to defend slaves. Constantine, for example, in 321 decreed that the church, not
merely the state, had the power to free slaves ("Manumissio in ecclesia"), and
he personally freed 1,250 of them.

In Spain, Alfonso X codified slavery in his *Siete partidas* (2: 57–59; partida 4,
title 12), in which many of the Roman laws were incorporated. Yet his laws were
more benign toward the slaves, granting them rights to choose their spouse
freely, to own things, and to buy their own freedom. He also dictated the circumstances in which slaves could be captured and specified who could be considered a slave: enemies captured in war, those born of slaves, and those who
agreed to be sold (Thomas 40).

The depth and breadth of these background discussions (essential to teaching this aspect of Las Casas) will depend on the students, yet we believe that
the materials used can be tailored to suit any level. After this introductory part,
students should be ready to engage with the two texts by Las Casas. The first,
the "Memorial de remedios" of 1516, attests to Las Casas's desires to remedy
Indian decimation and suggests, in his eleventh remedy, that black or other African slaves should be brought to Indian communities to work in mining (see
also Baptiste 22–23).[2] As Isacìo Pérez Fernández exhaustively demonstrates
with detailed yearly documentation, Las Casas was capitalizing on a transatlantic

slavery practice that had been in place since 1501 and on a labor replacement that was already being considered by *encomenderos*; he was specifically suggesting the importation to America of African slaves (black or white) from Castile (known as *ladinos*) and not people directly from Guinea or elsewhere in Africa (known as *bozales*), and his petition was similar to others being made at the time by officials, neighbors, and members of religious orders (*Fray Bartolomé de las Casas* 21–65).[3] The second Las Casas text for the class to consider is the *History of the Indies* (1527–63), in which the Dominican retracts his earlier stance, having realized that African slaves were unjustly captured and sold. He makes this new evidence available in those chapters dealing with the Portuguese and Castilian expansion into the Canary Islands and Africa (1: 90–148; bk. 1, chs. 17–27, in particular 1: 143–44; bk. 1, ch. 27) and, later, in those dealing with the Caribbean in the context of the sugar cane plantation and the presence of punitive plagues in the New World (3: 176–78, 273–76; bk. 3, chs. 102, 129).

When responding to accusations that continue to define Las Casas almost as a nineteenth-century *negrero* (as suggested by the Cuban writer Reinaldo Arenas in *El central* [1981] and by the Argentine Jorge Luis Borges 295–300), useful books to consult are Isacio Pérez Fernández's three important studies in relation to Las Casas, Africa, and the slave trade (*Bartolomé de la Casas*, "Estudio preliminar," and *Fray Bartolomé de las Casas*). With the express purpose of setting the record straight before the five-hundredth anniversary of the Columbian enterprise, Pérez Fernández dismantles once and for all the legend of Las Casas as promoter of the slave trade and resolves what has been seen as a contradictory stance toward human rights, which was thought to be biased against blacks (*Bartolomé de las Casas*). Although he is far from being the first to bring up these issues, Pérez Fernández makes a series of important points. First, the legend that Las Casas supported the slave trade was invented in Europe by white Enlightenment intellectuals in the second half of the eighteenth century, mainly by Cornelius de Pauw (*Recherches philosophiques*). In opposing Rousseau's "bon sauvage," De Pauw affirms that Las Casas conceived the plan of establishing a definitive trade of black slaves with America (Pérez Fernández, *Bartolomé de las Casas* 36–37). Second, the legend was perpetuated by Guillaume-Thomas François Raynal (*Histoire*), who followed Georges-Louis Leclerc, Comte de Buffon, as well as William Robertson and others (38–39). Third, the Spanish royal chronicler Antonio de Herrera had access to Las Casas's unpublished *History of the Indies*, and his report of 1601 (*Historia*, decada 2, bk. 2, ch. 20) contained a damaging statement that was later repeated by Fernández de Navarrete in 1825: "Casas por aliviar a los indios, autorizó y estableció el tráfico de los negros para las islas del Nuevo Mundo como si éstos no fuesen racionales" 'To mitigate Indian suffering, Casas authorized and established the trade of black slaves to the islands of the New World as if they were not rational beings' (qtd. in Pérez Fernández, *Bartolomé de las Casas* 33, 40).[4] Above all, Pérez Fernández's book debunks categorically the accusations made against Las Casas by past as well as recent writers.

Once Las Casas's position is clarified, further discussions of issues of slavery should bring into conversation the opinions of other colonial writers. One such author could be Bartolomé Frías de Albornoz, a Spanish lawyer who lived in Mexico. In his *Arte de los contratos*, published in Valencia in 1573, he questioned the legality of the centuries-old practice of enslaving war captives. Contrary to the usual excuse that enslaving heathens and Christianizing them saved their souls (as Prince Henry of Portugal claimed when he received his "royal fifth" from the more than two hundred slaves brought to Portugal in 1444), Frías de Albornoz thought that no African benefited from living as a slave in the New World and that the church could not justify the violence of the slave trade (Thomas 146). Nevertheless, on the issue of the Portuguese enslaving of Ethiopians, Frías de Albornoz was much more ambiguous than Las Casas, who categorically declared it illegal (Pérez Fernández, *Fray Bartolomé de las Casas* 194). In 1580 in Brazil, the Jesuit priest Miguel García (like the Dominican Antonio de Montesinos, who had condemned the ill treatment of Indians in Hispaniola) refused to confess slaveholders, as Las Casas prescribed in his *Rules for Confessors*. In Mexico, the historian Juan Suárez de Peralta, in his book *Noticias históricas de la Nueva España*, expresses surprise that there were not more voices protesting the treatment of African slaves, while there were many in favor of the Indians. For him, skin color was the only difference: "No había otra diferencia más de ser más subidos de color y más prietos" (50). His book, like Las Casas's, was not published until almost three centuries later, in 1878.

The writings of the Jesuits on the issue of slavery and blacks should be read polyphonically with Las Casas's. The opinions of the members of the Society of Jesus were by no means homogeneous. For instance, Fray Luis Lópes, one of the first Jesuits to arrive in Perú in 1567, doubted the legality of the conquest. Viceroy Toledo discovered in his possession a manuscript against his government and the Crown. It stated that no just war titles, legal papal bulls, or claims of the tyranny of the Incas could justify the possession of American territories and the domination of their people (Vargas Ugarte 151). These concerns were still evident in the second generation of Jesuits when Bartolomé de Hernández, after hearing Domingo de Soto in the famous debates in Salamanca, wrote to Saint Francisco de Borja stating his many doubts about the enterprise of the Indies. José de Acosta is perhaps the most important author one might use for a dialogical reading of Las Casas. Like the Dominican, Acosta writes a history of the Indies—his *Historia natural y moral de las Indias*. He also deals with the conversion of Amerindians and the rights and wrongs surrounding the conquest and evangelization in his *De procuranda Indorum salute*. His *catecismo* had direct bearings on how Indians were Christianized in Perú. For Acosta, Indians and blacks were equal when it came to the salvation of their souls and to the many moral issues pertaining to them.

Felipe Guaman Poma's *Nueva crónica y buen gobierno* is another important voice in the polyphonic reading of Las Casas and the Atlantic slave trade that opens up the subject of *castas*, along with the black and mulatto culture that flourished in the New World. Including this Andean writer helps illustrate geographic divergences in the Americas, where the experience of black slavery differs considerably, from the Andes to the Caribbean to Brazil. Guaman Poma implicitly accepts the institution of slavery, and his opinions on blacks and on slaves are clear and direct. For him, there are two kinds of slaves: the *bozales* recently arrived from Africa, and those whom he calls *criollos*, who are the subsequent generations born in the New World. He finds the *bozales* morally sound and endowed with all Christian virtues. From this kind of slave even saints are born, says Guaman Poma, citing the case of Saint Buenaventura. These slaves for him are worth twice as much as the *criollos*, who are contumacious sinners from birth and become criminals. "They are blacks worse than blacks" he states (718), making explicit his marked prejudice and accusing them of corrupting the *bozales* and the Indians. He gives many precise directives about how the *criollos* should be treated and governed. His main preoccupation is that these black *criollos* are raping the Indians, thus causing the Indian population to diminish (see, e.g., his section on "negros" [717–24]). An excellent introduction to the relevant issue of the *çastas* is also the Inca Garcilaso's *Comentarios reales*, which appears in the anthologized selection of "tipos de hombres americanos" in *Huellas de las literaturas hispanoamericanas* (Garganigo et al. 115–16). Addressing the *casta* system not only adds a visual element to undergraduate or graduate courses dealing with Las Casas but also can lead the discussion into political and social aspects of daily life in the colonial period. Ilona Katzew's *Casta Painting* and Magali Carrera's *Imagining Identity in New Spain* are useful sources for this topic. Many historians have written extensively about the *casta* system, particularly in Mexico and to a lesser extent in Perú.

The above contextualization is relevant for both the undergraduate and graduate classroom, but it is even more appropriate in a graduate setting to present Las Casas as the keystone of a Caribbean discourse on race and ethnicity that can be traced back to the nineteenth century. Some of the voices one could include are intellectuals and writers like the Dominican Republic's Manuel de Jesús Galván, the Cuban José Antonio Saco (*Historia de esclavitud*), and the twentieth-century Cuban ethnographer Fernando Ortiz (Introduction and *Contrapunteo*). We must also mention more-recent critical revisions of the Lascasian presence in Caribbean discourse by Antonio Benítez Rojo ("Bartolomé de Las Casas") and José Buscaglia Salgado. Las Casas's incursion in this history of ideas can be framed using the concepts of genealogy and appropriation.

In the Dominican Republic, or Hispaniola, the case of the Indian lord Enriquillo and his rebellion is paradigmatic, showing how nineteenth-century intellectuals, like Galván, appropriated colonial history, historical actors, and historical texts as propaganda for nation building. As it has been pointed out by Doris Sommer, among others, Galván's novel *Enriquillo* (1882) constructed a foundational fictional identity for the Dominican Republic that erased blackness and promoted a domesticated Indianness (in the form of Enriquillo) that was, in turn, tied to the civilizing mission of Hispanism (represented by the character of Las Casas). Las Casas had a decisive role in the pacification of Enriquillo, and he is featured in the novel as mediator, go-between in the love stories that occupy most of the book (Sommer, *Foundational Fictions* 21–22, 233–56). Las Casas cannot but be a conciliatory figure for the Dominican elite to which Galván belongs and whose national project would take the country back again to Spanish rule and away from the black republic of Haiti, a contaminating and invasive neighbor.

In Cuba, Saco gives Las Casas a privileged position. One can even argue that Saco's ethnographic gaze on the African other is mediated in part by Las Casas's gaze on the Amerindian. Saco's extensive historical, literary, and journalistic works reveal that he, like Las Casas, condemns the slave trade, and his comprehensive *History of Slavery* (four volumes appeared in 1875–79; the final two were published posthumously) uses Las Casas's historiographical works as one of his sources. Saco's condemnation might have responded not to an "authentic philanthropy or a truly democratic stance, but to the belief that abolition of slavery would allow the modernization of the sugar industry and consolidate the position of the Cuban *hacendados*" (Llorens 51). Nevertheless, his readings of Las Casas turned him against slavery and to a slightly different view of his black others. His desire to clear Las Casas's reputation regarding the black slave trade is an indication of how instrumental the Dominican became for his project.

From his exile in Spain and France, Saco waged an active campaign to print Las Casas's two monumental histories, *The History of Indies* and the *Apologética historia*. Although these are Las Casas's most impressive historiographical works, they were not published until the nineteenth century.[5] The *History* was overlooked by the Academia de la Historia, which decided to publish Gonzalo Fernández de Oviedo's history first, but, partly, because of the intervention of Saco, who envisioned Las Casas as an emblem of Hispanism, both histories were officially printed ("*Historia de las Indias*"). Las Casas offered a model of Hispanism that was perfectly digestible to the white *criollo* national project, the place where Saco positioned himself. Thus, such an appropriation allows for multiple identifications with Hispanism, a notion that is mediated and mitigated by a transatlantic figure whose dissenting position makes him usable.

When in the twentieth century Fernando Ortiz writes the prologue for the works of Saco, he follows the same path. Ortiz kept a bust of Las Casas on his desk and took ample notes from the friar's works. How much of Las Casas as a pristine foundational figure is already there in the works of Saco or how much of Las Casas is a projection of Fernando Ortiz's own genealogy for Cuba's process of "transculturation" is debatable. An ethnographer and one of Cuba's most prominent intellectuals, Ortiz not only feels the need to highlight Las Casas and his intellectual project in the 1932 prologue to Saco's volume on Indian slavery (Ortiz, Introduction), he inserts his own defense of Las Casas's stance regarding blacks in his master narrative *Contrapunteo cubano del tabaco y el azúcar* ("Cuban Counterpoint"; 300–55). Rightfully so, Ortiz makes Las Casas into a protagonist of Cuban cultural history along with the native tobacco and the Indians who smoked it, as well as the imported sugar and the black slaves who produced it. The notion of Las Casas as the initiator of the slave trade becomes crucial yet again, and Ortiz feels compelled to take the reader through the origins of the false accusation. He revisits Las Casas's own statements and emphasizes, like Saco did, that Las Casas regretted everything he believed early on in his career regarding African slaves once he learned of the illicit trade conducted by Portuguese and Castilians. Ortiz provides additional archival evidence of a continuous trade that had little to do with Las Casas, taking as point of departure Saco's critique that had already documented how the slave trade was in place even before Las Casas's first suggestion. Finally, Ortiz discredits Jesuits—who historically had received praise for their role in an antislavery genealogy—for not having gone as far as Las Casas had and for not formulating their critique as early as he did.

On one level, Ortiz's insistence responds, no doubt, to a long-standing misconception that surrounded the figure of Las Casas and to a certain degree on a conviction that Las Casas is an important piece in the history that he sets to tell. On another level, Ortiz's revisionist obsession, which places Las Casas along with "la cuestión negra" at the center, responds to Ortiz's consciousness of being the heir of the nineteenth-century *criollos* who hijacked Las Casas for their own national project. Ortiz's great contribution is the recognition that when it comes to Latin America, the Caribbean, and Cuban ethos, Las Casas stands as the most prominent foundational figure, without whom any progressive ethnographic work would have been impossible. For Ortiz, Las Casas cannot be dismissed, because the Dominican was the originator and transmitter of certain knowledge that anticipated modern notions of cultural relativity, international laws regarding wars among nations, and human rights. Most important, Las Casas is again, for Ortiz as he was for Saco, the redeemable face of Hispanism. Las Casas allows Caribbean intellectuals to resolve the *criollo* predicament. They can embrace blackness, *hibridez, mulatez,* and transculturation, as well as Hispanism and the colonial legacy of Spain—as long as it is embodied by Bartolomé de Las Casas.

Equally compelling to introduce to graduate students is Benítez Rojo's essay "Bartolomé de las Casas," reprinted in his *La isla que se repite* ("The Repeating Island"), as it offers an interesting (mis)reading of Las Casas's guilt in his *History of the Indies.* Here, Benítez Rojo explores the uncanny relation between the plague of ants that attacked Hispaniola and the plague of blacks that facilitated the birth of the sugar plantation in the Caribbean (69–147). Benítez Rojo sees in Las Casas a fundamental piece in his theorization of the Caribbean space as a meta-archipelago that repeats itself. Román de la Campa's general critique of Benítez Rojo's partial postmodernism and his mostly Cuba-centric corpus of Caribbean literature does not address in detail the function of Las Casas in the text, although de la Campa denies the Dominican the status of being proto-postmodern or proto-Caribbean (90–103). Malcolm Read's keen evaluation of this episode offers further insights in the shortcomings of Benítez Rojo's psychoanalytic approach to Las Casas by exposing the critic's theoretical flaws. For

Read, Benítez Rojo's version of Las Casas's guilt for having suggested bringing black slaves to the New World cannot be read in terms of the inversion of the master-slave dichotomy, in which it is the runaway black slaves who torment the white settlers.

Buscaglia Salgado's recent reflection on Las Casas in *Undoing Empire* accepts the arguments of Benítez Rojo and takes them as point of departure for his own. For Buscaglia Salgado, not only is Las Casas tied to the origins of the plantation and the *criollo* discourse but he also sets in motion the politics of what he calls *mulataje*, since black slavery yields to mulatto culture. Read's critique of Benítez Rojo also applies to Buscaglia Salgado's reading of the episode in the *History of the Indies*. Buscaglia Salgado sees Las Casas on the side of other victims, not the Indians or the blacks, but the European settlers (indianos). Thus, he projects in Las Casas a fear of the "black" plague that threatens to ruin his utopian vision of Indians and European farmers coexisting in peace. It is not accidental that Benítez Rojo sets up his version of a Lascasian Caribbean genealogy by quoting Saco, nor is the fact that Buscaglia Salgado builds up his transatlantic genealogy on the work of Saco as well, for any genealogy implies a retrospective gaze that always fragments or distorts the production of the Lascasian text. Although the reception of Las Casas is as rich as his innumerable contributions in the sixteenth century, we must warn students not to read Las Casas today through the eyes of the nineteenth century (e.g., Saco), helping them instead to be conscious of processes of appropriation, especially as it serves national and regional agendas. Ultimately, teaching the colonial period is a call to historicize, to return to the moment of production.

In the end, Las Casas's writings have a prominent place in intellectual genealogies that make texts from the colonial period relevant to other historical periods. They are a benchmark in a universal history of (anti)slavery, and they also have a place in the articulation of a unique transatlantic paradigm determined not only by European (anti)imperialist ideas but by the black slave trade. They play a role as well in the formulation of national imaginaries (such as the Dominican Republic's and Cuba's) as they come to terms with the thorny issue of race. These genealogies are complex and crucial but cannot replace the study of the primary texts—they can only complement it.

NOTES

[1] For a useful chronology of European interventions in the Atlantic and the Canaries as well as along the African coast, see Pérez Fernández ("Estudio preliminar" 145–87). Pérez Fernández concentrates on all interventions, political and military as well as religious, offering a useful list of all papal bulls issued to regulate religious activity in the region to prevent or justify slavery.

[2] We suggest Baptiste's study because it reproduces a version of the "Memorial" in both English and Spanish. The latest edition of the text appears in volume 13 of the *Obras completas* (23–40). On the eleventh remedy in question and related issues, see also the collection of essays edited by Victorien Lavou Zoungbo.

[3] Between his first interventions in 1516 through 1520 and his ultimate retraction, Las Casas requested African slaves again in 1531, 1542, and 1543 (Pérez Fernández, *Fray Bartolomé de las Casas* 73–75, 91–93). However, according to Pérez Fernández, Las Casas seemed to have had a change of mind after a trip to Lisbon in 1547—earlier than traditionally thought—hence his denunciation in his *History of the Indies* (Pérez Fernández, *Fray Bartolomé de las Casas* 112–23).

[4] Translations are ours unless otherwise noted.

[5] Nevertheless, Las Casas's unpublished histories were extensively circulated in manuscript form or plagiarized verbatim in the work of other historians, as demonstrated by Wagner and Parish and by Adorno ("Censorship" 812–27).

Teaching Liberation Theology:
The Legacy of Las Casas

Erik Camayd-Freixas

The challenge of showing historical figures' contemporary relevance to undergraduates and nonspecialists can be met in different ways. In teaching Las Casas, a particularly effective approach is to highlight his legacy in relation to the "recent" Latin American phenomenon of liberation theology. Then, the challenge when teaching the graduate student or specialist is how to relate, with philological rigor, two historical instances four hundred years apart. This task becomes an opportunity for reflecting on the history of theological social thought, hypothesizing about reasons for Iberian American Christianity's proclivity toward sociopolitical praxis, and broadly debating the social role of religion in transhistorical and cross-cultural perspective. Notions to explore include: the view of religion shared by Karl Marx, Herbert Spencer, Émile Durkheim, Max Weber, and Bronislaw Malinowski, who see it as a retardant of social change—the proverbial "opium of the people"; liberation theology as the product of foreign influences; its claims to signifying a complete break with the past; and its possible future.

I begin by examining the rise of liberation theology in mid-twentieth-century Latin America, particularly its claims to difference, and from that standpoint look back comparatively to the social and theological struggle under the colonial system in Las Casas's time. I find that this retrospective affords the class a closer understanding of the complex historical and intellectual situation of the colonial period. I also find core similarities between both movements, despite circumstantial and rhetorical differences. The pedagogical task is then to discover (and reconstruct) the historical and philological links that explain those similarities as being, more than mere coincidence, the tip of the iceberg, signs of continuity for what appears to be an underlying ideological and cultural current spanning Latin American intellectual history.

Liberation theology stakes two claims to difference: its theory rejects essentialist metaphysics and opens theology to historicism for a legitimate focus on earthly affairs; and its praxis demands radical structural changes in society, as opposed to mere reform, to solve the deep-seated problems of social injustice and inequality. I suggest, however, that these claims are not unique to liberation theology but are also operant in Lascasian ministry and pastoral strategy. My comparative approach touches on three topics: utopianism as a constant intersection of religious and social thought (Gutiérrez, *Teología* and *Las Casas*); legacy, the historical perspective, not of Las Casas the individual writer and activist but of the movement he spearheaded, which survived him by nearly three hundred years, projecting him as a precursor of contemporary Catholic social thought and practice; and heterodoxy, an inquiry into the influences on

Iberian Christianity in Las Casas's time, which blend spiritual and material concerns, leading to social engagement and political agency as inseparable aspects of spiritual leadership.

It should be emphasized that Las Casas was not an isolated voice. (In addition to Lewis Hanke's seminal work, see Ramón Xirau's anthology of social writings by sixteenth-century priests like Vasco de Quiroga, Juan de Zumárraga, and Bernardino de Sahagún). Yet Las Casas became an emblematic figure, as the most effective and relentless propagandist and the author of an international best seller: *Brevísima relación de la destrucción de las Indias* (*Brief Account of the Destruction of the Indies*). An *encomendero* in his youth, Las Casas traces his "conversion" to Fray Antonio de Montesinos's inflamed sermon of Easter Sunday, 1511. In a prophetic tone, Montesinos admonished the *encomenderos* of Hispaniola that they were in "mortal sin" because of the "cruelty and tyranny" they exercised against "these innocents"; further, he denied absolution to all who kept the Indians as slaves (*La destrucción* 8).[1] The scandal reached King Ferdinand, who suppressed Montesinos but promulgated a year later, as a vague concession, the controversial Laws of Burgos and the *Requerimiento*. Las Casas freed his own slaves and joined Montesinos's dissension in 1514; the following year, they traveled to Seville to lobby before the Council of Indies. In 1518, with the support of Cardinal Cisneros, Las Casas received permission to establish the first colony of free Indians, and in 1521, he sailed to Hispaniola with seventy Spanish farm workers, a few priests, and supplies to found the first fraternal (what we would now call utopian) society of the New World. Natives and Spaniards were to work the land side by side, under the guidance of the priests. The blueprint had been drawn in Las Casas's letters almost two years before Thomas More's *Utopia* was published, and Victor N. Baptiste argues that there is circumstantial evidence to suggest that More's *Utopia* could have been inspired by Las Casas's "Memorial de remedios para las Indias" (1516) (Baptiste's systematic comparison is appropriate for a student presentation; see also Herrero). Undermined by colonial interests, Las Casas's first utopian experiment failed. Nevertheless, it became the basis for his treatise *De unico vocationis modo* (c. 1538) and a second fraternal community he established with the help of friars Alonso de Talavera and Domingo de Vico in Guatemala, the Vera Paz, which lasted nineteen years. Along with the utopian "pueblo-hospitals" founded by Bishops Juan de Zumárraga and Vasco de Quiroga in Central America, the Lascasian project predated by more than four centuries the utopian experiment or "lay monastery" founded under the aegis of liberation theology by Father Ernesto Cardenal in Solentiname, Nicaragua.

Liberation theology's first claim to difference is its openness to historicism. Since the nineteenth century, a rift has widened between traditional Christian thought and modern historicism—the idea that human, ethical, and social values change with the times. Christian essentialism remits the order of things to universal principles established by revelation and elaborated on by metaphysics and theology. Accordingly, man is not a historical entity but the product of permanent human nature in the image and likeness of God. Influenced by Platonic dualism and Western idealism, traditional theology posits two realms: one, spiritual and eternal; the other, material and temporal. The spiritual realm is accorded absolute primacy: the hardship and injustice of earthly life are seen as insignificant, if the individual can attain salvation in the beyond—a model that breeds indifference toward social and historical projects.

In the twentieth century, European theologians like Teilhard de Chardin and Karl Rahner proposed a hermeneutic shift that places history at the center of theological concern (Silva Gotay 38–49), which has led some critics to erroneously ascribe Latin American liberation theology to foreign influences. Yet in Latin America the praxis of liberation preceded its theory. As in the Las Casas movement four hundred years earlier, the theology was developed later, in response to the need for reconciling doctrine with an a priori social practice dictated and justified by the circumstances. In both moments, action could not wait for theological justification. In 1962, when Juan Luis Segundo took the first theoretical steps toward a theology of liberation, he emphasized this same historicity:

> El dogma cristiano progresa. No por descubrimiento de verdades nuevas que se añadan a las reveladas, sino por el descubrimiento de nuevos sentidos, realidades más hondas encerradas en esas mismas verdades que Dios reveló. Y esos descubrimientos no los hacen especialistas en teología encerrados en gabinetes asépticos barajando silogismos, sino en el enfrentamiento de la Iglesia, inspirada por el Espíritu Santo, con las realidades históricas nuevas que solicitan una nueva y más profunda respuesta cristiana.   (28–29)

> Christian dogma evolves, based on the discovery not of new truths to be added to the revealed ones but of new and deeper meanings in those same truths revealed by God. And those discoveries are made not by specialists shuffling syllogisms in hygienic offices but when the church, inspired by the Holy Spirit, confronts new historical realities that demand a new and deeper Christian response.

Next to a theology of liberation, Segundo proposes the liberation of theology from Greek and Roman philosophical additions, preserved by European theology, and the restoration of theology's authentic historical meaning in the original Hebrew tradition—the meaning it had during primitive Christianity, when it constituted, among other things, a form of resistance of the Jewish people subjugated by the Roman Empire.

> La cosmovisión histórica y materialista con la cual Jesús y la iglesia primitiva interpretan la realidad y entienden su fe, es transformada por la influencia de la cosmovisión esencialista de la metafísica greco-romana

mediante ese proceso de "traducción" al lenguaje y a la filosofía de los "gentiles". De aquí las serias consecuencias sobre la ética y la política de la iglesia que hemos estado sufriendo hasta el día de hoy. El reino de Dios está concebido en los profetas y el nuevo testamento como un reino de estructura económica y política (la frase que se traduce "mi reino no es de este mundo", sabemos hoy que debe ser traducida "mi reino no es de este orden de relaciones sociales", o de "este tiempo"). . . . Mientras la *palabra* para los griegos viene a ser el *logos* que ellos definen como razón-idea, relacionada con el mundo de las ideas no históricas en el caso de Platón y con la estructura racional del universo en el caso de los estoicos, la *palabra* para los hebreos viene a ser el *dabar* que éstos otros definen como palabra-acontecimiento. . . . La salvación se desvincula de la creación. . . . La religión se refugia en la interioridad personal. . . . Esta es la cuestión que está en el fondo del rechazo de la teología europea y el nacimiento de la teología de liberación.   (Silva Gotay 73–80)

The materialist and historical worldview with which Jesus and the primitive church interpreted reality and understood their faith was transformed by the essentialist worldview of Greek and Roman metaphysics, by means of a process of "translation" into the language and philosophy of the "gentiles"; hence the consequences for the ethics and politics of the church, which affect us to this day. . . . The kingdom of God is conceived in the prophets and the New Testament as a kingdom of economic and political structure. The phrase translated as "my kingdom is not from this world" we now know should have been translated as "my kingdom is not from this social order" or "from this time." . . . Whereas the *word* for the Greeks meant *logos*, defined as reason-idea and related to Plato's nonhistorical realm and the stoics' rational order of the universe, for the Hebrews the *word* meant *dabar*, defined as word-deed. . . . [With this "translation"] salvation is dissociated from creation. . . . Religion withdraws to the individual's inner self. . . . This is the matter that is at the root of the rejection of Western theology and the rise of the theology of liberation.

Hellenized Christianity, mediated by Saint Augustine and Saint Thomas Aquinas, informed the reformist Christian-Democrat movement that flourished in Latin America (1930–70) among the followers of the French neo-Thomist Jacques Maritain. Anxious to distance itself from neo-Thomism after the failure of reformism, liberation theology insists on the aforementioned radical structural changes in society and presents its praxis as a complete break with the past. Yet, in asserting this difference, it overlooks its debt to the Lascasian movement, whose struggle for the abolition of the *encomienda* was no less radical, since it struck the backbone of the early colonial economic system. Liberation theology's claim to newness raises—and evades—the question of its links to previous Latin American Christianity. Its cultural identification is with primitive Hebrew

Christianity rather than Iberian, and its proponents cite only circumstantial, not cultural, reasons for its rise:

> En Europa se dan las condiciones teóricas pero no se dan las condiciones materiales, en el resto del "tercer mundo" se dan las condiciones materiales pero no se dan las condiciones teóricas porque no son predominantemente cristianos. En América Latina es el único lugar donde coinciden ambas condiciones para hacer posible el desarrollo de esta mutación.
> (Silva Gotay 324)

> In Europe the theoretical conditions existed but not the material conditions; in the rest of the "third world" the material conditions existed but not the theoretical conditions, because [the people] are not predominantly Christian. Only in Latin America do both conditions coincide to make this development possible.

But if, unlike in Europe, liberation praxis in Latin America preceded theory, one wonders how its adherents developed such a heartfelt, intuitive way of understanding their faith: whether there existed in Iberian Christianity certain dissident currents—closely linked to historical, earthly concerns—that left their mark on Latin American religiosity. A clue might be found, first, in the seven centuries of Islamic influence on Iberian Christianity. Contrary to primitive Christianity, which quickly succumbed to Greek and Roman cultural imperialism, Islam had plenty of time to develop its own style of life and thought around its doctrine, conserving the close ties between history and faith characteristic of its Semitic origins. This feature of the Arabic worldview inevitably came to be part and parcel of Latin America's heritage. After all, the Spanish has just reconquered Granada when Columbus discovered the New World.

Enrique Dussel points out only the negative aspect of this influence—the consolidation of theocratic ideology and the patronage of the Spanish Crown over the church:

> esa tendencia a unificar indisolublemente los fines del Estado y de la Iglesia. . . . La doctrina islámica del Califato exigía esta unidad, este monismo religioso-político. . . . El Patronato otorga a una nación el doble poder de colonizar y misionar, es decir, mezcla lo temporal y lo sobrenatural, lo político y lo eclesial, lo económico y lo evangélico, produciendo una teocracia expansiva y militar—de tipo más bien islámico que cristiano, pero frecuente en la Edad Media.
> (*Historia* 54–55)

> that tendency to inextricably merge the aims of church and state. . . . Islamic Caliphate doctrine demanded this unity, this religious-political monism. . . . The patronage grants a nation both colonial and missionary powers; that is, it mixes the temporal and the heavenly, the political

and the ecclesiastical, economics and the Gospel, producing an expansive
military theocracy—rather Islamic than Christian, though frequent in the
Middle Ages.

Yet this same confusion of realms, together with other historically bound influences, contributed to an environment of dissent among sectors of the Spanish
clergy who, like Las Casas and countless others who followed him during the
entire colonial period, were committed not to the high political spheres but to
the defense of grassroot communities.

Among the heterodox currents that converged on Iberian Christianity was the
conspicuous, though poorly studied, influence of the Jews converted to Christianity under inquisitorial pressure. The converts spread illuminist doctrines
based on the rather utopian idea of an earthly messianism, which led them
to dream of the church's historical return to the promised land of Jerusalem,
where humanity would at last found a society based on justice and freedom.
Although Spanish orthodoxy was a declared enemy of such Judaic ideas,

> la Iglesia de España encierra en su seno, desde fines del siglo XIV, una
> proporción notable de elementos venidos del judaísmo. . . . ¿Quién sabe
> si la inspiración religiosa y moral de los profetas no resurgía en ellos, flo-
> reciendo en inquietudes mesiánicas?   (Bataillon, *Erasmo* 70–71)

> the Spanish church harbors in its very core, since the late fourteenth
> century, a considerable proportion of elements issuing from Judaism. . . .
> Who knows if the prophets' religious and moral inspiration resurfaced in
> them, flourishing in messianic preoccupations?

Descendants of converted Jews were found throughout the empire, sometimes
in important positions in the church; among them, possibly Fray Bartolomé de
Las Casas and the Salamanca theologian and jurist Fray Francisco de Vitoria,
considered the "father of international law."[2]

Preceding Thomas More as they do, Las Casas's utopian ideas are likely to
be the influence of Jewish tradition, but with one important difference: Las
Casas's utopianism left behind the messianism of his forebears. Far from any
providential attitude, his treatises, based on theological and historical arguments, showed an early scientism and an advanced social understanding. Christian messianism declined in fifteenth-century Spain, such that by the time of
Las Casas, Jewish utopianism had lost its messianic character and acquired a
decidedly historical bent, by virtue of the seminal influence of renaissance humanism, which had made its way into Spain through Cardinal Cisneros's reform
and Erasmus's ideas. An immediate effect of humanism was the resurgence of
Aquinas's populist doctrines, which influenced Las Casas and Vitoria and challenged the foundation of theocratic power (Vitoria, *Escritos políticos*).

These heterogeneous elements point to a synthesis that, on the one hand,
preserves the Islamic blend of the spiritual and the temporal while rejecting

theocratic power and, on the other, aspires to the Jewish utopian ideal, no longer under messianism but as a humanistic historical project. Such is the basis for a dissident Iberian Christianity, which took shape in Spanish America as a response to material conditions of exploitation under colonial rule. The defense of Amerindian rationality by Las Casas and others was already an affirmation of human historicity. The European encounter with New World populations in a markedly different state of material and historical development prompted humanistic reflection along Aristotelian and Thomist lines, following a tradition propelled by Jewish and Arabic philosophers in medieval Spain, a tradition that had now taken root in the laic universities of Europe. If humankind's essence is immutable, as orthodoxy maintained, then those beings so different from the Europeans must be somewhat less than human, irrational beings incapable of understanding the faith, who could therefore be enslaved. The opposite tenet, the defense of native rationality, showcased by Las Casas's debate with Juan Ginés de Sepúlveda in the early 1550s, fully reflected the rise of modern historicism (now at the center of liberation theology), over and against the metaphysical essentialism of the Platonic-Augustinian tradition, which has remained at the core of the church's official conservative doctrine.

Liberation theology owes its self-concept as a break with the past to that official doctrine's historical role in legitimizing, first, monarchical power and colonial hegemony and, later, the interests of the oligarchy. Moreover, the figure of Las Casas was appropriated after the 1930s by neo-Thomism and superficially associated with the moderate position of the church after Vatican II (1962–65). Like most writers, Roberto Oliveros isolates Las Casas as a landmark in the history of the Latin American church, the second landmark being liberation theology, without apparent continuity, four hundred years later. Yet we are really before a far-reaching and organized movement, committed to the struggle for justice (Hanke, *Spanish Struggle*). Numerous clerics sent their complaints to Las Casas for lobbying and circulated manuscript copies of his treatises throughout the Caribbean and from Mexico to Perú (a good opportunity to have students research the social agency of priests in Latin American history—e.g., Bishop Julián Garcés, Bishop Juan de Zumárraga, and Fray Domingo de Santo Tomás). At the 1536 ecclesiastical conference in Mexico, Las Casas worked with Bishops Zumárraga and Garcés in drafting petitions to Pope Paul III on behalf of the Indians. Meanwhile, Fray Bernardino de Minaya, a major opponent of the tyrannical conquistador Francisco Pizarro in Perú, took the lobbying personally to Rome. His efforts, together with the influence of Las Casas, prompted the pope to promulgate in 1537 his influential bull *Sublimis Deus*, regarded as the Magna Carta of Indian rights, which proclaimed the Indians to be "true men, capable of receiving the Christian faith" (to be dispensed only through peaceful preaching and good example) and condemned their enslavement by declaring them entitled to "freedom" and "property." This papal bull, in turn, influenced the theologian Vitoria, whose disciples were spread throughout the kingdom opposing official orthodoxy: Alonso de la Vera Cruz in Mexico, Bartolomé de Ledesma in Perú, Domingo de Salazar and Miguel de Benavides in the Philippines, and Domingo de Soto and Melchor Cano in Spain. Vitoria, a colleague in Paris of Saint Ignatius Loyola (founder of the Jesuit order in 1540), had a seminal influence on the Jesuits, who led the liberation movement in the seventeenth and eighteenth centuries. From the universities they founded throughout the continent, the Jesuits disseminated the ideas of the "father of international law." To his doctrine on the equality of states (which included Indian nations), they added Father Juan de Mariana's doctrine on the equality of members of political society. And it was a Spanish Jesuit, Francisco Suárez (1548–1617), who developed the populist doctrines on the origin of monarchical power that Vitoria had left in embryonic state and according to which the authority of the king depends on the consent of the people, who may withdraw it and rebel against a tyrant. The Suárez doctrine was invoked two centuries later by leaders of Latin American independence like Gregorio Funes, Mariano Moreno, and Father Morelos (Furlong, *Los jesuitas*).

As to praxis, in 1608 the Jesuit Diego de Torres began in Santiago de Chile another wave of liberation with continental repercussions. Like the Dominicans of Hispaniola a century earlier, the Jesuits of Santiago put the Indians on wages and denied absolution to those who kept them in servitude. Father Torres went to Argentina that same year and extended the initiative to Tucumán, Santa Fe, and Asunción. Shortly after, the largest utopian experiment in history was begun: the Jesuit-Guaraní missions in Paraguay, which lasted 150 years until the general expulsion of the Jesuits by the Bourbon King Carlos III in 1767. These communities of free, wage-earning, and armed Indians built numerous churches, palaces, public buildings, and shipyards; fortified Buenos Aires, Asunción, and Montevideo; drove out Portuguese invaders in 1704; and repelled frequent English and Dutch attacks (Furlong). Even after their expulsion, Jesuits like Juan Pablo Viscardo became precursors of independence. His *Carta a los españoles americanos* (1798) inspired leaders of the revolutionary war (Batllori).

Many priests contributed notoriously to the struggles for independence, like Fathers Mier, Hidalgo, and Morelos in Mexico, and hundreds died in the revolutionary wars; we cannot isolate as a historical landmark a unique liberation movement that covered the entire continent over three hundred years. In French, British, and Dutch colonies, "material conditions" certainly existed, but not the "theoretical conditions," perhaps because of their hellenized Christianity, dissociated from historical circumstance. There is, however, a hundred-year hiatus between independence and liberation theology: although many priests participated in antislavery struggles and other social causes, there was no broad movement as before. The question is what happened with Iberian American Christianity after independence.

First, there was blind rejection in the new nations of everything Spanish, the influence of European anticlericalism took root, and by the 1850s the separation of church and state became a constitutional norm. Social matters were now in the hands of civil authorities. The growing secularization left entire countries without bishops. Moreover, the crown's patronage over the church ceased with independence, and so did the relative autonomy of the clerics. Now they answered directly to the Vatican, which made appointments and directed pastoral orientation. The empire was divided into twenty countries and the church fragmented, thus reducing the possibilities of support and expansion for minority movements. Finally, during the republican period and until twentieth-century Marxist critique and socialist agendas, there was no cogent, discernible utopian project of social transformation that could rally the historical awareness of Christians across the continent. Beginning in the late 1950s, however, with the Colombian revolutionary priest Camilo Torres Restrepo and later with the Colombian Golconda Group and the Chilean Sacerdotes para el Socialismo (Priests for Socialism), Christian coalitions once again joined social causes without worrying about theology, which would be developed afterward.

Thus, in the "new" liberation theology, the Hispanist recognizes the legacy of Las Casas, not because history repeats itself but because at times, culture achieves a vantage point that reveals its continuity with the past and, amid the heterogeneous present, sheds light on a possible future. Liberation theology has been one such vantage point.

NOTES

[1] All translations from Spanish are mine. Citations of the *Brevísima relación* refer to the edition published by Bouret in 1946, entitled *La destrucción de las Indias*.

[2] The much debated theory of Las Casas's Jewish ancestry, variously propounded by Marcel Bataillon (*Estudios*), Américo Castro, Manuel Giménez Fernández ("Fray Bartolomé de las Casas"), Claudio Guillén, and others since the mid-1960s, has received substantial and detailed support from Juan Gil. Gil finds that the family "de las Casas" of Seville, though claiming nobility under the name "Casaus," was censured by the Inquisition, such that even its most distinguished branch had to marry into converted Jewish families. Several documents link Fray Bartolomé to various siblings of the same surname, thereby invalidating an earlier theory that Las Casas may not have been his real name.

Las Casas and the Testimonial Narrative

Melvin S. Arrington, Jr.

One of the greatest challenges facing those who teach Bartolomé de Las Casas's writings is their historical remoteness. Since many students have trouble relating to literary selections from earlier periods, the question becomes, How do I make a sixteenth-century author's texts seem relevant? One of the best ways to accomplish this goal is by drawing comparisons to the contemporary *testimonio*. The works of the Dominican friar called the "Apostle of the Indians" represent excellent early examples of Spanish American social protest literature. His calls for justice are in many ways echoed by those voicing humanitarian concerns today regarding the plight of indigenous peoples. A useful approach is to view Las Casas as a precursor of liberation theology, politically committed literature in general, and the testimonial narrative in particular. By making comparisons with these topics, especially *testimonio*, students come to see Las Casas not as a remote figure of literary history but as a writer who speaks to real-world problems of their own times.

The modern-day *testimonio*, which has garnered widespread critical and popular attention, is a form of prose nonfiction that gives voice to the voiceless. It provides the poor and the oppressed with a vehicle for conveying their stories; these alternative narratives supplement and often run counter to the standard version of history. Miguel Barnet's *Biografía de un cimarrón* (1966) established the genre. It is the first-person account of Esteban Montejo, an elderly black man who in his youth had been a slave. Another indispensable *testimonio* is *Me llamo Rigoberta Menchú y así me nació la conciencia* (Burgos [1983]), the controversial life story of an indigenous woman from Guatemala who breaks the silence of the powerless by denouncing their exploitation at the hands of the government and the military.

George Yúdice defines "testimonio" as

> an authentic narrative, told by a witness who is moved to narrate by the urgency of a situation (e.g., war, oppression, revolution, etc.). Emphasizing popular, oral discourse, the witness portrays his or her own experience as an agent (rather than a representative) of a collective memory and identity. Truth is summoned in the cause of denouncing a present situation of exploitation and oppression or in exorcising and setting aright official history. (44)

John Beverley also provides a useful description of the genre:

> By *testimonio* I mean a novel or novella-length narrative in book or pamphlet (that is, printed as opposed to acoustic) form, told in the first person by a narrator who is also the real protagonist or witness of the events he

or she recounts, and whose unit of narration is usually a "life" or a significant life experience. Testimonio may include, but is not subsumed under,
any of the following textual categories, some of which are conventionally
considered literature, others not: autobiography, autobiographical novel,
oral history, memoir, confession, diary, interview, eyewitness report, life
history, *novela-testimonio*, nonfiction novel, or "factographic literature."
("Margin" 24–25)

When reading Las Casas we should keep in mind that the *testimonio* "always
signifies the need for a general social change in which the stability of the reader's world must be brought into question" (36). The demands the contemporary
testimonio makes on the reader bear a remarkable resemblance to the effects
Las Casas was trying to achieve in the sixteenth century. The likenesses are most
evident with regard to the scope and aim of these works and the narrative and
rhetorical techniques they employ. Las Casas, in his day, spoke for the innocent
victims of the *encomienda* system, the enslaved Indian laborers who, by virtue
of their condition, were unable to publicize their predicament. Most notably in
the *Brevísima relación de la destrucción de las Indias* and the *Historia de las Indias*, he often used first-person narrative to document the abuses he witnessed.
The text that best illustrates this link to the *testimonio* is the *Brevísima relación*, in which Las Casas vigorously protested the wrongdoings committed by
his countrymen against the New World's native inhabitants and appealed to the
Spanish monarch to rectify these injustices. On close examination of this work,
students quickly discover that some of its most salient features—its eyewitness
narration, accusatory tone, use of exaggeration for effect, and refusal to shy
away from graphic descriptions of violence—are also prominent characteristics
of testimonial literature.

The early chroniclers wrote on an array of topics, often focusing on strange
New World phenomena unfamiliar to Europeans, such as the customs and beliefs of the native inhabitants and the flora and fauna of the region. They used
a first-person voice for a number of reasons: to lend credibility to their claims,
to justify their actions, and, at times, to clarify and correct errors in earlier writings. The eyewitness element is of prime importance in colonial texts, as Rolena
Adorno has shown with regard to the accounts of Las Casas and Bernal Díaz
del Castillo ("Discursive Encounter"). Las Casas repeatedly cites authorities to
legitimize his claims; however, when he argues in defense of the Amerindians in
the *Brevísima relación*, the *Historia de las Indias*, and the *Apologética historia
sumaria*, he draws heavily on eyewitness reports:

Erudite works such as Gómara's history and Las Casas's *Apologética* are
exemplary and novel because they draw the traditions together, relying on
ancient authority and contemporary eyewitness testimony. The discursive
encounter of Spain and America was characterized by this conjunction of

history and law, the confluence of historical authority and juridical testimony.   (Adorno 228)

Although Las Casas was an eyewitness to many of the episodes he chronicles, he also frequently relates incidents he did not observe. However, even for those times when he was not a witness, he insists in the *Brevísima relación*: "Allí vide tan grandes crueldades" 'There I saw such great cruelty,' "estando yo presente" 'I being present,' "Otras cosas vide espantables" 'I saw other frightening things' (93–94); "yo soy testigo" 'I am a witness' (153); "he visto por mis mismos ojos" 'I have seen with my own eyes' (171).[1] On other occasions he simply issues a general statement—"dicen los testigos que . . ." 'the witnesses say that . . .' (168)—or references a specific source, as when he directly quotes the Franciscan friar Marcos de Niza, who offered "testimonio verdadero de algunas cosas que yo con mis ojos vi en aquella tierra" 'true testimony of some things that I saw with my own eyes in that land' (161). That Las Casas performed textual borrowings of Alvar Núñez Cabeza de Vaca (Adorno, "Discursive Encounter" 220–27) and many others (S. Arias, *Retórica* 75–77) is not significant in the context of Renaissance historiography. He needed to move his readers with accounts that posed serious threats to their worldview and reality—exactly what a testimony tries to accomplish.

Las Casas boldly accuses his fellow Spaniards of crimes against humanity, illustrating his charges of genocide with violent scenes of cruelty: the slaughtering of men, women, and children; tortures and mutilations; rapes. Equally shocking episodes appear all too frequently in *testimonios*. In the *testimonios*, the subaltern voice serves as a mouthpiece for the powerless by speaking out against their oppressors. Similarly, Las Casas functions as a surrogate subaltern by making accusations on behalf of those who are unable to speak out. In subject matter and tone his writings provide the framework for twentieth-century *testimonios* such as Menchú's that focus on themes of protest, resistance, and struggle. Las Casas's texts and many contemporary testimonial narratives have also had to endure a common burden: they have been objects of extraordinary scrutiny because of charges that they contain falsehoods and fabrications.

This point suggests another practical way to approach Las Casas: by placing his advocacy of the rights and dignity of indigenous peoples in the context of the attempts by Spanish authorities to grant privileged status to historical works at the expense of fictional ones, the so-called *historias fingidas*, or "lying histories," of the period. Colonial officials sought to prohibit the importation of all fictional writings into the New World because those works, especially the ever-popular novels of chivalry containing accounts of magic and monsters, were considered potentially harmful to the church's missionary efforts. According to Irving A. Leonard, "It was inevitable that there should be a mutual interaction between the contemporary historical events and creative literature, the imaginary influencing the real and the real the imaginary, thereby engendering a certain confusion in the minds of all" (27). It is, therefore, not surprising that the veracity and reliability of prose narratives were frequently called into question in colonial Spanish America.

An interesting case in point is *Los infortunios de Alonso Ramírez*, a seventeenth-century account penned by the Mexican baroque scholar Carlos de Sigüenza y Góngora. This first-person work, which relates the life story of a shipwreck victim, displays the trappings of a picaresque or a Byzantine novel. Did Sigüenza disguise an invented tale as a true account to avoid censorship? In other words, was *Los infortunios* just another one of the "lying histories," or was it actually a *crónica*? And what about the intercalated narrative in the Inca Garcilaso's *Comentarios reales* concerning Pedro Serrano, a Spaniard who found himself marooned on an island in the Caribbean? The author, who digresses from his discussion of the physical geography of the Andean empire to tell this tale, assures his readers that it is true, citing his source as corroborating evidence. These examples, which illustrate a major literary controversy during Spain's Renaissance and baroque periods, can help students see that readers during those eras often questioned the truthfulness of works purporting to be historical. The fact that contemporary readers have challenged the authenticity of modern *testimonios* forges another strong link with the literature of the early modern period.

One of the fundamental ironies associated with the *testimonio* is that, while ostensibly dealing with truth and reality, it also allows for considerable interplay between history and fiction. Indeed, as the firsthand accounts of Menchú and Las Casas bear out, truth is sometimes more symbolic than literal. Students eventually have to come to grips with the tension between history and fiction when they read these narratives. In his controversial critique of Menchú's life story, *Rigoberta Menchú and the Story of All Poor Guatemalans*, David Stoll, a Middlebury College anthropologist, demonstrates that key elements of her narrative are patently false. These charges have inspired a heated polemic in the pages of various academic publications (*PMLA*; *LASA Forum*, the newsletter of the Latin American Studies Association; *Lingua Franca: The Review of Academic Life*) between Stoll and Menchú's defenders. Arturo Arias, Stoll's most vocal and relentless opponent, has collected and published the views of some thirty participants (writers, journalists, and academics) in this bitter dispute in *The Rigoberta Menchú Controversy*. Interestingly, the accusations made by Las Casas also inspired fierce polemics, which climaxed in 1550 in Valladolid, Spain, in his much-celebrated debates with the noted humanist Juan Ginés de Sepúlveda. By examining the disputes engendered by the Dominican friar's claims in the light of current squabbles over Menchú's book, students can gain a greater appreciation for the provocative nature of the Lascasian texts.

Arias, in an article published in *PMLA*, charges Stoll with "strategic manipulation of information" and "ideological bias" ("Authoring" 76, 84) and criticizes him for attempting to invalidate Menchú's narrative by using the claims of other Guatemalans to contradict her. According to Arias, the concept of truth is problematic, and he questions "whether we can define fact in the Guatemalan context, where disseminating information often leads to torture and death" (76). In some situations, he concludes, it is simply impossible to know the truth. Arias, therefore, asserts that *testimonios* call for a kind of reading that differs radically from the way one reads fiction, a legal text, or a scientific report; they "demand a kind of affective, empathetic reading, in which individuals who enjoy guaranteed freedoms or hegemonic positions discover and sympathize with subaltern subjects" (86). In an interesting parallel, Las Casas, more than four centuries before the publication of Menchú's *testimonio*, was writing with the goal of not only informing his readers but also persuading them to read his texts in ways similar to those described by Arias.

It has been established that, in his zeal to protect the native peoples, Las Casas used hyperbole when documenting incidents of Spanish cruelty and also registered large numbers using exact figures when he reported casualties. As we now know through the work of many geographers and anthropologists—on which Charles Mann based his arguments in his compelling *1491*—scholarship has traditionally underestimated the Amerindian population at the time of contact, as well as the rapid demographic decline that began almost simultaneously with the arrival of the first Europeans. However, it is important to remember that Las Casas closely followed Aristotle's theoretical precepts on conveying truth. In the *Poetics*, for example, Aristotle recognizes the metaphoric value of placing the number of Odysseus's brave deeds at ten thousand; this was a highly effective way of conveying the idea that they were many (Potts 46–47). And so, to persuade with numbers, one must use specific figures.

What is at stake here is not just the issue of truth versus exaggeration or outright fiction but also a subtler distinction between an absolute, literal truth (one in which details of the account are factually accurate) and a symbolic or poetic truth (one that is substantially true, if not literally so). In opposition to Stoll, Doris Sommer advocates linking history to apologia. To illustrate her stance, she poses a question: "Do we dismiss the testimonies of genocidal holocaust in World War II because of controvertible details, when the incontrovertible fact of genocide is in the balance?" ("Las Casas's Lies" 238). In her view, "whether or not the information is accurate is beside the point" (239). In other words, as Las Casas and Menchú draw attention to the exploitation of native peoples and cry out for justice, they bear witness to situations that are, in essence, true, even though some of the details recounted are technically false. Sommer concludes that

> whatever the accurate numbers of dead Indians and victorious Spaniards, the ineluctable fact of history is that a short generation after the "discovery," Hispaniola's indigenous population was practically exterminated, and the rest of the Caribbean peoples were essentially wiped out soon afterwards.   (240)

Today, one is tempted to lay the blame for Las Casas's bending of the truth on his obsession with protecting the church's newest converts. Menchú, in contrast, points to her interviewer and editor, Elizabeth Burgos, as the one responsible for any erroneous content in her narrative. One can find interesting parallels in the roles played by source-informant and editor in these two cases. Specifically, the connection between Christopher Columbus and Las Casas (who transcribed the admiral's diaries and letters in *Historia de las Indias*) is fundamentally the same as the Menchú-Burgos relationship. Each one—Las Casas and Burgos—takes the words of another (Columbus and Menchú) and incorporates those words into the body of a text of his or her own fashioning. Students are thus left to ponder the reliability of the editor and to wonder how much of what is told can be attributed to this secondary author and what portion derives from information provided by the original source (Lindstrom; Denegri). These topics offer intriguing possibilities for engaging students in lively and meaningful classroom discussion.

In a seminar on testimonial-documentary narrative aimed at graduate students and advanced undergraduates, I present the writings of Las Casas as sixteenth-century examples of the *testimonio*. A study of his life and works offers valuable opportunities for examining sociopolitical and cultural issues such as slavery, genocide, colonialism, and imperialism. His texts also foster conversations about such topics as the ways in which societies view marginalized peoples, comparisons of depictions of the other in colonial writings and contemporary works, and the role of the church and clergy in promoting or thwarting social justice. In reading the works of Las Casas as *testimonio*, I encourage students to compare and contrast literary and aesthetic issues in his texts with those found in present-day works in the testimonial vein. Examples include the use of rhetorical techniques and tools of persuasion (e.g., hyperbole), the narrator's trustworthiness (especially given the difficulty or even impossibility of verifying charges of abuse and exploitation or number of casualties), justifications for inclusion of graphic descriptions of cruelty, and eyewitness accounts versus secondhand reports and hearsay.

The contemporary *testimonio* is a reinvention of social protest writing, a genre that has been a hallmark of Spanish American literature since its beginnings. Perhaps this explains why students can successfully relate Las Casas to Menchú and her *testimonio*; they often discover for themselves numerous similarities in terms of the authors' denunciatory tone, harsh critiques of government authorities and policies, eyewitness reporting, and documentation techniques. Students find these comparisons intriguing and worthy of investigation. Whether taught in undergraduate literature surveys and Spanish American culture and civilization courses or in graduate-level seminars, the works of Bartolomé de Las Casas continue to be viable and vibrant components of the Hispanic literature curriculum. Contemporary *testimonios* such as *Me llamo Rigoberta Menchú y así me nació la conciencia* and the writings of the Apostle of the Indians from the colonial era are kindred texts. When students consider Las Casas and Menchú in the light of the controversies that both authors generated, they have little difficulty connecting the dots.

NOTES

I follow André Saint-Lu's Spanish-language edition of Las Casas's *Brevísima relación* (Cátedra, 2005).

[1] All translations are mine unless otherwise indicated.

All about Las Casas: The Productive Dialogue between Literature and Film

Eyda M. Merediz

The demands that an increasingly overwhelming cinematic culture has put on literature professors are large—more so when students have to engage with the rich legacy of the colonial period, for which there are few specialized anthologies, at least in Spanish. Those of us who teach early modern Spanish-language literature often resort to our own selection of passages and texts in upper-division courses that explore the intermedial dialogue between literary texts and cinematic ones.

Such an exploration was practically impossible until just before 1992, the quincentenary of Columbus's arrival in the New World, when the production of films that adapted, appropriated, and elaborated on colonial figures, themes, and texts flourished considerably. Robert Stam's description of this phenomenon as a more sophisticated manifestation of Eurocentrism serves as a gateway into pedagogical and ideological inquiries that can lead in a variety of directions.

Most specialists of the colonial period, by now, have designed and taught a course in which the writings of Columbus are paired with one or two commercial movies made about his enterprise: Ridley Scott's *1492: The Conquest of Paradise* (1992) or John Glen's *Christopher Columbus: The Discovery* (1992; see, e.g., Lipsett-Rivera and Rivera Ayala). The 1561 letter of Lope de Aguirre to Philip II or the several chronicles that documented Aguirre's expedition in search of El Dorado are more enticing when compared with the 1972 Werner Herzog film *Aguirre: The Wrath of God* and Carlos Saura's *El Dorado* (1988; Stone, "Aguirre"; Holloway). Álvar Núñez Cabeza de Vaca's account of his life in the southwest United States, *Relación* (later known as *Naufragios*), is typically read in tandem with Nicolás Echeverría's parodic reelaboration of the narrative in the 1989 film *Cabeza de Vaca* (see Verdesio). The memoirs of Catalina de Erauso are explored alongside Emilio Gómez Muriel's 1945 movie, *La monja alférez*, also famous for its twentieth-century protagonist (the Mexican diva María Félix), or the 1986 Basque production of the same title directed by Javier Aguirre (see Velasco). Likewise, Sor Juana's *Respuesta a Sor Filotea de la Cruz* is illustrated by María Luisa Bemberg's cinematic rendition of the nun's predicaments in sixteenth–century Mexico in *Yo, la peor de todas* (1990) (see Ramírez; Miller; Stone, "Beyond").

This fruitful dialogue between literature and film must address the specific language of each medium. Most of our students have already been exposed to literary analysis, but the language of film requires further contextualization. I find it useful to assign the first three chapters of Sturken and Cartwright's *Practices of Looking* (or the first chapter of Gillian Rose's *Visual Methodologies*), which introduce students to analytic categories and schools of thought that have shaped our critical gaze. Another important dialogic relation, that of history and film, is addressed in the volume *Based on a True Story,* edited by Donald Stevens, which features thoughtful articles on many of the films mentioned above. In addition, readings from Mark Burkholder and Lyman Johnson's *Colonial Latin America* can complement the understanding of the historical background in which these early texts were produced.

How, then, can we integrate Bartolomé de las Casas into such a course on literature and film? First, I resist the sole assignment of the *Brevísima relación,* even though it might be the most popular work of Las Casas—or at least the most easily obtained, most cathartic, and most effective text for the classroom. Its rhetorical and editorial success eclipses the depth and complexity of other Lascasian texts that should be introduced in an upper-division course. Even if they are taught in fragments, they reflect a much wider scope of literature as it intersects with religion, politics, and the law. Thus, I often choose selections that depict Las Casas's early utopian thinking (from the "Memorial de remedios" [1516]), his historiographical rigor (from the *Historia de las Indias*), his anthropological stance (from the *Apologética historia*), his missionary program (outlined in *Del único modo*), and his political intervention with its critique of Spanish imperial rule in the Americas and advocacy for restitution (as it appears in the scholastic "Tratado de las doce dudas").

Most of these ideas resonate with films that do not necessarily represent the specific context in which Las Casas wrote. I suggest comparing Las Casas's writings with *The Mission* (Roland Joffé, 1986) or *Black Robe* (Bruce Beresford, 1991), both commercially available in North America. These films speak of later Jesuit evangelical missions, the first in Paraguay and the second in Quebec. *The Mission* explores how the Guaraní were caught in the midst of political conflicts among European powers, while *Black Robe* tells the story of the Jesuit missionaries among the Algonquin and Huron.[1] What the comparison loses in specificity it gains in offering a comparative hemispheric perspective that reveals the same rotten core; that is, the predicament of the Christian mission, with its underlying contradictions among utopian ideals, connections to projects of imperial expansion and colonization, and cultural miscommunication inherent in any interaction with Europe's others in the New World.

At times, however, I follow a different path involving a dramatic piece by the Catalan playwright Jaime Salom, who, circa 1992, took on Las Casas, a controversial subject difficult to revisit in Spain regardless of the angle that one takes, given his ill-conceived reputation of being a traitor to his own nation (*Las Casas* [available in English as *Bonfire at Dawn,* trans. Phyllis Zatlin]). Indeed, Salom dared to enter a terrain not explored since the 1960s and 1970s when Latin American dramatists like Enrique Buenaventura and Augusto Salazar Bondy took up the subject.[2] Salom's play, moreover, did not debut in Spain but in Mexico and was subsequently staged at the GALA Teatro Hispano in Washington, DC, during the conflict-ridden year of 1992.[3]

A full-scale production in Mexico and a modest one in Washington tell us, predictably enough, that Las Casas has crossed the Atlantic once more to achieve a literary recognition many times denied to him on the other side. Luckily for Salom, his play was turned into a film (entitled *Bartolomé de las Casas*), thereby potentially extending its reach beyond the audiences for the 1992 productions. This project, undertaken by Sergio Olhovich, who also staged the theatrical event in Mexico, was nevertheless a modest low-budget production of limited diffusion to date.

Salom's craftsmanship has been celebrated by critics who approve of his dramatic strategies, such as the use of simultaneous planes (upper and lower), which constantly interact to transition from one scene to the next. He has also been praised for the use of the doubling technique in which one actor plays two or more different characters—a recurring device in Salom's dramatic production (see Gómez 15–18 for a discussion of dramatic mechanisms). In his play *Las Casas*, the strategy unveils the systemic illness of the royal administration, which duplicates or can replicate itself endlessly (i.e., Ferdinand II and Charles V are played by the same actor). This doubling also extends to characters who somewhat mirror each other and who relate to Las Casas as allies or friends (e.g., the actor who plays Señor, Las Casas's Indian slave, also plays Señor's son, who appears at the end of the drama; the actor who plays Pedro de Rentería, Las Casas's close friend and co-owner of the Cuban *encomienda* [ownership he and Las Casas subsequently renounced], also plays Rodrigo de Andrada [or Ladrada], a fellow Dominican who often accompanied Las Casas until his final days).

Olhovich's obvious innovation involves the addition of a metacinematic frame that calls attention to the filmmaking process. This adaptation stands alone in an otherwise theatrically static set. As Cynthia Stone suggests, the film is too faithful to the original drama to use the cinematic medium to full effect. The merits of the film, as briefly pointed out by Stone, arise from its offering a cinematic "alternative to a monolithic image of Spanishness" that normally centers on "the Inquisitions and Counterreformation" ("Filming" 317). Olhovich, I would argue, goes beyond that; he copies Salom but with a revisionist eye, the corrective vision of those who have recovered Las Casas through a New World lens.

Olhovich adapts Salom's text, a dramatic image that is innovative in its own right, destined to desacralize Las Casas without taking away his powerful message.[4] More often than not, Las Casas gets trapped by fragmented or blurred portraits that flatten the nuances of his anthropological, religious, and political thinking; Salom, however, rises to the challenge and produces a mutable and undeniably human Bartolomé de Las Casas. During the first three acts, the playwright focuses on the early years of the conquest and colonization of America by tracing the transformation of Las Casas from a young Sevillian dreamer into a compassionate *encomendero* and then eventually into the advocate for the legal rights of the Indians—his ultimate and true humanitarian mission.

Salom presents Las Casas in contact with the bisexuality of his young Indian page, Señor, who has fallen in love with him in Seville. Señor's attachment produces in Las Casas a tremendous fear of desire but also a genuine love and the guilt that follows, when Señor dies working in the Caribbean mines after his master sent him away in obedience to a royal decree. Salom seems to attribute Las Casas's love for mankind to his love for one man (Ortega; Gómez 19–21). Thus, what Salom has done in a sense is to quasi queer Las Casas. This suggestive strategy is, in my view, merely a provocation designed to question the order of things with a concrete, contemporary concern, instead of presenting, for example, Las Casas's views on cannibalism. Gender bending becomes here the indicator for testing the audience's take on cultural alterity. This queering makes for a thorny point of class discussion, to which students inevitably react with passion (as Las Casas did against injustice), especially those with close ties to Latin America who cannot identify with such a fictionalized, "unholy" version of the Dominican friar.

Although the dramatist rocks the boat, he still makes sure that Las Casas shares the stage with a female lover, Petrilla, a Sevillian *tabernera* and whore who constantly tempts his flesh throughout the play and ends up marrying Las Casas's uncle, Gabriel, a greedy and vulgar *encomendero*. Las Casas assumes his chastity vows and remains chaste and committed to his religious and political causes, despite being haunted by both the memory of Señor and the presence of Petrilla.

Other aspects of the play are more faithful to Las Casas's worldview, as when Salom introduces Las Casas's oppositional ideas in defense of the Indians, either directly voiced by the character of the friar or echoed by another important historical and dramatic figure, Antonio de Montesinos, whose 1511 homily in Hispaniola helped prompt Las Casas's change of heart. By attributing Las Casas's well-known positions to senior Dominicans like Montesinos and Pedro de Córdoba, Salom establishes that Las Casas is not a lonely voice but part of a community of missionaries who paved his way to public recognition and agency.

Salom's shortcomings have to do with the depiction of the indigenous world. He presents arguments in favor of *mestizaje* (miscegenation, hybridity) in Las Casas's words and upholds the friar's reading of Aristotle to prove the civility of the Amerindians and their right to self-government. However, Salom engages in a conventional replica of primitivist topoi, or what can be colloquially called the "tarzanization" of the other. In this sense, he does not depart from a humorous device long practiced in Spanish National Theater, evocative of Golden Age use of *vazcuense* and *morisco* speech on the stage for comic relief. Señor, for instance, speaks in infinitives; not a single conjugated verb is present in his utterances (e.g., Salom 41). Moreover, he belongs to an invented tribe, the Zailos, that bears little resemblance to the Arawak (Taíno) populations of Hispaniola and Cuba, for whom no historical documentation exists regarding extensive bisexual practices: "Espíritu mujer, espíritu hombre, cuerpo mujer, cuerpo hombre, para Zailos, lo mismo" 'Spirit woman, spirit man, body woman, body man, for Zailos, the same' (43).[5] At the end of the play, Las Casas invokes the god of life who is called Tlatelolco (138), a Nahuatl toponym meaning "place of the earth mound" (still today the name of a neighborhood in Mexico City), and spends his last days in a senile delusional episode where all characters parade in front of him in the fourth act.

Olhovich's cinematic text revisits these problematic aspects of the drama in a more conscientious attempt to be historical and ethnically accurate for a more culturally sensitive Mexican audience. Tlatelolco, for example, becomes Tonatzin, the goddess of life. Olhovich also sanitizes Salom's text, considerably departing from Salom's provocatively gendered approach. Neither Las Casas nor entire indigenous communities could be queered in Mexico (certainly not before the 2001 film *Y tu mamá también*); thus, every suggestion of a bisexual natural inclination is substituted in the movie with a different kind of threat, an openly political stance that points to the illegality of the Spanish conquest—a much harder line to pursue in Spain and one Salom merely alludes to in his drama.

Salom gives no stage directions as regarding the physical appearance of Las Casas's character. Olhovich opts for a virile beard, an unusual element to use when representing the Dominican friar. Indeed, the most popular portrait of Las Casas, drawn in 1791 by the López Enguídanos brothers (*Retrato*) and re-produced ad infinitum, depicts him sideways as an elderly, clean-shaven, halo-bearing, pen-in-hand beatified historian in a multivolume library. This portrait does not differ much from the recently discovered and apparently authentic frontal portrait of Las Casas made during his lifetime by N. Albítez (Pérez Fernández, "Hallazgo"). Although realistic, Olhovich's choice seems odd (unless it is intended to counteract the emasculation of Las Casas in the play), and I use this cinematic portrayal as a point of departure to talk about the representation of Las Casas through time and space.

Toward the end of the class, in which we trace comparisons between the play and the film, I introduce a series of illustrations that provide an overview of the many verbal and visual portraits of Las Casas (see Pérez Fernández ["Hallazgo"] and Giroud 201–58 for a comprehensive selection). In reading Antonio de Remesal's and Agustín Dávila Padilla's histories of the Order of Preachers in the sixteenth century and the earliest indirect biographers of Las Casas, one discovers that there are no detailed physiognomic descriptions of the Dominican friar. Any vivid descriptions that exist date from the nineteenth century, when a certain connection between the friar and the fictional character of Don Quixote de la Mancha was established. As already noted by Marcel Batallion and André Saint-Lu (*El padre Las Casas* 308–09), José Martí, in his "El padre Las Casas" (1889), depicts Las Casas as the implicit combative image of Don Quixote, long-limbed, with an elongated nose, his clothes hanging off his frame as he fights all of Spain: "largo, de nariz larga, ropa que le caía y de pelea con toda España" (qtd. in Batallion and Saint-Lu 308–09)—a description inspired by that of Manuel de Jesús Galván in his novel *Enriquillo* (1882).[6] The Cuban ethnographer Fernando Ortiz, in his prologue to nineteenth-century scholar José Antonio Saco's work, also asserts:

[E]stas Américas hispánicas son hijas de Don Juan. . . . El vino a este Nuevo Mundo. No fue Don Quijote. Pero si alguna vez llegóse a estas

> Indias el caballero inmortal, a unas aventuras que olvidara Cide Hamete
> Benengeli, fue a no dudarlo, bajo el sayal de Bartolomé de las Casas.
> (Introduction xlix)

> These Hispanic Americas are the daughters of Don Juan. . . . He came to
> the New World, not Don Quixote. But if this immortal knight ever came
> to the Indies in some adventure forgotten by Benengeli, it was, without
> any doubt, disguised in the habit of Bartolomé de las Casas.

Ortiz adds that this association between the literary character and the historical
friar was established by a French writer, Marcel Brion, in his 1927 *Bartholomé de
las Casas, "Père des Indiens,"* also available in an English version (Ortiz xlix n40).

Ortiz further points out that the Spanish critic Manuel Serrano y Sanz, in his
1918 *Orígenes de la dominación española en América*, also compared Las Casas to Cervantes's character, stating that Las Casas had a "cerebro tan enfermo
como el de Don Quijote de la Mancha" (qtd. in Ortiz xlix n40). This notion that
Las Casas had "a sick brain (as Don Quixote did)" is echoed later in the infamous 1963 biography of the friar written by the prominent Hispanist Ramón
Menéndez Pidal, in which, following the primitive psychoanalytic apparatus of
the 1950s and early 1960s, Las Casas turns out to have a double personality, one
of them rather psychotic in his supposed anti-Spanishness. Pérez Fernández
reports as well a 1990 interview of the Spanish writer and Nobel Prize winner
Camilo José Cela, in which he gives Las Casas the epithet of "hysterical" (Pérez
Fernández, *Fray Bartolomé de las Casas* 8).

This general dichotomy in the reception of Las Casas has of course a more
nuanced history, in which some detractors can be found in Latin America and
sympathizers in Spain. Among Las Casas's Latin American detractors, one finds
the Argentinian Rómulo Carbia (who called Las Casas "loco . . . frenético") and
also the Peruvian intellectual Raúl Porras Barrenechea (Martínez Torrejón 75–
76). The Dominican's Spanish defenders can be traced back to Benito Jerónimo
Feijóo in the eighteenth century. He is followed by Fabié in the nineteenth
century and later by contemporaries of Menéndez Pidal such as Manuel María
Martínez, Giménez Fernández, and Pérez de Tudela Bueso, who, among others, contributed greatly to Lascasian studies in the 1950s and 1960s.[7]

Las Casas, I point out to students, serves Hispanism in two ways—or, better, in a split way, depending on the side of the Hispanic Atlantic from which
he is represented. Spain has often pursued a pathological dimension, while
Latin America has mostly followed a utopian, heroic one. Works like Salom's
and Olhovich's, although exhibiting certain characteristics of this tendency toward a split perception, help dismantle an increasingly disappearing dichotomy
by revealing a traveling iconographic figure engaged in constant crossings and
appropriations. These works attest to Las Casas's multifaceted and unstable
legacy, which continues to rise above nationalist and regionalist constructions to
embrace a far more complex Atlantic identity.

NOTES

My thanks to Cindy Stone for introducing me to the film about Las Casas and for all her help.

[1] See Saeger on the *The Mission* and Axtell on *Black Robe* for useful information on the films and their relation to history.

[2] As recent as 2004, New York City's Public Theater staged a successful English adaptation of another drama, *The Controversy of Valladolid*, by French screenwriter-dramatist Jean-Claude Carrière, who wrote the play originally in French in 1992 (*La controverse de Valladolid* [available in Spanish as *La controversia de Valladolid*, trans. Manuel Serrat]). Carrière had been working with the text in previous years and wrote the script for a film of the same title released commercially in France in 1991. Although the film is generally available, there is no subtitled version either in English or Spanish. Unlike Sergio Olhovich's 1992 production, *Bartolomé de las Casas*, *La controverse* is a first-rate, award-winning film that inspired the New York theatrical production. The shortcomings of both (film and play) are their reliance on some stereotypical misconceptions: a passionate Las Casas overpowers the logical and legally sound one. The Valladolid meeting, for example, is depicted in *La controverse* as a face-to-face debate between Las Casas and Juan Ginés de Sepúlveda. The subject of the quarrel in front of the pope's legate mistakenly centers on whether Indians were true human beings (who can laugh, appreciate beauty, and be impregnated) and whether they possess souls. Although historically inaccurate in many ways, the dramatization in the film is engaging and has great pedagogical potential. The English version of the play is further simplified, however, and less convincing.

[3] Zatlin-Boring discusses in detail the productions of the play.

[4] Klein inscribes the play in the tradition of the "epic theater" in both its Brechtian alienation and Artaudian sensorial understandings.

[5] All translations are mine. Zatlin-Boring modified Salom's text slightly when translating it for American audiences. She changes controversial passages of the first act, sanitizes this one (12), and translates *Zailos* as *Arawak* (11).

[6] For details of this relationship, see Cairo's critical edition of Martí's text (26n9).

[7] Regarding Las Casas's detractors, see Comas (518-31); Hanke and Giménez Fernández (316); and Martínez Torrejón's introduction to the *Brevísima relación* (64–79). Daniel Castro's *Another Face of Empire* (2007) can also be seen as part of a detracting tradition; here, the Lascasian pathology seems to be a sort of attention deficit disorder that prevents the cleric from finishing many of the projects that affected the indigenous population directly.

Las Casas and Early Modern Spanish and English Colonialist Discourses

Elizabeth Sauer

Studies of early modern Spanish, English, and select Continental colonialist writings on the New World offer various pedagogical opportunities for exploring cultural, political, and ethnographic representations and encounters. The suggestions for the comparative investigations proposed here promise to enrich the classroom experience of students studying early modern Europe. Central to these approaches are questions about Spanish and inter-European relations, as viewed through travel literature and histories that address such issues as national self-definition and the New World encounter. The three case studies presented here are framed by the writings and the received tradition of Bartolomé de Las Casas, including *Historia de las Indias*—a detailed account of the exploration and settlement of the New World by Spain to 1520 (printed in 1875)—*Apologética historia sumaria* (completed in 1559), and the popular, often-translated *Brevísima relación,* which appeared first in English in 1583 as *The Spanish Colonie.* Excerpts from Spanish and other European narratives and travel literatures stimulate pedagogical discussions about cross-cultural, transnational New World experiences and establish a basis for assessing the importance and controversial history of Las Casas's key writings in the European theater and the colonial world.

This tripartite investigation is designed for senior undergraduate or graduate literature or history courses on early modern England or Europe and would also complement the interests of students undertaking projects on American literature and history, the legacy of the colonial period, or the founding of the American nation. These approaches to teaching Las Casas can be extended to include Protestantism and Catholicism, Spanish-English-Continental religious conflicts, imperialisms, and debates on toleration and nationhood, as well as on the politics of translation in the early modern era. Las Casas's works lend themselves to various analyses—including historical, autobiographical, anthropological, political, and linguistic—and literary engagement involving examinations of the textual apparatus, experimentations with genre, questions of narrative voice, and textual appropriation. All these approaches inform the study of Las Casas, whose writings I locate in relation to his contemporaries. My classroom investigations are framed by three themes, illuminated by case studies: Documenting the first encounters: *Historia de las Indias*; European debates about the natives and national rights: *Apologética historia sumaria*; Reception history, textual representation, appropriation: the *Brevísima relación* and *The Spanish Colonie*.

Documenting the First Encounters

The exploration of early modern Spanish and English colonialist discourses begins most productively with the historicizing of the above-mentioned themes. The encounter with the Amerindians should be contextualized in terms of Spain's response to other groups marked by cultural, ethnic, and religious difference: the Muslim Moors, whom the Spaniards defeated in southern Spain (Granada) on 2 January 1492; and the Jews, who were expelled by the Catholic monarchs Ferdinand and Isabella. Following immediately on these events was the voyage of Christopher Columbus, who set sail on 3 August 1492. He claimed the land in accordance with Spain's legal entitlement to govern the Americas, which rested on *Inter caetera*, the bull of donation issued by Alexander VI. In 1493 the pope, a Spaniard, "donated" to the Castilian crown the lands unoccupied by a Christian ruler but also made that right provisional on the Spaniards' "induce[ment of] the peoples who live in such islands and lands to receive the Catholic religion, save that you never inflict upon them hardships and dangers" (qtd. in Pagden, Introduction xvi–xvii.).

The imposition of the colonizer's language on the New World and its inhabitants is a central feature of imperialism. "Your Majesty," explained the bishop of Ávila, who spoke on behalf of the scholar Elío Antonio de Nebrija after Nebrija presented to Isabella his Spanish *Gramática*—the first grammar of a modern European language ever produced: "language is the perfect instrument of empire" (qtd. in Trend 88). Naming and defining constitute the colonizing act that overwrites cultural difference. To illustrate this point, I ask students to read "The Letter of Columbus on the Discovery of America," which presents the first encounter—the charting, naming, and detailing of the New World and its inhabitants. The "Letter of Columbus" invites comparison with Las Casas's corresponding accounts in *Historia de las Indias*, which offer testimony of Columbus's voyages from documents relating to or written by Columbus that describe Spanish-native interactions and the settlement of the New World to 1520. In his report to the Spanish monarchs, Columbus, in an act of political and ideological hegemony, claimed the island of San Salvador for Spain. The corresponding narratives in the *Historia* are found in book 1, chapter 2, wherein Las Casas celebrates the explorer as pious, determined, and faithful to his sovereigns, and in book 1, chapters 39–40, in which Las Casas recounts Columbus's commemorative naming of the new Spanish empire (*Bartolomé de las Casas* 53).

In identifying selections from *Historia de las Indias* for classroom examination, I am guided by George Sanderlin's usefully organized edition of Las Casas. The excerpts Sanderlin includes from the prologue of the *Historia* outline the reasons for the writing of this history—namely, the recounting of the first encounters in the Indies (35; Prologue) and the edification of posterity. Questions about Las Casas's eyewitness testimony, authority, and perspective are central to the composition of his narrative, which focuses on the plight of the natives, uncharacteristic of other travel literature on the New World.

Theories of the liminal experience of wonder, expounded by Stephen Greenblatt, prove instructive in studying Las Casas. Wonder is "a central recurring feature in the early discourse of the New World . . . thrilling, potentially dangerous, momentarily immobilizing, charged at once with desire, ignorance, and fear"; wonder is "the quintessential human response to what Descartes calls a 'first encounter'" (Greenblatt, *Marvelous Possessions* 19, 20). Correspondingly, Las Casas's documented experience is designed to capture the "marvelous deeds in these Indies" and the history of the divine creation since the "time of God's merciful wonders ha[d] now arrived" (*Bartolomé de las Casas* 35, 37; bk. 1, ch. 2). The massacres, Las Casas would state in the *Brevísima relación*, not only "seem to have clouded and laid silence and oblivion upon all those other deeds" but also threatened to end the world (*An Account* 1).

Book 1, chapters 39 and 40 of the *Historia,* "San Salvador," present the experience of wonder from both sides—Indian and Christian: "The Christians stood looking at the Indians, marveling no less than the Indians marveled at them—wondering at the Indians' extreme mildness, artlessness, and trust in a people they had never known" (54). The anthology *The Literatures of Colonial America* by Susan Castillo and Ivy Schweitzer includes a cluster of accounts under "Native Views of the Conquest of Mexico" (62–71), among which is "The Omens Described by Muñoz Camargo" (1520), consisting of eight "wonders" that struck the natives with dread. "The Story of the Conquest as Told by the Anonymous Authors of Tlatelolco" was originally written in Nahuátl in 1528 and recorded by a Spanish Franciscan, Bernardino de Sahagún. The poetic laments and songs of sorrow artfully record the response to the arrival of Cortés in Mexico, which should be compared with the speeches Las Casas attributes to the Indians in the *Historia.*

Book 3, chapters 26, 29, and 30 of the *Historia,* "The Conquest of Cuba," describe the massive slaughters of the years 1511–13 under the command of Diego

Velázquez and his lieutenant, Pánfilo de Nárvaez. Las Casas, who was a member of Velázquez's expedition to Cuba in 1511–12, made the conquest the basis of his *Brevísima relación*. Other selections I assign from book 3 are chapters 27 and 115, on the character of Cortés—a secretary of Velázquez (the governor of Cuba). Cortés defied Velázquez's orders and, on 18 November 1518, left Cuba for the conquest of Mexico, mentioned above. I end the examination of the *Historia* by comparing it with an excerpt from Bernal Díaz del Castillo's 1568 *Historia verdadera de la conquista de la Nueva España* (pub. 1623). Like Las Casas, Bernal Díaz documents the experience of wonder, involving "both the failure of words—the stumbling recourse to the old chivalric fables—and the failure of vision, since seeing brings no assurance" (Greenblatt, *Marvelous Possessions* 133). Wonder is thus the confrontation of "an absolute difference" (131–32). In the narrative of Bernal Díaz, that difference is cannibalism—a heathen practice that is, however, as Michel de Montaigne will judge, less barbarous than the Spanish acts of torture ("Of Cannibals" 1077).

European Debates about the Natives and National Rights

The *Apologética historia sumaria* (the 1550s composition date is still subject to inquiry) was not published until 1909. The 1,350-page work compares the culture of the natives with the ancient Greeks, Romans, Egyptians, and Spaniards. Instructors might introduce this work by explaining the continuation and extension of its argument from *Historia de las Indias*. The section "A Description of Cuba" in the *Apologética* documents the physical environment of Hispaniola, the accounts having been derived from earlier chapters of the *Historia* that were transferred to the later work. Las Casas's comparative ethnography of the Americas and of the cultural and social practices of the indigenous communities aimed to demonstrate that the Indians were imbued with reason and that the civil society they developed was comparable to that of any Christian commonwealth.

The subject of the Indians' nature intrigued the Spaniards in Spain and America, who were generally convinced of the natives' potential for conversion and cultivation (Hanke, *Aristotle* 9). Proposals for the protection and welfare of the Indians were plentiful, and eventually arguments about the theological merits of conversion and the theory of natural servitude culminated in the famous debate between Las Casas and Juan Ginés de Sepúlveda at the ancient Spanish city of Valladolid in 1550–51, just before the printing of the *Brevísima relación*.

The argument from the *Apologética* takes up these concerns and addresses the question provoked by the Dominican father Antonio Montesinos's widely published sermon "Are Not the Indians Men?" delivered in the church of Santo Domingo in 1511. The account is included in *Historia de las Indias* (bk. 3, chs. 4–6): "Be assured that in your present state you can no more be saved than the Moors or Turks, who lack the faith of Jesus Christ and do not desire it," Montesinos warns his countrymen (*Bartolomé de las Casas* 81). Las Casas reiterates this point in the *Brevísima relación* by aligning the Spanish conquistadors' practices with those of Muslims. The civility practiced by the Indians stands in contrast. Chapters 40 through 58 of the *Apologética* associate Aristotelian standards for civil life with the kinds of prudence that the Indians exercise, as well as with the six classes of citizens they designated and the cities they built. Sanderlin's selections from chapters 43, 62, and 63 feature accounts of the second class of Indian citizens—craftspeople, producers of featherworks and silver products. The insights into Indian culture were intended to refute charges based on Aristotelian thought (the tenets of which Las Casas expertly supported) that Indians were natural slaves.

The comparative ethnographic and anthropological approach I invite involves analyses of several excerpted travel narratives from *The Literatures of Colonial America*: First, "The Letter of Pero Vaz de Caminha to King Manuel I, May 1, 1500," by Pero Vaz de Caminha, describes the Portuguese traveler's encounter with the native Brazilians—likely of the Tupinambá tribe. Second, Giovanni da Verrazzano's *Voyage of Verrazzano, Florentine Noble in the Service of François I, King of France, 1524* details the life and customs of New World natives, which Verrazzano compares with those of Orientals, particularly the Chinese. Students are asked to consider Vaz de Caminha's and Verrazzano's works in relation to "The Letter of Columbus" (addressed to Ferdinand and Isabella) and to Las Casas's appeals to the Spanish monarchy throughout his writings.

Another valuable text for comparing Las Casas's anthropological observations of the Indians to the views of his contemporaries is the *Dialogue for the Conversion of the Indians* (composed c. 1556–57). The Portuguese traveler Manuel da Nóbrega develops the subject of converting the Brazilian natives to Catholicism into a debate between a missionary priest, Brother Gonçalo Alvarez, and a blacksmith, Matheus Nogueira. The exchanges broach such issues as the Indians' alleged lack of civil organization and the appropriation of native languages for ideological control.

Fourth, *A Briefe and True Report of the New Found Land of Virginia* (1588; pub. 1598), by Thomas Harriot, the English surveyor and mathematical tutor to Sir Walter Raleigh, includes "Of the Nature and Maners of the People." This moralistic section, while surveying the natives' social structures and customs, focuses on the prospects for religious conversion. Harriot also conveys his contradictory position on the treatment of the Indians: he admits that the colonizers applied excessive force in their dealings with the natives, and yet, "because it was on their part justly deserved, the alteration of their opinions generally and for the most part concerning us is the lesse to be doubted."

I reserve for the end of our examination of Las Casas and anthropology a comparative analysis of the concluding sections in Las Casas's *Apologética* with the frequently anthologized "Of Cannibals," by Michel de Montaigne. This essay was published in 1580, 1588, 1595, each time with revisions; the first English translation appeared in 1603 by John Florio (in Montaigne, *The Essayes*).

Montaigne declared that *barbarous* meant foreign rather than uncivilized and condemned the European practice of torture as less humane than cannibalism. Anticipating this critique of the concept of barbarism, Las Casas in chapters 264 through 267 of the *Apologética* and in the epilogue to his text anatomizes the term, as defined by Aristotle, and identifies four categories and various subcategories thereof. In "not speaking our language well, nor understanding us," the natives are barbarous, Las Casas states, but "in this, we are as barbarous to them as they are to us" (146). Las Casas defamiliarizes the colonizer's language, thereby unsettling the dichotomous relationship between self and other used to justify European supremacy.

Reception History, Textual Representation, Appropriation

Linguistic appropriation is the theme of the third case study in my approach to teaching Las Casas. Featured here is the *Brevísima relación*—a graphic exposition of the barbarism and brutality of the Spanish conquistadors, produced in 1540-42, while Las Casas was lobbying the court of Charles V for reforms for the Indians and creating a climate for Charles's "emancipation proclamation"—the New Laws of 1542. The *Brevísima relación* resembled medieval chronicles with which Las Casas was familiar, its title being derived from the early Spanish accounts of the "destruction of Spain" describing Muslim conquests of Europe. Las Casas's title reveals his recognition of the tyrannical nature of the *Requerimiento*, which he repudiated on the basis that "those who war on infidels [nonbelievers] mimic Muhammad" (Casas, *The Only Way*, qtd. in Seed, *Ceremonies* 92).

The connections between the *Brevísima relación* and the *Historia de las Indias* effectively link the first and last segments of my pedagogical approach to Las Casas. Published in 1552, the *Brevísima relación* was translated during the sixteenth century into every major European language and served to entrench the image of Spanish conquest in the minds of Europeans. Its intentions were identical to those of the *Historia*, but it was designed to capture "the immediacy of the American experience" and to serve as an official report—in this case, to the monarch—in accordance with those produced by royal officers to document their activities in the Indies (Pagden, Introduction xxx, xxxi). As a "relación," the genre of Las Casas's work resembled that of other contemporaneous narratives: Diego de Landa's *Relación de las cosas de Yucatán*—the classical text on Mayan civilization—and Hernán Cortés's *Cartas de relación*, which, like Bernal Díaz's *Historia verdadera de la conquista de la Nueva España*, betrayed some admiration of Aztec culture.

An analysis of the *Brevísima relación*'s front matter again yields insights into the purpose of the work and the author's relationship to his royal addressee. In the "Prólogo" to Prince Philip ("Presentation by . . . Casaus, to the . . . lord Prince"), Las Casas justifies his entreaty on the basis that "this subject was not able to contain himself from supplicating with Your Majesty . . . that Your Majesty not . . . allow those terrible things that the tyrants . . . committed against those peaceable, humble, and meek Indian peoples" (*An Account* 3). He insists in turn that this "is a thing . . . which is most sorely needful and necessary so that God might make the entire estate of the royal crown of Castile prosper spiritually and temporally" (4)—not to mention economically and imperially, for Spain was squandering its chance to use conversion (as benign conquest) to establish its rightful sovereignty.

Selections from the *Brevísima relación* that I assign include the "Introduction to the Relation"—an overview of the forty-nine years of destruction and "infernal tyranny" wreaked by the insatiably greedy conquistadors on the more than twelve million innocent natives (*An Account* 7)—and "On the Island of Cuba" (discussed in reference to the *Historia* above), which describes the efforts of the Indians to appease the demonic Spaniards, who nevertheless "slew above three thousand" in a scene of unspeakable cruelty (20). Excerpts illustrating the acts of torture by the Spaniards in the penultimate chapter, "On the New Kingdom of Granada," allow for connections between the Spanish defeat of the Muslims in the Spanish city of Granada and their slaughter of the Indians in the New Granada of modern-day South America. Questions of narrative perspective, conventions of the travel narrative, uses of detail, the language of objectivity and credibility, and the effects of irony are central to this exploration and the ensuing examination of the text's reception history.

First appearing in English in 1583, the translated *Brevísima relación* was printed under the title *The Spanish Colonie*. The translation helped intensify English antipathy toward Catholics at a time of mounting fear of the Spaniards. A comparison of the front matter, on which classroom discussions might focus, reveals more obviously the differences between Las Casas's treatise and *The Spanish Colonie*. The title page of *The Spanish Colonie* indicates that the work is "nowe first translated into english, by M. M. S." But the epistle "To the Reader" states that the work is "faithfully translated by *James Aliggrodo*, to serve as a President and warning to the xii. Provinces of the lowe Countries." The reference is to a French translation by Jacques de Miggrode, from which the English version was produced. In the 1580s, the work was also translated into Dutch and served as propaganda against the Spaniards, so that, as its dedication "To the Reader" states, the persecuted Netherlanders might "consider with what enemie they are to deale" (2). Besides including an epistle "To the Reader," *The Spanish Colonie* has a long appendix: "The Authour his wordes farder to *king Philip*, then at the time of writing thereof, Prince of *Spayne*," featuring selections from the debates at Valladolid.

"To the Reader" situates Spain's history of atrocities in relation to that of the Goths and then the Turks; the translator states that "it seemeth that the Spaniardes have murdered and put to death in the Westerne Indies by all such meanes as barbarousnesse it selfe coulde imagine" (2). Students will discover that M. M. S. concentrates on the imperial competitor rather than on the victims of the imperial conquest. A large section is devoted to the history of Christian-Muslim conflict, in which context the English reader is asked to judge the justly executed assault against the Spaniards as revenge for persecution of the Indians. Translation thus becomes an act of interpretation, appropriation, and moral justification as the *Brevísima relación* is used against its original intention: the work is enlisted in the English campaign against the Spaniards that would culminate, five years after the printing of *The Spanish Colonie*, in the defeat of the Spanish Armada.

Teaching Las Casas in terms of related texts by his Continental and English contemporaries offers the instructor the opportunity to apply methodologies often lacking in English literature or history courses. Examined from suggestive comparative perspectives, these manageable case studies of *Historia de las Indias*, *Apologética historia sumaria*, and *Brevísima relación de la destrucción de las Indias* invigorate the classroom experience by engaging students in conversations about colonialist discourses and encounters in early modern historical, anthropological, and textual contexts.

NOTE

Quotations from Las Casas's *Brevísima relación* are from *An Account, Much Abbreviated, of the Destruction of the Indies* (trans. Andrew Hurley [Hackett, 2003]). Texts from *Historia de las Indias* and *Apologética historia sumaria* come from *Bartolomé de las Casas: A Selection of His Writings* (ed. George Sanderlin [Knopf, 1971]). I gratefully acknowledge the assistance of Christopher Stampone with the editing of this essay.

Las Casas and the American Literature Survey

Thomas Scanlan

At this moment in literary studies, there's nothing terribly radical about the suggestion that a survey course in American literature might include some of the writings of Bartolomé de las Casas. Until fairly recently, however, such a suggestion would have seemed, if not radical, at least unusual. Consider, for instance, that the third edition of the *Norton Anthology of American Literature* (1989 [Baym et al.]), which was—and still is—one of the most widely used anthologies for American literature survey courses, began its coverage of American literature with a selection from John Smith's *General History of Virginia, New England, and the Summer Isles* (1624). That American literature might have begun before the sailing of the *Mayflower* and that it might include texts written in languages other than English was an idea whose time had not yet arrived. Today, anyone contemplating teaching a survey course in American literature is confronted with a dizzying array of anthologies, almost all of which define American literature much more broadly—in both temporal and geographic terms—than would have been the case a mere two decades ago. Anyone who wants to measure the change should cast a quick glance at the table of contents of the seventh edition of the *Norton Anthology*, which now includes—and has included since the fourth edition was published in 1994—a short selection from Las Casas's *Brevísima relación de la destrucción de las Indias* (*A Short Account of the Destruction of the Indies*).

While I am delighted that Las Casas is now represented in major anthologies of American literature, I want to make the case in this essay for going beyond the anthology and assigning Las Casas's *Brevísima relación* in its entirety. (The availability of relatively inexpensive paperback translations of the *Brevísima relación* makes it an easy choice for instructors teaching in departments of English and American literature to require this text of their students.) While some scholars of Las Casas might argue that the *Brevísima relación* is not representative of Las Casas's whole career as a writer, thinker, and actor on the world stage, I want to suggest that the narrative is the ideal text to teach in the American literature survey. I make this suggestion for three reasons. First, Las Casas's remarkable text is a dramatic example of the ways in which the printed word shaped the colonial enterprises of European nations. The second reason to include Las Casas's *Brevísima relación* is its deep historical connection to the Anglo-American colonial project. The third reason is the way it resonates with one of the major themes of American literature. I would like to spend the bulk of this essay discussing this third strand, but before I turn to the thematic connections between the *Brevísima relación* and American literary history, I want to say a bit more about the first two features.

I always begin my early American literature courses by reminding my students that colonialism was a discursive phenomenon. That is, in addition to being a physical operation that required human beings to transport themselves and their material and equipment to far flung places, colonialism demanded documentation. Kings, queens, and other state officials had to rely on the written reports of their subordinates to make decisions about how best to use their finite resources. In the early stages of colonialism, these reports were often private documents that circulated among church and state officials who were involved in the colonial effort. Some of these private communications eventually saw wider circulation. For example, the translation and publication of Christopher Columbus's letter to Luis de Santángel made that document available to a trans-European readership. Sometimes, individual players in the colonial enterprise used publication as a means of building a wider base of support for a particular view or approach. An example of such leveraging would be Álvar Núñez Cabeza de Vaca's *Relación*. Although Cabeza de Vaca frames his account as a report to the king, he publishes it to promote his own career as a future leader of colonial expeditions. Like Cabeza de Vaca, Las Casas uses publication as a way of drawing attention to a cause. Although its publication forms part of the celebrated—and intricate—theological debate between Las Casas and the theologian and philosopher Juan Ginés de Sepúlveda, the *Brevísima relación*, which was printed in the vernacular, was also an attempt to appeal to an audience that would be wider than Spain's clerical elite. American literature is filled with examples of texts that changed the course of history, and Las Casas's *Brevísima relación* gives students one of the earliest examples of this phenomenon. In its simplicity and its rhetorical power, the text is comparable to such American classics as Thomas Paine's *Common Sense* and Harriet Beecher Stowe's *Uncle Tom's Cabin*.

In addition to serving as a locus classicus of the power of print in the promotion of a political agenda, the *Brevísima relación* bears a particular relationship to the English colonial enterprise. From the moment of its first translation and publication in English in 1583 (*The Spanish Colonie*), the account shaped the way that the English talked about their colonial endeavors. It is hard to overestimate the effect of this text on England's subsequent colonial undertakings. Not only was the impact almost immediate, it was long-lived: within a few years of the *Brevísima relación*'s first English publication, its depictions of Spanish misdeeds were widely circulated among English readers, and those misdeeds would be kept in the public view by the periodic republication of Las Casas's visceral text. It would be an overstatement to suggest that Las Casas singlehandedly changed the future prosecution of the English colonial effort. Nevertheless, it is fair to say that the widely reported Spanish atrocities loomed large in the minds of those who directed English colonial operations. Such prominent participants in the English colonial enterprise as Richard Hakluyt, Roger Williams, and John Eliot—to name just a few—all explicitly construct their visions for English colonial endeavor in direct opposition to what they saw as the cruel and violent behavior of the Spanish. There is indeed a good deal more to say on the direct connections between the *Brevísima relación* and subsequent English colonial undertakings, but my space is limited, and I would like now to turn to the thematic connections that one can draw between Las Casas and Anglo-American literature.

Three basic themes tie the *Brevísima relación* to other pieces of American literature. The first of these themes is the notion of individualism that figures largely in many American texts. Some writers celebrate the power and possibilities occasioned by the birth of the unchecked and unfettered individual in the modern world. Other writers, like Las Casas, look more cautiously on this development and offer a critique of unbridled individualism. My second theme is that of the status of European subjectivity in an expanding colonial world. While some texts confidently assert the implicit superiority of European culture and values, Las Casas gives voice to a more skeptical view that refuses to dismiss non-European cultures and societies as inherently inferior. Finally, I look at the *Brevísima relación* as an early instance of eyewitness testimonial—a subgenre that would become prevalent in Anglo-American writing in the centuries that followed. In my survey course of American literature, the *Brevísima relación* functions as a touchstone on these and other themes. Students who read the narrative in the context of the survey find particularly interesting the striking similarities between the arguments and strategies of Las Casas and those used by Anglo-American writers, some of whom are writing several centuries after the first publication of Las Casas's powerful text.

While the *Brevísima relación* is a complicated text that works on a number of different levels, three components of Las Casas's rhetorical strategy correspond roughly to the three themes I outlined above. The first of these is conveniently on display in a short, early passage: "The simplest people in the world," Las Casas writes, "unassuming, long-suffering, unassertive, and submissive—they are without malice or guile, and are utterly faithful and obedient to their own native lords and to the Spaniards in whose service they now find themselves" (*Short Account* 9–10). Las Casas presents his readers with a picture of a people who possess a natural, almost prelapsarian virtuousness. In contrast to the virtue and kindness shown by the natives, the Spaniards seem naturally endowed with a remarkable capacity for cruelty. In other words, unlike the natives, who seem to show selflessness at every turn, the Spaniards seem driven by a selfish individualism that leads to meanness and hatred. The second component of Las Casas's strategy is to refer frequently to the Spaniards as Christians. The effect of this subtle gesture is to force the reader to measure the behavior of both—the Spaniards and those whom they would subject to their power—against Christian ideals. Not surprisingly, the Spaniards come up short in this comparison. The result is that the Spaniards are represented as nominal Christians only—that is, as people who call themselves Christians while finding it within themselves to commit acts of unspeakable barbarity. The natives, on the other hand, are people who treat others with Christian virtue but lack the name Christian. By comparing the natives with the Spanish, Las Casas calls into question the assumed superiority of European culture and values. The final rhetorical feature I examine is the way Las Casas persistently calls attention to his status as an eyewitness to the events he is describing. Early in his narrative, for instance, Las Casas mentions "the eleven survivors I saw with my own eyes" (12). Such rhetorical markers can be found throughout Las Casas's text, as he reminds his readers that he is not a purveyor of a second- or thirdhand account but rather an observer who has witnessed these brutal acts with his own eyes.

While many American texts deploy one or more of the strategies on display in the *Brevísima relación*, I find that four texts seem to offer an especially close connection to Las Casas. In the remarkable *Key into the Language of America* (1643), Roger Williams offers his readers what he claims is a phrase book that will help them as they attempt to navigate their way through Algonquin language and customs. Embedded in this phrase book, however, is a stinging critique of the Massachusetts Bay Puritans who banished Williams from their territory. Like Las Casas, Williams published his tract in Europe to make his argument to a European audience. Williams also resembles Las Casas in the way that he frequently draws the attention of his readers to his own status as firsthand observer of the people he is describing. As an eyewitness, Williams deliberately draws unflattering comparisons between the cruelty of his countrymen and the kindness of the natives among whom they reside. In the first chapter of the *Key*, Williams comments, "There is a savour of *civility* and *courtesie* even amongst these wild *Americans*, both amongst *themselves* and towards *strangers.*" He follows this observation with a brief poem that ends with the following verse:

> If Natures Sons both wild and tame,
> Humane and Courteous be:
> How ill becomes it Sonnes of God
> To want Humanity?   (99)

In other words, like Las Casas, Williams has compared the behavior of his countrymen with that of the Indians, and he has found the behavior of the English lacking. Williams then goes on to describe a native society in which there are loving relations among family members and equally friendly relations among the families. "The wildest of them," he writes, "love societie" (128). And in his chapter entitled "*Of the Earth and the Fruits Thereof, & c.*," Williams describes how the natives help one another with large tasks: "When a field is to be broken up, they have a very loving sociable speedy way to dispatch it: All the neighbours men and women forty, fifty, a hundred & c, joyne, and come in to help freely" (170). In other words, instead of describing a lawless, uncivilized people, Williams gives his English readers a picture of a harmonious society governed by kindness and mutual affection. In contrast to the selfish individualism of the English, the reader finds the selfless communitarianism of the natives.

In a different sort of text, published almost 250 years after the *Brevísima relación*, the freed slave Olaudah Equiano makes use of rhetorical strategies that are remarkably similar to those used by Las Casas, despite the fact that Equiano is constructing an autoethnographic account. In the *The Interesting Narrative of Olaudah Equiano; or, Gustavus Vassa, the African, Written by Himself*, Equiano begins by painting a picture of the society into which he was born in Africa. Equiano proclaims, "We are almost a nation of dancers, musicians, and poets." He goes on to tell his readers, "Our manner of living is entirely plain; for as yet the natives are unacquainted with those refinements in cookery which debauch the taste" (14–15). The descriptions that Equiano gives echo those of Las Casas in offering us a picture of a people who possess a natural and simple virtue that governs every aspect of their behavior. He goes on to describe his first experience of slavery at the hands of a rival African tribe, whose members treat him with kindness and humanity. This stage of his life gives way to a much more difficult set of experiences as he is taken captive by Europeans and carried off to a life of slavery in America. In an implicit comparison of the two kinds of slavery he experiences, Equiano says of his first African captors, "In honor of those sable destroyers of human rights . . . I never met with any ill treatment, or saw any offered to their slaves, except tying them, when necessary, to keep them [from] running away" (29). In other words, like Las Casas and Williams, Equiano compares the behavior of the "civilized" Europeans with that of the supposedly savage Africans, and he finds the Europeans acting in a manner far more cruel and inhumane. In a climactic moment early on in his *Interesting Narrative*, Equiano confronts his English audience directly with the hypocrisy of slavery: "O, ye nominal Christians! Might not an African ask you, 'learned you this from your God, who says unto you, Do unto all men as you would men should do unto you?'" (38). Again, like Las Casas, Equiano tries to shame his captors by demanding that they ask themselves whether there is any way that Christ would condone their behavior.

In a text that returns to the question of the Anglo-American treatment of Native Americans, Catharine Maria Sedgwick attempts to challenge her readers' basic assumptions about race. Although Sedgwick sets her novel, *Hope Leslie,* in the seventeenth century, the immediate political context is the Indian removals begun by the American government during the 1820s. Like Las Casas, Sedgwick questions the moral superiority that implicitly informs the attitudes and policies of her government. Early in the novel, for instance, the male protagonist, Everell, says to Magawisca, "I can honour noble deeds though done by our enemies, and see that cruelty is cruelty, though inflicted by our friends" (46). Magawisca, an Indian child who has survived the Puritans' massacre of the Pequods, is seen by Everell to "embody nature's best gifts, and her feelings to be the inspiration of heaven" (53). Clearly influenced by the Romantic notion that the natural state of human beings was one of harmonious cohabitation, Sedgwick offers her readers Indian characters quite different from those people who were "represented as 'surly dogs' who preferred to die rather than live," as she says in her preface (6). In doing so, Sedgwick closely follows Las Casas's strategy of emphasizing the humanity and virtue of the Indians while reminding her readers that their white ancestors were capable of cruel actions at least equal to the cruelties perpetrated by the natives. It would be a misrepresentation of

Hope Leslie to say that it condemns American behavior with the same bluntness that the *Brevísima relación* condemns the misdeeds of the Spanish colonizers. But it does force its readers to confront the possibility that race might not be a good predictor of behavior. In *Hope Leslie*, Indians and Anglos both commit barbarous acts. And Indians and Anglos also both exhibit the natural human capacity for compassion and generosity. In so doing, Sedgwick follows a path down which Las Casas, Williams, and Equiano all traveled.

My final example of the legacy of Las Casas is Harriet Beecher Stowe's *Uncle Tom's Cabin*. Published during the decade preceding the Civil War, *Uncle Tom's Cabin* was written to achieve for enslaved African Americans what the *Brevísima relación* was intended to accomplish for the native inhabitants of the Spanish New World. Throughout *Uncle Tom's Cabin*, Stowe gives examples of African American humanity, and she contrasts that humanity with the cruelty of those white characters who hold and trade slaves. In following the lives of several of the enslaved African Americans, Stowe echoes Las Casas's rhetorical strategy in the *Brevísima relación*. Early on, in an oft-cited moment in the novel, Stowe practically forces her readers to accept the humanity of the slaves. Eliza, a slave who has just fled with her child from the same plantation where Uncle Tom was a slave, pleads with Mrs. Bird, a white woman, to help her continue on her journey out of bondage so that she will not be separated from her child. "Have you ever lost a child?" Eliza asks Mrs. Bird (72). This question elicits a cascade of feeling from Mrs. Bird, one of whose children has just died. Like Williams and Las Casas, who point to the strong feelings the native inhabitants have for their children as evidence of their humanity, Stowe allows her readers to identify with this helpless slave as she confronts the possibility of losing her child. In addition to emphasizing the humanity of the slaves, Stowe also follows Las Casas by exposing the hypocrisy of the Christian slaveholders. She does this by constructing unmistakable parallels between the life of Uncle Tom and that of Christ. The slaveholders, who simultaneously profess their Christian beliefs and perpetrate cruelties on their slaves, are made to look much like the Spanish colonizers in Las Casas, whose actions belie their self-proclaimed identity as Christians.

In this brief look at a handful of texts, we have seen how the *Brevísima relación* makes a prescient introduction to the issue of race in American literature. Las Casas's bold intervention in his country's debates about the obligations of colonizers anticipates the moves in a much larger argument that would take place on four continents over the next three centuries. As the predominantly white societies of European countries established colonies in far-flung places, they would have to ask themselves basic questions about the ways the colonial enterprise might be reconciled with their own notions of faith, justice, and individual responsibility. And the colonies that turned into nations—including the United States—were left to answer the same fundamental questions. I don't think there can be any dispute about the status of Las Casas's *Brevísima relación* as a quintessentially American text.

Las Casas in French and Other Languages

Jonathan Hart

Teaching Bartolomé de las Casas in a comparative context means considering notions of translation and intertextuality, as well as questioning how the texts enter the colonial archive (manuscripts and rare books).[1] Spain was to France and England an example, especially, in the colonization of the New World. The national, colonial, and imperial identities of France and England were bound up with the precedence of Spain in the New World and how figures like Columbus and Las Casas permeated their textual and political archive. More specifically, I balance the French and English emulation of Spain with their use of the Black Legend of that country. Texts that emphasized the heroism and riches of the Spanish empire far outweighed those that did not until the seventeenth century. Las Casas is a key part of a course on the comparative studies of the Americas, which should relate him to others—like Columbus, Jacques Cartier, and John Smith—who also came into contact with the indigenous peoples of the New World. My goal is to have North American students see their own colonial and present-day culture in the context of the Atlantic world and to enable them to understand the relation between the Anglo-American colonies and those of the Spanish, Portuguese, French, and Dutch.

As the French and English had to come to terms with Spain in Europe and the New World, they had to consider Spanish texts, and their identities became deeply tied to translations of those works. Translations into French and English early on were closely related: the first English translation of the *Brevísima relación* was from a French text. The revolt in the Netherlands was also a prominent field for the sowing of Las Casas's translations and the rise of the Black Legend. French translations appeared in Switzerland and the Netherlands, and it is on French and other related translations that I concentrate.

The "French" translations were at first for French-speakers who spread, with the Reformation, into other countries beyond France. Students discuss with me the typology of the Old World and the New (a prefiguration of one in the other, or a double image), in which the cruelty of the Spaniards in the New World was like their cruelty in the Netherlands. The Spanish mistreatment of the natives from 1492 became a warning for their later abuses in the Netherlands during the Dutch revolt (c. 1568–1648). My students are surprised to learn that Las Casas and the Black Legend were not simply vehicles for Protestants but were also an influence on French Catholics like Marc Lescarbot (in some ways the Richard Hakluyt of New France). Some of the ideological translation and editing of Las Casas's work is refractory and intricate and does not make for a linear tale. Students see that Las Casas is subject to various interpretations in different languages, by authors who translate and discuss his work among one another in an array of editions and in terms of religious, cultural, and linguistic rivalry. Moreover, students learn that translation is a political and religious instrument as well as a linguistic tool. Las Casas would have been horrified to see some of the uses to which the heretics and other enemies of Spain put his works. The *Brevísima relación* is the text that was chosen for translation into English and French: whether or not it is a fair summa of Las Casas's work, the account was the central focus in these languages, perhaps owing to its brief, polemical, and self-contained nature. This text is the nexus and crux of the representation and misrepresentation of Las Casas in French and English and some other European languages.

Teaching this material at the heart of the library or archive is key for students, whatever their level or field of study. I am able to call expert librarians who expose students to a range of editions, translations, and manuscripts. The collection becomes part of the course: its presence is about the students, whose learning is enhanced when they have the actual historical materials before them.

Libraries without the resource of early editions of Las Casas's texts and related works can substitute databases, facsimiles, microfilm, and digital collections. I ask the class to meet in the rare books section of the library so the students can see various editions, including early Spanish editions of Las Casas (1552, 1553), whose images and typography are always helpful and of special interest for students who know Spanish. With the text at hand, we are able to go over some differences of phrasing between the original and the translations in different languages.

Translations

The first translation we discuss is Jacques de Miggrode's 1579 French-language version, *Tyrannies et cruautez des Espagnols, perpetrées es Indes Occidentales, qu'on dit le Nouveau Monde*. Miggrode's translation of Las Casas's *Brevísima relación*—which was printed in Antwerp (1579), then in Paris (1582), and, finally, in Rouen (1630)—emphasizes the tyranny and cruelty of the Spaniards in its title. Miggrode includes in his address, "Au Lecteur," a frontal attack on the Spanish. However, he finally confesses that he likes individual Spaniards but not "their insupportable pride"[2] as a nation. In a hyperbolic mode, Miggrode proceeds in his discourse to address the reader directly about the genealogy of Spanish barbarity and cruelty, from the Goths through the Saracens to the Spaniards, all of whom killed millions—especially the Spaniards, who massacred the inhabitants in the West Indies, an area three times as large as Christendom. The slippage occurs when Miggrode speaks of "the nation" but chooses the plural "their pride" ("leur") instead of the singular "its" ("sa"), so that the Spanish nation is constructed as a collection of individuals (*ii recto–*ii verso). This formula is a familiar one: I like the individuals but not the country. Pride was the worst sin for a Christian. In a polemic, logical fallacies were masked in the emotive language of persuasion. If the attack appeared hateful, Miggrode could disclaim hatred as a motivation because he was simply calling on a Spaniard, Las Casas, who showed even more asperity in his attack on Spain. The propaganda on both sides of the wars of religion was bitter and displayed figuratively and textually what was literally a fight to the death.

Anyone who knows the *Brevísima relación* remembers the chapter on Venezuela, where Las Casas says of the Germans, to whom Charles V had granted this vast territory, "In my opinion, the Venezuela expedition was incomparably more barbaric than any we have so far described" (*Short Account* 96). Miggrode left this passage out of his translation of the text, fearing, perhaps, that the Germans might be taken for Protestants (whether they were or not) even more cruel than the Catholic Spaniards. In a more explicit elision, sometimes the word "cristianos" is rendered as "Espagnols" (Saint-Lu, *Las Casas indigeniste* 162–63). Something I ask my students to consider is whether the example of Spain was as much about staying alive in Europe as it was about death in the New World. Miggrode's address was there to awaken the provinces of the Netherlands from their sleep. Translating Las Casas was a way to draw the attention of the people of the Low Countries to the nature of their Spanish oppressors. Part of the suspicion of the Spanish among the French might have been derived from Miggrode's translation of Las Casas in 1579, which Lescarbot, who questioned the godliness and zeal of the Spaniards, made popular (Lescarbot even inflated Las Casas's number of native dead).[3] However, the *légend noire*, or Black Legend, was not the only view in France: two decades before, for instance, André Thevet (*Les singularitez* [1558]) thought that God had rewarded the Spanish with America for taking Granada (16–24).

The class also looks at subsequent versions with different outlandish titles that were part of the war of propaganda that surrounded rivalries in Europe, especially the revolt of the Netherlands. Las Casas was reprinted in French in 1620 and 1630. The first of these editions appeared in Amsterdam without any prefatory matter, not even the author's, and the second, in Rouen, reproduced almost all the material from Miggrode's editions of the 1580s, except the "Extract of the Privilege." In 1620, the year the English Pilgrims sailed from Holland, a French edition of Las Casas appeared there, relying largely on copper plates to tell a pictorial story of torture and cruelty on the title page and throughout the text.[4] The publisher, Jan Evertz Cloppenburg (also known as Jan Evertsoon or Jean Everhardts Cloppenburch) presented a typology of Spanish cruelty. He included two title pages set up in identical ways with the same pictures. The first, which introduced the first part of the book, was on the Low Countries (see illus.), and the second, about halfway through the volume, was about the New World and preceded Las Casas's account. The first title page included writing surrounded by pictures of men, women, and children being tortured. Philip of Spain presided at the top and center above the title, his vassals, Don John of Austria (to the king's right and to the reader's left) and the duke of Alba (on the other side), facing the title: the Spanish cruelty in the Netherlands was mirroring that in the New World. Like the readers of the time, the students

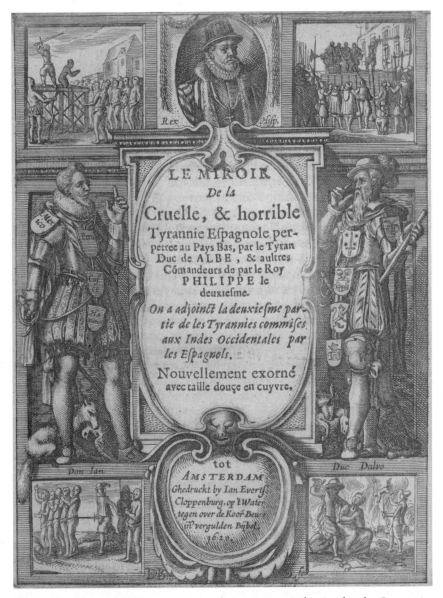

Frontispiece of *Le miroir de la tyrannie espagnole perpetree aux Indes Occidentales. On verra icy la cruaute plus que inhumaine, commise par les Espagnols, aussi la description de ces terres, peuples, et leur nature* (1620). The volume consists of two parts, each with its own title page: Johannes Gysius's account of the Spanish cruelty in the Low Countries, *Le miroir de la cruelle, et horrible tyrannie* (whose title page is displayed here); and Las Casas's account of Spanish cruelty in the New World, *Le miroir de la tyrannie espagnole perpetree aux Indes Occidentales.*

travel back from Spanish atrocities in Europe to those that happened previously in the New World. This symbolic correspondence was a central typology of the Old World and the New. Cloppenburg was asking the readers to see the Old World through the New World. This technique resembled the typology familiar to Christians at the time, in which they read the Old Testament through the New Testament. Images were as important as words in these translations, as were intertextuality and a kind of intericonography, all of which combined to affect the reader-viewer. In this version, the first title page introduced visual propaganda of scenes of Spanish brutality, images Cloppenburg arranged in typological correspondence to demonstrate that Spain was a universal tyrant that abused the Dutch in the same way it had mistreated the natives.

Cloppenburg's address to the reader illustrates as well an ideological struggle. Here, the publisher says that the Spaniards brought war and tyranny to the Low Countries under the same religious pretext they used to tyrannize the natives in the New World a hundred years before. The heretics and the Lutherans in the Netherlands had taken the place of pagans and idolaters in the New World. Cloppenburg cataloged the cruelty and subterfuge of the king of Spain and of the duke of Alba against Dutch Protestants, connecting the abuse of innocent peoples in the New World and the Old. In the service of delivering the people of the Low Countries from the Spaniards, Cloppenburg introduced Las Casas, a Catholic bishop, as a Spanish champion against cruelty and tyranny. In the typology of the Indies and the Netherlands, Las Casas was used as an inspiration in the fight against oppression and for liberty. In some of the engravings in Cloppenburg's edition, the inhabitants of the Netherlands are naked like the natives. The first part of the book then depicts the Dutch in words, and the second part describes the natives. The structure of the book is a reverse typology—a movement from present to past. The translation, which is from the Dutch, sometimes elaborates beyond Las Casas's original (to which Miggrode is closer) to make the Spaniards seem even crueler. The engravings of the Flemish artist Theodor de Bry, which had been in the Frankfurt Latin edition of Las Casas in 1598 (*Narratio regionum*), constituted part of this edition (as they did various Dutch translations), where they reinforced visually the worst atrocities in the text.

The other reprint of *Tyrannies* that we study is the Rouen version from 1630 that reproduces Miggrode's translation, demonstrating that demand for anti-Spanish tracts existed in France even after the wars of religion (see also Saint-Lu, *Las Casas indigeniste* 159–70). This version and that of 1642 (also published in Rouen) featured Las Casas on the title page. The 1642 edition presented its own brief preface and bears the permission of the Catholic church and the "Permission" granted by the king of France. The editor emphasizes "the inhuman cruelties practiced by the Spaniards (who call themselves good Christians and Catholics)" and swears that the narrative is "very certain and true" (Ã2r). Like Cloppenburg, this editor addressed the reader with the familiar *tu*, similar to the *thou* in English at the time, thereby creating a familiar bond with the reader, whom he began by addressing as a friend. The editor gave three reasons for the narrative's right to be taken as true: first, Las Casas was greatly respected for his experience in the Indies and his Christian compassion for the ill-treatment of the poor Indians ("pauvres Indiens" [Ã2v]), as well as for his book chronicling the abuses they suffered; second, the Dominican order esteemed Las Casas so much that they wrote several histories of the order that included extensive biographies of him; finally, the friar's view of Spanish cruelty was corroborated by Girolamo Benzoni (who lived fourteen years in the New World when Las Casas was alive) in his *Histoire nouvelle du Nouveau Monde*, translated from the Italian into the French. Further, the editor noted the *Short Account*'s many translations and its appearance throughout Western Europe: "The Dutch at once translated the book word for word into their language and into French. The Venetians also put it into Italian, and it spread through Italy to Spain in one volume" (Ã3r). According to this editor, no one had been able to contradict Las Casas, the authority on the matter of Spanish tyranny. The editor also provided reasons why the Spanish were tyrants in the New World: they wanted to master and settle the lands, and they came from a cruel, haughty, and proud ("superbe") nation (Ã4r, Ã4v). In his address to the reader, however, the book's raison d'être rose to the surface—Spain was the enemy of France: "if you are a good Frenchman, take this warning; if the Spaniard had the power over you that he usurped over the poor Indians, you would not be treated any more gently, and [let] this little book serve as an example to you" (Ã4v). Spain's behavior in the New World was a negative exemplum of what Spain might do in France. The Dutch, French, and English all used this strategy of reading Las Casas typologically to deploy America as a warning in Europe.

Las Casas was not the only source of the Black Legend: the title page of Urbain Chauveton's 1579 edition of Benzoni's *Histoire nouvelle du Nouveau Monde* (*La historia de Mondo Nuovo*, published in Venice in 1565) demonstrated that the Italians, too, fed this legend. This page stressed "the rude treatment" that the Spanish showed some of the "poor peoples" in the New World and indicated that the volume includes a "little history of a massacre" the Spaniards committed against the French in Florida. (See Nicolas Le Challeux's *Discours de l'histoire de la Floride* [1566]). Fifteen years later Theodor de Bry's illustrations in Frankfurt would indicate the participation of artists and printers in Germany in anti-Spanish tracts.[5] The French used Las Casas and Benzoni as providential scourges of the Spanish colonists in the New World, although even André Thevet, the royal cosmographer in France, attacked Benzoni and "his pal Léry" for lack of proper knowledge and experience of the New World (*André Thevet's North America* 161).

With translations came the migration of allusions and ideas among countries. For instance, supplementing Las Casas and Gonzalo Fernández de Oviedo, Richard Hakluyt the Younger, member of Francis Walsingham's circle and close to the court of Elizabeth I of England, referred in 1584 to Benzoni, using as his source the French preface of Chauveton's edition of Benzoni's text. In so doing,

Hakluyt displaced the experienced Benzoni, a severe critic of Spain and one of the contributors to the Black Legend, with his translator, who published in Protestant Geneva. French Protestant views of Spain were influential in Hakluyt's circle, and the Englishman marshaled them in arguments meant to sway the queen into challenging Spain's virtual monopoly in the New World. In Chauveton's version, which Hakluyt attributed to Benzoni (and translated and quoted in making his point), the Indians had logical reasoning without having studied logic, while the Spanish, more furious than lions and more dangerous than wild beasts, were cruel and devilish and had spoiled their country (Hakluyt 111; see also the Quinns' "Commentary" in Hakluyt's book [186–87]). Montaigne often took a similar view of the natives, a perspective related to the positive image that Las Casas, the explorer Jean de Léry, the Puritan missionary John Eliot, and Jean-Jacques Rousseau held of the indigenous peoples of the New World. This strand is but one of the textual and intertextual intricacies surrounding translations of Las Casas's *Brevísima relación* and related texts.

We also focus on the 1583 English version of Las Casas, *The Spanish Colonie*, a translation by M. M. S. of Miggrode's French version. (Miggrode's translation, as well as the Dutch version, *Seer cort verhael van d' Indien . . . uyte Spaensche overgeset* [Antwerp, 1578], served as propaganda against Spain.)[6] The class then explores another context for Las Casas's revival in English: the republican anti-Spanish propaganda campaign in the 1650s. In 1656, John Phillips's version of Las Casas, *The Tears of the Indians*, presented Spanish cruelty as an allegory for Cromwell's era. In it, Phillips stated that his affection for Cromwell had prompted him "to publish this Relation of the Spanish Cruelties," confident that God, "who hath put this Great Designe" in to the protector's hands, would bless the book (A4v–A6r).[7]

We continue to track this ongoing circulation of Las Casas translations in Europe, discussing versions such as *Popery Truly Display'd in Its Bloody Colours; or, A Faithful Narrative of the Horrid and Unexampled Massacres, Butcheries, and All Manner of Cruelties, That Hell and Malice Could Invent, Committed by the Popish Spanish Party on the Inhabitants of West-India* (published in London in 1689), which emphasized the horrors of Catholicism to an England that had just undergone a Protestant revolution in 1688. The title page announced that Las Casas had been translated into Latin, High Dutch, Low Dutch, and French and was "now Taught to speak Modern English," and the same old charges of the Black Legend reappeared in the volume (see the headers on pages 76 and 79).[8] The class also learns that the *Brevísima relación* was translated again during the buildup to the War of Spanish Succession and that the anonymous translator presented Las Casas's struggle as one of conscience and humankind's natural right to liberty and property against the inquisition, oppression, and tyranny of his Spain (see the preface in Las Casas, *A Relation* [published in London in 1699, n. pag.]). This edition was translated from the French version of J. B. M. Morvan de Bellegarde[9] (Saint-Lu, *Las Casas indigeniste* 168–69; Allison 42; Steele 107–08, 175–76). The relation of French and English editions of Las Casas is an intricate maze that has branches in other countries like the Netherlands, creating a sustained intertextuality that endured centuries.

Intertextuality at Play

As we dig deeper into the issues of translation and politics, the class discussions focus on comparing the colonies of the New World. Las Casas, as an editor of Columbus and as someone who prefigured the work of Léry, Montaigne, and William Shakespeare on European-native contacts, is an important figure for North American students to locate in relation to their own history and culture as well as the Atlantic basin's. A comparative study with Las Casas as centerpiece helps students better understand their own traditions and some of the Hispanic influences then and now. The ethnographic writings of Las Casas, Thevet, Léry, Montaigne, and others use foreign cultures to criticize European culture (Peter Burke calls the practice the "Germania syndrome," after Tacitus's *Germania*, which uses the manly German barbarians to reproach the effeminate Romans [Burke 46]). Depicting natives was a way of criticizing European behavior in Europe, the New World, and elsewhere, and the otherness of the past provides a critique that guards against stereotyping or oversimplifications in the present.

Léry's *Histoire d'un voyage faict en la terre du Bresil, autrement dite Amerique* (1578, rev. 1580) was about his voyage to Brazil in 1556. Over time, editions of Léry expanded, especially the section on cannibalism, which came to include Las Casas's description of the Spanish cruelty in the New World. The material from Las Casas had soon grown so much that Léry created a new chapter for it (compare the editions of 1599 and 1611). Sensational cruelty, by the Spanish or the natives, was obviously in demand and sold books, a profitable (and thus easily overlooked) aspect of the Spanish conquest. In "Des cannibales" (1580), from the *Essays*, Montaigne talks with several New World natives who traveled to Rouen when Charles IX of France was there, and the essayist asks what they found most remarkable. The natives then make satirical observations on kingship (wondering why men would obey a boy as a leader), poverty, inequality, and social class (surprised that the poor do not take the rich by the throats and burn down their houses). With the students, I discuss Montaigne as developing in part from Las Casas and Léry, especially in terms of his comments about Spain in "Des coches" ("Of Coaches"), which have been relatively neglected. Whereas in the essay on cannibals Montaigne emphasizes the French and Europeans in relation to the New World, "Des coches" represents the Spanish. In it, Montaigne compares the classical world positively with his own day, asking why the new lands could not have been conquered under the Greeks and Romans, who would have brought the peoples virtue instead of teaching them European avarice and "all sorts of inhumanity and cruelty, to the example and pattern of our customs" (*Essais* 3: 399).[10] Instead, in search of pearls and pepper, the Europeans exterminated nations and millions of people, which Montaigne deems "mechanicall victories": Florio, Montaigne's translator in English, rendered the passage "Oh mechanical victories, oh base conquest" (*Montaigne's Essays* 2: 314).[11]

Montaigne's reference to the New World is meant to chastise the Spanish, the king of Castile, and the pope, all of whom are mentioned in the description of the usual Spanish ceremony of possession in which the Spaniards, searching for a mine, tell the natives that their king is "the greatest Prince in the inhabited earth, to whom the Pope, representing God on earth, had given the principality of all the Indies." The Spaniards explain that they want the natives to be tributaries: to yield up food, medicine, and gold; believe in one God; and acknowledge the truth of the Spanish religion (*Essais* 3: 399). The noble king of Mexico is subjected to Spanish cruelty and torture, which diminishes Spain and not the victim (3: 401). Florio stressed this contrast by applying the epithet "barbarous mindes" to the Spanish torturers (*Montaigne's Essays* 2: 317). Strangely, these and other atrocities were, Montaigne reports, a source of Spanish pride: "We have from themselves these narratives, for they not only admit but extol and publish them."[12] According to Montaigne, the Spaniards exceeded the force necessary in conquest and had met with providential justice in the form of civil war and the seas' swallowing up some of their treasure (*Essais* 3: 401–02). Taken in context, then, Montaigne's comments on the Spaniards and their treatment of the natives can be seen in the light of those by Las Casas, Léry, and others as a critical position Europeans could take in relation to their own colonization, politics of expansion, and relations with other peoples, especially in the New World.

The same can be said about Shakespeare: *The Tempest*, like Montaigne's essays, is brilliant, but it too is indebted to earlier works. A couple of examples help students see the importance of context for great texts. When Gonzalo speaks about an ideal commonwealth in act 1, scene 1, he draws on Montaigne's description of cannibals, which owes something to the writings of Columbus, Las Casas, and others, although Shakespeare has Antonio and Sebastian scorn Gonzalo's speech, thus creating friction between the ideal and the satirical. Caliban opens act 2, scene 2, with a curse on Prospero, who now has power over Caliban and the island that Caliban and his mother, Sycorax, found and claimed much earlier. (In act 1, scene 1, Caliban tells Prospero, "This island's mine, by Sycorax my mother, / Which thou takest from me.") Whereas Caliban mistakes the English Trinculo for a spirit, Trinculo does not know what to make of Caliban—is the island native man or fish? In England, Trinculo says, a monster makes a man rich, because there, when people "will not give a doit to relieve a lame beggar, they will lay out ten to see a dead Indian" (1.2.32–34). At this point, students are encouraged to make connections among this key Shakespearean text, Las Casas's writings, and Montaigne's passages about Indians who were brought back to France (similar to those John Cabot and Martin Frobisher took to England). As Frank Kermode states in his edition of Shakespeare, in England, as Indians became more familiar, they replaced the wild man in pageants and masques

(145–47n62; Sauer 13, 15). Caliban performs a parodic first encounter between natives and Europeans when he asks Stephano if he has dropped from heaven, a recurring trope from Columbus onward among Europeans, who think the indigenous peoples consider them to be gods (2.2.137–40). It is this attitude of superiority that Las Casas, Léry, Montaigne, and Shakespeare were opening up for debate.

Las Casas's *Brevísima relación* and its many translations and appropriations have become a means of understanding European-native encounters in a comparative setting. Reading Las Casas in comparison with Léry, Montaigne, Hakluyt, Shakespeare, Lescarbot, and others—those we have not had time to discuss include Jacques Cartier, Samuel de Champlain, Samuel Purchas, William Strachey, and Robert Johnson—unveils the process of intertextuality that lies at the heart of the European and Atlantic colonial discourse.

NOTES

[1] A good resource for all teachers of Las Casas and other writers representing the New World is *European Americana* (Alden). See also my *Representing the New World*.

[2] "Je confesse n'avoir jaimais gueres aimé la nation en general, à cause de leur orgueil insupportable; com-bien que ie ne laisse de louër & aimer aulcuns excellens personages qu'il y a entre eux" (*2r–v). This quotation comes from the French-language edition published in 1579 in Antwerp, available online through Gale (http://galenet.galegroup .com) and now the most available copy. (My thanks to Stephen Ferguson, Curator of Rare Books at Princeton, for pointing this out to me.) In general, references to the *Tyrannies* in this essay are, unless otherwise noted, to the 1582 Paris edition, because that was the volume to which I originally had access. This 1582 edition, printed by Guillaume Julien, is based on (and has the same title as) the 1579 Antwerp edition, which translated the original Spanish edition of 1552 (published in Seville as *Brevíssimma relación*). Other editions appear as *Histoire admirable des horribles insolences, cruautez, et tyrannies exercees par les Espagnoles és Indes Occidentales*: probably Geneva, 1582; Lyons, 1594. Saint-Lu identifies the 1594 Lyons edition, noting that it included the canceled title page of the 1582 edition and was based on the 1579 Antwerp translation (*Las Casas indigeniste* 164). All translations are mine, unless otherwise indicated.

[3] See, for instance, book 1, chapter 17, of the edition of 1618 in the accessible Grant translation of Lescarbot (Grant, *History of France* 1: 125–30). Lescarbot uses a rhetorical flourish to highlight not simply the vast numbers of dead but also the number of incidents of cruelty in Las Casas's text: "This good bishop, unable to endure all these cruelties and a hundred thousand others, made remonstrances and complaints thereon to the King of Spain." Moreover, Lescarbot claims, "what I have said is a small parcel of the contents of the book of this author," whom, he emphasizes, the Spaniards themselves cite (1: 30).

[4] *Le miroir de la tyrannie espagnole* (the Amsterdam edition of 1620) composes part 2 of Johannes Gysius, *Le miroir de la cruelle, et horrible tyrannie espagnole perpetree au Pays Bas . . . On a adjoinct la deuxiesme parties de les tyrannies commise aux Indes Occidentales par les Espagnoles*. The next version is *Tyrannies et cruautez des Espagnols*

(published in Rouen by J. Cailloué in 1630). The French edition of 1620 is translated from the two-part Dutch edition of the same year—*Den spiegel der Spaensche tijrannije-geschiet in West-Indien* (published in Amsterdam by J. E. Cloppenburg). The French edition transposes the two parts. Part 2, by Las Casas, has a special title page with the title *Le miroir de la tyrannie perpetree aux Indes Occidentales*. Gysius's work includes a reference to the massacre of the French in Florida by the Spaniards and also to the Spanish treatment of the Indians. In other words, the French reverses the two parts, which are as follows in the Dutch edition: part 1 was first published in Dutch in Antwerp in 1578 under the title *Seer cort verhael vande destructie van d' Indien . . . uyte Spaensche overgeset*. This was a translation of the edition of Las Casas's *Brevíssima relación* published in Seville in 1552. Part 2 has the title *Tweede deel van de spieghel der Spaensche tyrannye* and is an abridged version of Johannes Gysius's *Oorsprong en voortgang der Nederlandtschen bercertin,* published in Leyden in 1616.

⁵ Chauveton's 1579 volume also included Nicolas Le Challeux's *Discours . . . de la Floride* (first published in Dieppe in 1566), an account of the Spanish massacre of the French in Florida. The 1565 massacre was one of the events that turned the rhetoric of the Huguenots against Spain.

⁶ See the foreword by the anonymous editor of the March of America Facsimile Series reprint of *The Spanish Colonie* (Foreword Q2r).

⁷ In 1656, Edward Leigh's Latin *Treatise of Religion and Learning* relayed Las Casas's account of the destruction of the Indies, and in 1658, the *King of Spain's Cabinet* discussed the cruelties of the Spaniards in America.

⁸ The intertextuality of translations related to the French versions of Las Casas's *Brevissima relación* can be seen through the following thread. The 1579 French translation of the 1552 Spanish original was used for the English translation of 1583. The de Bry Latin version of 1598 (*Narratio*), with the now famous illustrations, was based on that French translation of 1579. But there were other later French translations of this text by Las Casas. The 1620 French translation of Gysius (which contained Las Casas) was from the Dutch edition of 1620 (*Tweede* [based on the Dutch original of 1616 (*Oorsprong*)]). The 1697 French translation (*La decouverte*) translated only six of the nine books from Las Casas and was the basis for the English translation of 1699. In this article about early French translations of this text by Las Casas, we can see there are three, two that spawn other translations and one that is from the Dutch.

⁹ Casas, *La decouverte des Indes Occidentales, par les Espagnols* (trans. J. B. M. Morvan de Bellegarde, published in Paris in 1697). Bellegarde's version was reprinted with *Relation curieuse des voyages du Sieur de Montauban* in Amsterdam in 1698.

¹⁰ All citations from the *Essais* are from the 1588 edition, unless otherwise indicated.

¹¹ Montaigne's sentence ends simply after "mechaniques victoires" (*Essais* 3: 399). This original is now available online at Gallica from the Bibliothèque nationale de France in Paris (http://gallica.bnf.fr). My thanks to Stephen Ferguson for calling my attention to this electronic version.

¹² "Nous tenons d'eux-meſmes ces narrations, car ils ne les aduouent pas ſeulement, ils les preſchent & publient" (*Essais* 3: 401). For "aduouent" in this sentence, in another translation I have used "confess," and I might well take "preſchent" as "preach" to continue this religious theme, but I have chosen not to be as literal here, as it makes the English more idiomatic. See Hart 119.

Bartolomé de Las Casas and His Counterparts in the Luso-Brazilian World

Lúcia Helena Costigan

When I teach courses on colonial Latin America, one of the most popular texts among undergraduate and first-year graduate students is the *Brevísima relación de la destrucción de las Indias*. After reading the narratives that describe the atrocities committed by the Spanish conquerors and colonizers against the Indians, students are often delighted to find out that someone in the sixteenth century had the courage to demand from the king immediate attention to the abuses against the indigenous people of the New World. As we discuss the text, two questions commonly arise: Besides Las Casas, did other missionaries defend the natives? Since Las Casas was so determined to condemn the exploitation of the Indians, why didn't he defend the slaves brought from Africa?

Keeping these questions in mind while analyzing the text provides an opportunity to extend the discussion beyond the scope of the *Brevísima relación*. Instructors can also take advantage of students' curiosity to introduce texts by subjects of the Iberian world such as Fernando Oliveira (1514–81?), a Portuguese New Christian who entered the Dominican order but later abandoned it to become a naval captain, and Antonio Vieira (1608–97), a Jesuit who was born in Portugal but who spent most of his life in Brazil. Similar to Las Casas, these two Lusitanian figures openly criticized their Iberian contemporaries who abused and persecuted American Indians, black Africans, and other subaltern groups.

Because they wrote in Portuguese, Oliveira and Vieira are not well known by scholars of colonial Latin American studies. To contextualize the readings and discussions of the texts by these Luso-Brazilian writers, I use chapters of books such as James Lockhart and Stuart Schwartz's *Early Latin America: A History of Colonial Spanish America and Brazil*, which offers insights into the sugar plantation economy that characterized Brazil and the Caribbean area during the sixteenth and the seventeenth centuries. The book contrasts the experience of the Portuguese conquerors and colonizers with that of the Spaniards in the New World. To highlight the influence of the classical and humanist thinkers on Las Casas and Vieira, I rely on works such as Lewis Hanke's *Aristotle and the American Indians* (1959), Santa Arias's *Retórica, historia y polémica* (2001), and Alcir Pécora's "Vieira e a condução do índio ao corpo místico do império português" (2005).

To address Las Casas's position on African slavery in the New World, I have students read excerpts from *Historia de las Indias*, written during the first half of the sixteenth century but published only in 1875. Since the work consists of three large volumes and is not as readily available as the *Brevísima relación*, I place on the course's Web page chapters 102 and 121 from the third volume, in which Las Casas, in an attitude of regret and repentance, elaborates on the sufferings of black slaves on the plantations of Santo Domingo and Hispaniola. Students learn much from reading Las Casas's views on the exploitation of Africans and his criticism of the Portuguese colonizers for their slave raids in Africa alongside texts such as Oliveira's *Arte da guerra do mar, De instauranda aethiopum salute* by Alonso de Sandoval (1576–1652), and sermons by Vieira. Because Sandoval's book is large and because its prolix language and many errors make it difficult to read, I select passages that invite comparison with Las Casas, Oliveira, and Vieira. Margaret Olsen's *Slavery and Salvation in Colonial Cartagena de Indias* provides a critical interpretation on Sandoval's thinking and enhances comparative studies on missionaries who worked with African slaves. Olsen's study helps broaden the scope of the course through its focus on New Granada, an area of the New World that occupies a marginal position compared with that of New Spain and Peru in the curriculum of colonial Latin American studies.

Taking as point of departure primary and secondary readings related to Las Casas's *Historia de Indias* and to Sandoval's *De instauranda aethiopum salute*, I introduce students to passages from Oliveira's and Vieira's condemnations of the Iberian and Iberian American exploitation of Indians and black Africans during the sixteenth and the seventeenth centuries. My primary goal is to offer fresh insights on texts that help expand the horizons of colonial Latin American studies, which often limits its discussions to texts written in Spanish. Adding works by other Iberian or Iberian American writers to the syllabus brings new and interesting dynamics to the class: the texts present a broader and more inclusive view of early Latin America and give students the opportunity to undertake in-depth comparative analyses of similarities and differences within it.

Oliveira, an outspoken Dominican priest of Jewish origin, seems to have been one of the first Iberian subjects who openly questioned his sixteenth-century European contemporaries for taking advantage of "just war" to enslave Indians and black Africans and to expand their imperial domains in Africa, Asia, and America. In addition, he seems to have been the first Portuguese writer who used the pen to condemn slavery as an institution. In 1555, when Las Casas was still editing his *Historia de las Indias* (in which he concluded that slavery of black Africans was as unjust as Indian slavery), Oliveira published his daring treatise *Arte da guerra do mar*, in which he criticized those who engaged in the "just war" of conquest.

Born in Portugal in 1514, this contemporary of Las Casas remains unknown by many scholars of the early modern–colonial period. Oliveira's social criticism against slavery and his stance on the justice of the wars waged against non-Christians is clearly spelled out: in chapter 3 of the first part of *Arte da guerra*, the author energetically condemns the wars instigated by Christians against the "unfaithful" people:

> Não podemos fazer guerra justa aos infieys que nunca foram cristãos, como são os mouros, judeus e gentios que conosco querem ter paz e não

tomaram nossas terras, nem por alguma via prejudicam a cristandade. Porque com todos he bem que tenhamos paz se for possível, como diz o apóstolo Sam Paulo, e para isso de nossa parte façamos quanto em nos for, que de nós se espera exemplo de paz e paciencia fundada em fé que Deos nos vingará e fará justiça.   (xxvi; pt. 1, ch. 3)

We cannot make just war against the unfaithful who have never been Christians, like the Moors and Jews and gentiles who wish to be at peace with us and who have never taken over our lands by any means to the detriment of Christianity. It is important that we have peace, as the apostle Saint Paul preaches. We should do everything possible to give examples of peace and patience based on the faith given to us by God. If we do not do this, God will punish us.[1]

Here, similar to the argument found in Las Casas's books, Oliveira asserts that just war should respond strictly to Augustinian principles and that Europeans who do not comply with such principles commit mortal sin and will be punished by God. Besides condemning the slavery of non-Christians who do not pose a threat to the Portuguese empire, Oliveira also condemns the persecution of people such as Jews and Muslims, who lived peacefully in Europe and did not pose a threat to Christianity. Isacio Pérez Fernández, however, has argued that Oliveira defended African slaves only implicitly, whereas Las Casas does so explicitly; Oliveira does not openly name slavers or slaves—calling them Christians and infidels instead—while Las Casas directly accuses nations (e.g., the Portuguese and Castilian) and specifically defends Indians and Africans (*Fray Bartolomé de las Casas* 163–67).

The unorthodox thinking in *Arte da guerra do mar* saw Oliveira incarcerated by the Inquisition four months after its publication. The proceedings of trial 5813, found in the archives of Torre do Tombo, in Lisbon, describe him as a heretic and list his crime as "Judaism." The account also indicates that he participated in the auto-da-fé that was held in Lisbon on 24 September 1559 (*Processo*). From this date onward, Oliveira fades into obscurity.

In the seventeenth century the Jesuit Antonio Vieira followed Oliveira and Las Casas in condemning slavery of the Indians and abuses against African slaves. Vieira, considered to be the most eloquent Baroque writer and preacher of the seventeenth century, is known by some specialists in colonial Latin American literature as the author who provoked the crisis that Sor Juana Inés de la Cruz experienced in her later years, since her "Carta atenagórica" contains a sharp critique of Vieira's 1650 "Sermão do mandato" (*Obras completas* 1: 49–85). However, because most of Vieira's ideas were expressed in the Portuguese language, this powerful preacher and writer of the Iberian American world still remains in the margins of the colonial Latin American canon. Vieira, like Las Casas, was born on the Iberian peninsula but spent a great part of his life in the New World, where he refuted the ideas and behavior of those who used the Aristotelian doctrine of natural slavery to justify the wars and subjugation of Amerindians and black Africans. Condemnation of the slave-hunting expeditions in the Amazons and of other abuses committed against the Indians can be found in Vieira's "Sermão da Primeira Dominga da Quaresma," delivered in the capital of Maranhão on the first Sunday of Lent in 1653 (3: 1–22), and his "Sermão Décimo Quarto," preached in a sugar mill of Bahia in 1633, denounces the exploitation and maltreatment of black Africans (4: 283–317).

To support his refutation of the theory of natural slavery, Vieira drew on classical and scholastic writings, particularly sixteenth-century humanists such as Antonio de Montesinos, Juan Luis Vives, and Francisco de Vitoria, who believed that "all men originally were free, since individual liberty is a right conceded by God as an essential attribute of man" (Hanke, *Aristotle* 40). Although there is no mention of Las Casas in Vieira's writings, it is almost certain that Vieira had some knowledge of Las Casas's work with the Indians. Since the Luso-Brazilian Jesuit was a well-read man and had traveled extensively through Europe as a diplomat to the Portuguese king, Dom João IV, who reigned over the Lusitanian world between 1640 and 1656, Vieira likely would have been familiar with the *Brevísima relación* and with the effect that the bishop of Chiapas's notorious book had on the Protestant world.

Like Las Casas, Vieira was an ardent defender of the Amerindians and played a decisive role in curtailing the colonizers' abuses of the natives. His devotion to the cause of the indigenous inhabitants of the New World can be seen throughout the sermons that he preached in Brazil, particularly during the years 1652 to 1662, when he worked as a superior of the Jesuit missions in the Amazons. While there, he worked closely with caciques to defend the numerous indigenous groups that lived in the region and used the pulpit to condemn the Portuguese colonizers for their exploitation of the natives. In his "Sermão da Primeira Dominga da Quaresma," for example, the baroque preacher warns the Portuguese colonizers about the material and spiritual consequences that they will have to bear because of the mortal sin they committed by enslaving the Indians:

> Sabeis, cristãos, sabeis, nobreza e povo do Maranhão, qual e o jejum que quer Deus de vos esta quaresma? Que solteis as ataduras da injustiça, e que deixeis livres os que tendes cativos e oprimidos. Estes são os pecados do Maranhão, estes são os que Deus me manda que vos anuncie: Annuntia populo meo scelera eorum—Cristãos, Deus me manda desenganar—vos, e eu vos desengano da parte de Deus. Todos estais em pecado mortal, todos viveis e morreis em estado de condenação, e todos vos ides diretos ao inferno. Já lá estão muitos, e vós também estareis cedo com eles, se não mudardes de vida.   (1: 10–11)

Do you know, Christians—do you know, nobility and people of Maranhão—what kind of fast God desires from you this Lent? That you loose the bonds of injustice and that you let those whom you hold captive and oppressed go free. These are the sins of Maranhão. These are the sins that God sends to announce to you: "declare to my people their transgression." Christians, God sends me to free you from deceit, and I free you from deceit on behalf of God. You all live and die in a state of damnation and go directly to hell. Already many [settlers] are there, and you too will soon be with them unless you change your lives.

This sermon and others by Vieira are excellent texts to read alongside Las Casas's works: they offer opportunities to discuss the issue of the defense of the Indians and to compare different literary styles and genres that proliferate in the sixteenth century and with the baroque rhetoric of the seventeenth century. (Given the importance of religious figures and writings, sermons are a crucial part of this literary corpus.)

Even if Sandoval's *De instauranda* "stands alone as the earliest document that seeks to make historical, philosophical, and cultural sense of the Africa-Europe encounter in a New World context," as Olsen posits (3), Sandoval was not the only one who wrote in defense of black slaves in early Latin America. Vieira, a contemporary of Sandoval and a grandson of a black woman from the Azores, was a pioneer in defending the humanity and dignity of African slaves in Portuguese America and one of the first missionaries in the New World who preached and published texts condemning the white masters' many abuses. In fact, Vieira's defense of black slaves seems to go beyond Sandoval's and Las Casas's. As early as 1633, Vieira was preaching to African slaves who worked on the sugar plantations of northeast Brazil. In the sermons addressed to the slaves that belonged to the Brotherhood of Our Lady of the Rosary, the Luso-Brazilian missionary expresses perplexity and frustration in face of the social violence that he observed in the plantations, and in an emotionally charged rhetorical argument directed toward their masters, he asks:

> Estes homens não são filhos do mesmo Adão e da mesma Eva? Estas almas não foram resgatadas com o sangue do mesmo Cristo? Estes corpos não nascem e morrem, como os nossos? Não respiram o mesmo ar? Não os cobre o mesmo céu? Não os aquenta o mesmo sol?   (4: 330)

> Are not these men children of the same Adam and the same Eve? Were not these souls saved by the blood of the same Christ? Are not these bodies born, and do they not die just like ours? Do they not breathe the same air? Does not the same sky cover them? Does not the same sun warm them?

In his "Sermão 14," preached in 1633 to the African slaves of a sugar plantation in Bahia, the baroque Jesuit sees their sacrifice comparable to the one that Christ suffered on the cross:

Em um engenho sois imitadores de Cristo crucificado: *Imitatoribus Christi crucifixi*, porque padeceis em um modo muito semelhante o que o mesmo Senhor padeceu na sua cruz, e em toda a sua paixão. A sua cruz foi composta de dous madeiros, e a vossa em um engenho e de três. Também ali não faltaram as canas, porque duas vezes entraram na Paixão: uma vez servindo para o ceptro do escárnio, e outra vez para a esponja em que Lhe deram o fel.   (4: 305)

In a sugar mill, you are imitators of the crucified Christ: because you suffer in a way similar to what Christ himself suffered on the cross, and with all his passion. His cross was composed of two wooden beams, and yours, by innovation, of three. The canes were not lacking there either, for they entered twice in the Passion: serving as the scepter of scorn and again as a sponge, absorbing their bitterness.

Despite his condemnation of the injustices of the colonizers, Vieira did not attack the institution of slavery, a paradox that characterizes Renaissance and baroque thought. As the passage suggests, Vieira was sorry for the sufferings of the slaves, but he preached to them conformity and sacrifice. Like many Spanish missionaries, nevertheless, Vieira believed that the suffering endured by the African slaves in the sugar plantations would result in the salvation of their souls and therefore was better than the life they had in Africa, without Christianity.

Some critics have used Vieira's sermons condemning the injustices inflected on the Indian and black slaves to portray the Jesuit as a revolutionary thinker ahead of his time. Alfredo Bosi, for example, takes advantage of a passage of the same sermon—in which Vieira compares the work of the African slaves to that of bees, who produce sweet honey not for themselves but for others—to establish a subtle association between Vieira and Karl Marx:

Marx diria dois séculos depois: "Por certo, o trabalho humano produz maravilhas para os ricos, mas produz privação para o trabalhador. Ele produz palácios, mas choupanas é o que toca ao trabalhador. . . . Ele produz beleza, porém para o trabalhador só fealdade."   (144)

Two centuries later, Marx would say: "Certainly, the work of man produces marvels for the rich, but it produces hardships for the worker. It produces palaces, but leaves only shacks for the worker. . . . It produces beauty, but for the worker only ugliness."

In contrast to this type of anachronistic interpretation, Pécora presents a more balanced view of Vieira: "Vieira, como os escolásticos, reconhece, por meio de argumentos de fé e razão, a injustiça do cativeiro, mas considera maior o ganho da salvação eterna, advindo do reconhecimento da nova fé, do que o custo em si do cativeiro" 'Vieira, like scholastic thinkers, recognizes, through arguments of faith and reason, the injustice of captivity but considers the gain of eternal salvation to be greater, coming from the recognition of the new faith, than the cost of captivity itself" (90). Pécora's argument coincides with Thomas M. Cohen's: commenting on Luis Palacin's thesis that Vieira pushed the limits of the *consciência possível* (social consciousness) of the Luso-Brazilian world, Cohen argues that "Vieira stays strictly within those limits. . . . [H]is underlying message is that human greed makes the defense of slavery in its present form an untenable position for Christians" (113–14).

One can trace the humanist and scholastic arguments that inspired Las Casas and Vieira and argue that neither was proposing total equality among all people in the world. What they defended was a fair and just treatment of subaltern subjects like the Indians and the African slaves. Each also believed that Indians and black slaves, despite their differences, deserved entrance into the Christian community and that the best way to save them was by preaching the Gospel, giving them good examples, and treating them with dignity. Las Casas, did not believe in evangelization with the use of force, but he accepted slavery insofar as it was the result of a just war—which, however, excluded the indigenous population of the Atlantic world as well the Africans unjustly traded (see his *De unico vocationis modo* and *Historia de las Indias*). The Dominican also saw the relation between sovereign nations as one of equality, where the imposition of a new European sovereign could not take place without the consent of the New World subjects (Pennington; Adorno, "Intellectual Life").

Vieira's ideas compare favorably with Las Casas's propositions. The many sermons and letters in which Vieira overtly criticizes the Portuguese elite seem to outshine Las Casas (and Sandoval) in exposing the cruelty of the colonizers against the black Africans, and his vehement attacks on the tyranny and greed of the Portuguese, along with the prophetic texts and letters that he wrote to members of the Crown encouraging the end of the Inquisition and the return of the Jews to Portugal, resulted in his own persecution. During a period of almost thirty years, Vieira was summoned several times by the inquisitors, and from 1665 to 1667 he was incarcerated by the Portuguese Inquisition. In 1674, perhaps to save the Jesuit missionary, the pope suspended the actions of the Tribunal of the Holy Office in Portugal and exempted Vieira from the sentences imposed on him. Seven years later, he was allowed to return to Brazil. As a result of his so-called heretic ideas and because in 1694 he opposed the system of *repartimento* (forced labor) of the Indians by the settlers of São Paulo known as *bandeirantes*, Vieira was denied active voice as a preacher and missionary. He died on 18 July 1697. Two years before his death, Zumbi dos Palmares (1630–95), the black leader of the first organized slave uprising in the Americas, was assassinated, but there are no writings by Vieira protesting the Zumbi's murder or the destruction of Palmares, a large community of runaway slaves that existed in the Americas during the seventeenth century. Perhaps the Jesuit had been effectively silenced by then.

Revisiting Las Casas and comparing him with other missionaries of the Luso-Brazilian world helps shed light on thinkers of the Iberian world who are still marginalized in the canon of colonial Latin American studies. As the editors of the *Encyclopedia of Contemporary Latin American and Caribbean Cultures* observe:

> Despite the existence of innumerable histories of Latin American and Caribbean art, literature, and music, for example, their development is not and cannot be seen in isolation from one another, or indeed from any of the multiple behaviors and practices through which human beings apprehend, make sense of, organize, and represent the world.
>
> (Balderston, González, and López xix)

The best way to broaden our understanding of Latin American and Caribbean cultures is to include the study of early modern Iberia and the colonial Iberian-American world as a whole.

NOTES

References to Las Casas's *Historia de las Indias* are to the version edited by Agustín Millares Carlo (Fondo de Cultura Económica, 1951).

[1] All translations are mine unless otherwise indicated.

NOTES ON CONTRIBUTORS

Rolena Adorno is Reuben Post Halleck Professor at Yale University. Her books include *Guaman Poma: Writing and Resistance in Colonial Peru* (1986); the award-winning *Álvar Núñez Cabeza de Vaca: His Account, His Life, and the Expedition of Pánfilo de Narváez* (1999), with Patrick C. Pautz; *The Polemics of Possession in Spanish American Narrative* (2007); and *De Guancane a Macondo: Estudios de literatura hispanoamericana* (2008). She is a member of the American Academy of Arts and Sciences.

Santa Arias is associate professor of Spanish at the University of Kansas. She has published *Retórica, historia y polémica en el Nuevo Mundo: Bartolomé de las Casas y la tradición intelectual renacentista* (2001), coedited *Mapping Colonial Spanish America: Identity, Culture, and Experience* (2002), and is working on "Spaces of Conversion in Colonial Spanish America: From Sacred Texts to Contested Territories." Her coedited volume *The Spatial Turn: Interdisciplinary Perspectives* is forthcoming.

Melvin S. Arrington, Jr., is professor of Spanish at the University of Mississippi. He is the author of articles on Spanish American literary topics, including studies of the Inca Garcilaso, Sor Juana, Palma, Borges, Fuentes, García Márquez, Vargas Llosa, and Cardenal. He is the cotranslator (with Robert M. Levine) of *I'm Going to Have a Little House: The Second Diary of Carolina María de Jesús* (1997).

Erik Camayd-Freixas is associate professor of Spanish at Florida International University. He has written *Realismo mágico y primitivismo* (1998) and coedited *Primitivism and Identity in Latin America* (2000), with José E. González. He has published numerous articles in international journals and collective volumes and is editing a volume on the topic of orientalism and identity in Latin America.

Lawrence A. Clayton is professor of history at the University of Alabama, Tuscaloosa. His publications related to the colonial period include *The DeSoto Chronicles* (1993), *The Shipyards of Colonial Guayaquil* (1980), and many journal articles. He has lectured on Las Casas in international forums in Chile, Nicaragua, and the United States and is finishing a biography of the Dominican friar (forthcoming).

Lúcia Helena Costigan is associate professor of Portuguese and Latin American literature at Ohio State University, Columbus. Her publications include *A sátira e o intelectual criollo na colônia: Gregório de Matos e Juan del Valle y Caviedes* (1991) and several edited volumes such as *Diálogos da conversão: Missionários, índios, negros e judeus no contexto ibero-americano do período barroco* (2005), *From "Excessive Friendships" to Cannibalism Revisited: Brazilian and Spanish American Literary and Cultural Encounters* (2005), and the coedited volume *Lusophone African and Afro-Brazilian Literatures* (2007).

Viviana Díaz Balsera is associate professor of Spanish at the University of Miami and the author of *Calderón y las quimeras de la culpa: Alegoría, seducción y resistencia en cinco autos sacramentales* (1997) and *The Pyramid under the Cross: Franciscan Discourses of Evangelization and the Nahua Christian Subject in Sixteenth-Century Mexico* (2005). Her articles on colonial and Golden Age studies have appeared in *Colonial Latin*

American Review, Journal of Spanish Cultural Studies, Revista de Estudios Hispánicos, Neophilologus, and *Hispanófila,* among others.

Angelica Duran is associate professor of English and comparative literature at Purdue University. She is the author of *The Age of Milton and the Scientific Revolution* (2007) and several articles on sixteenth- and seventeenth-century British literature, natural philosophy and science, and educational reforms and has edited *A Concise Companion to Milton* (2007). Her current projects are *Milton among Spaniards, The Great Instauration,* and *Milton in Hispanoamerica.*

Regina Harrison is professor of comparative literature and Spanish at the University of Maryland, College Park. She is the author of *Signs, Songs, and Memories: Translating Quechua Language and Culture* (1989; MLA Kovacs Book Award; honorable mention LASA Book Award). She has also filmed and scripted two videos; her *Mined to Death* received the LASA Award of Merit in Film (2006). A Guggenheim Memorial Foundation fellowship sponsored her book project on Spanish-Quechua confession manuals and the analysis of indigenous conversion in the viceroyalty of Peru.

Jonathan Hart is professor of English and comparative literature at the University of Alberta. His publications include *Representing the New World* (2001), *Columbus, Shakespeare, and the Interpretation of the New World* (2002), *Comparing Empires* (2003), *Contesting Empires* (2005), *Interpreting Cultures: Literature, Religion, and the Human Sciences* (2006), and *Empires and Colonies* (2007).

Ruth Hill is professor of Spanish with an affiliation in American studies at the University of Virginia. She has written two books, *Scepters and the Sciences in the Spains: Four Humanists and the New Philosophy (ca. 1680–1740)* (2000) and *Hierarchy, Commerce, and Fraud in Bourbon Spanish America* (2005), and has published articles in the *Journal of Spanish Cultural Studies, Comparative Literature,* and *Revista Iberoamericana.* Her next book manuscripts are entitled "Critical Race Theory in Latin American (Con)Texts" and "Aztecs, Incas, and Other White Men: A Hemispheric History of Hate."

Carlos A. Jáuregui is associate professor of Latin American literature and anthropology at Vanderbilt University. His publications include: *Canibalia* (2006; recipient of a Casa de las Americas Award); *The Conquest on Trial: Carvajal's Complaint of the Indians in The Court of Death* (2008); *Coloniality at Large: Latin America and the Postcolonial Debate,* edited with Enrique Dussel and Mabel Moraña (2008); *Heterotropías: Narrativas de identidad y alteridad latinoamericana,* coedited with Juan P. Dabove (2003); and *Querella de los indios en las "Cortes de la Muerte" (1557)* (2002).

Sara L. Lehman is assistant professor of Spanish at Fordham University. Her specializations include colonial and travel literatures and foreign language pedagogy. She has presented and published extensively on pedagogy through ACTFL, Prentice-Hall, and National Textbook Corporation. Her critical edition of Antonio Vázquez de Espinosa's *Tratado verdadero* is forthcoming, and she is working on a monograph on socioeconomics and morality in colonial Latin American narratives.

Laura A. Lewis is professor of anthropology at James Madison University. She is the author of *Hall of Mirrors: Power, Witchcraft, and Caste in Colonial Mexico* (2003; Erminie Wheeler-Voegelin Best Book Award, American Society for Ethnohistory, 2004) and numerous articles. She was awarded a National Endowment for the Humanities

Fellowship (2007–08) and a John Simon Guggenheim Memorial Foundation Fellowship (2002–03) and is currently working on her second book, *History, Race, and Place in the Making of Black Mexico.*

Eyda M. Merediz is associate professor of Spanish at the University of Maryland, College Park. Her publications include a critical edition of Lope de Vega's play *Los guanches de Tenerife* (2003) and a book, *Refracted Images: The Canary Islands through a New World Lens: Transatlantic Readings* (2004). She is working on a coedited volume on the intersections of transatlantic and Latin American studies (*Otros estudios transatlánticos: Lecturas desde lo latinoamericano*) as well as a monograph on Bartolomé de Las Casas.

Kathleen Ann Myers is professor of Spanish at Indiana University, Bloomington. Her research interests include colonial Latin American history and culture, women's autobiographical writing, the chronicles, and history and representation. She has written *Word from New Spain* (1993), *A Wild Country out in the Garden* (1999), *Neither Saints nor Sinners* (2003), and *Fernández de Oviedo's Chronicle of America: A New History for a New World.* Her current project is entitled *In Cortés's Shadow: From Veracruz to Mexico City.*

Kristy Nabhan-Warren is associate professor in the department of religion at Augustana College. She is the author of *The Virgin of El Barrio: Marian Apparitions and Mexican American Catholic Activism* (2005) and of several articles on Mary in Latino/a cultures, millennialism, and apparitional culture. She is engaged in a book-length study of the *Cursillo de Cristianidad* movement among Mexicans and Mexican Americans and in the United States.

Song No is assistant professor of Spanish at Purdue University. He has written articles on transatlantic topics and colonial orality, especially on Titu Cusi Yupangui and Inca Garcilaso de la Vega. His *Cien años de contrahegemonía: Un análisis de transculturación y heterogeneidad cultural* will appear in 2008. He is writing a book on the ideological resistance of Latin American intellectuals against Western cultural imperialism.

José Rabasa is professor at the University of California, Berkeley. He is the author of *Inventing America: Spanish Historiography and the Formation of Eurocentrism* (1993) and *Writing Violence on the Northern Frontier* (2000). In addition to several edited volumes, he is working on two books: "Pre-Columbian Pasts and Indian Presents" (pictography, alphabetical writings in Nahuatl, comparative studies, and radical relativism) and "Zapatismo Insurrections."

Luis Fernando Restrepo is professor of Latin American literature and director of comparative literature and cultural studies at the University of Arkansas, Fayetteville, where he specializes in colonial Latin America. His publications include *Un nuevo reino imaginado: Las elegías de varones ilustres de Indias* (1999) and *Antología crítica de Juan de Castellanos* (2004). He has been a visiting professor at the Universidad Javeriana and the Universidad de Antioquia, Colombia.

Verónica Salles-Reese is associate professor of Spanish at Georgetown University. Her publications include *From Viracocha to the Virgin of Copacabana* (1997) and the recently edited *Remembering the Past, Rethinking the Future* (2005). Her research and teaching interests concentrate on colonial Latin America, the viceroyalty of Peru,

Audiencia of Charcas, colonial art, and women's literature. She is working on a book entitled "Daily Life in Colonial Peru" and on Jesuit cosmopolitism.

Elizabeth Sauer is professor of English at Brock University, where she was awarded a Chancellor's Chair for Research Excellence. She has published *Barbarous Dissonance and Images of Voice in Milton's Epics* (1996) and *"Paper-Contestations" and Textual Communities in England, 1640–1675* (2005) and has edited or coedited ten volumes, most recently *Milton and Toleration* (2007). Sauer currently holds a Social Sciences and Humanities Research Canada Council grant to complete a book on toleration and nationhood in Milton's England.

Thomas Scanlan is associate professor of English at Ohio University, Athens. He is the author of *Colonial Writing and the New World: Allegories of Desire* (1999). He has published extensively on early American literature, and his new project, "Pursuing Happiness in the Early Years of the American Republic," examines the ways that writers and ordinary people wrote and thought about happiness.

David F. Slade is assistant professor of Spanish at Berry College, where his scholarly work concentrates on eighteenth-century transatlantic studies. He is coauthor (with Jerry Williams) of a critical edition of religious works by Pedro de Peralta Barnuevo, *The Devout World of Peralta Barnuevo:* La galería de la omnipotencia *and* Pasión y triunfo de Cristo *by Pedro Peralta Barnuevo* (forthcoming). He is working on a book about the founding of the Archivo General de Indias and other archival projects of the eighteenth-century Hispanic Atlantic.

Karen Stolley is associate professor of Spanish at Emory University. She is the author of *El lazarillo de ciegos caminantes: Un itinerario crítico* (1992). She has contributed to *The Cambridge History of Latin American Literature* and has published in *Colonial Latin American Review* and *Revista de Estudios Hispánicos*, among others. Her current book-length project is on the topic of domesticating discourse in eighteenth-century rewritings of colonial narrative.

Cynthia L. Stone is associate professor of Spanish at the College of the Holy Cross. Her research focuses on the interface between words and images in a variety of media, from Mesoamerican codices to films set in the colonial period. She is the author of *In Place of Gods and Kings: Authorship and Identity in the "Relación de Michoacán"* (2004), and she is currently completing a new English translation of the *Relación de Michoacán*.

Gustavo Verdesio is associate professor of Spanish and American culture at the University of Michigan, Ann Arbor. He has published *Forgotten Conquests: Re-reading New World History from the Margins* (2001) and coedited *Colonialism Past and Present* (2002). He is working on a book-length project on indigenous territorialities, another on Argentinean pop culture and counterculture in the 1960s and 1970s, and a third on classical and indigenous ruins (a material culture analysis of the built environment).

Margarita Zamora is professor of Spanish and Latin American, Caribbean, and Iberian studies at the University of Wisconsin, Madison. Her publications include *Language, Authority, and Indigenous History in the "Comentarios reales de los Incas"* (1988), *Reading Columbus* (1993; Katherine Singer Kovacs Prize, 1994), and the coedited *Cuba: Contrapuntos de cultura, historia y sociedad / Counterpoints on Culture, History, and Society* (2007).

SURVEY PARTICIPANTS

Rolena Adorno, *Yale University*
Maureen Ahern, *Ohio State University, Columbus*
Melvin S. Arrington, Jr., *University of Mississippi*
Erik Camayd-Freixas, *Florida International University*
Raquel Chang-Rodríguez, *Graduate Center, City University of New York*
Lawrence A. Clayton, *University of Alabama, Tuscaloosa*
Lúcia Helena Costigan, *Ohio State University, Columbus*
Viviana Díaz Balsera, *University of Miami*
Angelica Duran, *Purdue University*
Roberto González Echevarría, *Yale University*
Regina Harrison, *University of Maryland, College Park*
Jonathan Hart, *University of Alberta*
Ruth Hill, *University of Virginia*
Carlos A. Jáuregui, *Vanderbilt University*
Adriana Johnson, *University of California, Irvine*
Mónica Klien, *Georgetown University*
Sara L. Lehman, *Fordham University*
Laura A. Lewis, *James Madison University*
Raúl Marrero, *University of Richmond*
Yolanda Martínez–San Miguel, *University of Pennsylvania*
Kathryn McKnight, *University of New Mexico, Albuquerque*
Mariselle Meléndez, *University of Illinois, Urbana*
Kathleen Ann Myers, *Indiana University, Bloomington*
Kristy Nabhan-Warren, *Augustana College*
Song No, *Purdue University*
José Rabasa, *University of California, Berkeley*
Luis Fernando Restrepo, *University of Arkansas*
Verónica Salles-Reese, *Georgetown University*
Elizabeth Sauer, *Brock University*
Thomas Scanlan, *Ohio University, Athens*
David F. Slade, *Berry College*
Karen Stolley, *Emory University*
Cynthia L. Stone, *College of the Holy Cross*
Daniel Torres, *Ohio State University, Athens*
Gustavo Verdesio, *University of Michigan, Ann Arbor*
Paul Vickery, *Oral Roberts University*
Thomas Ward, *Loyola College*
Margarita Zamora, *University of Wisconsin, Madison*

WORKS CITED

Abbott, Don Paul. *Rhetoric in the New World: Rhetorical Theory and Practice in Colonial Spanish America*. Columbia: U of South Carolina P, 1996.

Abercrombie, Thomas A. "Tributes to Bad Conscience: Charity, Restitution, and Inheritance in Cacique and *Encomendero* Testaments." *Dead Giveaways: Indigenous Testaments of Colonial Mesoamerica and the Andes*. Ed. Susan Kellogg and Matthew Restall. Salt Lake: U of Utah P, 1998. 249–91.

Abrams, M. H. *A Glossary of Literary Terms*. 8th ed. Boston: Heinle, 2005.

Abril Castelló, Vidal. "La bipolarización Sepúlveda–Las Casas y sus consecuencias: La revolución de la duodécima duda." *La ética en la conquista de América: Francisco de Vitoria y la Escuela de Salamanca*. Ed. Demetrio Ramos et al. Corpus Hispanorum de Pace 25. Madrid: Consejo Superior de Investigaciones Científicas, 1984. 229–88.

Acosta, José de. *De procuranda Indorum salute*. Madrid: Misionera, 1952.

———. *Historia natural y moral de las Indias*. 1590. Ed. Edmundo O'Gorman. Mexico: Fondo de Cultura Económica, 1962.

Actualidad de Bartolomé de las Casas. Mexico: Fomento Cultural Banamex, 1975.

Adorno, Rolena. "El arte de la persuasión: El Padre Las Casas y Fray Luis de Granada en la obra de Waman Poma de Ayala." *Escritura, teoría y crítica literarias* 4.8 (1979): 167–89.

———. "Censorship and Its Evasion: Jerónimo Román and Bartolomé de las Casas." *Hispania* 75 (1992): 812–27.

———. "Colonial Reform or Utopia? Guaman Poma's Empire of the Four Parts of the World." Jara and Spadaccini, *Amerindian Images* 346–75.

———. "Los debates sobre la naturaleza del indio en el siglo XVI." *Revista de estudios hispánicos* 9 (1992): 47–66.

———. "Discourses on Colonialism: Bernal Díaz, Las Casas, and the 20th Century Reader." *MLN* 103 (1988): 239–58.

———. "The Discursive Encounter of Spain and America: The Authority of Eyewitness Testimony in the Writing of History." *William and Mary Quarterly: A Magazine of Early American History and Culture* 49 (1992): 210–28.

———. *Guaman Poma: Writing and Resistance in Colonial Peru*. 1986. 2nd ed. Austin: U of Texas P, 2000.

———. "The Intellectual Life of Bartolomé de las Casas." Andrew M. Mellon lecture. Tulane Univ., New Orleans. Fall, 1992. *The Guaman Poma Website*. 29 May 2007 <http://www.kb.dk/permalink/2006/poma/info/en/frontpage.htm>. Path: Resources; 1992c.

———. *The Polemics of Possession in Spanish American Narrative*. New Haven: Yale UP, 2007.

———. "The Politics of Publication: Bartolomé de las Casas's *The Devastation of the Indies*." *New West Indian Guide* 67 (1993): 285–92.

Afanasiev, Valeri. "The Literary Heritage of Bartolomé de las Casas." Friede and Keen 539–78.

Agamben, Giorgio. *Homo Sacer: Sovereign Power and Bare Life*. Trans. Daniel Heller-Roazen. Stanford: Stanford UP, 1998.

———. *The Open: Man and Animal*. Trans. Kevin Attell. Stanford: Stanford UP, 2004.

Aguirre: The Wrath of God. Dir. Werner Herzog. Anchor Bay, 1972.

Alden, John, ed. *European Americana: A Chronological Guide to Works Printed in Europe Relating to the Americas, 1493–1776*. Vols. 1–5. New York: Readex, 1980–97.

Alexander VI. *Inter caetera: European Treaties Bearing on the History of the United States and Its Dependencies to 1648*. Ed. Frances Gardiner Davenport. Washington, DC, 1917. *The Papal Bulls as Pertaining to the Americas*. 9 Aug. 2007 <http://www.bullsburning.itgo.com/essays/Caetera.htm>.

Alfonso X. *Siete partidas*. Vol. 2. Madrid: Imprenta Nacional del Boletín Oficial del Estado, 1985.

Allison, A. F. *English Translations from the Spanish and Portuguese to the Year 1700: An Annotated Catalogue of the Extant Printed Adaptations, Excluding Dramatic Adaptations*. London: Dawson of Pall Mall, 1974.

André-Vincent, Philippe I. *Bartolomé de las Casas, prophète du Nouveau Monde*. Paris: Tallander, 1980.

———. *Las Casas, apôtre des Indies: Foi et liberation*. Paris: Tallandier, 1975.

Ankersmit, F. R. *History and Tropology: The Rise and Fall of Metaphor*. Berkeley: U of California P, 1994.

Arenas, Reinaldo. *El central (Poema)*. Barcelona: Seix Barral, 1981.

Arias, Arturo. "Authoring Ethnicized Subjects: Rigoberta Menchú and the Performative Production of the Subaltern Self." *PMLA* 116 (2001): 75–88.

———, ed. *The Rigoberta Menchú Controversy*. Minneapolis: U of Minnesota P, 2001.

Arias, Santa. "Bartolomé de las Casas's Sacred Place of History." Arias and Meléndez, *Mapping* 121–36.

———. *Retórica, historia y polémica: Bartolomé de las Casas y la tradición intelectual renacentista*. Lanham: UP of America, 2001.

Arias, Santa, and Mariselle Meléndez, eds. *Mapping Colonial Spanish America: Places and Commonplaces of Identity, Culture, and Experience*. Lewisburg: Bucknell UP, 2002.

Aristotle. *The Politics*. Ed. Stephen Everson. Cambridge: Cambridge UP, 1988.

———. *The Rhetoric and the Poetics of Aristotle*. Trans. W. Rhys Roberts and Ingram Bywater. Introd. Edward P. J. Corbett. New York: Modern Lib., 1984.

Arrom, José Juan. "Bartolomé de las Casas, iniciador de la narrativa de protesta." *Imaginación del Nuevo Mundo: Diez estudios sobre los inicios de la narrativa hispanoamericana*. Mexico: Siglo XXI, 1991. 47–62.

Augustine of Hippo. *The City of God*. Trans. Marcus Dods. New York: Random, 1950.

———. *Confessions*. Trans. E. B. Pusey. *Augustine of Hippo*. Ed. J. J. O'Donnell. U of Pennsylvania. 8 Nov. 2006 <http://ccat.sas.upenn.edu/jod/augustine/>. Path: Texts and Translations, English Translation (Pusey).

———. *On Christian Doctrine*. Trans. and introd. D. W. Robertson. New York: Macmillan, 1989.

Avalle-Arce, Juan Bautista. "Las hipérboles del Padre Las Casas." *Dintorno de una época dorada*. Madrid: Porrúa Turanzas, 1978. 73–99.

Axtell, James. "*Black Robe*." *Past Imperfect: History According to the Movies*. Ed. Ted Mico, John Miller-Monzon, and David Rubel. New York: Henry Holt, 1995. 78–81.

Azaustre, Antonio, and Juan Casas. *Manual de retórica española*. Barcelona: Ariel, 1997.

Balderston, Daniel, Mike González, and Ana M. Lopez. Introduction. *Encyclopedia of Contemporary Latin American and Caribbean Cultures*. Ed. Balderston, González, and López. New York: Routledge, 2000. xiii–xxii.

Baptiste, Victor N., ed. *Bartolomé de las Casas and Thomas More's* Utopia: *Connections and Similarities. A Translation and Study*. Culver City: Labyrinthos, 1990.

Barilli, Renato. *Rhetoric*. Trans. Giuliana Menozzi. Minneapolis: U of Minnesota P, 1989.

Barkley, Elizabeth F., K. Patricia Cross, and Claire Howell Major. *Collaborative Learning Techniques: A Handbook for College Faculty*. San Francisco: Jossey-Bass, 2005.

Barnet, Miguel. *Biografía de un cimarrón*. Havana: Inst. de Etnología y Folklore, 1966.

Barreda, Jesús Ángel. "Aproximación histórica." Casas, *Obras completas* 2: i–xvi.

Bartolomé de las Casas. La leyenda negra. Dir. Sergio Olhovich. Soc. Cooperativa de Producciones José Revuelta SLC, 1992.

Bataillon, Marcel. "The Clérigo Casas, Colonist, and Colonial Reformer." Friede and Keen 353–440.

———. *Erasmo y España*. Mexico: Fondo de Cultura Económica, 1950.

———. *Estudios sobre Bartolomé de las Casas*. Barcelona: Península, 1976.

———. *Etudes sur Bartolomé de las Casas*. Paris: Centre de Recherches de l'Institut d'Études Hispaniques, 1965.

Bataillon, Marcel, and André Saint-Lu. *El padre Las Casas y la defensa de los indios*. Barcelona: Ariel, 1976.

———. *Las Casas et la défense des Indiens*. Paris: Julliard, 1971.

Batllori, Miguel. *El abate Viscardo*. Caracas: Inst. Panamericano de Geografía e Historia, 1953.

Baudot, Georges. "Amerindian Image and Utopian Project: Motolinía and the Millenarian Discourse." Jara and Spadaccini, *1492* 375–400.

Bauer, Ralph, ed. *The Colonial Americas, 1492–1820*. Vol. 1 of *Thomson Anthology of American Literature*. Forthcoming.

Baym, Nina, et al., eds. *The Norton Anthology of American Literature*. 3rd. ed. New York: Norton, 1989. 7th ed., 2007.

Benítez Rojo, Antonio. "Bartolomé de Las Casas: Entre el infierno y la ficción." *MLN* 103 (1988): 239–58.

———. *La isla que se repite*. Hanover: Ediciones del Norte, 1989.

Benjamin, Walter. "The Task of the Translator." *Illuminations*. Trans. Harry Zohn. New York: Harcourt, 1968. 69–82.

Benning, Sadie. "If Every Girl Had a Diary." *Sadie Benning Videoworks*. Dir. Benning. Vol. 1. Videocassette. Video Data Bank, 1990.

Benton, Lauren. *Law and Colonial Cultures: Legal Regimes in World History, 1400–1800*. Cambridge: Cambridge UP, 2002.

Benzoni, Girolamo. *Histoire nouvelle du Nouveau Monde, contenant en somme ce que les Hespagnols ont fait jusqu'a présent aux Indes Occidentales, et le rude traitement qu'ils font à ces pauvres peuples-la*. Trans. and ed. Urbain Chauveton. Geneva: Vignon, 1579.

———. *La historia de Mondo Nuovo*. Venice: Appresso Francesco Rampazetto, 1565.

Bermann, Sandra, and Michael Wood, eds. *Nation, Language, and the Ethics of Translation*. Princeton: Princeton UP, 2005.

Bernand, Carmen, and Serge Gruzinski. *De la idolatría: Una arqueología de las ciencias religiosas*. Mexico: Fondo de Cultura Económica, 1992.

Betances, Ramón Emeterio. "Cuba." 1874. *Peregrinos de la libertad.* Ed. Félix Ojeda Reyes. Río Piedras: U de Puerto Rico, 1992. 32–54.

———. *Les deux Indiens: Episode de la conquête de Borinquen*. Toulouse: Bonnal et Gibrac, n.d. [c. 1853].

———. *Los dos indios. Episodio de la conquista de Borinquen*. Trans. Carmen Lugo Filippi. San Juan: Centro Hostosiano, 1998.

Betanzos, Juan de. *Narratives of the Incas*. Austin: U of Texas P, 1996.

Beuchot, Mauricio. *Bartolomé de las Casas 1484–1566*. Madrid: Orto, 1995.

———. *Los fundamentos de los derechos humanos en Bartolomé de las Casas*. Barcelona: Anthropos, 1994.

Beverley, John. "The Margin at the Center: On *Testimonio*." Gugelberger 23–41.

———. *Una modernidad obsoleta: Estudios sobre el barroco*. Los Teques: Fondo Editorial ALEM, 1997.

Bhabha, Homi K. *The Location of Culture*. London: Routledge, 1995.

Black Robe. Dir. Bruce Beresford. Vidmark, 1991.

Bolaños, Álvaro Félix. "The Historian and the Hesperides: Fernández de Oviedo and the Limitations of Imitation." *Bulletin of Hispanic Studies* 72 (1995): 273–88.

———. "El líder ideal en el libro de caballerías y las crónicas de Indias de Gonzalo Fernández de Oviedo." Diss. U of Kentucky, 1988.

———. "A Place to Live, A Place to Think, and a Place to Die: Sixteenth-Century Frontier Cities, Plazas, and *Relaciones* in Spanish America." Arias and Meléndez, *Mapping* 275–93.

Bolívar, Simón. "Carta de Jamaica." Bolívar, *Doctrina* 55–75.

———. "Discurso de Angostura." Bolívar, *Doctrina* 101–27.

———. *Doctrina del libertador*. Ed. Manuel Pérez Vila. 3rd ed. Caracas: Ayacucho, 1983.

———. "The Jamaica Letter: Response from a South American to a Gentleman from This Island." Bolívar, *El Libertador* 12–30.

———. *El Libertador: Writings by Simón Bolívar*. Trans. Frederick H. Fornoff. Ed. David Bushnell. Oxford: Oxford UP, 2003.

———. "Manifiesto de Cartagena." Bolívar, *Doctrina* 8–17.

Borges, Jorge Luis. "El espantoso redentor Lazarus Morell." *Historia universal de la infamia. Obras completas*. Buenos Aires: Emecé, 1974. 295–300.

Bosi, Alfredo. *Dialética da colonização*. 2nd ed. São Paulo: Companhia das Letras, 1992.

Brading, David A. *The First America: The Spanish Monarchy, Creole Patriots, and the Liberal State, 1492–1867*. Cambridge: Cambridge UP, 1991.

———. *The Origins of Mexican Nationalism*. Cambridge: Cambridge UP, 1985.

Brion, Marcel. *Bartholomé de las Casas, "Père des Indiens."* Paris: Plon, 1927.

———. *Bartolomé de las Casas, "Father of the Indians."* Trans. Coley B. Taylor. New York: Dutton, 1929.

Brooks, Peter. *Troubling Confessions: Speaking Guilt in Law and Literature*. Chicago: U of Chicago P, 2000.

Brown, B. F. "Natural Law." *New Catholic Encyclopedia*. 2nd ed. Vol. 10. Detroit: Thomson; Washington: Catholic U of Amer., 2003. 179–96.

Buenaventura, Enrique. "Un requiem por el Padre Las Casas." *Teatro*. Bogota: Tercer Mundo, 1963. 8–84

Burgos, Elizabeth. *Me llamo Rigoberta Menchú y así me naciô la conciencia*. Mexico: Siglo XXI, 2000.

Burke, Peter. *Montaigne*. Oxford: Oxford UP, 1981.

Burkholder, Mark A., and Lyman L. Johnson. *Colonial Latin America*. 1990. 4th ed. Oxford: Oxford UP, 2001.

Buscaglia Salgado, José F. *Undoing Empire: Race and Nation in the Mulatto Caribbean*. Minneapolis: U of Minnesota P, 2003.

Bushnell, David, and Neil Macaulay. *The Emergence of Latin America in the Nineteenth Century*. New York: Oxford UP, 1988.

Butler, Judith. *Precarious Life: The Powers of Mourning and Violence*. London: Verso, 2004.

Cabeza de Vaca. Dir. Nicolás Echeverría. Iguana, 1989.

Cabeza de Vaca, Álvar Núñez. *The Narrative of Cabeza de Vaca*. 1542. Ed. and trans. Rolena Adorno and Patrick Charles Pautz. Lincoln: U of Nebraska P, 2003. Trans. of *Relación/Naufragios*.

———. *Relación*. 1542. *Álvar Núñez Cabeza de Vaca: His Account, His Life, and the Expedition of Pánfilo de Narváez*. By Rolena Adorno and Patrick Charles Pautz. Vol. 1. Lincoln: U of Nebraska P, 1999. 14–279.

Cabrera de Córdoba, Luis. 1611. *De historia, para entenderla y escrivirla*. Ed. Santiago Montero Díaz. Madrid: Inst. de Estudios Políticos, 1948.

Cain, Kathleen Shine, Albert C. DeCiccio, and Michael J. Rossi. *Exploring Literature: A Collaborative Approach*. Boston: Allyn, 1993.

Cain, William, ed. *American Literature*. New York: Penguin, 2004.

Cairo, Ana, ed. *El padre Las Casas. Edición crítica*. By José Martí. Havana: Centro de Estudios Martianos, 2001.

Cañizares-Esguerra, Jorge. *How to Write the History of the New World: Historiographies, Epistemologies, and Identities in the Eighteenth-Century Atlantic World*. Stanford: Stanford UP, 2001.

Capturing the Friedmans. Dir. Andrew Jarecki. 2003. DVD. HBO Documentary, 2003.

Carbia, Rómulo D. *Historia de la Leyenda Negra hispanoamericana.* Madrid: Espasa Calpe, 1944.

Carozza, Paolo. "From Conquest to Constitutions: Retrieving a Latin American Tradition of the Idea of Human Rights." *Human Rights Quarterly* 25 (2003): 281–313. *Bartolomé de las Casas.* Ed. Lawrence Clayton and Edward Cleary. 2005. 23 July 2007 <http://www.lascasas.org/carrozo.htm>.

Carrera, Magali. *Imagining Identity in New Spain.* Austin: U of Texas P, 2003.

Carrière, Jean-Claude. *La controversia de Valladolid.* Trans. Manuel Serrat. Barcelona: Península, 1998.

———. *The Controversy of Valladolid.* Trans. Richard Nelson. New York: Dramatists Play Service, 2005.

Carrió de la Vandera, Alonso. *El lazarillo de ciegos caminantes.* Caracas: Ayacucho, 1985.

Carro, Venancio D. *Bartolomé de las Casas y las controversias teleológico-jurídicas de Indias.* Madrid: Maestre, 1953.

Casas, Bartolomé de Las. *An Account, Much Abbreviated, of the Destruction of the Indies, with Related Texts.* Trans. Andrew Hurley. Introd. Franklin W. Knight. Indianapolis: Hackett, 2003.

———. *An Account of the First Voyages and Discoveries Made by the Spaniards in America Containing the Most Exact Relation Hitherto Publish'd, of Their Unparallel'd Cruelties on the Indians, in the Destruction of above Forty Millions of People: With the Propositions Offer'd to the King of Spain to Prevent the Further Ruin of the West-Indies.* London: Printed by J. Darby for D. Brown, 1699.

———. *Apologética historia sumaria.* Ed. Vidal Abril Castelló et al. Casas, *Obras completas,* vols. 6–8.

———. *Apologética historia sumaria.* 1527–60. Ed. Edmundo O'Gorman. 2 vols. México: U Nacional Autónoma de México, 1967.

———. *Apologética historia sumaria.* Ed. Manuel Serrano y Sanz. Vol. 113. Madrid: Nueva Biblioteca de Autores Españoles, 1909.

———. *Apología.* Ed. Ángel Losada. Casas, *Obras completas,* vol. 9.

———. *Apología, o Declaración universal de los derechos del hombre y de los pueblos.* Ed. Vidal Abril Castelló et al. Valladolid: Junta de Castilla y León, Consejería de Educación, 2000.

———. "Aquí se contienen unos avisos y reflas para los convesores. . . . " Casas, *Obras escogidas* 5: 235–50.

———. *Aquí se contiene una disputa.* Seville: Sebastián Trujillo, 1552.

———. *Bartolomé de las Casas: A Selection of His Writings.* Trans. and ed. George Sanderlin. New York: Knopf, 1971.

———. *Breve relación de la destrucción de las Indias Occidentales presentada a Felipe II, siendo Príncipe de Asturias, por Fray Bartolomé de las Casas del Orden de Predicadores, Obispo de Chiapa.* Ed. Servando Teresa de Mier. Philadelphia: Juan J. Hurtel, 1821. Madrid: Biblioteca Nacional, 2006. *Biblioteca Virtual Miguel de Cervantes.* 25 Nov. 2006 <http://www.cervantesvirtual.com/servlet/SirveObras/12479514321225063632457/index.htm>.

———. *Brevísima relación de la destrucción de África. Preludio de la destrucción de Indias. Primera defensa de los guanches y negros contra su esclavización.* Ed. Isacio Pérez Fernández. Salamanca: San Esteban, 1989.

———. *Brevísima relación de la destrucción de las Indias.* Ed. Trinidad Barrera. Madrid: Alianza, 2005.

———. *Brevísima relación de la destrucción de las Indias.* Ed. Isacio Pérez Fernández. Bayamon: U Central de Bayamon, Centro de Estudios de los Dominicos del Caribe, 2000.

———. *Brevísima relación de la destrucción de las Indias.* 1982. Ed. André Saint-Lu. Madrid: Cátedra, 2005.

———. *Brevísima relación de la destrucción de las Indias.* Ed. Consuelo Varela. Madrid: Castalia, 1999.

———. *Brevísima relación de la destruición de las Indias.* Ed. José Miguel Martínez Torrejón. Alicante: U de Alicante, 2006.

———. *Brevísima relación de la destruycción de las Indias.* Ed. Jean-Paul Duviols. Buenos Aires: Stockero, 2006.

———. *Brevíssima relación de la destruyción de las Indias.* Seville: Sebastián Trujillo, 1552.

———. "Cláusula del testamento que hizo el obispo de Chiapa, don fray Bartolomé de las Casas." 1564. Casas, *Obras escogidas* 5: 538–41.

———. *La decouverte des Indes Occidentales, par les Espagnols.* Trans. J. B. M. Bellegarde. Paris: André Pralard, 1697.

———. *De las antiguas gentes del Perú.* Ed. Marcos Jiménez de la Espada. Madrid: Tipografía de Manuel G. Hernández, 1892. *Biblioteca Virtual Miguel de Cervantes.* 2000. 25 Nov. 2006 <http://www.cervantesvirtual.com/servlet/SirveObras/01305086466137942200802/index.htm>.

———. *Del único modo de atraer a todos los pueblos a la verdadera religión.* 1942. Trans. Atenógenes Santamaría. Ed. and with fwd. and notes by Agustín Millares Carlo. Introd. Lewis Hanke. Mexico: Fondo de Cultura Económica, 1975.

———. *De l'unique manière d'évangéliser le monde entier.* Trans. Marianne Mahn-Lot. Paris: Éditions du Cerf, 1990.

———. *La destrucción de las Indias.* Paris: Bouret, 1946.

———. *De unico vocationis modo.* Ed. Paulino Castañeda Delgado and Antonio García del Moral. Casas, *Obras completas*, vol. 2.

———. *The Devastation of the Indies: A Brief Account.* Trans. Herma Briffault. Baltimore: Johns Hopkins UP, 1992.

———. "Entre los remedios." 1552. Casas, *Obras escogidas* 5: 69–119.

———. *Histoire admirable des horribles insolences, cruautez, et tyrannies exercees par les Espagnoles és Indes Occidentales . . . et nouvellement traduite et mise en langue françoise [par Jacques de Miggrode], pour l'utilité des bons François et l'instruction des mauvais.* Lyons, 1594.

———. *Histoire admirable des horribles insolences, cruautez, et tyrannies exercees par les Espagnols és Indes Occidentales . . . fidelement traduite par Jacques de Miggrode.* [Geneva]: G. Cartier, 1582.

———. *Historia de las Indias*. Ed. Agustín Millares Carlo. Introd. Lewis Hanke. 3 vols. México: Fondo de Cultura Económica, 1951.

———. *Historia de las Indias*. Ed. Isacio Pérez Fernández et al. Casas, *Obras completas*, vols. 3–5.

———. *Historia de las Indias*. Ed. André Saint-Lu. 2 vols. Caracas: Ayacucho, 1986.

———. *History of the Indies*. Trans. and ed. Andrée Collard. New York: Harper, 1971.

———. *In Defense of the Indians*. 1974. Trans. Stafford Poole. DeKalb: Northern Illinois UP, 1992.

———. *Indian Freedom: The Cause of Bartolomé de las Casas, 1484–1566: A Reader*. Ed. and trans. Francis Patrick Sullivan. Kansas City: Sheed, 1995.

———. "Joint Memorial to Philip" 1560. Casas, *Indian Freedom* 328–33.

———. "Last Will and Testament." Casas, *Indian Freedom* 353–56.

———. "Memorial de despedida al Consejo de Indias." Casas, *Obras escogidas* 5: 536–38.

———. "Memorial de remedios para las Indias." 1516. Casas, *Obras escogidas* 5: 5–27.

———. "Memorial de remedios para las Indias." 1518. Casas, *Obras escogidas* 5: 31–35.

———. *Le miroir de la tyrannye espagnole perpetree aux Indies Occidentales. On verra icy la cruaute plus que inhumaine, commise par les Espagnols, aussi la description de ces terres, peuples, et leur nature*. Amsterdam: Jan Evertsz Cloppenburg, 1620.

———. *Narratio regionum indicarum per hispanos quosdam devastatarum verissima*. Trans. and illus. Theodor de Bry and Jean Israêl de Bry. Frankfurt am Main: Hispali, Hispanicè, 1598.

———. *Obras completas*. Ed. Paulino Castañeda Delgado. 14 vols. Madrid: Alianza, 1988–98.

———. *Obras escogidas de fray Bartolomé de las Casas*. Ed. Juan Pérez de Tudela Bueso. Biblioteca de Autores Españoles 95, 96, 105, 106, 110. Madrid: Atlas, 1957–58.

———. *The Only Way: A New Restored Version*. Trans. Francis Patrick Sullivan. Ed. Helen Rand Parish. Mahwah: Paulist, 1992.

———. *Popery Truly Display'd in Its Bloody Colours; or, A Faithful Narrative of the Horrid and Unexampled Massacres, Butcheries, and All Manner of Cruelties, That Hell and Malice Could Invent, Committed by the Popish Spanish Party on the Inhabitants of West-India together with the Devastations of Several Kingdoms in America by Fire and Sword, for the Space of Forty and Two Years, from the Time of Its First Discovery by Them*. London: R. Hewson, 1689.

———. "Quaestio theologalis." Ed. Antonio Larios Ramos and Antonio García del Moral y Garrido. Casas, *Obras completas* 12: 229–408.

———. *A Relation of the First Voyages and Discoveries Made by Spaniards in America*. London: D. Brown and A. Bell, 1699.

———. *Rules for Confessors*. Casas, *Indian Freedom* 281–89.

———. *Seer cort verhael van d'Indien . . . uyte Spaensche overgeset.* Antwerp, 1578.

———. *A Short Account of the Destruction of the Indies.* Ed. and trans. Nigel Griffin. Introd. Anthony Pagden. New York: Penguin, 1992.

———. *The Spanish Colonie; or, Briefe Chronicle of the Acts and Gestes of the Spaniardes in the West Indies, called the Newe World, for the Space of XL. Yeeres.* London: Thomas Dawson for William Brome, 1583.

———. *Tears of the Indians.* Trans. John Phillips. London: Nath. Brook, 1656.

———. *Los tesoros del Perú [De thesauris qui reperiuntur in sepulchris indorum].* 1563. Ed. and trans. Ángel Losada. Madrid: Consejo Superior de Investigaciones Científicas, 1958.

———. "Tratado de las doce dudas." 1564. Casas, *Obras escogidas* 5: 478–536.

———. *Tratados de fray Bartolomé de las Casas.* Ed. Juan Pérez de Tudela Bueso. 2 vols. Mexico: Fondo de Cultura Económica, 1965.

———. "Twelve Problems of Conscience (1564)." Casas, *Indian Freedom* 333–53.

———. *Tyrannies et cruautez des Espagnols commises es Indes Occidentales, qu'on dit le Nouveau Monde.* Trans. Jacques de Miggrode. Rouen, 1642.

———. *Tyrannies et cruautez des Espagnols, commises es Indes Occidentales qu'on dit le Nouveau Monde. Briefuement descrite en espagnol.* Trans. Jacques de Miggrode. Rouen: Jacques Cailloué, 1630.

———. *Tyrannies et cruautez des Espagnols commises es Indes Occidentales, qu'on dit le Nouveau Monde . . . traduitte . . . par Jacques de Miggrode.* Rouen: J. Cailloué, 1630.

———. *Tyrannies et cruautez des Espagnols, perpetrées es Indes Occidentales, qu'on dit le Nouveau Monde.* Trans. Ja[c]ques de Miggrode. Antwerp: François de Ravelenghien, 1579.

———. *Tyrannies et cruautez des Espagnols perpetrées es Indes Occidentales quon dit le Nouveau Monde: Brievement descrites en lettre castillane par l'evesque Don Frere Bartelemy De Las Casas . . . fidelement traduites par Jackques De Miggrode.* Paris: Guillaume Julien, 1582.

Casas, Bartolomé de Las, and Thomas Harris. *Popery and Slavery Display'd Containing the Character of Popery, and a Relation of Popish Cruelties . . . to Which Are Added, the Demands of the Pope and Pretender, on This Nation.* London: C. Corbett, 1745.

Castañeda, Felipe. *El indio: Entre el bárbaro y el cristianismo: Ensayos sobre filosofía de la conquista en Las Casas, Sepúlveda y Acosta.* Bogota: Alfaomega Colombiana, 2002.

Castillo, Susan, and Ivy Schweitzer, eds. *The Literatures of Colonial America: An Anthology.* Oxford: Blackwell, 2001.

Castro, Américo. "Fray Bartolomé de las Casas o Casaus." *Cervantes y los casticismos españoles.* Madrid: Alianza, 1975. 190–227.

Castro, Daniel. *Another Face of Empire: Bartolomé de Las Casas, Human Rights, and Ecclesiastical Imperialism.* Durham: Duke UP, 2007.

Certeau, Michel de. *Heterologies: Discourse on the Other.* Trans. Brian Massumi. Minneapolis: U of Minnesota P, 1986.

Cervantes, Fernando. *The Devil in the New World: The Impact of Diabolism in New Spain*. New Haven: Yale UP, 1994.

Cervantes Saavedra, Miguel de. *The History of the Most Renowned Don Quixote of Mancha, and His Trusty Squire Sancho Pancha*. Trans. John Phillips. London: Thomas Hodgkin, 1687.

Chang-Rodríguez, Raquel, and Malva E. Filer, eds. *Voces de Hispanoamérica: Antología literaria*. 3rd ed. Boston: Thomson-Heinle, 2004.

Charlevoix, Pierre-François-Xavier de. *Histoire de l'Isle Espagnole ou de S. Domingue*. 2 vols. Paris: F. Didot, 1730–31.

Chodorow, Nancy J. *The Reproduction of Mothering: Psychoanalysis and the Sociology of Gender*. Berkeley: U of California P, 1978.

Christopher Columbus: The Discovery. 1992. Dir. John Glen. VHS. Warner Home Video, 1994.

Cicero, Marcus Tullius. *On the Ideal Orator [De Oratore]*. Introd. and trans. and with notes by James M. May and Jakob Wisse. New York: Oxford UP, 2001.

Clarkson, Thomas. *An Essay on the Slavery and Commerce of the Human Species*. London: J. Phillips, 1786. *Eighteenth Century Collections Online*. Gale Group. 28 Oct. 2006 <http://galenet.galegroup.com/servlet/ECCO>.

Clavijero, Francisco Javier. *Historia antigua de México*. Ed. Mariano Cuevas. Mexico: Porrúa, 1991.

Clendinnen, Inga. *Aztecs*. New York: Cambridge UP, 1991.

———. "Disciplining the Indians: Franciscan Ideology and Missionary Violence in Sixteenth-Century Yucatán." *Past and Present* 94 (1982): 27–48.

Clifford, James. "Introduction: Partial Truths." *Writing Culture: The Poetics and Politics of Ethnography*. Ed. Clifford and George E. Marcus. Berkeley: U of California P, 1986. 1–26.

Cohen, Thomas M. *The Fire of Tongues: Antonio Vieira and the Missionary Church in Brazil and Portugal*. Stanford: Stanford UP, 1998.

Colección de documentos inéditos relativos al descubrimiento, conquista y organización de las antiguas posesiones españolas de América y Oceanía. Vol. 31. Madrid, 1864–84. 42 vols.

Colección documental del descubrimiento. Vol. 2. Ed. Juan Pérez de Tudela Bueso. Madrid: Real Acad. de la Historia, 1994.

Colón, Cristóbal. *Diario de Colón: Edición facsímil del "Libro de la primera navegación y descubrimiento de las Indias."* Ed. Carlos Sanz. Madrid: Bibliotheca Americana Vetustissima, 1962.

———. "Diario del primer viaje." *Los cuatro viajes. Testamento*. Ed. Consuelo Varela. Madrid: Alianza, 2004. 39–199.

———. "El primer viaje." Los cuatro viajes *del Almirante y sus* Testamento. Ed. Ignacio B. Anzoátegui. Madrid: Austral, 1971. 15–154.

Columbus, Christopher. *The Diario of Christopher Columbus's First Voyage to America, 1492–93*. Ed. and trans. Oliver Dunn and James E. Kelley, Jr. Norman: U of Oklahoma P, 1989.

———. "The Letter of Columbus on the Discovery of America." Castillo and Schweitzer 24–27.

Comaroff, Jean, and John Comaroff. *Of Revelation and Revolution: Christianity, Colonialism, and Consciousness in South Africa*. Vol. 1. Chicago: U of Chicago P, 1991.

Comas, Juan. "Historical Reality and the Detractors of Father Las Casas." Friede and Keen 487–537.

Conley, Tom. "De Bry's Las Casas." Jara and Spadaccini, *Amerindian Images* 103–31.

Connell, Robert W. *Gender and Power: Society, the Person and Sexual Politics*. Sydney: Allen, 1987.

———. *Masculinities*. Sydney: Allen, 1995.

Control Room. Dir. Jehane Noujaim. Magnolia / Noujaim Films, 2004.

La controverse de Valladolid. Dir. Jean-Daniel Verhaeghe. Arte Vidéo: Koba Films, 1992.

Conway, Martin A. "Past and Present: Recovered Memories and False Memories." *Recovered Memories and False Memories*. Ed. Conway. New York: Oxford, 1997. 150–92.

Cortés, Hernán. *Letters from Mexico*. Ed., trans., and introd. Anthony Pagden. Introd. John Elliott. New Haven: Yale UP, 2001.

———. "The Third Letter." Cortés, *Letters* 160–281.

Cortijo Ocaña, Antonio. "Creación de una voz de autoridad en Bartolomé de las Casas: Estudio del Prólogo de la *Historia de Indias*." *Revista Iberoamericana* 61.170–71 (1995): 219–29.

Creed, Kevin A. "The Pamphleteer's Protestant Champion: Viewing Oliver Cromwell through the Media of His Day." *Essays in History* 34 (1992). 10 Sept. 2007 <http://etext.virginia.edu/journals/EH/EH34/creed34.html>.

Cromwell, Oliver. "Speech at the Opening of Parliament, 1656." Maltby 54–62.

Culler, Jonathan. *A Very Short Introduction to Theory*. Oxford: Oxford UP, 2000.

d'Anghiera, Peter Martyr. *De orbe novo, the Eight Decades of Peter Martyr d'Anghera*. Introd. and notes by Francis Augustus MacNutt. New York: Putnam's, 1912.

Davies, Nigel. *The Aztec Empire*. Norman: U of Oklahoma P, 1987.

———. *Human Sacrifice in History and Today*. New York: Morrow, 1981.

Dávila Padilla, Agustín. *Historia de la fundación y discurso de la provincia de Santiago de México de la Orden de Predicadores*. 1596. 3rd ed. Introd. Agustín Millares Carlo. Mexico: Academia Literaria, 1955.

de la Campa, Román. *Latinamericanism*. Minneapolis: U of Minnesota P, 1999.

Delgado, Mariano. "Las Casas en Alemania." *Anuario de historia de la iglesia* 7 (1998): 422–29.

———. "Moralische Unruhe angesichts des Unrechts. Bartolome de las Casas, 1484–1566." *Barmherziger Bund* 1 (2000): 16–57.

Denegri, Francesca. "Testimonio and Its Discontents." *Contemporary Latin American Cultural Studies*. Ed. Stephen Hart and Richard Young. London: Arnold, 2003. 228–38.

Denglos, J. Introducción. Casas, *Obras completas* 11.2:v–xlviii.

Díaz del Castillo, Bernal. *Historia verdadera de la conquista de la Nueva España.* 2 vols. Mexico: Porrúa, 1960.

———. *History of the Conquest of New Spain.* 1623. Castillo and Schweitzer 40–62.

El Dorado. Dir. Carlos Saura. Grupo Editorial Mundografic, 1988.

Durán Luzio, Juan. *Bartolomé de las Casas ante la conquista de América. Las voces del historiador.* Heredia, Costa Rica: Editorial de la Universidad Nacional, 1992.

Dussel, Enrique. *Historia de la iglesia en América Latina.* Barcelona: Nova Terra, 1972.

———. "Núcleo simbólico lascasiano como profética crítica al imperialismo europeo." *Bartolomé de las Casas (1474–1974) e historia de la iglesia en América Latina.* Ed. Dussel. Barcelona: Cehila / Nova Terra, 1976. 11–17.

———. *The Underside of Modernity.* Atlantic Highlands: Humanities, 1996.

"Ecclesiasticus." *Christian Apologetics and Research Ministry.* Ed. Matthew J. Slick. 1996–2006. 3 Dec. 2007 <http://www.carm.org/lost/sirach.htm>.

Eggensperger, Thomas. *Bartolomé de las Casas.* Mainz: Grünewald, 1991.

———. *Der Einfluss des Thomas von Aqui auf das politische Denken des Bartolome de las Casas im Traktat "De imperatoria vel regio potestate."* Münster: LIT, 2001.

Eguiara y Eguren, Juan José. *Bibliotheca mexicana.* 1755. Ed., introd., and trans. Benjamín Fernández Valenzuela. Introd. Ernesto de la Torre Villar and Ramiro Navarro de Anda, general eds. 5 vols. Mexico: U Nacional Autónoma de Mexico, 1986–90.

Eire, Carlos M. N. *From Madrid to Purgatory: The Art and Craft of Dying in Sixteenth-Century Spain.* New York: Cambridge UP, 1995.

Elliott, John H. *Empires of the Atlantic World: Britain and Spain in America, 1492–1830.* New Haven Yale UP, 2006.

———. *The Old World and the New, 1492–1650.* Cambridge: Cambridge UP, 1970.

En el quinto centenario de Bartolomé de las Casas. Madrid: Inst. de Cooperación Iberoamericana, 1986.

Equiano, Olaudah. *The Interesting Narrative of Olaudah Equiano; or, Gustavus Vassa, the African, Written by Himself. The Classic Slave Narratives.* Ed. Henry Louis Gates. New York: Mentor, 1987. 1–182.

Espinosa Medrano, Juan de. *Apologético en favor de don Luis de Góngora.* Ed. Mariella Byrne et al. Lima: Pontificia U Católica del Perú, Fondo Editorial, 1973.

Espinosa Soriano, Waldemar. *Los Incas: Economía, sociedad y estado en la era del Tahuantinsuyo.* Lima: Amaru, 1987.

Estrade, Paul. *José Martí: Los fundamentos de la democracia en la América Latina.* Madrid: Doce Calles, 2000.

Estrade, Paul, and Félix Ojeda Reyes. *Ramón Emeterio Betances: El anciano maravilloso.* Rio Piedras: U de Puerto Rico, 1995.

Evans, J. Martin. *Milton's Imperial Epic: Paradise Lost and the Discourse of Colonization.* Ithaca: Cornell UP, 1996.

Fabian, Johannes. *Time and the Other: How Anthropology Makes Its Object.* New York: Columbia UP, 1983.

Fabié, Antonio María. *Vida y escritos de don fray Bartolomé de las Casas*. 2 vols. Madrid: M. Ginesta, 1879.

Ferm, Robert L. *Issues in American Protestantism: A Documentary History from the Puritans to the Present*. New York: Anchor, 1969.

Fernández de Oviedo, Gonzalo. *Historia general de las Indias*. Seville: Juan Cromberger, 1535.

———. *Historia general y natural de las Indias*. Ed. Juan Pérez de Tudela Bueso. Biblioteca de Autores Españoles. 5 vols. Madrid: Atlas, 1992.

———. "Proemio." Fernández de Oviedo, *Historia general y natural* 1: 111.

———. *Sumario de la natural historia de las Indias*. Ed. José Miranda. Mexico: Fondo de Cultura Económica, 1950.

Fletcher, Harris Francis. *The Intellectual Development of John Milton*. Urbana: U of Illinois P, 1956.

Foreword. *The Spanish Colonie*. By Bartolomé de Las Casas. Trans. M. M. S. March of America Facsimile Series 8. Ann Arbor: University Microfilms, [1966.]

1492: The Conquest of Paradise. Dir. Ridley Scott. Paramount, 1992.

Fraser, Howard M. "*La edad de oro* and José Martí's Modernist Ideology for Children." *Revista Interamericana de Bibliografía / Inter-American Review of Bibliography* 42 (1992): 223–32.

Freitas Neto, José Alves de. *Bartolomé de las Casas: Narrativa trágica, o amor cristão e a memória americana*. São Paulo: AnnaBlume, 2003.

Friede, Juan. *Bartolomé de las Casas: Precursor del anticolonialismo*. Mexico: Siglo XXI, 1974.

———. "Las Casas and Indigenism in the Sixteenth Century." Friede and Keen 127–237.

Friede, Juan, and Benjamin Keen, eds. *Bartolomé de las Casas in History: Toward an Understanding of the Man and His Work*. DeKalb: Northern Illinois UP, 1971.

Furlong, Guillermo. *Los jesuitas y la escisión del reino de Indias*. Buenos Aires: Amorrortu, 1960.

Galmés, Lorenzo. *Bartolomé de las Casas*. Madrid: Biblioteca de Autores Cristianos, 1982.

Galván, Manuel de Jesús. *Enriquillo: Leyenda histórica dominicana (1503–1533)*. Mexico: Porrúa, 1976.

García, Gustavo G. "La invención 'ética' del sujeto indígena en la *Brevísima relación de la destruición de las Indias*." *Revista Iberoamericana* 3.12 (2003): 7–24.

García Icazbalceta, Joaquín, and Rafael Aguayo Spencer. *Don Fray Juan de Zumárraga*. Vol. 3. Mexico: Porrúa, 1947.

Garcilaso de la Vega [El Inca]. *Comentarios reales de los Incas*. 1609, 1617. *Obras completas del Inca Garcilaso de la Vega*. Ed. Carmelo Sáenz de Santa María. Vols. 2–4. Biblioteca de Autores Españoles 132–34. Madrid: Atlas, 1960–65.

———. *La Florida del Inca*. 1605. Introd. and ed. Mercedes López-Baralt. Madrid: Espasa Calpe, 2003.

————. *Royal Commentaries of the Incas and General History of Peru*. Trans. Harold V. Livermore. Austin: U of Texas P, 1987.

————. "Tipos de hombre americano." Garganigo et al. 115–16.

Garganigo, John, et al. *Huellas de las literaturas hispanoamericanas*. Upper Saddle: Prentice, 1997.

Gauderman, Kimberly. *Women's Lives in Colonial Quito: Gender, Law, and Economy in Spanish America*. Austin: U of Texas P, 2003.

Geertz, Clifford. "Thick Description: Notes toward an Interpretive Theory of Culture." *The Interpretation of Cultures*. New York: Basic, 1973. 3–32.

Gerbi, Antonello. *The Dispute of the New World: The History of a Polemic, 1750–1900*. Trans. Jeremy Moyle. Pittsburgh: U of Pittsburgh P, 1973.

————. *La naturaleza de las Indias nuevas: De Cristóbal Colón a Fernández de Oviedo*. Mexico: Fondo de Cultura Económica, 1978.

Gibaldi, Joseph. *MLA Handbook for Writers of Research Papers*. 6th ed. New York: MLA, 2003.

Gil, Juan. "La familia de fray Bartolomé de las Casas." *Los conversos y la inquisición sevillana*. Vol. 3. Seville: U de Sevilla; Fundación El Monte, 2001. 452–66.

Gil Fernández, Luis. *Panorama social del humanismo español (1500–1800)*. Madrid: Tecnos, 1997.

Gilligan, Carol. *In a Different Voice: Psychological Theory and Women's Development*. Cambridge: Harvard UP, 1982.

Gillner, Matthias. *Bartolomé de las Casas und die Eroberung des indianischen Kontinents: Das friedensethische Profil eines weltgeschichtlichen Umbruchs aus der Perspektive eines Anwalts der Unterdrückten*. Stuttgart: Kohlhammer, 1997.

Giménez Fernández, Manuel. *Bartolomé de las Casas*. 2 vols. Seville: Escuela de Estudios Hispanoamericanos, U de Sevilla, 1953.

————. "Fray Bartolomé de las Casas: A Biographical Sketch." Friede and Keen 67–125.

Giroud, Nicole. *Une mosaïque de Fr. Bartholomé de las Casas (1484–1566): Histoire de la réception dans l'histoire, la théologie, la société, l'art et la littérature*. Fribourg: Editions U Fribourg Suisse, 2002.

Gladden, Washington. *Recollections of Washington Gladden*. Whitefish: Kessinger, 2007.

————. *Social Salvation*. Eugene: Wipf, 2004.

Gómez, María Asunción. "Estrategias dramáticas para una reescritura de la historia: *Las Casas. Una hoguera en el amanener* de Jaime Salom." *Explicación de textos literarios* 23.2 (1994–95): 13–22.

Gómez Peña, Guillermo, and Roberto Sifuentes. *Temple of Confessions: Mexican Beasts and Living Santos*. New York: PowerHouse, 1996.

Gorriti, Juana Manuela. *Veladas literarias de Lima, 1876–1877*. Buenos Aires: Imprenta Europea, 1982.

Graffigny, Françoise de. *Letters from a Peruvian Woman*. Trans. David Hornacker. Ed. and intro. Joan DeJean and Nancy K. Miller. New York: MLA, 1993.

Grant, W. L., trans. *The History of New France*. By Marc Lescarbot. 3 vols. Toronto: Champlain Soc., 1907–14.

Greenblatt, Stephen. *Marvelous Possessions: The Wonder of the New World*. Chicago: U of Chicago P, 1991.

———, ed. *New World Encounters*. Berkeley: U of California P, 1993.

Griffiths, Nicholas. Introduction. *Spiritual Encounters*. Ed. Griffiths and Fernando Cervantes. Lincoln: U of Nebraska P, 1999. 1–41.

Grodsinsky, Sergio. "Los perros en el descubrimiento y la conquista de América." *El alano español*. 2000. 21 Aug. 2007 <http://www.spanish-alano.com/america .htm>.

Guaman Poma de Ayala, Felipe. *El primer nueva corónica y buen gobierno*. 1615. Ed. John V. Murra and Rolena Adorno. Trans. Jorge L. Urioste. 3 vols. México: Siglo XXI, 1992.

Guerra, José (*See also* Mier, Servando Teresa de). *Historia de la revolución de Nueva España*. 1813. 2 vols. México: Fondo de Cultura Economica, 1986.

Gugelberger, Georg M., ed. *The Real Thing: Testimonial Discourse and Latin America*. Durham: Duke UP, 1996.

Guillén, Claudio. "Un padrón de conversos sevillanos (1510)." *Bulletin Hispanique* 65 (1963): 49–89.

Gutiérrez, Gustavo. *En busca de los pobres de Jesucristo*. Lima: Inst. Bartolomé de las Casas, 1992.

———. *Fray Bartolomé de las Casas y la teología de la liberación: Entrevista a Gustavo Gutiérrez*. Interview with Mario A. Rodríguez León. Toa Alta: Convento Santo Domingo de Guzmán, 1989.

———. *Las Casas: In Search of the Poor of Jesus Christ*. Trans. Robert R. Barr. Maryknoll: Orbis, 1993.

———. *Teología de la liberación: Perspectivas*. Salamanca: Sígueme, 1972.

Gysius, Johannes. *Oorsprong en voortgang der Nederlandtschen becerten*. [Leyden, 1616].

———. *Tweede deel van de spieghel der Spaenishe tyrannye*. Amsterdam: J. E. Coppenburg, 1620.

Hakluyt, Richard. *A Particuler Discourse concerninge the Greate Necessitie and Manifolde Commodyties That Are Like to Growe to This Realme of Englande by the Westerne Discoveries Lately Attempted*. 1584. Ed. David B. Quinn and Alison Quinn. London: Hakluyt Soc., 1993.

Hanke, Lewis. *All Mankind Is One; a Study of the Disputation between Bartolomé de las Casas and Juan Ginés de Sepúlveda in 1550 on the Intellectual and Religious Capacity of the American Indians*. DeKalb: Northern Illinois UP, 1974.

———. *Aristotle and the American Indians: A Study in Race Prejudice in the Modern World*. Bloomington: Indiana UP, 1959.

———. *Bartolomé de las Casas. Pensador político, historiador, antropólogo*. Buenos Aires: Eudeba, 1968.

———. Introducción. Las Casas, *Del único modo* xvii–lx.

———. "Las Casas, historiador." Introduction. Casas, *Historia de las Indias* ix–lxxxvi.

———. *The Spanish Struggle for Justice in the Conquest of America*. 1949. Dallas: Southern Methodist UP, 2002.

Hanke, Lewis, and Manuel Giménez Fernández. *Bartolomé de las Casas, 1474–1566, Bibliografía crítica y cuerpo de materias para su estudio.* Santiago: Fondo Histórico y Bibliográfico José Toribio Medina, 1954.

Hardt, Michael, and Antonio Negri. *Empire.* Cambridge: Harvard UP, 2001.

Harriot, Thomas. *A Briefe and True Report of the New Found Land of Virginia.* Castillo and Schweitzer 99.

Harrison, Regina. "Cultural Translation in the Andes: The Case of the Pregnant Penitent." *Latin American Indian Literatures* 11 (1995): 108–28.

———. "The Theology of Concupiscence: Spanish-Quechua Confessional Manuals in the Andes." *Encoded Encounters: Race, Gender, and Ethnicity in Colonial Latin America.* Ed. Francisco Javier Cevallos et al. Amherst: U of Massachusetts P, 1994. 135–53.

Hart, Jonathan. *Representing the New World: English and French Uses of the Example of Spain.* New York: Palgrave, 2001.

Hartsock, Nancy. *Money, Sex, and Power: Toward a Feminist Historical Materialism.* New York: Longman, 1983.

Hennessy, A. P. "Satisfaction of Christ." *New Catholic Encyclopedia.* Vol. 12. 2nd ed. Detroit: Thomson; Washington: Catholic U of Amer., 2003. 701–04.

Herrera y Tordesillas, Antonio de. *Historia general de los hechos de los castellanos en las islas y tierra firme del Mar Océano.* 1601–15. 4 vols. Madrid: U Complutense, 1991.

Herrero, J. "More and Vives: Christian Radical Thought and the Renaissance." *Spain: Church-State Relations.* Chicago: Loyola U of Chicago P, 1983. 17–36.

Hodgen, Margaret T. *Early Anthropology in the Sixteenth and Seventeenth Centuries.* Philadelphia: U of Pennsylvania P, 1964.

Hodgkins, Christopher. "The Uses of Atrocity: Satanic Spaniards, Hispanic Satans, and the 'Black Legend' from Las Casas to Milton." *Reforming Empire: Protestant Colonialism and Conscience in British Literature.* Columbia: U of Missouri P, 2002. 54–76.

Holloway, Thomas H. "Whose Conquest Is This, Anyway? *Aguirre: The Wrath of God.*" Stevens 29–45.

Holy Bible. Illus. and designed by Barry Moser. New York: Viking Studio, 1999.

Hurley, Andrew. "A Note on the Text and the Translation." Casas, *An Account* li–lv.

Hurtado, Albert, and Peter Iverson, eds. *Major Problems in American Indian History: Documents and Essays.* 2nd ed. Boston: Houghton, 2001.

I Confess. Dir. Alfred Hitchcock. 1953. DVD. Warner, 2004.

"The Interrogation of Michael Crowe." *The System.* Prod. Carolyn Kresley. 2001. Videocassette. Courtroom Television Network, 2002.

Jara, René, and Nicholas Spadaccini, eds. *Amerindian Images and the Legacy of Columbus.* Hispanic Issues 9. Minneapolis: U of Minnesota P, 1992.

———, eds. *1492–1992: Re/Discovering Colonial Writing.* Hispanic Issues 4. Minneapolis: Prisma Inst., 1989.

Jáuregui, Carlos. *The Conquest on Trial: Carvajal's Complaint of the Indians in* The Court of Death. Pennsylvania State UP, forthcoming.

Jerningham, Edward. *The Fall of Mexico, a Poem*. London: Scott, for J. Robson, 1775. *Eighteenth Century Collections Online*. Gale Group. 28 Oct. 2006 <http://galenet.galegroup.com/servlet/ECCO>.

Johnson, Michael P., ed. *Reading the American Past: Select Historical Documents*. Vol. 1: *To 1877*. New York: Bedford–St. Martin's, 2002.

Jordan, Winthrop. *White over Black: American Attitudes towards the Negro, 1550–1812*. New York: Norton, 1977.

Josaphat, Carlos. *Las Casas: Todos os dereitos para todos*. São Paulo: Loyola, 2000.

Juana Inés de la Cruz. "Carta atenagórica." *Obras completas*. Mexico: Perrúa, 1997. 811–27.

Katzew, Ilona. *Casta Painting: Images of Race in Eighteenth-Century Mexico*. New Haven: Yale UP, 2004.

Keen, Benjamin. *Essays in the Intellectual History of Colonial Latin America*. Boulder: Westview, 1998.

———. "The Legacy of Bartolomé de Las Casas." *Ibero-Americana Pragensia* 11 (1977): 57–67.

Kennedy, George A. *Classical Rhetoric and Its Christian and Secular Tradition from Ancient to Modern Times*. Chapel Hill: U of North Carolina P, 1980.

King, Edward, Viscount Kingsborough, *Antiquities of Mexico*. London: H. Bohn, 1831.

The King of Spain's Cabinet Divulged; or, A Discovery of the Prevarications of the Spaniards. London: J. H. for J. S., 1658.

Klein, Dennis A. "Epic Theater of the Conquest: Jaime Salom's *Las Casas. Una hoguera en el amanecer* and Peter Shaffer's *The Royal Hunt of the Sun*." *Estreno* 18.2 (1992): 34–36.

Klor de Alva, J. Jorge. "Sahagún and the Birth of Modern Ethnography: Representing, Confessing, and Inscribing the Native Other." *The Work of Bernardino de Sahagún: Pioneer Ethnographer of Sixteenth-Century Mexico*. Ed. Klor de Alva, H. B. Nicholson, and Eloise Quiñones Keber. Austin: U of Texas P, 1988.

Knight, Franklin. Introduction. Casas, *An Account* xi–l.

Kotzebue, August von. *Pizarro in Peru; or, The Death of Rolla*. Trans. Thomas Dutton. London: W. West, 1799. *Eighteenth Century Collections Online*. Gale Group. 28 Oct. 2006 <http://galenet.galegroup.com/servlet/ECCO>.

Krickeberg, Walter. *Las antiguas culturas mexicanas*. Mexico: Fondo de Cultura Económica, 1990.

Lahontan, Louis Armand de Lom d' Arce, Baron de. *Dialogues curieux entre l'auter et un sauvage de bons sens qui a vovagé. . . .* Baltimore: Johns Hopkins P, 1931.

Lakoff, George. *Moral Politics: How Liberals and Conservatives Think*. Chicago: U of Chicago P, 2002.

Las Casas entre dos mundos: Congreso Teleológico Internacional, Lima, 26–27–28 de agosto de 1992. Lima: Instituto Bartolomé de las Casas; CEP, 1993.

Lavou Zoungbo, Victorien, ed. *Las Casas face à l'esclavage des Noirs: Vision critique du Onzième Remède (1516) / Las Casas frente a la esclavitud de los Negros: vision crítica del Undécimo Remedio (1516)*. Perpignan: Centre de Recherches Ibériques et Latino-américaines de l'U. de Perpignan; PU de Perpignan, 2001.

Lawall, Sarah, ed. *The Norton Anthology of Western Literature.* 8th ed. New York: Norton, 2006.

Le Challeux, Nicolas. *Discours de l'histoire de la Floride, contenant la trahision des Espagnols.* Dieppe: J. Le Sellier, 1566.

Leigh, Edward. *A Treatise of Religion and Learning, and of Religious and Learned Men.* London: A. M[iller] for C. Adams, 1656.

León, Nicolás. "Códice del Ilmo. D. Fr. Bartolomé de las Casas existente en la Biblioteca Pública del Estado de Oaxaca." *Anales del museo michoacano* 2 (1889): 177–79.

Leonard, Irving A. *Books of the Brave.* Berkeley: U of California P, 1992.

León Pinelo, Antonio de. *Epítome de la biblioteca oriental y occidental, náutica y geográfica.* 1629. Madrid: F. Martínez Abad, 1737–38.

Lepore, Jill. *Encounters in the New World: A History of Documents.* New York: Oxford UP, 2000.

Léry, Jean de. *Histoire d'un voyage faict en la terre du Bresil, autrement dite Amerique.* 2nd ed. Geneve: A. Chuppin, 1580. Rpt. Geneva: Droz, 1975.

———. *Histoire d'un voyage faict en la terre du Bresil, autrement dite Amerique.* 4th ed. Geneve: Pour les Heritiers d'Eustache Vignon, 1599.

———. *Histoire d'un voyage faict en la terre du Bresil, autrement dite Amerique. . . .* Geneve: V. Vignon, 1611.

———. *Histoire d'un voyage faict en la terre du Bresil, autrement dite Amerique.* Geneva: Pour les Heritiers d'Éustache Vignon, 1578.

Lewis, Laura. *Hall of Mirrors: Power, Witchcraft, and Caste in Colonial Mexico.* Durham: Duke UP, 2003.

Lindstrom, Naomi. *The Social Conscience of Latin American Writing.* Austin: U of Texas P, 1998.

Lipsett-Rivera, Sonya, and Sergio Rivera Ayala. "Columbus Takes On the Forces of Darkness; or, Film and the Historical Myth in *1492: The Conquest of Paradise.*" Stevens 13–28.

Llano Zapata, José Eusebio de. *Memorias históricas, físicas, apologéticas de la América Meridional.* 1761. Lima: Imprenta y Librería de San Pedro, 1904.

Llorens, Irma. *Nacionalismo y literatura. Constitución e institucionalización de la "República de las letras cubanas."* Serie América 2. Lleida: Asociación Española de Estudios Literarios Hispanoamericanos, U de Lleida, 1998.

Llorente, Juan Antonio, ed. *Colección de las obras del venerable Obispo de Chiapa, don Bartolomé de las Casas.* 2 vols. Paris: Casa de Rosa, 1822.

Lockhart, James, and Stuart B. Schwartz. *Early Latin America: A History of Colonial Spanish America and Brazil.* Cambridge: Cambridge UP, 1983.

Lohmann Villena, Guillermo. "La restitución por corregidores y encomenderos: Un aspecto de la incidencia lascasiana en el Perú." *Anuario de estudios americanos* 23 (1966): 21–89.

López Enguídanos, Tomás, and José López Enguídanos. *Retrato de Fray Bartolomé de las Casas.* Madrid: La Imprenta Real, 1791. [Drawn by J. López Enguídanos. Steel-engraved by T. López Enguídanos. Plate 346 x 250mm].

Lorenzana, Francisco Antonio. *Historia de Nueva España, escrita por su esclarecido conquistador Hernán Cortés; Aumentada con otros documentos y notas por Francisco Antonio Lorenzana*. 1770. Mexico: U de Castilla–La Mancha; Miguel Ángel Porrúa, 1992.

Losada, Ángel. Introducción. *Apología*. 1551. Las Casas, *Obras completas* 9: 11–42.

———. *Fray Bartolomé de las Casas a la luz de la moderna crítica histórica*. Madrid: Tecnos, 1970.

Luis de Granada. *Los seis libros de la retórica eclesiástica, o de la manera de predicar. Obras*. Biblioteca de Autores Españoles 11. Madrid: Atlas, 1945. 487–642. Vol. 3 of *Obras de R. P. M. Fray Luis de Granada*. 3 vols. 1944–45.

Luther, Martin. "The Freedom of a Christian." *Martin Luther's Basic Theological Writings*. Ed. Timothy F. Lull. 2nd ed. Minneapolis: Fortress, 2005. 386–411.

———. "Ninety-Five Theses." *Martin Luther's Basic Theological Writings*. Ed. Timothy F. Lull. Minneapolis: Fortress, 2005. 40–46.

Lynch, John. *Simón Bolívar: A Life*. New Haven: Yale UP, 2006.

———. *The Spanish American Revolutions (1808–1826)*. New York: Norton, 1986.

Lyotard, Jean-François. *The Differend: Phrases in Dispute*. Trans. Georges Van Den Abbeele. Minneapolis: U of Minnesota P, 1988.

Mahn-Lot, Marianne. *Las Casas moraliste. Culture et foi*. Paris: Cerf, 1997.

Maltby, William S. *The Black Legend in England: The Development of Anti-Spanish Sentiment, 1558-1660*. Durham: Duke UP, 1971.

Mann, Charles C. *1491: New Revelations of the Americas before Columbus*. New York: Knopf, 2005.

"Manumissio in ecclesia. *Codex Theodosianus* 4.7.1." *Theodosiani libri XVI*. Ed. Theodor Mommsen and Paul M. Krueger. Dublin: Weidmann, 1970–71. 179.

Maravall, José Antonio. "La utopía político-religiosa de los franciscanos en Nueva España." *Estudios americanos* 1 (1949): 199–227.

Marchese, Angelo, and Joaquín Forradellas. *Diccionario de retórica, crítica y terminología literaria*. 5th ed. Barcelona: Ariel, 1997.

Marcus, Raymond. "Las Casas in Literature." Friede and Keen 581–600.

Marcus, Robert D., David Burner, and Anthony Marcus, eds. *America Firsthand: Readings from Settlement to Reconstruction*. 6th ed. New York: Bedford–St. Martin's, 2004.

Marin, Louis. *Utopics: Spatial Play*. Trans. Robert A. Vollrath. Atlantic Highlands: Humanities P Intl., 1984.

Martí, José. "Betances." *Martí y Puerto Rico*. Ed. Carlos Alberto Montaner. Río Piedras: San Juan, 1970. 34–35.

———. *La edad de oro*. Miami: Universal, 2001.

———. "El padre Las Casas." 1889. Cairo 11–24.

———. "Las ruinas indias." Martí, *La edad* 125–39.

Martínez, Manuel M. *Fray Bartolomé de las Casas*. Madrid: La Rafa, 1958.

Martínez Torrejón, José Miguel. "Estudio introductorio." Casas, *Brevísima relación de la destruición de las Indias* [ed. Martínez Torrejón] 12–97.

McFarlane, Anthony, and Eduardo Posada-Carbó, eds. *Independence and Revolution in Spanish America: Perspectives and Problems*. London: Inst. of Latin Amer. Studies, U of London, 1999.

Mendieta, Jerónimo de. *Historia eclesiástica indiana*. 1596. Mexico: Consejo Nacional para la Cultura y las Artes, 1997.

Menéndez Pidal, Ramón. *El Padre Las Casas, su doble personalidad*. Madrid: Espasa, 1963.

Merediz, Eyda M. *Refracted Images: The Canary Islands through a New World Lens: Transatlantic Readings*. Medieval and Renaissance Texts and Studies 276. Mediterranean Studies, Monographs, and Texts 3. Tempe: Center for Medieval and Renaissance Studies, 2004.

Merrim, Stephanie. "The Apprehension of the New in Nature and Culture: Fernández de Oviedo's *Sumario*." Jara and Spadaccini, *1492* 165–99.

———. "The Castle of Discourse: Fernández de Oviedo's Don Claribalte (1959) or 'Los correos andan más que los caballeros.'" *MLN* 97 (1982): 329–46.

———. " 'Un Mare Magno e Oculto': Anatomy of Fernández de Oviedo's *Historia general y natural de las indias*." *Revista de estudios hispánicos* 11 (1984): 101–19.

Mier, Servando Teresa de (*See also* Guerra, José). "Apologia del doctor Mier." *Memorias*. Vol. 1. Mexico: Porrúa, 1971. 3–222.

———. "Discurso preliminar." Casas, *Breve relación de la destrucción de las Indias Occidentales* iii–xxxv. *Biblioteca Virtual Miguel de Cervantes*. 4 Apr. 2006 <http://www.cervantesvirtual.com>.

———. "Idea de una constitución dada a las Americas." *Obras completas*. México: U Nacional Autónoma de Mexico, 1967.

Mignolo, Walter. "Cartas, crónicas y relaciones del descubrimiento y la conquista." *Historia de la literatura Hispanoamericana. Época Colonial*. Madrid: Cátedra, 1982. 57–116.

Milhou, Alain. "El concepto de la destrucción en el evangelismo milenario franciscano." *Los franciscanos en el Nuevo Mundo*. Actas del II Congreso Intl. Madrid: Deimos, 1988. 297–315.

———. "Las Casas frente a las reivindicaciones de los colonos de la isla Española (1544–1561)." *Historiografía y bibliografía americanistas* 19-20 (1976): 11–66.

Miller, Denise. "María Luisa Bemberg's Interpretation of Octavio Paz's Sor Juana." *An Argentine Passion: María Luisa Bemberg and Her Films*. Ed. John King, Sheila Whitaker, and Rosa Bosch. London: Verso, 2000. 137–73.

Mills, Kenneth, and Anthony Grafton. Introduction. *Conversion: Old Worlds and New*. Ed. Mills and Grafton. Rochester: U of Rochester P, 2003. ix–xvii.

Milton, John. *Of Education. The Riverside Milton*. Ed. Roy Flannagan. Boston: Houghton, 1998. 977–86.

The Mission. 1986. Dir. Roland Joffé. DVD. Warner Home Video, 2003.

La monja alférez. Dir. Javier Aguirre. Tripictures, 1986.

La monja alférez. Dir. Emilio Gómez Muriel. Clasa Films Mundiales, 1945.

Montaigne, Michel de. "Des cannibales." *Essais. Livre I.* Paris: Garnier-Flammarion, 1969. 251–63.

———. *Essais de Michel Seigneur de Montaigne.* Paris, 1588. Rpt. as *Les Essais de Montaigne: reproduction typographique de l'exemplaire annoté par l'auteur et conservé à la Bibliothèque de Bordeaux avec un avertissement et une notice par M. Ernest Courbet.* 3 vols. Paris: Imprimerie Natl., 1906–31.

———. *Essais de Michel Seigneur de Montaigne.* Paris, 1580.

———. *The Essayes or Morall, Politike and Millitarie Discourses of Lo Michaell de Montaigne.* Trans. John Florio. London: Val. Sims for Edward Blount dwelling in Paules Churchyard, 1603.

———. *Montaigne's Essays.* Trans. John Florio. Ed. J. I. M. Stewart. 2 vols. London: Nonesuch, 1931.

———. "Of Cannibals." Ed. Constance Jordan and Clare Carroll. *The Longman Anthology of British Literature.* Vol. 1. Gen. ed. David Damrosch. New York: Longman, 1999. 1077–78.

Montúfar, Alonso de. Letter to Philip II. June 1560. Legajo 115. Archivo Histórica, Colección Francisco de Paso y Troncoso. Biblioteca Nacional de Antropología e Historia, Mexico City.

More, Thomas. *Utopia.* Ed. George M. Logan and Robert M. Adams. Cambridge: Cambridge UP, 2002.

Moreiras, Alberto. "Ten Notes on Primitive Imperial Accumulation: Sepúlveda, Las Casas, and Fernández de Oviedo." *Interventions* 2 (2000): 343–63.

Mortara Garavelli, Bice. *Manual de retórica.* 2nd ed. Madrid: Cátedra, 1991.

Motolinía [Toribio de Benavente]. "Carta de fray Toribio de Motolinía al Emperador Carlos V. Enero 2 de 1555." Motolinía, *Historia* 295–316.

———. *Historia de los indios de la Nueva España.* 1969. Ed. Edmundo O'Gorman. 5th ed. Mexico: Porrúa, 1990.

———. *History of the Indians of New Spain.* Trans. Francis Borgia Steck. Washington: Acad. of Amer. Franciscan Hist., 1951.

———. *Memoriales o libro de las cosas de la Nueva España y de los naturales de ella.* Ed. Edmundo O'Gorman. Mexico: U Nacional Autónoma de México, 1971.

Muldoon, James. *The Americas in the Spanish World Order: The Justification for Conquest in the Seventeenth Century.* Philadelphia: U of Pennsylvania P, 1994.

———. "Medieval Canon Law and the Conquest of the Americas." *Jahrbuch für Geschichte Lateinamerikas* 37 (2000): 10–22.

Mulford, Carla, et al. *Early American Writings.* Oxford: Oxford UP, 2002.

Muñoz, Juan Bautista. *Colección Muñoz.* Comp. Maxine Emert. New York, 1941. New York Public Lib.

———. *Historia del Nuevo Mundo.* Madrid: Viuda de Ibarra, 1793.

———. *Relación de documentos de fray Bartolomé de las Casas.* Diversos-Colecciones 29, N. 19. 21 Jan 1784. Archivo Hist. Nacional, Madrid. *Archivos Españoles en Red.* 28 Oct. 2006 <http://aer.mcu.es/sgae/index_aer.jsp>.

Myers, Kathleen Ann. *Fernández de Oviedo's Chronicle of America: A New History for a New World.* Austin: U of Texas P, forthcoming.

Nicholson, Henry B. "Religion in Pre-Hispanic Central Mexico." *Handbook of Middle American Indians.* Ed. Robert Wauchope. Vol. 10. Austin: U of Texas P, 1971. 395–446.

Nóbrega, Manuel da. *Dialogue for the Conversion of the Indians.* Castillo and Schweitzer 81–92.

Nuix, Juan. *Reflexiones imparciales sobre la humanidad de los españoles en las Indias contra los pretendidos filósofos y políticos. Para servir de luz a las historias de los señores Raynal y Robertson.* 1783. Madrid: Col. Cisneros, 1944.

O'Gorman, Edmundo. "Estudio preliminar." Casas, *Apologética historia sumaria* 1: vii–lxxix.

———. *Fundamentos de la historia de América.* Mexico: Imprenta Universitaria, 1942.

Oliveira, Fernando. *Arte da guerra do mar.* 1555. Lisboa: Marinha, 1983.

Oliveros, Roberto. *Liberación y teología, génesis y crecimiento de una reflexión.* Lima: Centro de Estudios Peruanos, 1977.

Olsen, Margaret. *Slavery and Salvation in Colonial Cartagena de Indias.* Gainesville: UP of Florida, 2005.

O'Meara, Thomas F. *Thomas Aquinas, Theologian.* Notre Dame: U of Notre Dame P, 1997.

Orique, David Thomas. "*Confesionario: Avisos y reglas para confesores* by Bartolomé de las Casas: A Translation and Introduction to Its Historical Context and Legal Teaching." Master's thesis. Dominican School of Philosophy and Theology. 8 Aug. 2001. *Western Dominican Province.* Feature archives 2003. 18 Nov. 2006 <http://www.opwest.org/Archive/2003/200303_OriqueThesis/200303_01_oriquethesis.htm>.

Ortega, José. "La figura heroica de las Casas en *Las Casas. Una hoguera en el amanecer* de Salom." *Estreno* 18.2 (1992): 37–38.

Ortiz, Fernando. *Contrapunteo cubano del tabaco y el azúcar.?* Introd. Julio Le Riverend. Caracas: Ayacucho, 1978.

———. Introduction. Saco, *Historia de la esclavitud* 1: vii–lv.

———. "La leyenda negra contra Bartolomé de las Casas." *Cuadernos americanos* 11.5 (1952): 146–84.

Outram, Dorinda. *The Enlightenment.* Cambridge: Cambridge UP, 1995.

Pagden, Anthony. "Dispossessing the Barbarian." *The Languages of Political Theory in Early Modern Europe.* Ed. Pagden. Cambridge: Cambridge UP, 1987. 79–98.

———. *European Encounters with the New World: From Renaissance to Romanticism.* New Haven: Yale UP, 1993.

———. *The Fall of Natural Man: The American Indian and the Origins of Comparative Ethnology.* Cambridge: Cambridge UP, 1982.

———. Introduction. Las Casas, *Short Account* xii–xl.

———. "Ius et Factum: Text and Experience in the Writings of Bartolomé de las Casas." Greenblatt, *New World* 85–100.

———. *Lords of All the World: Ideologies of Empire in Spain, Britain, and France, c.1500–c.1800.* New Haven: Yale UP, 1995.

———. *Spanish Imperialism and the Political Imagination, 1513–1830*. New Haven: Yale UP, 1990.

Palacios Rubios, Juan López de. *Requerimiento*. 1513. *History 130-01: Latin American History to 1825—Resources*. Comp. Marcelo J. Borges. History Dept., Dickinson College. 9 Feb. 2006. 13 Aug. 2007 <http://www.dickinson.edu/~borges/Resources-Requerimiento.htm>.

Palencia-Roth, Michael. "The Cannibal Law of 1503." *Early Images of the Americas: Transfer and Invention*. Ed. Jerry M. Williams and Robert E. Lewis. Tucson: U of Arizona P, 1993. 21–63.

Parish, Helen Rand. Introduction. Casas, *Only Way* 9–58.

———. *Las Casas as Bishop: A New Interpretation Based on His Holograph Petition in the Hans P. Kraus Collection of Hispanic American Manuscripts*. Washington: Lib. of Congress, 1980.

Parish, Helen Rand, and Harold E. Weidman. "The Correct Birthdate of Bartolomé de las Casas." *Hispanic American Historical Review* 56 (1976): 385–403.

———. *Las Casas en México: Historia y obra desconocidas*. México: Fondo de Cultura Económica, 1992.

Parra, Félix. *Friar Bartolomé de las Casas*. Museo Nacional de Arte, Mexico City, Mexico.

Paul III. *Sublimis Dei*. 29 May 1537. *Papal Encyclicals Online*. 2000–06. 14 Nov. 2006 <http://www.papalencyclicals.net/Paul03/p3subli.htm>.

———. *Sublimis Deus*. 1537. *Documentos para el estudio de la historia de la Iglesia en la América Latina*. Ed. Fernando Gil. Pontificia U Católica Argentina. 1998–2003. 13 Aug. 2007 <http://usuarios.advance.com.ar/pfernando/DocsIglLA/Paulo3_sublimis.htm>.

Pauw, Cornelius de. *Recherches philosophiques sur les américains; ou, Mémoires intéressants pour servir a l'histoire de l'espèce humaine*. 2 vols. Berlin: Georges Jacques Decker, 1768–69.

Pécora, Alcir. "Vieira e a condução do índio ao corpo místico do império português (Maranhão, 1652–1661)." *Diálogos da conversão: Missionários, índios, negros e judeus no contexto ibero-americano do período barroco*. Comp. Lúcia Helena Costigan: Campinas: Unicamp, 2005. 83–98.

Pennington, Kenneth J., Jr. "Bartolomé de las Casas and the Tradition of Medieval Law." *Church History* 39.2 (1970): 149–61.

El pensamiento lascasiano en la conciencia de América y Europa. Mexico: U Nacional Autónoma de Mexico, 1994.

Pérez Fernández, Isacio. *Bartolomé de las Casas: ¿Contra los negros? Revisión de una leyenda*. Madrid: Mundo Negro; Mexico: Esquila, 1991.

———. *Cronología documentada de los viajes, estancias y actuaciones de Fray Bartolomé de las Casas*. Bayamon: Centro de Estudios de los Dominicos del Caribe, U Central de Bayamón, 1984.

———. "Estudio preliminar." Casas, *Brevísima relación de la destrucción de Africa* 11–187.

———. *Fray Bartolomé de las Casas, O. P. De defensor de los indios a defensor de los negros*. Salamanca: San Esteban, 1995.

————. "Hallazgo de un retrato auténtico del P. Las Casas." *Studium* 32 (1992): 245–80.

————. "Identificación del bien y favor de los indios, de fray Bartolomé de las Casas." *Escritos del Vedat* 12 (1979): 247–302.

————. *Inventario documentado de los escritos de Fray Bartolomé de las Casas.* Bayamón: Centro de Estudios de los Dominicos del Caribe, U Central de Bayamón, 1981.

————. "Sobre la fecha y el lugar de redacción del 'primer libro' de Fray Bartolomé de las Casas." *Ciencia Tomista* 105 (1978): 125–43.

Phelan, John Leddy. *The Millennial Kingdom of the Franciscans in the New World.* 2nd ed. Berkeley: U of California P, 1970.

Philip II. "Ordenanzas de descubrimiento, nueva población y pacificación de las Indias dadas por Felipe II, el 13 de Julio de 1573, en el bosque de Segovia." *Teoría y leyes de la Conquista.* Ed. Francisco Morales Padrón. Madrid: Ediciones de Cultura Hispánica del Centro Iberoamericano de Cooperación, 1979. 489–518.

Phillips, Edward. "The Life of Mr. John Milton." *Early Lives of Milton.* Ed. Helen Darbishire. London: Constable, 1932. 49–82.

Phillips, William D., and Carla Rahn Phillips. *The Worlds of Christopher Columbus.* Cambridge: Cambridge UP, 1992.

Plato. *Republic.* Ed. Francis Cornford. Oxford: Clarendon, 1941.

Potts, L. J. *Aristotle on the Art of Fiction.* London: Cambridge UP, 1968.

Processo 5813 da Inquisção de Lisboa. Ms. 7283. Instituto dos Arquivos Nacionais da Torre do Tombo, Lisboa, República Portuguesa.

Purchas, Samuel. *Hakluytus Posthumus; or, Purchas His Pilgrimes: Contayning a History of the World in Sea Voyages and Lande Travells by Englishmen and Others.* 1625. 20 vols. Glasgow: J. MacLehose and Sons, 1905–07.

Quint, David. *Epic and Empire: Politics and Generic Form from Virgil to Milton.* Princeton: Princeton UP, 1993.

Quintilian. *Institutio Oratoria / The Orator's Education.* Trans. Donald A. Russell. Vol. 3. Cambridge: Harvard UP, 2002. 5 vols.

Rabasa, José. *Inventing America: Spanish Historiography and the Formation of Eurocentrism.* Norman: U of Oklahoma P, 1993.

————. "Utopian Ethnology in Las Casas's *Apologética.*" Jara and Spadaccini, *1492* 263–90.

————. *Writing Violence on the Northern Frontier: The Historiography of Sixteenth-Century New Mexico and Florida and the Legacy of Conquest.* Durham: Duke UP, 2000.

Ramírez, Susan E. "I, the Worst of All: The Literary Life of Sor Juana Inés de la Cruz." Stevens 47–62.

Rauschenbusch, Walter. *Christianity and the Social Crisis.* Whitefish: Kessinger, 2007.

————. *A Theology for the Social Gospel.* Louisville: Westminster–John Knox, 1997.

Raynal, Guillaume-Thomas. *Histoire philosophique et politique des établissements et du commerce des Européens dans les deux Indes.* 6 vols. Amsterdam, 1770.

————. *A Philosophical and Political History of the Settlements and Trade of the Europeans in the East and West Indies.* Trans. J. O. Justamond. 8 vols. London:

W. Strahan and T. Cadell, 1783. *Eighteenth Century Collections Online*. Gale Group. 28 Oct. 2006 <http://galenet.galegroup.com/servlet/ECCO>.

Read, Malcolm K. "Benítez Rojo and Las Casas's Plague of Ants: The Libidinal Versus the Ideological Unconscious." *Diacritics* 32.2 (2002): 60–85.

Real Academia de la Historia. *Catálogo de la coleccion de don Juan Bautista Muñoz.* 3 vols. Madrid: Maestre, 1954–56.

Reeser, Todd W., and Steven D. Spalding. "Reading Literature/Culture: A Translation of 'Reading as a Cultural Practice.' " *Style* 36 (2002): 659–76.

Remesal, Antonio de. *Historia general de las Indias Occidentales y particular de la gobernación de Chiapa y Guatemala.* 1619. Ed. Carmelo Sáenz de Santa María. 2 vols. Madrid: Atlas, 1964–66.

Renov, Michael. "Video Confessions." *The Subject of Documentary.* Minneapolis: U of Minnesota P, 2004. 191–216.

Rich, Adrienne. *Of Woman Born: Motherhood as Experience and Institution.* New York: Norton, 1976.

Rivera-Pagán, Luis N. "A Prophetic Challenge to the Church: The Last Word of Bartolomé de las Casas." Inaugural lecture as Henry Winters Luce Professor in Ecumenics and Mission. Princeton Theological Seminary. 9 Apr. 2003. *Bartolomé de las Casas.* Ed. Lawrence Clayton and Edward Clearly. 2005. 18 Nov. 2006 <http://www.lascasas.org/Rivera_Pagan.htm>.

———. *A Violent Evangelism: The Political and Religious Conquest of the Americas.* Louisville: Westminster–John Knox, 1992.

Robertson, William. *The History of America.* 1777. 5th ed. 3 vols. London, 1788.

Rodríguez, Rodney. *Momentos cumbres de las literaturas hispánicas.* Upper Saddle River: Pearson, 2004.

Román Enviado, José Antonio. "Samuel Ruiz: 'Sólo alguien con los ojos tapados' puede negar el zapatismo." *La jornada* 17 Jan 2005. 5 Apr. 2006 <http://www.jornada.unam.mx/2005/01/17/006n1pol.php>.

Román y Zamora, Jerónimo. *República de Indias idolátricas y gobierno en México y Perú.* 1569. Madrid: V. Suárez, 1897.

Rosati, Hugo. "Los misioneros." *América y la irrupción europea.* Pontificia Universidad Católica de Chile. 2004. 25 Oct. 2006 <http://www.puc.cl/sw_educ/historia/conquista/parte3/html/h53.html>.

Rose, Gillian. *Visual Methodologies: An Introduction to the Interpretation of Visual Materials.* London: Sage, 2001.

Rowe, John Howland. "The Renaissance Foundations of Anthropology." *American Anthropologist* 67 (1965): 1–20.

Ruddick, Sara. *Maternal Thinking: Toward a Politics of Peace.* Boston: Beacon, 1989.

Ruiz de Alarcón, Hernando. *Aztec Sorcerers in Seventeenth-Century Mexico: The Treatise on Superstitions.* Trans. Michael D. Coe and Gordon Whittaker. Albany: State U of New York, Albany, Inst. for Mesoamerican Studies, 1982.

Saco, José Antonio. *Historia de la esclavitud de los indios en el Nuevo Mundo.* Introd. Fernando Ortiz. 2 vols. Havana: Cultural, 1932.

———. "La *Historia de las Indias* por fray Bartolomé de las Casas y la Real Academia de la Historia." *Revista Hispano-americana* 12 Feb. 1865. 109.

Saeger, James Schofield. "The Mission and Historical Missions: Film and the Writing of History." Stevens 63–84.

Sahagún, Bernardino de. *Florentine Codex: General History of the Things of New Spain.* Ed. and trans. Arthur J. O. Anderson and Charles E. Dibble. 12 vols. Santa Fe: School of Amer. Research; Salt Lake City: U of Utah P, 1953–82.

———. *Historia general de las cosas de la Nueva España.* Mexico: Porrúa, 1986.

Said, Edward. *Orientalism.* New York: Vintage, 1978.

Saint-Lu, André. "Fray Bartolomé de Las Casas." *Historia de la literatura hispanoamericana.* Ed. Luis Iñigo Madrigal. Vol. 1. Madrid: Cátedra, 1992. 117–25.

———. Introduction. Casas, *Brevísima relación de la destrucción de las Indias* (ed. Saint-Lu) 11–57.

———. *Las Casas indigeniste: Études sur la vie et l'œuvre du défenseur des Indiens.* Paris: L'Harmattan, 1982.

———. *La Vera Paz, esprit évangélique et colonisation.* Paris: Centre de Recherches Hispaniques, 1968.

Saint-Lu, André, Raymond Marcus, et al. *Estudios sobre fray Bartolomé de las Casas.* Seville: U de Sevilla, 1974.

Salazar Bondy, Augusto. *Bartolomé o de la dominación.* Lima: Peisa, 1977.

Salom, Jaime. *Bonfire at Dawn.* Trans. Phyllis Zatlin. University Park: Estreno, 1992.

———. *Las Casas. Una hoguera en el amanecer.* Madrid: Inst. de Cooperación Iberoamericana, 1986.

Sandoval, Alonso de. *De instauranda aethiopum salute. El mundo de la esclavitud negra en America.* Bogota: Empresa Nacional de Publicaciones, 1956.

Sauer, Carl Orwin. *Sixteenth-Century North America: The Land and the People as Seen by the Europeans.* Berkeley: U of California P, 1971.

Schwaller, John B. Rev. of *A Violent Evangelism: The Political and Religious Conquest of the Americas,* by Luis Rivera-Pagán. *Hispanic American Historical Review* 75 (1995): 107–09.

Sedgwick, Catharine Maria. *Hope Leslie.* 1827. Ed. Mary Kelley. New Brunswick: Rutgers UP, 1987.

Seed, Patricia. *American Pentimento: The Invention of Indians and the Pursuit of Riches.* Minneapolis: U of Minnesota P, 2001.

———. *Ceremonies of Possession in Europe's Conquest of the New World.* Cambridge: Cambridge UP, 1995.

Segundo, Juan Luis. *Función de la iglesia en la realidad rioplatense.* Montevideo: Barreiro y Ramos, 1962.

Sepúlveda, Juan Ginés de. *Apología.* 1550. Ed. Ángel Losada. Madrid: Nacional, 1975.

———. *Historia del Nuevo Mundo.* Madrid: Alianza, 1996.

———. *Tratado sobre las justas causas de la guerra contra los indios.* Mexico: Fondo de Cultura Económica, 1941.

Serna, Jacinto de la. "Manual de ministros de indios para el conocimiento de sus idolatrías, y extirpación de ellas." *Anales del Museo Nacional de México.* 6 vols. Mexico: Imprenta del Museo Nacional, 1892. 261–475.

Serrano y Sanz, Manuel. *Orígenes de la dominación española en América.* Madrid: Bailly-Baillière, 1918.

Shakespeare, William. *The Tempest*. Ed. Frank Kermode. London: Methuen, 1958.

Shawcross, John T. *The Arms of the Family: The Significance of John Milton's Relatives and Associates*. Lexington: UP of Kentucky, 2004.

Shuffleton, Frank. "The American Enlightenment and Endless Emancipation." *Teaching the Literatures of Early America*. Ed. Carla Munford. New York: MLA, 1999. 155–69.

Sidney, Philip. *A Defence of Poetry*. Ed. J. A. Van Dorsten. Oxford: Oxford UP, 1986.

Sigüenza y Góngora, Carlos de. *Los infortunios de Alonso Ramírez. Obras históricas*. Mexico: Porrúa, 1960. 1–75.

Silva Gotay, Samuel. *El pensamiento cristiano revolucionario en América Latina y el Caribe*. Rio Piedras: Cordillera-Sígueme, 1983.

Slater, T. "Restitution." *Catholic Encyclopedia*. 1913. *New Advent*. Ed. Kevin Knight. 2007. 1 Dec. 2007 <http://www.newadvent.org/cathen/00002a.htm>.

Smith, Karl. "Cooperative Learning: Making 'Groupwork' Work." Sutherland and Bonwell, *Using* 71–82.

Solórzano Pereira, Juan de. *De Indiarum Iure*. 1629–72. Madrid: Consejo Superior de Investigaciones Científicas, 1994–2001. 3 vols.

Someda, Hidefuji. *Apología e historia. Estudios sobre fray Bartolomé de las Casas*. Lima: Pontificia U del Perú, 2005.

Sommer, Doris. *Foundational Fictions: The National Romances of Latin America*. Berkeley: U of California P, 1991.

———. "Las Casas's Lies and Other Language Games." A. Arias, *Rigoberta Menchu* 237–50.

Soto, Domingo de. *Aquí se contiene una disputa o controversia*. Casas, *Tratados* 1: 217–86.

———. "Traslado de un sumario que . . . coligió el muy reverendo y doctísimo padre, maestro fray Domingo de Soto." 1551. Casas, *Obras escogidas* 5: 295–308.

Stam, Robert. "Eurocentrism, Polycentrism, and Multicultural Pedagogy: Film and the Quincentennial." *Late Imperial Culture*. Ed. Román de la Campa, E. Ann Kaplan, and Michael Sprinker. New York: Verso, 1995. 97–121.

Steele, Colin. *English Interpreters of the Iberian New World from Purchas to Stevens: A Bibliographical Study, 1603–1726*. Oxford: Dolphin, 1975.

Stephenson, Marcia. *Gender and Modernity in Andean Bolivia*. Austin: U of Texas P, 1999.

Stevens, Donald F., ed. *Based on a True Story: Latin American History at the Movies*. Wilmington: SR Books, 1997.

Stoler, Ann Laura. "Developing Historical Negatives: Race and the (Modernist) Visions of a Colonial State." *From the Margins: Historical Anthropology and Its Futures*. Ed. Brian Keith Axel. Durham: Duke UP, 2002. 156–88.

———. "'In Cold Blood': Hierarchies of Credibility and the Politics of Colonial Narratives." *Representations* 37 (1992): 151–89.

Stoll, David. *Rigoberta Menchú and the Story of All Poor Guatemalans*. Boulder: Westview, 1999.

Stone, Cynthia L. "Aguirre Goes to the Movies: Twentieth-Century Visions of Colonial-Era *Relaciones*." *Bridging Continents: Cinematic and Literary Representations of Spanish and Latin American Themes*. Ed. Nora Glickman and Alejandro Varderi. Tempe: Chasqui, 2005. 24–35.

———. "Beyond the Female Gaze: María Luisa Bemberg's Sor Juana Inés de la Cruz." *CiberLetras* 13 (2005). 6 Nov. 2006 <http://www.lehman.cuny.edu/ciberletras/v13/stone.htm>.

———. "The Filming of Colonial Spanish America." *Colonial Latin American Review* 5 (1996): 315–19.

Stowe, Harriet Beecher. *Uncle Tom's Cabin*. 1851. New York: Norton, 1994.

Sturken, Marita, and Lisa Cartwright. *Practices of Looking: An Introduction to Visual Culture*. Oxford: Oxford UP, 2001.

Suárez de Peralta, Juan. *Noticias históricas de la Nueva España*. Madrid: M. G. Hernández, 1878.

Sullivan, Francis P. "Textual Appendices." Casas, *Only Way* 211–43.

Sutherland, Tracey E., and Charles C. Bonwell. "The Active Learning Continuum: Choosing Activities to Engage Students in the Classroom." Sutherland and Bonwell, *Using* 3–16.

———, eds. *Using Active Learning in College Classes: A Range of Options for Faculty*. New Directions for Teaching and Learning 67. San Francisco: Jossey-Bass, 1996.

Symposium Fray Bartolomé de las Casas. Trascendencia de su obra y doctrina. Mexico: U Nacional Autónoma de México, 1985.

"Teaching Bartolomé de Las Casas." Session 646. MLA Annual Convention. Loews Philadelphia, Philadelphia. 30 Dec. 2004.

"Teaching Bartolomé de Las Casas beyond the *Brevísima relación*." Session 451. MLA Annual Convention. Washington Hilton, Washington. 29 Dec. 2005.

Thevet, André. *André Thevet's North America; A Sixteenth-Century View*. Ed. Roger Schlesinger and Arthur Stabler. Kingston: McGill-Queen's UP, 1986.

———. *Les singularitez de la France antarctique autrement nommée Amérique et de plusieurs terres et isles découvertes de notre temps*. Paris: Chez les héritiers de Maurice de la Porte, 1558.

Thomas, Hugh. *The Slave Trade: The Story of the Atlantic Slave Trade, 1440–1870*. New York: Touchstone, 1997.

Thomas Aquinas. *Summa theologica*. Trans. Fathers of the English Dominican Province. 2 vols. Westminster: Christian Classics, 1981.

"Three Men and Adena." *Homicide: Life on the Streets*. NBC. 3 March 1993.

Thurner, Mark, and Andrés Guerrero, eds. *After Spanish Rule: Postcolonial Predicaments of the Americas*. Durham: Duke UP, 2003.

Todorov, Tzvetan. *The Conquest of America*. New York: Harper, 1984.

Torquemada, Juan de. *Monarquía indiana*. 1615. Mexico: U Nacional Autónoma de México, 1995.

Trend, John Brande. *The Civilization of Spain*. Oxford: Oxford UP, 1944.

Trexler, Richard C. *Sex and Conquest*. Ithaca: Cornell UP, 1995.

Trillo, Mauricio Tenorio. "Essaying the History of National Images." Thurner and Guerrero 58-86.

Truth Commissions Digital Collection. United States Institute of Peace. 2005. 13 Feb. 2006 <http://www.usip.org/library/truth.html>.

Ulloa, Daniel. *Los predicadores divididos*. Mexico: Colegio de México, 1977.

Una hoguera al amanecer. By Jaime Salom. Dir. Hugo Medrano. GALA Teatro Hispano, Washington. 8 Feb. 1992.

Vargas, José M. *Bartolomé de las Casas: Su personalidad histórica*. Quito: Santo Domingo, 1974.

Vargas Machuca, Bernardo de. *Apologías y discursos de las conquistas occidentales*. Ed. María Luisa Martínez de Salinas. Valladolid: Junta de Castilla y León, 1993.

———. *Milicia y descripción de las Indias*. Bogotá: Fondo de Promoción de la Cultura, Banco Popular, 2003.

Vargas Ugarte, Ruben. *Historia de la Compañía de Jesús en el Perú*. Burgos: n.p., 1963.

Vaz de Caminha, Pero. "The Letter of Pero Vaz de Caminha to King Manuel I, May 1, 1500." Castillo and Schweitzer 33–34.

V centenario del primer viaje a América de Bartolomé de las Casas: 1502–2002. Seville: Junta de Andalucía; Consejería de la Presidencia; Consejería de Cultura, 2003.

Velasco, Sherry. *The Lieutenant Nun: Transgenderism, Lesbian Desire, and Catalina de Erauso*. Austin: U of Texas P, 2001.

Verdesio, Gustavo. "Cabeza de Vaca: Una visión paródica de la épica colonial." *Nuevo texto crítico* 10 (1997): 195–204.

Veres, Luis. "El marco de la ficción en la 'Brevísima relación de la destrucción de las Indias' de Fray Bartolomé de las Casas." *Espéculo: Revista de estudios literarios* 3.9 (1998): 1–11. 21 Aug. 2007 <www.ucm.es/info/especulo/numero9/bcasas.html>.

Verrazzano, Giovanni da. *Voyage of Verrazzano, Florentine Noble in the Service of François I, King of France, 1524*. Castillo and Schweitzer 34–36.

Vickery, Paul S. *Bartolomé de las Casas, Great Prophet of the Americas*. New York: Newman, 2006.

Vieira, Padre Antonio. *Obras completas. Sermões*. 15 vols. Porto: Lello, 1959.

Vigne Pacheco, Ana. "El padre Las Casas entre los modernistas." *Caravelle: Cahiers du monde hispanique et luso-brésilien* 76-77 (2001): 475–83.

Vitoria, Francisco de. "De indis et de jure belli." *Relectiones*. 1917. Ed. Ernest Nys. Buffalo: Hein, 1995.

———. "De temperantia." *Obras de Francisco de Vitoria: Relecciones teológicas*. Ed. Teófilo Urdánoz. Madrid: Biblioteca de Autores Cristianos, 1960. 1004–69.

———. *Escritos políticos*. Buenos Aires: Depalma, 1967.

———. "On the Evangelization of the Unbelievers." Vitoria, *Political Writings* 341–51.

———. *Political Writings*. Ed. Anthony Pagden and Jeremy Lawrance. Cambridge: Cambridge UP, 1991.

Voltaire [François-Marie Arouet]. *Alzira*. Trans. Aaron Hill. London: John Osborn, 1736. *Eighteenth Century Collections Online*. Gale Group. 28 Oct. 2006 <http://galenet.galegroup.com/servlet/ECCO>.

———. *An Essay on Universal History, the Manners, and Spirit of Nations, from the Reign of Charlemaign to the Age of Lewis XIV*. Trans. Nugent. 2nd ed. 4 vols.

London: J. Nourse, 1759. *Eighteenth Century Collections Online*. Gale Group. 28 Oct. 2006 <http://galenet.galegroup.com/servlet/ECCO>.

Wagner, Henry Raup. "My Original Plan Changes." Foreword. Wagner and Parish xxi–xxv.

Wagner, Henry Raup, and Helen Rand Parish. *The Life and Writings of Bartolomé de las Casas*. Albuquerque: U of New Mexico P, 1967.

Wardropper, Bruce W. "*Don Quixote*: Story or History?" *Modern Philology* 63 (1965): 1–11.

Wertheimer, Eric. *Imagined Empires: Incas, Aztecs, and the New World of American Literature, 1771-1876*. Cambridge: Cambridge UP, 1999.

White, Hayden. "The Noble Savage Theme as Fetish." *First Images of America: The Impact of the New World on the Old*. Ed. Freddy Chiappelli, Michael J. B. Allen, and Robert L. Benson. Berkeley: U of California P, 1976. 121–35.

———. "Rhetoric and History." *Theories of History: Papers Read at a Clark Library Seminar*. Los Angeles: Williams Andrew Clark Memorial Lib., 1978.

Widdifield, Stacie G. "Dispossession, Assimilation, and the Image of the Indian in Late-Nineteenth-Century Mexican Painting." *Art Journal* 49.2 (1990): 125–32.

Wilkinson, Alec. "Mr. Apology." *"Mr. Apology" and Other Essays* Boston: Houghton, 2003. 225–45.

Williams, Raymond. *Keywords: A Vocabulary of Culture and Society*. Rev. ed. New York: Oxford, 1983.

Williams, Ritva. "Biblical justifications for slavery." E-mail to Kristy Nabhan-Warren. 25 Jan. 2006.

Williams, Robert A., Jr. *The American Indian in Western Legal Thought*. Oxford: Oxford UP, 1990.

Williams, Roger. *A Key into the Language of America*. 1643. Ed. John J. Teunissen and Evelyn J. Hinz. Detroit: Wayne State UP, 1973.

Winthrop, John. "A Model of Christian Charity." *Puritan Political Ideas, 1558–1794*. Ed. Edmund S. Morgan. New York: Bobbs, 1965. 75–93.

Xirau, Ramón. *Idea y querella de la Nueva España*. Madrid: Alianza, 1973.

Yo, la peor de todas. 1990. Dir. María Luisa Bemberg. DVD. First Run Features Home Video, 2003.

Young, Robert J. C. *Postcolonialism: An Historical Introduction*. London: Blackwell, 2001.

Yúdice, George. "Testimonio and Postmodernism." Gugelberger 42–57.

Zamora, Margarita. *Reading Columbus*. Berkeley: U of California P, 1994.

———. "Todas son palabras formales del Almirante: Casas y el *Diario de Colón*." *Hispanic Review* 57 (1989): 25–41.

Zatlin-Boring, Phyllis. "Bartolomé de las Casas en el escenario contemporáneo: La perspectiva de Jaime Salom." *España y América en sus literaturas*. Ed. María Ángeles Encinar. Madrid: Inst. de Cooperación Iberoamericana, 1993. 17–39.

Zavala, Silvio. *La encomienda indiana*. 1935. 3rd ed. Mexico: Porrúa, 1992.

———. *La filosofía política de la conquista de América*. Mexico: Fondo de Cultura Económica, 1947.

INDEX OF NAMES

Modern Language Association of America
Approaches to Teaching World Literature
Joseph Gibaldi, series editor

Achebe's Things Fall Apart. Ed. Bernth Lindfors. 1991.
Arthurian Tradition. Ed. Maureen Fries and Jeanie Watson. 1992.
Atwood's The Handmaid's Tale *and Other Works*. Ed. Sharon R. Wilson,
   Thomas B. Friedman, and Shannon Hengen. 1996.
Austen's Emma. Ed. Marcia McClintock Folsom. 2004.
Austen's Pride and Prejudice. Ed. Marcia McClintock Folsom. 1993.
Balzac's Old Goriot. Ed. Michal Peled Ginsburg. 2000.
Baudelaire's Flowers of Evil. Ed. Laurence M. Porter. 2000.
Beckett's Waiting for Godot. Ed. June Schlueter and Enoch Brater. 1991.
Beowulf. Ed. Jess B. Bessinger, Jr., and Robert F. Yeager. 1984.
Blake's Songs of Innocence and of Experience. Ed. Robert F. Gleckner and
   Mark L. Greenberg. 1989.
Boccaccio's Decameron. Ed. James H. McGregor. 2000.
British Women Poets of the Romantic Period. Ed. Stephen C. Behrendt and
   Harriet Kramer Linkin. 1997.
Charlotte Brontë's Jane Eyre. Ed. Diane Long Hoeveler and Beth Lau. 1993.
Emily Brontë's Wuthering Heights. Ed. Sue Lonoff and Terri A. Hasseler. 2006.
Byron's Poetry. Ed. Frederick W. Shilstone. 1991.
Camus's The Plague. Ed. Steven G. Kellman. 1985.
Writings of Bartolomé de Las Casas. Ed. Santa Arias and Eyda M. Merediz. 2008.
Cather's My Ántonia. Ed. Susan J. Rosowski. 1989.
Cervantes' Don Quixote. Ed. Richard Bjornson. 1984.
Chaucer's Canterbury Tales. Ed. Joseph Gibaldi. 1980.
Chaucer's Troilus and Criseyde *and the Shorter Poems*. Ed. Tison Pugh and
   Angela Jane Weisl. 2006.
Chopin's The Awakening. Ed. Bernard Koloski. 1988.
Coleridge's Poetry and Prose. Ed. Richard E. Matlak. 1991.
Collodi's Pinocchio *and Its Adaptations*. Ed. Michael Sherberg. 2006.
Conrad's "Heart of Darkness" and "The Secret Sharer." Ed. Hunt Hawkins and
   Brian W. Shaffer. 2002.
Dante's Divine Comedy. Ed. Carole Slade. 1982.
Defoe's Robinson Crusoe. Ed. Maximillian E. Novak and Carl Fisher. 2005.
DeLillo's White Noise. Ed. Tim Engles and John N. Duvall. 2006.
Dickens' David Copperfield. Ed. Richard J. Dunn. 1984.
Dickinson's Poetry. Ed. Robin Riley Fast and Christine Mack Gordon. 1989.
Narrative of the Life of Frederick Douglass. Ed. James C. Hall. 1999.
Early Modern Spanish Drama. Ed. Laura R. Bass and Margaret R. Greer. 2006

Eliot's Middlemarch. Ed. Kathleen Blake. 1990.

Eliot's Poetry and Plays. Ed. Jewel Spears Brooker. 1988.

Shorter Elizabethan Poetry. Ed. Patrick Cheney and Anne Lake Prescott. 2000.

Ellison's Invisible Man. Ed. Susan Resneck Parr and Pancho Savery. 1989.

English Renaissance Drama. Ed. Karen Bamford and Alexander Leggatt. 2002.

Works of Louise Erdrich. Ed. Gregg Sarris, Connie A. Jacobs, and James R. Giles. 2004.

Dramas of Euripides. Ed. Robin Mitchell-Boyask. 2002.

Faulkner's The Sound and the Fury. Ed. Stephen Hahn and Arthur F. Kinney. 1996.

Flaubert's Madame Bovary. Ed. Laurence M. Porter and Eugene F. Gray. 1995.

García Márquez's One Hundred Years of Solitude. Ed. María Elena de Valdés and Mario J. Valdés. 1990.

Gilman's "The Yellow Wall-Paper" and Herland. Ed. Denise D. Knight and Cynthia J. Davis. 2003.

Goethe's Faust. Ed. Douglas J. McMillan. 1987.

Gothic Fiction: The British and American Traditions. Ed. Diane Long Hoeveler and Tamar Heller. 2003.

Grass's The Tin Drum. Ed. Monika Shafi. 2008.

Hebrew Bible as Literature in Translation. Ed. Barry N. Olshen and Yael S. Feldman. 1989.

Homer's Iliad *and* Odyssey. Ed. Kostas Myrsiades. 1987.

Ibsen's A Doll House. Ed. Yvonne Shafer. 1985.

Henry James's Daisy Miller *and* The Turn of the Screw. Ed. Kimberly C. Reed and Peter G. Beidler. 2005.

Works of Samuel Johnson. Ed. David R. Anderson and Gwin J. Kolb. 1993.

Joyce's Ulysses. Ed. Kathleen McCormick and Erwin R. Steinberg. 1993.

Works of Sor Juana Inés de la Cruz. Ed. Emilie L. Bergmann and Stacey Schlau. 2007.

Kafka's Short Fiction. Ed. Richard T. Gray. 1995.

Keats's Poetry. Ed. Walter H. Evert and Jack W. Rhodes. 1991.

Kingston's The Woman Warrior. Ed. Shirley Geok-lin Lim. 1991.

Lafayette's The Princess of Clèves. Ed. Faith E. Beasley and Katharine Ann Jensen. 1998.

Works of D. H. Lawrence. Ed. M. Elizabeth Sargent and Garry Watson. 2001.

Lessing's The Golden Notebook. Ed. Carey Kaplan and Ellen Cronan Rose. 1989.

Mann's Death in Venice *and Other Short Fiction.* Ed. Jeffrey B. Berlin. 1992.

Marguerite de Navarre's Heptameron. Ed. Colette H. Winn. 2007.

Medieval English Drama. Ed. Richard K. Emmerson. 1990.

Melville's Moby-Dick. Ed. Martin Bickman. 1985.

Metaphysical Poets. Ed. Sidney Gottlieb. 1990.

Miller's Death of a Salesman. Ed. Matthew C. Roudané. 1995.

Milton's Paradise Lost. Ed. Galbraith M. Crump. 1986.

Milton's Shorter Poetry and Prose. Ed. Peter C. Herman. 2007.

Molière's Tartuffe *and Other Plays*. Ed. James F. Gaines and
    Michael S. Koppisch. 1995.

Momaday's The Way to Rainy Mountain. Ed. Kenneth M. Roemer. 1988.

Montaigne's Essays. Ed. Patrick Henry. 1994.

Novels of Toni Morrison. Ed. Nellie Y. McKay and Kathryn Earle. 1997.

Murasaki Shikibu's The Tale of Genji. Ed. Edward Kamens. 1993.

Nabokov's Lolita. Ed. Zoran Kuzmanovich and Galya Diment. 2008.

Poe's Prose and Poetry. Ed. Jeffrey Andrew Weinstock and Tony Magistrale. 2008.

Pope's Poetry. Ed. Wallace Jackson and R. Paul Yoder. 1993.

Proust's Fiction and Criticism. Ed. Elyane Dezon-Jones and
    Inge Crosman Wimmers. 2003.

Puig's Kiss of the Spider Woman. Ed. Daniel Balderston and Francine Masiello.
    2007.

Pynchon's The Crying of Lot 49 *and Other Works*. Ed. Thomas H. Schaub. 2008.

Novels of Samuel Richardson. Ed. Lisa Zunshine and Jocelyn Harris. 2006.

Rousseau's Confessions *and* Reveries of the Solitary Walker. Ed. John C. O'Neal
    and Ourida Mostefai. 2003.

Shakespeare's Hamlet. Ed. Bernice W. Kliman. 2001.

Shakespeare's King Lear. Ed. Robert H. Ray. 1986.

Shakespeare's Othello. Ed. Peter Erickson and Maurice Hunt. 2005.

Shakespeare's Romeo and Juliet. Ed. Maurice Hunt. 2000.

Shakespeare's The Tempest *and Other Late Romances*. Ed. Maurice Hunt. 1992.

Shelley's Frankenstein. Ed. Stephen C. Behrendt. 1990.

Shelley's Poetry. Ed. Spencer Hall. 1990.

Sir Gawain and the Green Knight. Ed. Miriam Youngerman Miller and
    Jane Chance. 1986.

Song of Roland. Ed. William W. Kibler and Leslie Zarker Morgan. 2006.

Spenser's Faerie Queene. Ed. David Lee Miller and Alexander Dunlop. 1994.

Stendhal's The Red and the Black. Ed. Dean de la Motte and Stirling Haig. 1999.

Sterne's Tristram Shandy. Ed. Melvyn New. 1989.

Stowe's Uncle Tom's Cabin. Ed. Elizabeth Ammons and Susan Belasco. 2000.

Swift's Gulliver's Travels. Ed. Edward J. Rielly. 1988.

Thoreau's Walden *and Other Works*. Ed. Richard J. Schneider. 1996.

Tolstoy's Anna Karenina. Ed. Liza Knapp and Amy Mandelker. 2003.

Vergil's Aeneid. Ed. William S. Anderson and Lorina N. Quartarone. 2002.

Voltaire's Candide. Ed. Renée Waldinger. 1987.

Whitman's Leaves of Grass. Ed. Donald D. Kummings. 1990.

Wiesel's Night. Ed. Alan Rosen. 2007.

Works of Oscar Wilde. Ed. Philip E. Smith II. 2008.

Woolf's To the Lighthouse. Ed. Beth Rigel Daugherty and Mary Beth Pringle. 2001.

Wordsworth's Poetry. Ed. Spencer Hall, with Jonathan Ramsey. 1986.

Wright's Native Son. Ed. James A. Miller. 1997.